THE
OXYRHYNCHUS PAPYRI
VOLUME LIV

PA3315
.08
v.54
arab

THE
OXYRHYNCHUS PAPYRI
VOLUME LIV

EDITED WITH TRANSLATIONS AND NOTES BY

R. A. COLES

H. MAEHLER

P. J. PARSONS

WITH CONTRIBUTIONS BY

J. M. BREMER   R. J. D. CARDEN

Graeco-Roman Memoirs, No. 74

PUBLISHED FOR
THE BRITISH ACADEMY
BY THE
EGYPT EXPLORATION SOCIETY
3 DOUGHTY MEWS, LONDON WC1N 2PG
1987

PRINTED IN GREAT BRITAIN
AT THE UNIVERSITY PRINTING HOUSE, OXFORD
AND PUBLISHED FOR
THE BRITISH ACADEMY
BY THE EGYPT EXPLORATION SOCIETY
3 DOUGHTY MEWS, LONDON WC1N 2PG

ISSN 0306-9222

ISBN 0 85698 093 5

© EGYPT EXPLORATION SOCIETY 1987

PREFACE

THIS volume offers the traditional mixture of literature and documents. Professor Maehler has prepared for publication an extensive but very fragmentary and tantalizing commentary on Anacreon (**3722**); we join with him in acknowledging the valuable preliminary work of Dr R. J. D. Carden. Mr Parsons is responsible for the remainder of the literary texts (**3723–6**). All these have elegiac connections; the most intriguing is the collection of epigram incipits festooning a recipe for cough mixture (**3724**). Professor J. M. Bremer of the University of Amsterdam has collaborated in the edition of **3723.**

The documents (**3727–76**) have been selected and edited by Dr Coles to illustrate the work of the *curator* of Oxyrhynchus, from the new earliest reference to the post in AD 303 up to the early 340s. A list of the holders forms Appendix I. Various groups of price declarations submitted to his office give new information about the currency inflation of the early fourth century, see Appendix III. There is much of interest in the incidental detail, from high politics to daily routine: notice the consular vagaries of AD 325 (**3756** 26 n.), and the *curator*'s day off, changed by Constantine from pagan Thursday to Christian Sunday (**3741** introd., **3759** introd. and 38 n.).

Dr Helen Cockle has compiled the usual indexes with more than usual speed and alertness. Dr Coles himself made Index XIII, Corrections to Published Papyri, an addition suggested to us by reviewers. The Oxford University Press continues to deserve our admiration and gratitude; the skills which it displays on our behalf are rare indeed.

March 1987

P. J. PARSONS
J. R. REA
General Editors
Graeco-Roman Memoirs

CONTENTS

TABLE OF PAPYRI

I. NEW LITERARY TEXTS

II. OFFICIAL DOCUMENTS

* All dates are AD.

LIST OF PLATES

NUMBERS AND PLATES

NOTE ON THE METHOD OF
PUBLICATION AND ABBREVIATIONS

THE method of publication follows that adopted in Part XLV. As there, the dots indicating letters unread and, within square brackets, the estimated number of letters lost are printed slightly below the line. The texts are printed in modern form, with accents and punctuation, the lectional signs occurring in the papyri being noted in the *apparatus criticus* where also faults of orthography, etc., are corrected. Iota adscript is printed where written, otherwise iota subscript is used. Square brackets [] indicate a lacuna, round brackets () the resolution of a symbol or abbreviation, angular brackets ⟨⟩ a mistaken omission in the original, braces {} a superfluous letter or letters, double square brackets ⟦⟧ a deletion, the signs ` ´ an insertion above the line. Dots within brackets represent the estimated number of letters lost or deleted, dots outside brackets mutilated or otherwise illegible letters. Dots under letters indicate that the reading is doubtful. Lastly, heavy arabic numerals refer to Oxyrhynchus papyri printed in this and preceding volumes, ordinary numerals to lines, small roma numerals to columns.

The use of arrows (→, ↓) to indicate the direction of the fibres in relation to the writing has been abandoned for reasons put forward by E. G. Turner, 'The Terms Recto and Verso' (*Actes du XVᵉ Congrès International de Papyrologie* I: Papyrologica Bruxellensia 16 (1978) 64–5), except when they serve to distinguish the two sides of a page in a papyrus codex. In this volume most texts appear to accord with normal practice in being written parallel with the fibres on sheets of papyrus cut from the manufacturer's roll. Any departures from this practice which have been detected are described in the introductions to the relevant items.

The abbreviations used are in the main identical with those in E. G. Turner, *Greek Papyri: an Introduction* (2nd edn., 1980). It is hoped that any new ones will be self-explanatory.

I. NEW LITERARY TEXTS

3722. COMMENTARY ON ANACREON

Inv. no. unrecorded   Fr. 15 12.5 × 12.8 cm   Second century

On the verso of a month-by-month account, written in a large upright hand of the late first or early second century AD, are the remains of a commentary on some of Anacreon's sympotic songs, written in a small practised bookhand with some cursive features, especially at line-ends, which slopes slightly to the right; it must have been written in the second century, perhaps in its second half rather than in the first. It is very similar to that of **2802**, a commentary on Alcman.

Spaces between columns are narrow (little more than 1 cm in frr. 15, 16, 17, 25) but top and bottom margins are fairly generous (in fr. 29 there is a margin at the foot of the column of at least 3.5 cm). A rough breathing seems to occur only once (fr. 26. 4, combined with an accent?). There are few instances of elision marks, all of them, it seems, in quotations: frr. 1. 5; 4. 2; 5. 3; 17 i 16, 18 (doubtful: 17 ii 16; 21 i 8; 56. 9; 57. 3). Punctuation is rare (frr. 3. 6; 83. 3). A dicolon is used to mark the end of the lemma (frr. 1. 27; 2. 9; 4. 1; 9. 6; 83. 3) and perhaps, more generally, to separate quotation and comment (frr. 15 i 1, 3, ii 10; 16 ii 6; 25 i 6, 7; 28. 3; 90. 9; 102. 7); sometimes a blank space is left to indicate this (frr. 1. 5, 25; 2. 1, 4; 3. 6; 5. 10; 17 ii 7). In fr. 25 col. ii, a number of lines have been marked by diplai, also fr. 51 ii 8 and fr. 54 ii 23. A reference-mark, possibly to an omitted line, occurs at fr. 51 ii 9–10, and a very puzzling sign is found at fr. 25 ii 17 (see n.). The scribe uses no abbreviations, except a raised horizontal for final ν (frr. 1. 6; 2. 3; 17 i 2; 25 i 5; 87. 10); also $\bar{\delta}$ for $\delta\acute{\epsilon}$ in fr. 16 i 6 and perhaps in fr. 73. 8 (unless there it is the numeral, see the note), $\bar{\mu}$ for $\mu\acute{\epsilon}\nu$ at fr. 15 ii 13 (?). Diaeresis occurs only once ($\ddot{\upsilon}\delta a$[fr. 15 ii 9). The quotation in fr. 17 i 13–19 suggests an average of 27 or 28 letters to the line.

The attribution of the poetic text to Anacreon rests on the certain or probable occurrences of known lines. Certain quotations are: An. 38 Gentili (*PMG* 396) = fr. 15 ii 1 and An. 91 (*PMG* 380) = fr. 29. 2; probable: An. 135 (*PMG* 454) = fr. 2. 1; An. 114 (*PMG* 403) = fr. 15 i 3; An. 117 (*PMG* 377) = fr. 15 i 5; An. 8 (*PMG* 372) = fr. 27. 6a; possible: An. 35 (*PMG* 400) = fr. 2. 3; An. 47 (*PMG* 401) = fr. 52. 5. Fragments of Anacreon's poetry have been preserved in XXII **2321, 2322**, LIII **3695**.

Mention of the poet's name at fr. 1. 19, 15 i 18, 27. 7, 39. 4, and 73. 10 confirms the attribution, as does the content of most of the recognizable lemmata, which seem for the most part to be concerned with erotic and sympotic matters. Dialect and metre (ionics, choriambs, aeolic verses) point in the same direction. Unfortunately, the gain, as far as new lines or words of Anacreon are concerned, is very modest.

The fragments of this papyrus were assembled by Mr Edgar Lobel, who also made a number of joins. They were subsequently transcribed by Mr Richard Carden. Between 1970 and 1976, Dr Walter Cockle revised and annotated Mr Carden's manuscript; he also transcribed the accounts on the recto.[1] His suggestions are mentioned in the notes. Mrs Margaret Maehler has contributed a number of observations on the content, in particular on the quotations; the identification of fr. 17 i 13–19 as Hes. *Th.* 183 ff. is due to her. I am greatly indebted to all of them, especially to Mr Carden, whose accurate transcription of the text and meticulous descriptions of traces and uncertain letters have proved immensely helpful and have greatly facilitated my task. I have checked Mr Carden's readings and descriptions against the papyrus; the resulting changes have for the most part been insignificant, and I have therefore, as a rule, not recorded them as such.

In the diplomatic transcript which follows, I have marked the lemmata by the use of upright type.

fr. 1 7.4 × 18.6 cm

```
              ] . [                    ]                 7 [
              ] . υν . . [             ]                 } [
              ]      [                 ]                 2 [
          ]ατουτωνεμφα[ . . ] . ιτ .                    7 [
     5    ]νδ'απεπριμηναβιον· οιον                      ) [
          ]εταφορααποτωνποιμνιῶ                         S [
          ]νητοντωνχειρων[ . ]ωθ . αι                     [
          ] . χρομεςτουδ . [ . . . . ]ει . . [ ]ς         [
          ] . χ[ ]ειληλεγε . [       ] . ερ . [
     10   ]παροιμιαν . . [           ] . ω . [
```

2] . , overhang perhaps of ϲ   . . [, bit of an upright, then a short fairly upright trace intersected at top by a diagonal ascending from left   4]ατ, end of a stroke descending from the left; of τ, only the right part of the crossbar and stalk can be seen: perhaps χ   At line-end a horizontal mark more resembling the tongue of ε than the sign for ν (cf. l. 6); if ε, it will have been raised above the level of the other letters   7 θ . , stroke leaning slightly to right, turning more sharply right at top, and apparently continuing round in a loop to rejoin the upright—though the length of this does not commend ρ; then αι or δι, and a diagonal mark well below the line   8] . κ, horizontal mark on line touching back of κ   I think ς correct, though there is what seems like a diagonal running up from the end of the tongue of ε through the left corner of the next letter, like a deletion   δ . [, speck touching top of δ: apostrophe? Another trace at same level on the other side of a short break, and a faint trace below this: ε?   9] . χ, speck at mid-level   . [, a letter with rounded lower left corner   ] . ε, short upright with speck to left of top   10 . . [, faint upright followed at a short interval by bit of diagonal ascending to right, at upper level: κ, or ν? Then lower half of another upright   ] . , υ, or perhaps τ; ει possible but not much suggested

---

[1] The recto text, unfortunately, by its very nature does not help much to establish the order of the fragments, which remains quite uncertain, except where colour or fibre patterns suggest proximity.

]. . [.]ελα[]εκμ[. .]οχου. []. μ. ν. [

]. . εποημα[.]. . φαι. [   ]. ο. . [

]γεγονεναι. . [. . . .]. . . [   ]ται. . [

]απεποι. . [. .]. [. .]. [.]παι[.]. . []. [

15   ]. η. . . ν[. .]cτου[]π. []. [   ]. [

]υποαρ[.]cτοφαν[. . .]α[

    ]κλε^α. ντιφερ. . . [

]. επ[.]χειληδο. ει. [.]. [

]ακρεωνεcτινγαρ. ο[

20   ]υρωνεπιχε[.]λη. c[

]. . λκαιον δ. [. . . .]επ[

]αυτοεπιχειλ. . [.]ε. []. . [

]ει[]ωνδ. λοι. χει. ειι. [

    ]ονοτικαιτωκοριωcπ[

25   ]. αναναγεχι τοcημ[

]. ερωcκακετρυγηc. [

]. το: [

]. ιουcαπ[

    ][[α]]ουτο[

    ]ηδια[

      ]τ[

·   ·   ·   ·

11]. ., foot of upright below line, a speck higher and slightly to the right: ν? Then 2 strokes one above the other, the lower more or less horizontal, upper ascending to right: ο or top half of ε would fit, or δ? Above κ, mark like a tiny c   ν. [, upright   ]. μ, trace level with top of μ   12]. . ε, scattered traces including base of upright, on line   ι. [, foot of a stroke perhaps ascending slightly to right   ο. . [, upright; top of a tall stroke, perhaps not quite upright; below this, 2 specks suggesting a diagonal ascending to right   13]. . .[, 2 uprights followed by a small loop—this possibly to be connected with a dimly visible stroke below the line a little to the right, as φ, though the loop would be larger than that of the specimens in ll. 4, 6   ι. .[, perhaps top of ζ, then upright   14 ι., top of small circle   15]., base of upright   η., lower half of upright   ]. .[, in first space, γ or τ   16 Of ν, only a foot   17 Over ε, what looks like an abnormally large rough breathing with a smaller one in its upper angle: α?   ρ. ., possibly an upright, then apparently bits of 2 uprights: second trace not compatible with ζ (i.e. not αντιφεριζ-)   18 ι. [, I think, the beginning of a diagonal ascending to right, hooked at base   ]. [, left side of a small arch   19 ρ., 2 specks level with tops of letters: τ might fit   23 ει[, possibly a trace just to right of the top of this upright, which could suggest rather ν than ι; but it is very faint   δ., trace on line, worm-hole, trace level with tops of letters   . χ, colon or small upright   ει, for ι, γ or π possible   ι. [, hook at mid-level   24 π[, or χ; not τ   26 . [, left side of small circle

4 δι]ὰ τούτων ἐμφαί[ν]ει? For ἐμφαίνειν 'to indicate', cf. Schol. Pind. *Ol.* 7. 173a, *Py.* 1. 47b, etc.

5 ?τό]νδ' ἀπεποίμηνα βίον: double choriambs are frequent in Anacreon, e.g., An. 91 (*PMG* 380), 85 (*PMG*

381b), 109 (*PMG* 382), 110. 1 (*PMG* 383. 1), 82 (*PMG* 388), 108 (*PMG* 389), 107 (*PMG* 412). The verb, ἀποποιμαίνειν, is not attested elsewhere, but cf. Man., *Apotel.* 4. 419 βίον διαποιμαίνοντες. The metaphor is also discussed in fr. 28. 3 ff.

5–6 οἷον [διῆγον· ἡ μ]εταφ. would fill the gap.

8].κρομες would be very puzzling—a Doric ending, 1st person plural? The alternative seems to be ἀκρομέστου 'brim-full', not so far attested but a possible form, cf. ἀνάμεστος, πάμμεστος, ἡμίμεστος. This would suggest a bowl or cup and might find support in χείλη in the next line, if χ can be read there; cf. Semon. 24 Diehl (27 West). At the end,]ειλης (Carden) is unlikely as η cannot be read;]ειαρ[ο]ς seems possible.

12]ε πεποημα[could be An. 57 (99 D.) οἰνοπότης δὲ πεποίημαι.

14 πεποιθ.[: ω[possible, θ almost certain.

16 ὑπὸ Ἀρ[ι]στοφάν[ους]: An. 28 (*PMG* 408) shows that Aristophanes wrote a commentary on Anacreon (Cockle).

17]κλε^α: if the raised letter was α, it may suggest an abbreviation, possibly a name (Κλέαρχος?, see fr. 57. 4 n.), followed by a form of ἀντιφέρειν or ἀντιφέρεσθαι.

18–19 ἐπ[ὶ] χείλη δοκεῖ λ[έγειν (?) . . . . . ὁ Ἀν]ακρέων. If so, ἐπὶ χείλη could be part of a lemma, cf. l. 20.

19 ἐστὶν γὰρ τὸ [ὅλον?

21 .λκαιον: I cannot verify the letter preceding λ.

23 δηλοῖ χεῖ ἐπὶ seems possible.

24 γεγ]ονότι, δηλ]ονότι, or]ον ὅτι?

25]. αν ἀνάγεαι: apparently part of a lemma; then: τὸ σημ[εῖον ὅτι . . .?

26 Ἔρως κακέ, τρυγης.[or κάκ' ἐτρύγησε (e.g., ἄνθη), cf. *AP* 12. 256 (Meleager).

fr. 2   6 × 6.5 cm

```
                          .        .              .
                          ]  [    ][
                  ]θεραπωνεμηνεν ελ   [
                   ]υτοναποτουςυμποςιου        [
                   ].νδροναπιρνταουνῡ           [
                  ]προπεςων ομενδι               [
          5       ]. ς βελτειρνφηςινεπ[].  [
                  ]. ερωτικων·τοδεμεν            [
                  ]. ενγαροιδακαιλειαν   [
                  ]τιοτιμεθυςθειςπαρα[
                      ]υδρου :ν[[πεταρτ...[
          10          ]εφ.[ ]...[  ]..[
                          .        .         .
```

3]. , speck on line close to edge of ν   ρ is very inflated: its appearance would be explained if the scribe first wrote ι, then converted it by adding a curved right side of matching height   4 δι, for ι the last stroke is anomalous, bulging out to the right   5]. , a squat trace on and below the line, with vertical extension, and suggestion of ink going left from centre; from upper end a stroke curves out to right, upwards, and then back on itself; I cannot explain these traces   6]. , trace level with tops of letters, top of an upright suggested   7]. , stroke descending vertically from upper level, then curving out to right, turning up just short of the line: μ?   8]τι, stroke running horizontally near the line, then ascending vertically   9 Deletion by horizontal line rather below mid-level, from π as far as the writing extends   τ . . . , in first space, top and bottom of a tall upright; two indefinite traces at mid-level, then perhaps τ   10 φ. [, small circle, and possibly a tail-stroke below: either ο or ρ looks likely   ]. . . [, tallish upright (ι?) with a stroke joining top diagonal from left; then the upper left part of a circle; then a trace above the general level

1–3] θεράπων ἔμηνεν is evidently lemma. The comment may have been something like ἔλ[εγεν ἐμμανῆ a]ὐτὸν ἀπὸ τοῦ cυμποcίου [ἐπὶ τὸν Πυθόμ]ανδρον ἀπιόντα, οὗ νῦ(ν) κτλ.; cf. An. 35 (*PMG* 400). (ἔλ|[εγε(ν) would be wrong word-division (but see on ll. 4–5, and on fr. 3. 5); to the right above λ the top layer of papyrus has broken away; if there was a raised ε (ελ[ε] = ἔλε(γε)?), it is lost). If this comes anywhere near the truth, the θεράπων who 'has driven mad' may be Eros (cf. Sappho 159 *LP*, where Aphrodite calls Eros her servant), unless it is a boy as in Theoc. 5. 90f. = An. 135 (*PMG* 454) οἰνηρὸc θεράπων?

4 προπεcών: very probably lemma, but in what sense? Is it paraphrased by ἀπιόντα? Ll. 4–8 seem to suggest that the verb may refer to someone suffering either from love or from drink.

4–5 ὁ μὲν δι[(answered, it seems, by τὸ δέ in l. 6) may be part of a discussion (on the meaning of προπεcών?) involving Didymus, who may have said that the word refers to erotic passion (ἐπὶ [παθημάτων τῶ]ν ἐρωτικῶν would fill the gap), whereas the author of this commentary thinks that a quotation from Menander (τὸ δὲ Μεν|[άνδρειον, with wrong word-division? or μέν|[τοι?) suggests drunkenness (μεθυcθείc, l. 8). If this is right, Didymus is not the author of this commentary. Didymus is not the only scholar's name which could be supplied, but he is the only one known to have written on Anacreon (cf. Sen. *Ep.* 88. 37; M. Schmidt, *Didymi . . . fragmenta*, p. 384) that will fit.

7 τὸ] μὲν γὰρ οἶδα καὶ λ{ε}ίαν (cf. βέλτειον l. 5) could be part of an iambic trimeter; for καὶ λίαν, cf. Men. fr. 758. The quotation seems to recur below in fr. 6. 6.

9]νδρου: the dicolon suggests that this may be part of the lemma; if An. 35 (*PMG* 400), quoted above, is relevant to this passage, Πυθομά]νδρου may be worth considering.

fr. 3   5 × 7.5 cm

```
                .      .     .
        ].[    ].[ ].[
        ]αικαι·διδͅωcοτε[. ]ϵ [
                  θ
        ]θελωναρθμιοcειν      [
        ]ρτιcταιγαρηδιανͅοια [
   5    ]εμφεαι περιουμεμφ[
        ]αcτͅα τυρᾳννα ˙ολογο [
        ]ͅιομαπυλͅᾳ. ει[. ]προcκ. [
        ]γπυνθανͅο. . . . . νͅς[
        ]. ͅο[]υc[
  10    ].[ ].[
        ]. [
      traces of c. 3 more lines
```

The short gap which appears repeatedly on the right-hand side would suggest that these were the ends of lines, if it were not clear from ll. 5, 7 that this cannot be the case; the surface does not *seem* to have been removed here; therefore the scribe for some reason jumped a strip   1 First trace, speck on line; second, stroke slanting slightly to right, joined by one from right at base   2 Between και and δ a short thick upright or narrow circle which may be a superscript o   Above final ϵ, attached to top of it, a dim upright hooked to right at top: offset?   3 The superscript θ has a thick diagonal line through lower half   4 Of]ρ only the loop is visible, ͅο possible   After final α, a dull dot on line, perhaps not significant   6 Second ν seems to have been deleted by a slanting line through middle   γο, o small, and attached to the end of the cross-piece of γ   7]ι, only upper half of this stroke survives: ν also possible   υ apparently written over o   λͅα or λͅϵ   8 ͅο. . . etc., dispersed traces on floating fibres   About 3 more lines on a narrow strip, the surface of which is almost entirely rubbed away

2 τε[ ]ε: there is space for one narrow letter (not μ). ὅτε [δ]έ seems possible.

3 Lemma: ἐ]θέλων ἄρθμιος εἶν|[αι?, cf. Thgn. 1312. (εἶν|[έοισιν would conform to Anacreontic metre, but the word-division would be awkward.)

4 The γάρ needs a short remark, e.g. ἄτοπον· οὐκ ἀπή]ρτισται γὰρ ἡ διάνοια|[πρὸς τὰ ἑπόμενα *vel sim.*

5 μ]έμφεαι is obviously lemma, then perhaps περὶ οὗ μέμφ|[εται ἄδηλον (for another possible case of wrong syllabification, see fr. 2. 4–5 n.).

6–7]αστα τύραννα·: if τύραννα (n. plur.) paraphrases the preceding word, this cannot have been δυν]άστα (voc.); possibly ἀπέλ]αστα 'unapproachable' (Simon. 29 B.?), or βι]αστά 'violent', if the scholion continued with something like ὁ λόγο[ς δὲ νοεῖ καὶ ἄ]νομα. (Dr Leofranc Holford-Strevens suspects a scribal error for τύραννε.)

8]γπυνθανο . . . . : = ἐ]κπυνθ.?

fr. 4   3.6 × 6.2 cm

```
                    .       .      .        .
              ]. :ϲυνεβη μ[
              ]. ταδ'αφεντε . . [
              ]ψειϲαφεντ[
              ]ϲϲωϲαρετη[
         5    ]ετιος ητοι . [
              ]. ϲικελιανα . τ[
              ]ουϲ[. .]. . . . [  ]κι . . [
              ]ατα[          ]νβ̄κα[
              ]μα[           ]αϲεωϲ[
        10                   ]      [
                            ]απτα[
                    .     .      .     .
```

1]. , part of crossbar, with suggestion of vertical descending from left end   2]. , trace level with top of τ; branch of υ slightly suggested   . . [, top of a stroke slanting a little forward to right, descending from tongue of ε; then, after a short space, apex of triangle   4 ωϲ corrected from ιϲ?   5 . [, traces suggest π, set rather low and with a speck above it, unaccounted for   6]. , speck at mid level, close to back of ϲ   α . , speck at mid-level   7]. . ., upper half of stroke leaning slightly to right, with traces of ink to right at top and middle; top of diagonal descending to left; upper half of a more curved stroke, perhaps the left arc of a circle, then 2 specks above the general level   . . [, diagonal ascending to right, then dispersed traces at mid-level   9 for μα perhaps ν . α

2–3 ταδ' αφεντες . [may be part of a lemma, paraphrased in the next line (e.g., τὰς τέρ]ψεις ἀφέντες).

6]. ϲικελίαν: so far, the only reference to Sicily in Anacreon is 31 (*PMG* 415).

fr. 5   3.2 × 6.4 cm

·   ·   ·

].αλ.[
]εδεαντι[
]υαρμ'ελαα [
]ουϲιουϲαϲ [
5   ].ϲεπιτον [
]ιϲκαιπαλ [
]ακαιβακ [
]υτοϲ παρθε[
]αρμαϲιν [
10   ]χαιτηϲ τηϲ[
]ων [
]ν [

·   ·   ·

    1]., stroke running along line, then ascending to right diagonally, finally horizontal: θ with crossbar extended beyond the body of the letter?   .[, upright slanting slightly to right, followed by lower half of a second upright (the upper half dim, but suggested) on the break; to left of middle of the first appears to be a short horizontal; between the 2 uprights is a suggestion of this continuing: possibilities seem to be ψ. [, or η[, of which I slightly favour the former   3 α [, more rounded than the preceding specimen—open at top; or ω with right-hand bow higher than left, and the right-hand side of it now lost   5]., 2 arcs of a small circle, o most suggested, possibly α   9 ρ, the tail has disappeared except, I think, for a faint speck, the foot

    3]υ ἄρμ' ἐλάᾳ: lemma, cf. *Il.* 23. 335 ἐλάαν ϲχεδὸν ἄρμα καὶ ἵππουϲ.
    7–8 καθ]ὰ καὶ Βακ[χυλίδηϲ· Διὸϲ ὑψιμέδο]υτοϲ παρθέ[νοι (Bacch. 1. 2)?
    10]χαιτηϲ: possibly part of a compound (ὑψιχαίτηϲ and χρυϲοχαίτηϲ appear in Pindar), and a lemma or quotation.

fr. 6   4 × 5.7 cm

·   ·

]..[.].το[
]απελλ.υμε[
]δρανφηϲι.[
].υοϲαντι[
5   ].υθρην[

    1].τ, upright with the suggestion of ink to the left half-way down: η?   2]α, or λ?   πε, for ε possibly α   λ., base of a small circle, apparently with a bit of ink descending to line from lower right, upsetting the possibility of o   4]., a tail descending below the line, with suggestion of a fork at the top   5]., top half of a diagonal ascending to right, hooked to right at lower end: ε might fit

].ρ[]οιδαχ[
]αθ[]ειργμ[
].α[.]γελλ[
].[.]...δ[
10   ]...ρ[
　　·　　　·　　·

6]., top of upright ascending above the line, close to ρ　　8]., apparently top of a diagonal from left　　9-10 Very rubbed, and I can make little of the traces; the second letter before δ is possibly υ; and possibly this, the next letter, and δ are all deleted by a horizontal line　　10]., λ? Then upper half of a stroke leaning over to right, at top, where it is joined by an upright　　.ρ, trace at mid-level slanting down to left

2 If]απελλου, An. 188 (*PMG* 957) may be relevant here, possibly also fr. 86. 2 below (]ελληcιαι.[); Ἀπελλοῦ would then be part of the paraphrase (in Anacreon, the genitive would have been Ἀπελλέου). Alternatively, one might think of πελλός 'dark', or the gloss ἀπελλόν· αἴγειρος in Hsch. a 5949.
  6 Perhaps the same line as in fr. 2. 7 above.
  7 κ]αθ' εἰργμ[όν?, cf. An. 65 (*PMG* 346 fr. 4. 5).

fr. 7　　　　　　　　　　3.8 × 5.4 cm

　　　　·　　　·　　·
]γ.[
].ν.[
]αεκα[
]cεατ[
5　]ωcαυτ[
]υ γαρτεκα[
]ερωτοc[
]θεινκαι..[
]..με.[]αι..[
10　].αποκε[
　　·　　　·　　·

1 .[, little hook open to right at upper level　　2]., foot of stroke curled back to left at bottom .[, trace on line　　8 after και, specks on line; above this, smudgy trace on a displaced scrap　　9].., upper half of a very small circle, on the line; then γ, or more likely c　　ε., apparently a stroke descends from tongue of ε—this will be ι; then either a short space or the surface has been stripped　　..[, traces obscured by a blot: first letter includes a loop, perhaps ο or α; second apparently a V, i.e. cursive υ?　　10]., trace at mid-level

fr. 8   0.8 × 4.5 cm

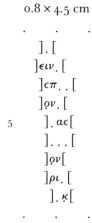

          ·   ·   ·

         ] . [
         ]ειν . [
         ]cπ . . [
         ]ọν . [
5   ] . αc[
         ] . . . [
         ]ọν[
         ]ρι . [
         ] . κ[

          ·   ·

1 Foot of upright, perhaps below the line   2 . [, speck at mid-level   3 . . [, I think, bow of α; then possibly ο, or ρ: traces on fibres which may be displaced   4 . [, fairly upright stroke, perhaps with ink going right from centre   5] . , short stroke leaning to the right   6 Perhaps only 2 letters, only tops visible: first the top of an upright, followed shortly by that of a diagonal from the left, perhaps κ   8 . [, a loop suggesting rather left side of ω than α   9] . , I think part of an upright, and a speck just to left of its lower end

fr. 9   4.5 × 4.2 cm

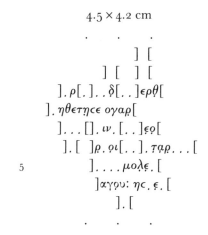

          ·   ·

            ] [
        ] [   ] [
   ] . ρ[.] . . δ[. .]ερθ[
   ] . ηθετηcε ογαρ[
     ] . . . [] . ιν . [. .]εọ[
     ] . [   ]ρ . οι[. .] . ταρ . . . [
5   ] . . . . μολε . [
     ]αγου: ηc . ε . [
         ] . [

        ·   ·   ·

The piece is very worm-eaten, and the surface in part badly rubbed: tentative version   1] . ρ, mark at mid-level   ] . . , top right of a (small ?) circle; a mark suggesting overhang of c, and below it a trace on the line   2 ρ[or ɩ[3] . ɩ, ν . [, specks level with tops of letters   4 ρ . , perhaps υ   6 ε . [, upright apparently turning over to right at top

fr. 10   1.9 × 2.9 cm   fr. 11   1 × 1 cm

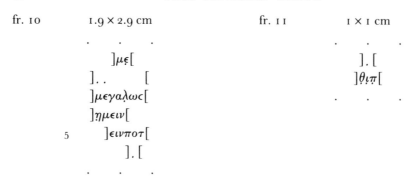

```
            ]με[                              ]. [
        ]. .        [                      ]θιπ[
        ]μεγαλωϲ[
        ]ημειν[
  5       ]εινποτ[
          ]. [
```

     2]. ., apparently a small circle joined at top left by a horizontal   To the right, end of another horizontal at upper level

fr. 12   1.5 × 2 cm   fr. 13   1.4 × 1.2 cm

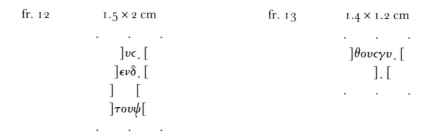

```
        ]υϲ. [                          ]θουϲγυ. [
        ]ενδ. [                          ]. [
        ]      [
        ]τουψ[
```

     1 . [, in ligature with top end of ϲ, a stroke descends vertically to mid-level, then turns sharply right and slightly upwards   2 . [, lower left of a circle (or rounded bow of α?) off the line

     1 . [trace ascending from left of an upright   2 Upper half of an upright

fr. 14   7.4 × 6.1 cm

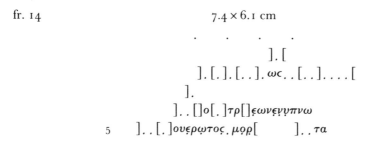

```
                      ]. [
        ]. [. ]. [. .]. ωϲ. .[. .]. . . .[
        ].
        ]. .[]ο[. ]τρ[]εωνεγυπνω
  5     ]. .[. ]ουερωτοϲ. μορ[      ]. .τα
```

     The piece is very tattered and rubbed   1 Foot of upright, below the line   2 . .[, perhaps ει, or η?   ]. . . ., speck on the line, foot of upright and a trace a little to the right at mid-level, then possibly a low-set τ, with some ink (from the next letter?) at the right end of the crossbar   To the right of ll. 2–5, what resemble remains of a coronis in the left margin of the following column

]υτ[   ]νθναν . . ην . [

]ν . . λλατον . ρ . α . [

]φν[.]ει . . τριτο[

]ε . . [   ] . ον[.] δνϲτρ . [

10a   ] . . αν . [

10   ] . [.] . . [[η]]κν . ρονε . [

] . [.]ε . [

. . . .

6 ν . . , apex, of a triangle? bit of a diagonal ascending to right   . [, I think, left side of ω   7 ν . . , 2 traces on the line   . ρ . , traces each side of ρ suggest α   . [, speck on line   8 ι . . , 2 or 3 letters: the second, 3 specks one above the other, looks like ε or θ   9] . ο, foot of a diagonal descending from left   . [, foot of diagonal ascending to right   10a ν . [, possibly η   10 ε . [, apex of a triangle   11 . [, top of a diagonal descending to the right

9 δνϲτρα[: a form of δνϲτράπελοϲ 'difficult to deal with'?

10 κνπρογεν[: a form of Κνπρογενήϲ, cf. *PMG* 949; Alc. 296b. 1; Stesich., *Suppl. lyr. gr.* 104. 6; Sol. 24.1 G. (26. 1 W.); frequent in Theognis.

fr. 15   12.5 × 12.8 cm

. . . .

col. i   col. ii

top of col.   top of col.

] . [.] . ϲ:πετ^α φερ'υδωρφερ οιν[

]τηκεαμο   κτικονδηλοι[]και[

]τοϲ:αϲημω̄   αγεπαραλαμβανο[

]χειμαζομαι   πων̇φερεεπηνεγκ[

5   ]ρονδεμνϲι   το . αγεειρητοτοδιε[

]ιοχενο   οτιπροτερον[] ενχει[

]τονειπεν   πρωτονν . νμεν . [

] . νδειππο   τονοιν . νκαιη[

] . πονϲποι   λεγωντρειϲϋδα[

Col. i.   1] . [, more or less horizontal stroke on line, slanting slightly up to right   ] . , trace at upper level with vertical extension; below and right, speck on line   After τ apparently λ (or α?) written off the line— though the top stroke seems to be in a different ink   7]τ, or γ   8] . , top of an upright   9] . , foot

Col. ii.   5 ο . , some smudging and tearing: the letter seems to have a diagonal right side, slanting up to right: cursive upsilon suggested   6 ενχ, surface darkened, ink smudged, only to be deciphered uncertainly   7 ν . ν, smudge in bottom left of space, speck above and right: if ο, exceptionally bulky   μ, some extraneous ink suggests that μ has been made by correction of another letter   . [, a crossbar on the break: γ[?

10   ]. ωϟ χεϟ.   οιϟου: μεθυ[]. [. .]. . . . [

               ]   . . []τοκατακοι. [.]. [.]ε. . . [

           ]δηνχ[]. [.]ϲ   ϲω[]φρονιϲθαϊ[. . . . (.)]υν . [

      ] ϟ[. . .]. . ειϲαυτ. .[]. ạ   τ[.]ϟτοδεομ̄. .[]. . θαυ   [

      ] .[. . .] . []α εϲτιν μεν   ναχεινωϲκομενωϟτϙ[

15   ]ρτιεκτουεναντιοϟ   ϲθαιεπειγαϙϙιαλλ[.]. ανθ[

       ]ην. ϲ[]ϟ[]. αλιφηνεκπλη   ϲιναυτωϲδεφηϲιδοκε. [   ]

       ]ιει. β[.]ϟ[]λευτεϲυβωτα   εικοτωϲεπηνεγ. [   ]. ϙ. [   ]

       ]. . . [   ]αμωοανακρε[   ]φϙποιωκαιμετε. [   ]

             ]ϟϙ[.] τουτοδι[   ]. [

20   ]τ ευ[. .]. [

              ]. . . [

                 .   .   .   .

Col. i. 10]., trace below tops of letters, loop of ρ would fit   ϟ., short upright on line, then one descending below the line and flourished to right—a cursive ε?   12 Over ν, what seems to be ω, but faint   ]. [, upper half of upright hooked to right at top   13]. ., first, speck rather below line, second, horizontal stroke at mid-level   τ. ., speck level with top of τ, speck in next space slightly lower   ]. α, to right of space, the top of, apparently, a diagonal from left   14 . [, on line, hook open upwards and to right; above and right, a bit of a stroke slanting down to right (or upper right part of circle)   Apparently nothing between α and ε, though possibly surface lost: the gap is rather longer than normal between words 16 ff. left ends of these lines (on a detached fragment) very rubbed   19 δ small and rounded, possibly ϙ

Col. ii. 10]. [, two traces close together level with tops of letters, perhaps ο; probably no letter lost between preceding ν and this   ]. . . . [, lower half of upright, base of α or perhaps λ, lower part of a stroke slightly leaning to right, speck off the line, base of a stroke tailing off to left   11 . . [, stroke rising at a shallow angle from line to right; above right end of this a vertical trace; then top of upright   κο, a dot under ο, presumably not significant   ε. . ., in second space what looks like right half of a squarely made η; then a large bow open to right: perhaps δ   12 . [, diagonal descending from left, turning back to left at mid-level: δ suggested   14 ο[or ω[15]. , a bit, it seems, of an upright (fibre may be displaced) 17 . [, upright (the mark as of a stroke ascending to right from centre of this is not ink; but κ might still be read; the upright is on the break)   ]. , horizontal stroke level with tops of letters   . [, upper half of diagonal ascending to right, turning over at top (though this is on the break and perhaps illusory)

Col. i. 1 πετ^α: the raised α suggests abbreviation; πέτα(λα) (of a victor's wreath?) seems a possibility, as a reference to mules follows in l. 5 below.

2]τηκεα μο or]τηκε ἄμ' ο? The former might be λεπ]τήκεα 'fine-pointed', cf. Hsch. λ 676 λεπτήκεα· λεπτῆϲ ἐργαϲίαϲ ποιηθέντα (of thin gold leaves?).

3-4 An. 114 (*PMG* 403) ἀϲήμων ὑπὲρ ἑρμάτων φορεῦμαι (φορέομαι Page); χειμάζομαι might then be paraphrase.

5 Apparently = An. 117 (*PMG* 377) ἱπποθόρον (-θόρων Bergk) δὲ Μυϲοὶ εὑρεῖν (εὗρον Bergk) μίξιν ὄνων. If so, μυϲι may be a slip (read Μυϲ⟨ο⟩ί). Bergk's conjecture ἱπποθόρων could well be an ancient variant, as Hsch. ι 828 suggests (ἱπποθόροϲ· ὄνος ἵππους βιβάζων).

6 If the lemma ended with ὄνων, the commentator may have said something like, e.g., αἱ γὰρ ἵππο]ι ὀχευό[μεναι ὑπ' ὄνων ἡμιόνους ἔτικ]τον.

8-9 τὴν μίξ]ιν δὲ ἱππο[θόρον λέγει ὅτι ἐγκύους τὰς ἵ]ππους ποι[εῖ?

12 γ[έ]ϟ[ο]ϲ or γ[ό]ϟ[ο]ϲ seem possible (γ[έ]ϟ[υ]ϲ less likely, as a trace of υ would be visible).

16 Perhaps κατ' ἀποκοπ]ὴν ἦ ϛ[υ]γαλιφήν, such as at An. 86 (*PMG* 385) ἐκ ποταμοῦ 'πανέρχομαι, cf. An. 36. 12 (*PMG* 395) and 188 (*PMG* 957).

17 Lemma: βουλευτὲ ϲυβῶτα (obviously coined after Εὔμαιε ϲυβῶτα, *Od.* 14. 55 etc.); for βουλευτός = βουλευτής, one might compare Hsch. β 928; Latte, however, warns: *a grammaticis ex αβουλευτοϲ ficta v. Arcad.* 84, 5.

18-19 ἐν C]άμῳ ὁ Ἀνακρέ[ων?

Col. ii. 1-5 φέρ' ὕδωρ φέρ' οἶν[ον ὦ παῖ = An. 38 (*PMG* 396), almost certainly the opening verse of a song; is this the poem commented on, or is it being quoted in connection with fr. 33 (*PMG* 356) ἄγε δή, φέρ' ἡμῖν ὦ παῖ κτλ.)? And is φέρε an imperative, followed by another imperative (ἔνεικον), or is it, like ἄγε in An. 33, an ἐπίρρημα παρακελευϲτικόν (cf. DT 19, i 82. 1 Uhlig)? The choice seems to be between (*a*) ὅτι προϲτα]|κτικὸν (sc. τὸ φέρε) δηλοῖ καὶ [τὸ ἄγε δή, φέρ' ἡμῖν, ἐν ᾧ τὸ] | ἄγε παραλαμβάνῳ[ν καὶ ἐπιρρηματικῶϲ εἰ]|πὼν 'τ(ὸ) 'φέρε ἐπήνεγκ[εν· ἢ ἐνταῦθα (sc. in fr. 38) ἀντὶ] | τοῦ ἄγε εἴρητο, or (*b*) οἶν[ον· ὅτι φέρε οὐ προϲτα]|κτικόν, δηλοῖ καὶ [ἄλλη ᾠδή, ἐν ᾗ τὸ] | ἄγε παραλαμβάνῳ[ν κτλ. . . . ἐπήνεγκ[εν· ἐκεῖ γὰρ ἀντὶ] | τοῦ ἄγε εἴρητο (sc. τὸ φέρε). Cf. Schol. Ar. *Nub.* 218 ϲημαίνει πλείονα τὸ φέρε· νῦν μὲν οὖν τὸ ἄγε δηλοῖ.

5-6 πρῶτον εἶπε (*vel sim.*)] ὅτι πρότερον ἐνχεῖ[ν ὕδωρ εἰώθαϲι or something similar, cf. Athen. 11. 782 a ἔθος ἦν πρότερον ἐν τῷ ποτηρίῳ ὕδωρ ἐμβάλλεϲθαι, μεθ' ὃ τὸν οἶνον. Athenaeus quotes An. 38 (*PMG* 396) and Hes. *Op.* 595-6 (see below, ll. 8-10).

7-10 πρῶτον ν.ν: not νῦν, hardly νιν, but what else? Then, μὲν χ[ὰρ seems possible; perhaps μὲν χ[ὰρ τὸ ὕδωρ ἐνέχεον, μεθ' ὃ] τὸν οἶνον· καὶ 'Η[cίοδος ϲυναινεῖ δεῖν] λέγων "τρεῖϲ ὕδα[τος προχέειν τὸ δὲ τέτρατον ἱέμεν] οἴνου" (*Op.* 596): the quotation would make the line too long, but it may have been shortened. See also fr. 88. 3-4.

10-12 There seems to be a contrast here between drunkenness (μεθυ[) and having learnt self-control ([ϲε]ϲωφρονίϲθαι); in 11, ὡς τὸ κατακοιμ[ᾶϲθαι?

13 τοδεοϋ: τόδε· ὁ μ(έν), or τὸ δεόμ(ενον)? As μ(έν) is usually μ̄, the latter seems more likely; cf., however, δ̄ = δέ in fr. 16 i 6.

14 ἀ]|ναγεινωϲκομένων τῷ[ν?

15 [ϲεϲωφρονί]ϲθαι again? Then, ἐπεὶ γὰρ οἱ ἄλλοι ἄνθ[ρωποι?

16 αὐτὸϲ or αὔτωϲ? δοκέω[seems possible (if αὐτόϲ can be read, δοκέω[may be lemma).

17].ọ.[:]τὸ δ[έ seems possible; if right, it may have introduced another lemma.

18 μέτει[μι or μετέρ[χομαι?

fr. 16   9 × 12 cm

col. i

].. [

]α.ειωπα

].θενηκαι

]ζοντο

5   ]τηφαι.

col. ii

].[].[..].το[

.[.]αιπερπ..[

ω..ϲεπιθεμ[

ρα.προϲαγορε[

5   ποιηϲθαιτοϱνο[

Col. i. 1]., foot of upright   2 α., beginning of diagonal ascending to right from rather below the line   Above and to right of πα, smudges of ink, offset from another sheet?   3]., I think overhang of ϲ   5 The final letter apparently iota deleted by 2 horizontal strokes flourished out to the right

Col. ii. 1].[, base of upright descending below the line   ].τ, the three points of a triangle, λ or α suggested   2 .[, hook on or below line, open upwards and to right, suggesting α or ω   π, might be read as ιτ, perhaps better; then speck on line; then traces resembling left side of μ   3 Two specks of ink in the left margin against this line are perhaps accidental   .ϲ, probably back of α

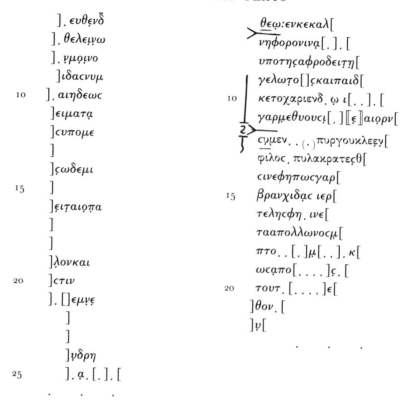

Col. i.

```
       ]. ευθενδ̄
       ]. θελεινω
       ]. νμοινο
       ]ιδασνυμ
10     ]. αιηδεως
       ]ειματα
       ]ςυπομε
       ]
       ]ςωδεμι
15     ]
       ]ειταιορπα
       ]
       ]
       ]λονκαι
20     ]ςτιν
       ]. []εμνε
       ]
       ]
       ]υδρη
25     ]. α. [.]. [
```

Col. ii.

```
        θεω:ενκεκαλ[
      ⟩ νηφορονινα[.]. [
        υποτηςαφροδειτη[
        γελωτο[]ςκαιπαιδ[
10      κετοχαριενδ. ω ι[..]. [
        γαρμεθυουςι[.][ε]αιορν[
   2⟩   ςυμεν...(.)πυργουκλεςυ[
        φιλος. πυλακρατεςθ[
        ςινεφηπωςγαρ[
15      βρανχιδας ιερ[
        τελησφη. ινε[
        τααπολλωνοςμ[
        πτο..[.]μ[..]. κ[
        ωςαπο[....]ς. [
20      τουτ. [....]ε[
        ]θον. [
        ]υ[
```

Col. i. 7]λ, equally α 8]., stroke descending from level with tops of letters, curving down and out to left 14]ς, o might be read: if so its right side has entirely disappeared 17 ff. perhaps only 1 line clear 21]. [, small *v*-shaped mark level with tops of letters Above and to left of ε, trace like a small 'short' mark 22 ff. again perhaps only 1 line clear 25]., stroke slanting at a shallow angle up to right from mid-level ˆ[, lower half of an upright]. [, junction of a diagonal descending from left end and an upright, perhaps belonging to separate letters

Col. ii. 7]. [, a small circle, cut off at bottom: o, or perhaps ρ; in the left margin between this and the next line apparently a diple obelismene, though not the same as that between ll. 11 and 12, nor in the normal position 10 δ., after δ, at a short interval, mark like a small apostrophe]. [, foot of upright 12 *v*..., surface damaged: in left of first space middle part of a fairly upright stroke, above and right a stroke angled to right: ε would fit these traces; then a longish upright with suggestion of ink to right and left at top; just to right of this, a trace on line, perhaps accidental *v*[, I should say *v* rather than *ι*. [, though the two strokes do not quite meet at the apex 13 ς., stroke beginning as a horizontal at mid-level, then hooked up at right end: right-hand half of a small ω? 16 *ι*, a tiny horizontal trace level with tops of letters, which would fit as overhang of ς 18 o., at first sight μ, but the curved middle stroke joins the second vertical near the bottom, not at the top, so that *v* seems a possibility . [, π or χ]., trace of ascending diagonal joined to top of vertical 20 . [, diagonal ascending to the right, curved over and down at top, a thick black stroke; if α is intended, it will have been larger than the normal 21 . [, upright

Col. i

3 ἀ]ςθενῆ?

5 αὐ]τῇ φαι[[ι]]||[ν-?

6 ἐν]τεῦθεν δ(έ)? Cf. μ̣ in fr. 15 ii 13 above.

7 ἦ]λθ' ἐλεῖν ω: quotation?

8 ς]ὺν μουνο- or ν]ῦν μοι νο-? In either case, this may be a lemma or a quotation.

9-10 Perhaps τὰς κυανωπ]ίδας νύμ[φας, cf. An. 14 (*PMG* 357) (Cockle).

10]καὶ ἡδέως may paraphrase εὐμενής in An. 14. 6 (*PMG* 357. 6).

11 If εἵματα, it might be part of a quotation from Homer.

16 δ]εῖται ὁ πα-?

21]εμνε[might be μ]έμνε[ο or τ]έμνε[ται.

24 ὕδρη or -ο]υ δρη-? In either case, this is likely to be a lemma or a quotation.

Col. ii

4-5 πε]ποιῆσθαι τὸ ὄνο[μα?

6 ἐγκεκαλ[υμμένος? Cf. Thgn. 1045 (for ἐνκ-, cf. Βρανχίδας l. 15 below).

7 στεφα]νηφόρον, δαφ]νηφόρον or the like.

8-9 μετὰ] γέλωτος καὶ παιδ[ιᾶς, cf. X. *Cyr.* 2. 3. 18.

9-10 εἴρη]κε τὸ "χαρίεν δ' ὦ . [? χαρίεν κτλ. seems to be part of a quotation, cf. An. 23 (*PMG* 402).

12 Cὺ μὲν ἐχ (or εν) πύργου κλεεν[νοῦ: obviously the opening verse of a new poem, after the coronis.

13 Πυλάκρατες: the name is not attested in Pape-Benseler. A pun on Πολύκρατες?

15-17 Βρανχίδας ἱερ[έας τοῦ Ἀπόλλωνος? An. 53 (*PMG* 426) also refers to Milesians, but is an iambic trimeter. The reference to Aristotle ([Ἀριστο]τέλης) may be to the same passage as that in Athen. 12. 523f. (Arist. fr. 557 Rose), i.e. to the story of Polycrates consulting the oracle of Apollo about whether or not to enter into an alliance with the Milesians (Schol. Ar. *Plut.* 999; Diod. 10. 25. 2).

17 τὰ Ἀπόλλωνος μ[αντεύματα?

fr. 17   8 × 9 cm

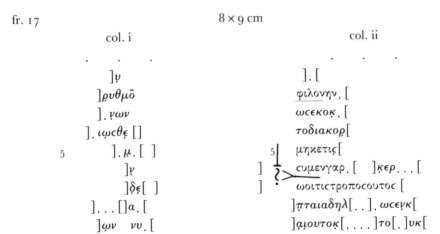

col. i   col. ii

.   .   .   .   .   .

]ν   ]. [

]ρυθμο̄   φιλονην. [

]. γων   ωcεκοκ. [

]. ιωcθε []   τοδιακορ[

5   ]. μ. [ ]   5   μηκετιс[

]ν   ] ⸓ ? cυμενγαρ. [   ]κερ. . . [

]δε[ ]   ]   ωοιτιστροποcουτοс [

]. . . []α. [   ]πταιαδηλ[. .]. ωсεν̣κ[

]ων   νυ. [   ]α̣ιουτοκ[. . . .]το[.]υκ[

Col. i. 1 If upsilon, cursive form   3]., two specks on or just below line   4]., speck on line   5]., top of upright   . [, hook on line, and a speck above: perhaps α   7]δε[, a small apex, then left side (shallow curve) of a circle   9 ω irregular: either the left half was made separately, or it represents another letter (which *might* be ε)

Col. ii. 2 ν. [, after ν what looks like a high point, then a little to the right a dot just below the line   3 . [, speck level with top of κ   6 . [, dot on line   . . . [, perhaps c with thickened overhang, then a diagonal as for left side of λ (no trace of right side), then perhaps ι; below the last two letters ink, I think not significant   9 κ, lower half missing, but the fork is too deep to be suggestive of υ

```
10   ]εφολο[                    10   αλλακ.[
     ]υτοιδα[                        cac.[
     ]τεκαιϲυ                        δραμη[
     ]ν μελιων                       των[
     ]ιγαρραθα                       τοκο[
15   ]εϲϲαιπα                   15   ηα.[]ο[
     ]μενωνδ'                        δ'α[
     ]τεκρατε                      ⸖ λα[
     ]υμφαϲτ'                        ].[
     ]ναγαιαν
20   ]υ.ο̣κε[]
```

Col. i. 12   υ[, cursive form   18 τ, no trace of right side of crossbar.

Col. ii. 10 .[, a dot level with top of κ—not, I think, α   11 .[, dot just below line; above and right, a trace just above general level   15 Speck next to foot of α; to the right of a narrow break, a speck level with tops of letters   16 Surface damaged, and interpretation of these traces must be hazardous

Col. i. 2] ῥυθμό(ν): cf. An. 99. 2 (*PMG* 416. 2) ῥυϲμούϲ.

12 Presumably]τε καὶ ϲύ (even though the κ looks rather like χ): quotation? = Archil. fr. 196a. 18 West, *Delectus ex iambis et elegis Graecis*.

13–19 quote Hes. *Th*. 183–5, 187:

> Ἡϲίοδοϲ γάρ φηϲι περὶ τῶ]ν Μελιῶν
> καλουμένων νυμφῶν· ὅϲϲα]ι γὰρ ῥαθά-
> μιγγεϲ ἀπέϲϲυθεν αἱματό]εϲϲαι, πά-
> ϲαϲ δέξατο Γαῖα· περιπλο]μένων δ'
> ἐνιαυτῶν γείνατ' Ἐρινῦϲ] τε κρατε-
> ρὰϲ μεγάλουϲ τε Γίγανταϲ ν]ύμφαϲ τ' (l. θ')
> ἃϲ Μελίαϲ καλέουϲ' ἐπ' ἀπείρο]να γαῖαν·

The omission of l. 186 seems to support Goettling's rejection of that line.

20]υ.ο̣κε: the ο might be part of ω, but the trace preceding it seems to rule out το]ῦ Ὠκε[ανοῦ (in Callim. fr. 598, a nymph, Melia, is a daughter of Oceanus, cf. schol. Pind. *P*. 11.5 and Apollod. 2. 1. 1.

Col. ii. 2 φίλον ἦν .[may be lemma.

3 ἐκοκ.[: a form of κοκκύζω? (If this were ὥϲ⟨τ⟩ε κόκκ[υξ = An. 105 (*PMG* 437), it would suggest διὰ κόρ[ον in the next line).

5–6 may be part of a quotation, not necessarily from Anacreon.

7 ωοι: 'The glyconic line requires this to be a disyllable at the verse beginning. A vocative plural like Κῷοι is ruled out by the requirements of word division (see W. Crönert, *Memoria Graeca Herculanensis* 10–28), which do not allow a word to be split after a single consonant when the next line begins with a vowel. However, the Aeolic form ὦοι for the interjection ὠοιοί is suggested by A.D. περὶ ἐπιρρημάτων §§ 537. 32–538. 3 (Bekker, *Anecdota Graeca* ii): καθάπερ οὖν τῷ πόποι τὸ παπαί παράκειται καὶ τῷ ὀτοτοί τὸ ἀταταί, οὕτωϲ καὶ τῷ ὠοιοί τὸ ὠαιαί, ὅπερ ϲυναλειφθὲν καὶ ἐν βαρείᾳ τάϲει γινόμενον παρ' Αἰολεῦϲίν ἐϲτιν ὦαι· διότι καὶ τὸ ῑ πρόϲκειται, κράϲεωϲ γενομένηϲ καὶ προϲλήψεωϲ' (Cockle).

τίϲ τρόποϲ οὗτοϲ; 'What kind of behaviour is this?', cf. Soph. *Ichn*. 120 τίϲ ὑμῶν ὁ τρόποϲ;

7–8 [γέγρα]πται? (for γέγραπται at the beginning of a comment, cf. fr. 25 ii 11 below); ἄδηλ[ο]ϲ ὡϲ? ἐνκ[may be a form of ἐγκαλεῖν, or ἐγκαλύπτειν (cf. αδηλ[-).

fr. 18   1.5 × 5 cm

· · ·

]β[
]．υλ．[
]ϲυν．[
]．λιη[
5   ]．ϲι[．]α[
]θεοιϲ．[
]λλωγ[
]αμιω[
]εξα．[
10   ]．ορ[]ι[
]ε[．]．[

· · · ·

2]．, foot of upright descending below line, with speck of ink left where it breaks off, at mid-level　．[, short diagonal ascending to right, joined at top by diagonal *from* right; apex, of λ?　　3 ．[, the rather blunt apex of a triangle　　4]., short stroke, apparently upright　　5 Of α[, only the loop survives, possibly ω　　6 ．[, short stroke slanting a little to right, in upper part of space, apparently unattached: a high stop? or, connecting a speck below and right, beneath the line, φ?　　9 ．[, beginning of a diagonal ascending from line to right　　10]., small loop on the line, very squashed and elongated if *o*; perhaps top of β set very low　　11]．[, top of a diagonal ascending from left

8 ϲ]αμίων? τ]αμιῶν?

fr. 19   2.5 × 5.5 cm

top of column

]ι διαγαϲτα[
]καιαυτοναδ[
]κοιχεⁱλειδον[
]．τατεκγα．[
5   ]ϲ θρην．[
]．ζωαετ[
]γνεγραψ[
]οξα．[

· · ·

1 γ, a vertical, then, detached from it, a semicircle open at the top　　4]., speck level with top of τ　　κγα．[, speck below line to left of space, speck on line, top of letter　　5 ．[, lower half and top of upright, perhaps ink going right from middle—but this is on the break and perhaps illusory　　6 α, a small specimen, possibly δ　　8 ．[, γ or π (or τ?)

1 διαναcτα[: a form of διανίcταμαι 'to get up' (of someone woken up by swallows?), cf. *Anacreontea* 10 W.

3]κοι χε⁺λειδόν[εc: cf. A. fr. 53 N² = 246d Radt πεδοίκου χελιδόνοc. I cannot account for the suprascript iota, unless it is χείλει δον[.

4–6 τὰ τέκνα. [--χελιδόνο]c θρηνη[τικά ἐcτι--]. ζῷα? Cf. *Anacreontea* 25 W.

fr. 20   2.5 × 5.5 cm

```
              .        .       .
        ]         [
        ]         [
        ] . . εντρα[
        ]του ελαγγ[
        ]εκτεινειντ . [
        ]αρισταρχος . [
   5    ]τονειθυ[
         ] . ηλον[
        ]ειξεως . . [
        ]ληγορειεχ[
        ]μιον    [
  10    ]η . ουγ . [
              .        .       .
```

Above what I have marked as l. 1 there is ink which appears not to be letters of preceding lines but most likely offsets: the probability of this is strengthened by the patch of smudging which has rendered the first 2 letters of l. 1 illegible   1] . ., badly smudged; from the mess emerge the lower half of an upright on the left, and the upper part of one on the right   2 ου, after υ a dot, rather high for a high point, probably not significant   γγ, upsilon slightly enlarged and irregular; of ν, only the first apex   3 . [, speck on line   4 . [, speck level with top of c   5 ι, suggestion of ink going right at top, but this is on a break; I do not think the rest of the stroke suggests υ   6] . , a small horizontal trace off the line   8 χ[, or π   10 For ϙ, perhaps ρ

3] ἐκτείνειν τὴ[ν cυλλαβήν 'to measure the syllable long'.

4 λ[έγει seems possible. Athen. 15. 671 F, quoting An. 19 (*PMG* 352), refers to Aristarchus' commentary on that poem; see also on fr. 33. 7 below.

6]δηλον[seems possible.

7 e.g., ἀποδ]είξεως τ[? The word is used as a rhetorical term, e.g. in VII **1012** fr. 1 ii. 22, see G. Fanan, *SCO* 26 (1977) 193.

fr. 21   5 × 5.7 cm

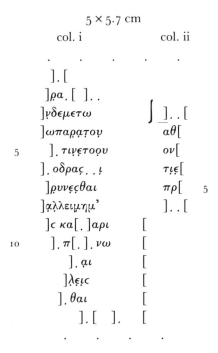

col. i   col. ii

    · · · · ·

```
          ]. [
          ]ρα. [ ].. 
          ]νδεμετω        ⌡ ].. [
          ]ωπαρατου        αθ[
    5     ]. τινετορυ       ον[
          ]. οδρας.. ι      τιε[
          ]ρυνεϲθαι         πρ[      5
          ]αλλειμημ᾿        ].. [
          ]ϲ κα[. ]αρι     [
   10     ]. π[.]. νω       [
          ]. αι            [
          ]λειϲ            [
          ]. θαι           [
          ]. [  ].         [
```

    · · · · ·

Col. i. 2 .[, an upright, with top missing, intersected at mid-level by a diagonal descending to right: κ possible   5]., right side of a circle broken at top: perhaps ω, but side of ν also possible   For γ, perhaps μ   6]., trace at mid-level   ϛ.., lower part of an upright apparently intersected by a stroke from left; above this, a trace above general level: combine as ε? Then foot of an upright, hooked to left at base   7]ρ, only right side of loop visible   10]. π, trace above general level   13]., tip of horizontal level with tops of letters   14]. [, top of diagonal ascending from left, or of upright turning left at top

Col. ii. 1 to the left, a vertical line which looks like the lower part of a coronis   6]., top of a stroke ascending from left, flattening out to right: ε? A speck to right of this, a little lower than top

Col. i. A small fragment numbered separately by Mr Lobel 'joins end of col. i 2–3 and provides coronis before col. ii. 1 (recto and verso fibres match)' (Cockle).

5]. τινετο ου (]ω possible, not]ϲ): very puzzling; if τιμ could be read, it might be a vocative, but no suitable name offers itself.

6 ἀ]ποδρὰϲ ἐπί?

7 βα]ρύνεϲθαι (of accents)?

8 ἀλλ᾿εἰ or β]άλλει μή μ(ε)? (after μ, a curved stroke descending from right to left, suggesting a large elision mark), apparently part of a lemma (for βάλλειν, cf. An. 13 (*PMG* 358) and *Anacreontea* 26. 7, 35. 16 W.)

9 ὡ]ϲ κα[ὶ] Ἀρι-.

10]επ[ι]χνω would fit the traces.

fr. 22

3·5 × 5 cm

col. i   col. ii

.   .   .   .   .

```
      ]. .            [
      ]ν             [
      ].             α[
      ]ου            . [
  5   ]ν             ϲ. [
      ]ϲω            κ. [
      ]. μα̣        [[υ]]. [      5
      ]υ
      ]. .          7  τε̣ρπ[
       ]  [            ]ηπαρθεν̣[
                       ]αρ. [
```

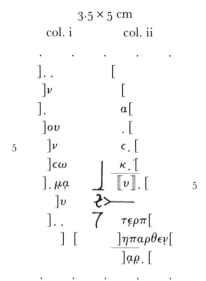

.   .   .   .

Col. i. 1]. ., upright with suggestion of ink going left at top; lower half of an upright with foot much higher than the preceding: τ̣?   3]. , μ, or . ι̣, or η?   7]. , apex of δ or λ   9 in second space, upper half of a diagonal ascending from left, turning upwards at end

Col. ii. 2 . [, bow, as of α, but the upper stroke is hooked out to left at top; perhaps ε, θ?   3 . [, bow, of α?   4 . [, another, more open, bow on line, but damaged   5 υ apparently deleted by a horizontal line through middle; next, a hook at mid-level, open to right and above; the deletion perhaps continues; to right of this, a speck off the line   6 ε̣, or α̣?   8 . [, a thick rather curved stroke: left side of a circle set off the line?

'Possibly fr. 22 belongs directly above fr. 21 so that the traces of the coronis abut, but I cannot certainly confirm this from verso fibres' (Cockle). The recto side would not be against the combination.

Col. ii. 6 τερπ[may be the opening line of a poem; cf. fr. 34. 1 below.

fr. 23   3.8 × 5.5 cm   fr. 24   1.4 × 4 cm

```
          ·        ·                         ·        ·
        ]ια[                              ]. [
        ]ιδ. [                            ]ρ. [
        ]ξηcω[                            ]αιητ[
        ]ενηνδ[                           ]εεαν[
5       ]ωςαπο. [                    5    ]ητοδ[
        ]τηνμας. η. [                     ].....ο[
        ] απειλυ[.].. [                   ].. ερ. [
        ]παραλαβοντ[                      ]. [
             ]    [                       ].. [
             ]    [                         ·        ·
```

Fr. 23

2 . [, upright   5 . [, trace level with top of letters   6 ς., speck at mid-level   . [, broad curve which would fit right side of ν in this hand

7 απειλυ[.].. [Garden: I cannot rule out απειλες[.

Fr. 24

2 . [, stroke leaning not very sharply to right   5 Of δ, only faint outline of left side   6]...., upright with faint traces of a cross-piece on either side, not extending far; then dispersed traces, rather suggesting ε; then top and bottom of a tall upright; at mid-level rather far off to be related, a stroke curving upwards from the horizontal   7 . ε, an upright   . [, left end of a crossbar, and two specks on the line below

fr. 25   10.5 × 17.6 cm

col. ii

```
              ·      ·          ·
              ]. θ. [
            ]. ειδοιτεις[
            ]. ςιε[]νων[
            ].. []α⟦κ⟧ γεται ε [
                     νγγτας[
    ]. [   ]. [   ]. vac[.]εν φοβ[          5
```

Col. ii. 1]., short upright with specks to left at top and to right at bottom   . [, trace off the line   2]., hook open to left   3]., upright with ink to right at centre—the surface is damaged: η would be possible   For ςι, possibly π   4].. [, top of a diagonal ascending from left, then a broad foot of diagonal on line ascending to right—perhaps the beginning of α   5]. ν, a horizontal at mid-level touching left side of ν: ε?

]τασφοβο. []αξιας[.]. .[]αρ[

]εϲπολιν ηλθον οιον ο. [

col. i   ]ωεπιϲχετικονγαρπραξ[

]οειρηκαμεν

.   .   .   .   ]. νυνϲυμεγορχεορ η. [10

]. [   ]χραπταιειϲγυναικαερωϲ[

]ουπ. [. . . . .]π. [   ]δερηϲϲ. υϲε. []μεγοϲδ. .[

]. .[]ειν[. . .]α[.]υτο [   ]ειο. [   ]εμι[

]α[.]φι[.]ολονητοι [   ]ϲ. [   ]τι[

5   ]. . αιϲεπα[. .]φοτερω̄   ]μπ[   ]εμ[15

]ηηβη: ω[]ραιαινο   ]. .μ. [   ]. [

]. αοινοι: κ[[ο̅ι̅]]μαι   ϲειληνω[   ]. [

]. ερ[]ηρε[. .]ειπαρα   221   τεραφη[

]. .ᵉυ̣ᵛ[. .]τητος   π. ωνι[

10   ]ερτικα. [. . .]δ. .ο. [ ] > []ρωγγρα[20

]τιωτ[. . . . .]ειν [ ] > [.]ειληγ[

Col. i. 1]. [, foot of upright   2 .[, trace on line   ]π., either π or .ι (in which case the first letter could be γ, τ, or ϲ); then top and a lower trace of an upright extending some way above general level   3]. .[, two feet on line   5]. ., speck on line, perhaps the end of a diagonal descending from left? Then foot of upright, for which the spacing suggests ι   α[. .], space for 2 letters: if only μ stood here, it will have been a rather wider specimen than normal   6 ω[], room for one letter, but by comparison with spacing above, probably no letter lost   7]., speck off the line   νο, possibly α was written, more probably a rather elongated ο   ι:, apparently ι though the upper point has merged with the top of the upright   οι deleted, ω written above   8]., speck at upper level   9]. ., traces consonant with top half of ε and then ρ, though the two letters would be further apart than usual when in ligature   10 .[, a small and roughly square letter open at the bottom: if π, a blotchy specimen; for ω, rather large and angular   δ. ., lower part of an upright descending below the line, then base of a diagonal from the left apparently turning upwards at right end: the two traces perhaps to be combined to ν   ο., lower part of an upright descending below the line, curved to left at foot   11 τ[, though the surface is apparently clear and intact for the space of 3 or 4 letters, writing appears to have been lost; no traces show

Col. ii. 6 Of]τ, only the right side   ο.[, two traces which would fit a cursive υ   ]. ., upright, upright with signs of a crossbar to left and right; then another, unconnected, upright curved slightly to left at foot, suitable for γ   7 .[, speck level with top of ο   10]., trace suggests upper half of a rather small η   .[, trace level with top of η in left of space   12 ϲ., trace at mid-level suggesting beginning of a diagonal ascending to right, but conceivable tip of ο?   ε., speck level with tip of tongue of ε   ευ, ν is suggested, but the right-hand stroke which should show stops short   . .[, tops of two apparently upright strokes   13 ει, ι represented by lower half of a thickish upright   .[, lower part of a stroke slanting slightly to the right, and possibly turning right at base   14 .[, foot of a stroke slanting slightly to the right   16]. ., foot, of upright? Then a little hook at upper level   .[, two specks on line   ]. [, crossbar linked to a curve which suggests the left side of ω   18 Of τ, the upright appears to project above the crossbar   19 π., trace suggests an upright turning right at top

]επ.[.......].πρ.[ ] > α[

]προετιθετ. > ρ.[

]...ρασδεκαι > .[

15   ].cαρδιc.[]δυνα > .[25

]μοιρας..[..]βα > .[

].κατα.η[..].νιε > ε[

]ψαικ[ ]..[.]νται > η[

]..τρ[......]αν > .[

20   ].[   ].[].ω   ορ.[30

]ηνι   αρ[

]ν–   ..[

]εγ   τοι[

].   πρ[

25   ]κυθε   ει[35

]εερα   γε.[

].εν.[ρ.[

].[

·   ·   ·   ·   ·

Col. i. 12 π.[, a point at mid-level   ].π, a speck level with top of π   .[, trace on line, suggesting foot of diagonal ascending to right   13]π, foot of upright   τ., the trace suggests either ο or ε   14]..., trace at mid-level and speck above; foot of a stroke upright at first, then slanting away to right; upper half of diagonal ascending to right   δε, apex of triangle, tip of diagonal ascending from left   15]., top of upright   .[, trace level with tops of letters   16 Of ι, only foot on line   ..[, speck off the line; diagonal ascending to right, angled more sharply towards top   17]., upright   α., small δ or possibly ο   ]., short stroke rising from line to mid-level: could be right side of ω   18].[, speck level with tops of letters, then bit of an upright   19].., trace rather above the general level, then upper half of an upright or stroke curving to left a little at top; above this, two specks of ink, perhaps accidental   20].ω, short upright leaning slightly to right, and hooked to right at foot: hardly c, possibly ι   21 To right of end of this line, a considerable amount of (offset?) ink   27]., thin stroke rising diagonally from left to touch back of ε at mid-level   .[, foot of diagonal ascending to right   28 A hook at upper level, open to right and downwards

Col. ii. 23 .[, trace off the line   24 .[, lower half of a diagonal ascending to right   25 .[, lower half of upright   26 .[, perhaps the left corner of δ   29 .[, top of a circle   30 .[, a stroke slanting slightly to the right, perhaps with ink to right top and bottom   36 .[, below the line, foot of diagonal ascending to right   37 .[, speck on the line

Col. i. 4 ἀ[μ]φί[β]ολον?

6 ω[]ραιϙινο: ὧραι αἰνο- (or ὡραῖαι): beginning of lemma? The gap after ω would suffice for one letter (ὣ [γ]ραῖαι?, but one would expect to see a trace of γ joined to ρ).

9 ευν[rather than ευμ[(εὐμ[αρό]τητοc hardly possible).

15–16 Perhaps] ἡ Cάρδιc ἥ[c] δυνά-[cτηc? (cf. *Anacreontea* 8. 1–2 W.) . . .]μοίρας τ[οῦ] βα-[cιλέωc.

25]κυθε: Κυθέ[ρεια?

Col. ii. 5–6 ʼνῦν τὰcʼ ἐν φόβ[ῳ οὔcαc . . .]τας φόβου ἀξίας? Or φρ]ένας [μ]ὲν φοβ[εράc, cf. *PMG* 346 fr. 1. 2–3 (Rea)?

7 ἐc πόλιν ἦλθον: lemma?

8 ἐπιcχετικόν: used as a medical term ('constipating'); could it also refer to a sceptical approach to a story? Or to the creating of a pause in the rhythm?

9 [πρ]οειρήκαμεν (sc. the commentator)?

10 [ἄγε δ]ὴ νῦν cὺ μὲν ὄρχεο would make an ionic dimeter; it may be the opening line of a poem.

11–12 ἔρωc [. . . τῆc] δέρηc cοῦ cει[ό]μενοc δ. .[: is the Love-god himself being shaken by the charm of a girl's neck?

17 cειληνῳ[: cf. l. 21 below; possibly to be connected with An. 102 (*PMG* 462) (Cockle), but more probably a reference to Silenus.

17–18 e.g., πα]τέρα φη[cίν (*scil.* Anacreon)? or κα]/τερ⟨ρ⟩άφη[, cf. Hsch. χηλᾶc· ῥάπτηc, πλέκτηc, and *PMG* 462 (Rea)? The sign to the left of l. 18 looks like **ϡϡ|** and certainly not like the usual coronis; its meaning is not clear.

21–9 The diplai against these lines seem to indicate that the passage is misplaced.

fr. 26   2.5 × 5.4 cm

⋅   ⋅

]. .[

] τητ[]. [

] αγεκα[

] καιτιε̆τ. [

5   ] εθα. .[

6a   ]εαρι. [

6   ] την ạ[

] ωcου. []υ. [

————

] κατạκοι[

] δειcạκ[

10   ] μεν. [

] θοc. [

] νωρ[

]. α. .[

⋅   ⋅   ⋅

1 Trace on line, base of stroke descending below the line, slanting up to right   6a Inserted, possibly by the first hand   .[, horizontal stroke level with the tops of letters   6 τ, or possibly φ: the crossbar is on a break; for τ, the letter is set rather low   7 υ. [, short upright intersected at mid-level, where it is broken off, by a stroke from right; a speck to right level with this intersection, and another above this .[, trace level with top of υ   9 ạ, a triangular letter: foot of a diagonal rising from left to right, and beginning and end of a second diagonal descending from left to right   13]., a horizontal rather lower than the top of α

8–9 A form of κατακοιμᾶcθαι (cf. fr. 15 ii 11), glossed καθεύ]|δειc?

fr. 27   4 × 4.6 cm

```
                    .          .
          ]δ̣[ ] . . [
      ] . [ . . ] . θα̣ι̣[
        ] . . [ . . . ]ιφει̣[
  ]αλινεπ[ . ]φ[ ]ε . . [
5         ]χ̣α̣ρτουτο̣ . [
6a              ]ϛυρυπυλη[
6         ] . ταυτηνα̣ . [
          ]νακρεοντο̣ϲαν[
          ] . ημεκεινε̣ . [
          ]ερηγυναικα̣ . [ . ] . [
10        ]καϲ αιμ̣ . [
          ] . . . . [
                    .          .
```

2] . θ, thickish trace on line; above and right, a speck: ϲ suggested, but it would not be typical 3] . . [, upright; shorter upright with crossbar to right, perhaps left also; then perhaps lower half of η 4 ε . , short upright descending from mid-level: ι, ρ? (there is a speck to right of top, which could be connected); then another speck, a little lower 5-7 These four lines are crowded close together; it seems impossible to say whether any of them in particular was a later insertion, though 6a seems to have been given the least space 5]χα, trace of horizontal level with tops of letters, then cusp of triangular letter linked to the following rho in a flat curve . [, speck at mid-level 8] . , two specks, close together on line . [, upright descending below line 9 More cursive 10 . [, perhaps α, surface damaged 11 In third space, a small circle.

4 π]άλιν ἐπ[ι]φέρε[ι?
6 The suprascript Εὐρυπύλη[ν evidently refers to ταύτην; she is mentioned in An. 8 (*PMG* 372).
8] μή μ' ἐκεῖ νει̣[? (cf. fr. 21. 8 above), or μή με κείνει (l. κίνει) 'don't touch (provoke?) me' (Eurypyle speaking?), cf. Eup. fr. 233. 3 K.

fr. 28   7.6 × 6.5 cm

```
                ·        ·        ·
                    ].  .  .[
             ] . τηχροα[]α . [
            ]ις: απεποιμ[ ]ην[
            ]ταφοραντηντωγ[
    5       ]ε τ αсτουсυθωτ[ . ]υ . . [
            ]α[ . . ]βιοτοcαμ[ . ] . [] . . . ει εντ . [
            ]          [        ]        [
            ] . . λλη[ . ]τοπ . [ . . ]ερονανεια[
            ] . [ . ] εα[ . ] . [ . . ]ιανα[ . . ]τουκατα [
                                               |εωс
    10      ] . [ . ]λα[        ]сα[    ][[  . νυ ]]ε . . [
            ]υ τ[         ] . [
            ] . . [
            ] . [
                ·       ·        ·        ·
```

1 In second space, foot of stroke descending well below the line, curving to left; base of a shorter upright with apparently some ink to right from foot   2] . , thinly drawn stroke descending from upper level in a curve to the right; a trace below and left suggests a diagonal descending to the left: α?   . [, top of a curved letter, possibly ϲ or ρ   5 υ is larger than normal, being written over ω   θ rather than β   6 . ε, thin stroke slanting up a little from horizontal, at mid-level   . [, speck just below tops of letters   8] . , short horizontal at upper level, joined at right end by a short upright: π?   . λ, short stroke at mid-level slanting up slightly from horizontal   π . [, upright (?) curved to right at top   9] . [.]ε, the first trace suggests a very small δ   α[.] . [, the trace may represent the right side of ν   υ abnormal: the stalk projects into the bowl making it look rather like ψ   10 . . [, short horizontal just above mid-level; upright, followed by a speck above the general level   13 τ or π

3 Cf. fr. 1. 5 (quotation rather than lemma).
4 τὴν με]ταφορὰν τὴν τῶν [ποιμνίων?
8 Ἀ]πελλῆ[] τὸ πρ[ότ]ερον?, see on fr. 6. 2.

fr. 29   4 × 5.5 cm

> .   .   .
>]τωκλ. . ϲιϲο[. .] . [
>]μειδιοωνπρ[
>]ληροϲμεν επ[
>] . νδε επιτουι[
>   foot of column

1 λ . , λ followed by a vertical (or possibly μ?); then speck at mid-level, trace on line followed by lower half of a diagonal from the left (these two traces to be combined—as λ?)   4] . , speck level with top of ν

2 An. 91 (PMG 380) χαῖρε, φίλον φῶϲ, χαρίεντι μειδιόων προϲώπωι (cf. LIII **3695** fr. 17. 3).

fr. 30   2.8 × 4.2 cm

>   .   .
>] . [. . . .] . [
>] . [. .]γηϲ[] . . . [
>]ενη []μεχριτου[
>]εναϲ ταπει[
> 5   ]φιβολονδε . [
>] . ριδοϲ^τη^ϲα . [
>]υταλοιπαξ[
>] . ε[ ]επ[
>   .   .

1 In second space, possibly ϲ, but traces perhaps to be divided between 2 letters   2 . . . [, two little traces at upper level, then a thin horizontal at mid-level not quite touching next trace, an upright; speck to right of upper part of this—perhaps to be combined with it, to make ρ; then an apostrophe-like mark, on the break   3 Of μ, only the right upright survives   4 ι[, isolated dot on line   5 Of φ, there remain the top of a quite tall upright, and lower, not quite attached, a short stroke angled slightly upwards from horizontal towards the right   . [, a short upright descends from tongue of ε, rather too short for ι, perhaps side of π?   6] . , minute trace level with top of ρ   τ and ϲ raised, bases level with top of η   . [, a little hook on line, suggesting base of ϲ   7 for ξ[, perhaps ζ[8] . , bit of a diagonal ascending to left (λ or δ); above the ε which follows, 2 dots, possibly accidental

5 ἀμ]φίβολον δὲ π[ῶϲ (or π[ότερον), cf. fr. 25 i 4.
6 Ἀϲτ]ερίδοϲ?, cf. An. 188 (*PMG* 957).
7]ν τὰ λοιπὰ ξ[(or λοιπάζ[εται?) rather than ϲκ]ύταλοι παξ[.

fr. 31   2.6 × 4.3 cm

```
              ·     ·    ·
              ]. [
              ]. [
              ]τ[
            ]τιμε[
      5     ]πο ϲειδ[
            ]ϲαδετ[].λ.[
            ]̄         []̄  [
            ]         []. ω[
                      ] . [
          ·        ·        ·
```

1 Loop, of α?   2 Diagonal ascending to right   4 Tongue of ε is irregular, a speck with vertical extension   6].λ.[, traces of the top of a diagonal ascending to right and of a horizontal (ε?) joined to a letter which has been corrected to λ, followed by a small curved letter (ε or ο)

5 e.g. ἀ]πὸ ϲ{ε}ιδ[ήρου (Rea), cf. PMG 347 fr. 1.7? The space after πο seems to rule out Ποϲειδ[.

fr. 32   3.7 × 5.7 cm

```
          ·     ·         ·
    ]..[].[ ]..[     ].[
    ].[].[ ]νε[]..[.].[
    ]ηϲεν[..]..[..]..μω.[
    ]εδ.ιμι.ειμαι[
 5  ]χιτωνα [
    ]            [
    ]            [
    ]            [
          ·        ·
```

1]..[, in second space, a stroke slanting rather to right of vertical, crossed below mid-level by a horizontal   2].[¹, speck on line   ].[², longish upright with ink going to right (and left?) at top   ].[³, narrow μ?   3 .[, foot, well below line   4]ε, bottom of a curved letter, ε or ϲ   after δ, trace of a diagonal ascending to right   μ rather than η   ι., two letters (ιϲ), or one (κ)?

5]χιτωνα: cf. An. 115 (*PMG* 399).

fr. 33

6.6 × 5.3 cm

```
                    ·      ·    ·        ·
         ]. θε. [. .]τερα η. [
         ]. νθην[.]νομαδι. . .[
         ]ονειδρϲενγεω[]δ[. .]. . . α. . .[
         ]ρα. υπερεϲ.[. . . . .]γα[. .]η   [
    5    ]α. . . . .[]. . .ιο. . .ν[]θηϲ      [
    6    ]π.μμ.[.]. .τεροιφαιν[.]νται  [
    7a         ].υτρ[.]αυτη
    7b    ].α. ου. .[. .].ϲγαραυτηϲ μαιναδαϲϰαλει [
                          οϲ      α
    7    ]. . . . .[. .]ιϲταρχειοϲαθετει        [
         ]. οιητηπ[.]ριηνειεπρ. [
          ]φ. . . .νπροϲαφρο     [
   10     ]εϲθαιπαρατιθε     [
         ]. αϰαϲα. ϰαιουψυ  [
          ]ειϲατ. υμει   [
              ·    ·     ·    ·
```

Surface has suffered badly from tearing and abrasion   1 After θε, a long upright (ρ[?])   .[, hook off the line, would fit e.g. α   2]., trace on line   ν[.], a speck below this gap, probably not connected with a letter   . . .[, upright, smudge on line, bit of a diagonal off the line, ascending to the right   8 The last two letters in cursive, perhaps πρα?   11]., speck rather below level of top of α

5 Possibly οἰνάνθης, cf. l. 2]ανθην.

7b In the second of the two inserted lines, οϲ has been added after γαρ and αυτης changed to αυτας.

7 Ἀμμώ]νιος ὁ [Ἀρ]ιϲτάρχειοϲ?, cf. Schol. A *Il.* 10. 397–9.

9–10 πρὸς Ἀφρο-[δίτην: cf. fr. 16 ii 8.

fr. 34   3 × 5.1 cm

top of column

]τερπεν . . ια[.] . . . [

]εραναι . υ . [

]ρυπ⟦δι̅ ⟧οι[
    ⟦αρ⟧

]τραι[] . . [

5   ] . . [ ]αδι[

] . τουτα[

7   ]νοc . [

8a   ] . . . [

8   ] . α . [

.   .   .

1 ν . . , upright, then a short horizontal off the line, suitable for tongue of ε   2 ι . , lower half of an upright leaning slightly to the right   . [, dispersed traces suitable for a short upright   6] . , upright   8] . , upright   . [, small circle above a break at mid-level—c suggested

fr. 35   1.5 × 1.5 cm

.   .   .

]ηρ . [

]χιc . . [

] . . . δ[

.   .   .

1   . [, speck on line   3] . . . , με, then top of an upright

fr. 36   2 × 3.8 cm

.   .   .

] . . ι [

] . φηc . [

] . τι[

] . . [] . . ε[

5   ] . . . . [

] . οιμ . [

] . . [

.   .   .

2] . , trace on line   . [, dim traces compatible with an upright (ι?)   3] . , possibly α   6] . ,
top of a curved letter: c?   . [, foot of an upright

fr. 37   2.9 × 2 cm

                    .   .
              ].. []. []. [. . .]. [
              ].. εβουλ[
              ]..: εϛκ.[
              ].νεκομ..τ..[
        5   ]δε[.]α..[
              ]ϛα[].[
                    .   .   .

2].., foot of upright; traces on line and, a little to right, at mid-level   3].., αϛ would fit the traces   .[, a hook at mid-level and a trace above: ε?   4]., trace on line   For ϰ, possibly υ: the stalk and right or upper arm can be seen, but neither a lower arm of ϰ nor the top of the upright, nor, if υ, the left arm   μ.., dispersed traces along the line of a diagonal ascending to the right, and a firmer trace at the top, perhaps descending again: α might fit; then upper part of a circle at mid-level   5 α., diagonal ascending steeply to right

That fr. 37 belongs under fr. 34 is suggested by the colour of the verso fibres (Cockle).

fr. 38   1 × 2 cm

                    .   .
                      ].[
                      ].διε[
                      ].ε.[
                      ]το[
        5   ]π.[
                    .   .

2]., back of λ or α   3]., three specks around the line   5 .[, traces on the break of another crossbar, slightly higher

fr. 39   3 × 1.6 cm

                    .   .
                      ].[
                      ].[]..[
                      ]ν[]ϰ..α[
                      ]ϰρεοντ.[
                    .   .

2].[, upright   ].., first trace: foot of upright and top of upright, its top intersected by a stroke descending diagonally to the right; second trace, upright   3 ϰ.., apparently a stroke slanting up from line to mid-level, in ligature with a υ-shaped letter (cursive υ?)   4 .[, trace above the general level

fr. 40   3 × 3 cm

```
            .              .
          ]λ[
          ]εαμο . [
          ](vac.) . [
          ] . οι[ . ]ε[
    5     ]καιτακ . [
          ] . ια [
            .      .      .
```

1 for λ, possibly χ   2 . [, lower part of a diagonal ascending to the right, beginning well below the line   4] . , bit of a stroke level with the tops of letters, angled like an acute accent   5 . [, speck level with top of κ

fr. 41   1.4 × 1.4 cm

```
          .      .      .
        ]κα . [
        ] . αγα[
          .      .      .
```

1 . [, μ or ν?   2] . , κ would fit the traces   α[or δ[?

fr. 42   1.8 × 3.5 cm

```
    .         .      .
          ]ς . [
          ]ι [
          ] . . . [
          ]      [
    5     ] . . . [
          ] . . [] . [
          ]τ ο . [
          ] . αι . [
            .      .
```

fr. 43   1.8 × 0.9 cm

      .   .   .

].....[

]εθ[.]..[

      .   .   .

fr. 44

Two fragments (1.6 × 2.6 cm and 2 × 2.2 cm), aligned by Lobel; the gap between them must be uncertain

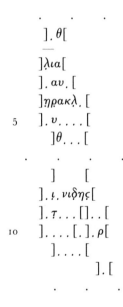

<pre>
          .   .   .
        ].θ[
        ]λια[
        ].αυ.[
        ]ηρακλ.[
   5   ].υ....[
        ]θ...[
          .   .   .   .
        ]   [
        ].ι.νιδης[
        ].τ...[]..[
  10   ]....[.].ρ[
        ]....[
              ].[
          .   .   .
</pre>

2 above λι, a horizontal stroke, curved slightly upwards   3]., possibly μ, of which the right leg is lost   .[, upright, and a speck just to the right of it at mid-level   5]., γ or τ   6 .[, left half of a circle   7 Blank   9 τ..., αδι would fit the traces   .[, hook on line, suggesting α   10]....[, ϛτον (or μ) would fit the traces   11 In second space, upper part of a tallish upright

fr. 45   1 × 1 cm   fr. 46   2 × 0.6 cm

$$. \qquad . \qquad\qquad\qquad . \qquad .$$

]ννϲι[   ]...ο[
]εξ[

$$. \qquad . \qquad . \qquad\qquad\qquad . \qquad .$$

fr. 47   2.7 × 1.6 cm   fr. 48   2 × 1.7 cm

$$. \qquad\qquad . \qquad\qquad\qquad . \qquad .$$

].[   ].[   ]εν[
]ρο...ει[   ].[]..ερηνφ[
]...ϲ[   ]..[.]..ν.ια.[
].[   ]...[

$$. \qquad . \qquad . \qquad\qquad\qquad . \qquad .$$

2 ο.., part of a short upright apparently beginning off the line; there follows another upright, hooked to the left at top in a way suggestive of ν in this hand: but the gap between the two is rather wide   3]..., a horizontal level with tops of letters; then dispersed traces, a small circle, and bit of an upright

2 e.g. ἡμετ]έρην φ[ιλίην or φ[ιλότητα? See below, fr. 50. 15; cf. Thgn. 600, 1102, 1278b.

fr. 49   1.2 × 4.6 cm

$$. \qquad . \qquad . \qquad .$$

].ξ[
].ο.[
]..ω[
].[].[
5   ]λα..[
]ν.ιϲω[
]τομα.[
].ι.[]εο[

$$. \qquad\qquad . \qquad\qquad .$$

This fragment is made up of two small scraps joined by Dr Cockle in 1975 (the recto fibres match)   1]., end of a diagonal ascending to right, joined to upright   2 .[, corner of α or δ   3].., diagonal ascending to right, then a circular letter open at the top   4].[, a very odd letter: a diagonal ascending to right but turning back horizontally at the top, intersected by a large curve open on the left   After the gap, a trace of a flat ω or a very sloping ν   7 .[, ν or μ rather than λ   8]., trace of horizontal level with tops of letters (ϲ, γ, τ)   .[, a letter curved at the top like a cursive π, joined to a diagonal ascending to the right; two letters may be represented

fr. 50   3.6 × 8.7 cm

· · ·

]ϲμε.[..].[
]τουτω[.]δ[
].ται τ. ιϲ[
    ων̈
].⟦εϲκα[]⟧.[
5   ]υϲνι.[
]δρωνλ[
]⟦.γεια.[
]ο.ϊϲτο[
]γοϲαποτ[
10]μι⟦μ⟧ναν[
]ενεινινα[
]νεαυτηϲ[
    επι
].εν⟦δι⟧αχρ[
].εξεωϲται.[
15].[]φιλοτητας[
]ελλει.ον[
].[..]ω[]ϲενϲ[
]αταλαμ⟦ι⟧.[
    δε
]ουμενο[

· · ·

1]ϲ, lower half of ϲ (or perhaps ε)   .[, lower half of upright followed by trace on line   ].[, upright apparently intersected near base by a stroke from below and left   3]., trace level with tops of letters   τ., trace level with top of τ, perhaps to be combined with it as π—but the spacing, and a suggestion that the crossbar projects to left of upright, make τ preferable   ϲ[, back of a curved letter—ϲ likely (τριϲ[?)   4 ω above line, most uncertain: it may be damaged or itself have been deleted   .[, trace rather below tops of letters   7 ⟦., upright   8 ο., a thin horizontal at mid-level, possibly the top stroke of ϲ, which this scribe often makes separately and sometimes exaggerates: but one would expect the lower part of the letter to appear   13]., on the break, β suggested, but the traces may be misleading   14]., bit of a diagonal ascending to the right   .[, speck on line   16 ι., dispersed traces suggesting α   of ν, only apex between upright and diagonal descending to the right can be seen: this may represent 2 letters; if so, ιν[or ιχ[would be possible   17].[, lower part of upright perhaps intersected at mid-level by stroke to right   18 .[, trace on line

fr. 51   4 × 6.7 cm

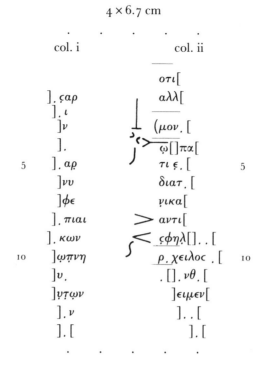

col. i   col. ii

```
                        οτι[
  ].ϲαρ                 αλλ[
  ].ι                   ―――
  ]ν                    (μον.[
  ].                    ―――――
                        ω[]πα[
5 ].αρ                  τι ϛ.[        5
  ]νυ                   διατ.[
  ]φε                   νικα[
  ].πιαι              > αντι[
  ].κων               < ϛφηλ[]..[
10 ]ωπνη                ρ.χειλοϲ.[    10
  ]υ.                    .[].νθ.[
  ]υτων                 ]ειμεν[
  ].ν                   ]..[
  ].[                   ].[
```

Col. i. 1]., trace seeming to rise from line to mid-level; then I think rather ϲ than γ, though the upright is hooked only very slightly to the right at base   2]., a stroke leaning rather to the right of vertical and bending to the right (and slightly downwards?) at top   5]., tip of an upright level with the tops of the letters   8]., I should say ι with diaeresis (and not e.g. υ) though there is some uncertainty since the left-hand of the two dots is darker than the other, and is right on the break   9]., speck level with top of κ   11 After υ, a short upright intersected just below the top by a stroke to the right

Col. ii. 1 There is a little upright stroke attached to the top of o, but I would hesitate to interpret it as part of a breathing   3 .[, base of an upright intersected towards mid-level by a horizontal to the right   4 Of ω, only the left edge is visible   5 .[, base of a stroke descending below the line   9 ϛ blotted and/or deleted   ]..[, hook on line, perhaps loop of α; then a speck below the line   10 ρ., trace on line as of tiny cusp   .[, horizontal stroke off the line   11 .[]., an upright, then traces of a letter apparently occupying very little space, i.e. o   12 Above the right leg of μ, a dot of ink not accounted for

Col. i. 8 If]ϊ, it might suggest ἐπί (cf. ἴπεϲ, *Od.* 21. 395)

Col. ii. 4 ὦ πα[ῖ, as in An. 15. 1 (*PMG* 360)?, cf. also An. 33 (*PMG* 356) and 38. 1 (*PMG* 396).

9–10 The sign opposite the paragraphos between l. 9 and 10 may be a reference to a line that had been omitted but was added in the margin; cf. Bacch. 11. 106 (col. 22 of the 1897 facsimile edn.).

10 ρα, hardly ρι: cf. Mimn. 10. 7 G. (11a. 3 W.) 'Ὠκεανοῦ παρὰ χείλεϲ' (χεῖλοϲ Bergk).

fr. 52   4.4 × 4.5 cm

```
                    .        .     .
       ]. [. ]ε. [. . ]εα. [. . . . ]ν. [
       ]ϲμε[. . ]βοιεν την[
       ]. . . . ρ. . αταρχο[
         ]. ο. . . . []αλληγορι[
    5    ]. . . ( . )ληφθα. []χα. . [
       ]. οντεϲ βαϲτα. []. . [
       ]. ο. [. . ]φοι. ερων[
                ]ιτοοχανον[
                             ]. [
              ]. ε[]. [  ]. [
    10          ]. [    ]. . . [
                    .      .      .
```

1 α. [, foot of upright hooked to right at bottom   3 ρ. ., upper half of a diagonal ascending to the right, followed by an upright (κ?)   4]. ο, a horizontal level with the top of ο   5]. . (.), first, top of a round letter, then trace of a triangular letter (α or δ); the end of its diagonal might also be the foot of an upright:]ρελλ seems possible   α. [, trace level with the tops of letters (ι possible)   α. . [, two traces which would combine as a short upright, a trace near top level, then base of an upright   6]. ο, before ο, another small circle, like that of ρ   α. [, left end of a horizontal level with tops of letters   ]. . [ligature of α or ε with ι   7]. , speck level with top of ο   . [, a longish upright on the break   . ε, an upright intersected by a curve (ψ possible); ε in its cursive form, or just possibly α

2 [λά]βοιεν (space does not allow με̣[ν λά]β-) τὴν[.
5 [πα]ρε̣ι̣λῆφθα̣ι [ὅ]χανο̣ν [: probably a comment on An. 47 (*PMG* 401).
6]ροντεϲ βαϲταζει[
7]φοι. ερων or]φοι. αρων: λό]φοι ψαρῶν ('dapple-grey', of horses)?

fr. 53a + b   4.7 × 5 cm

top of column

```
          a              b
     ]. θν. . [    ]ε. ι[. ]ορο. [
     ]. ν. [       ]ιν[]τ. []. [. . ]. ξ[]. [
     ]  [     ]  [  ]                 [
```

fr. 53a + b. 4 was aligned with fr. 52. 1 by Mr Lobel. While his combination of frs. 53a + b looks almost certain, their connection with fr. 52 does not rest on a clear pattern of the recto fibres   1]. , tip of upright   . . [, apex with suggestion of some ink to right, then a speck on the line; the width of the following gap is undetermined   ε. ι, room for perhaps 2 letters   . [, a trace off the line   2 ν. [, lower part of a diagonal ascending to the right   3 The line is blank (though the space is rather less than would be expected if a line had been lost)

].το.[]χια.[]ονται.[
5]ηρε[].ιτιδ[.]φιληγ[
]νν[.]εκτ.ν..[.].[
]ω.[
]ν.[

· · ·

4]., trace of horizontal level with top of τ ϙ.[, speck below line α.[, foot of diagonal ascending to right, beginning below the line 5].ι, trace level with tops of the letters Of ν[, the final upright cannot be seen and λ is theoretically possible 6 After τ, the surface is badly damaged: in the first space ϙ and in the fourth space θ[are possibilities 7 ω.[, upper left part of a (not small) circle

fr. 53a + b The combination of the two scraps is not quite certain.
4].τοι (οὐ]τοι?) χιάζονται.[(sc. οἱ ϲτίχοι).
5 τί δ[ὲ] φίλην [λέγει? This might refer to An. 93.3 (*PMG* 373) or 108.1 (*PMG* 389), or to a lost verse.

fr. 54   3.2 × 11.2 cm

· · · · ·

col. ii

αμφ.[
χε.[
col. i   ρν.[
]νϲ   παλιγ[
]   λωε[5
]ρα   ρειν δ[
]ρος   λοι..[
5]ετα   ..τ[
]κ.   παι[
]..   θε.[10
].η   τη[
].   π[11
]   επι

Col. i. 6 Trace after κ resembles cursive υ 7].., the traces are rather blurred: the lower half of a diagonal descending from left; then two halves of a rather large circle, facing one another but not joined together 8 for η, perhaps ει

Col. ii. 1 .[, trace at mid-level 2 .[, stroke swinging from mid-level down and to left 3 .[, crossbar 5 First letter apparently an enlarged λ, but ν might be read 10 There is a thin stroke across θ and extending to the back of ε, in addition to the crossbar—rather insubstantial for a deletion 11 Above the deleted π, τη[or τιϲ[has been added

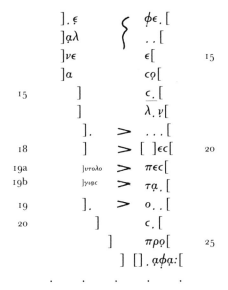

Col. i. 11]., short upright, perhaps turned to left at top (π?)

Col. ii. 13 .[, part of an upright   14 ..[, trace on line in left of first space, a speck higher and to right, then a υ-shaped trace off the line   17 .[, hair-line trace of upper part of an upright   19 first letter perhaps λ or κ, then a speck at mid-level, then a loop or left arc of a circle

Col. i

19 The end of the second of the two inserted lines might follow immediately on the first: τα]υτολογίας?

fr. 55   1.9 × 3.2 cm

```
        · ·
      ] . . [
      ] . α . . [
      ]εκαυθ[
      ]υθην[
  5   ]αυτω[
      ] . νμα[
      ] . cμ[
      ] . . [
        ·   ·   ·
```

1 Speck on line, then what resembles a small and careless μ   2]., speck level with tops of letters, a horizontal at mid-level, stopped on right by an upright; there is ink as of strokes going to the right from this at 2 points, above and below middle; small εκ might fit these traces   .[, rather long horizontal on the line: δ and part of another letter?   6]., a trace at mid-level   7]., trace off the line

fr. 56   1.3 × 3.7 cm

```
               .   .   .
          ]. αιν. [
          ]. καμ[
          ]μετ. [
          ]νεγαρ[
     5    ]ηοδε[
          ]νοργι[
          ]νακαν[
          ]ασαγρ. [
          ].. υ'δ[
    10        ].. [
               .       .
```

1]., trace rising a little from the line to touch tip of α; above this, a speck at mid-level   . [, lower part of upright descending well below line   2]., speck on line   3 . [, trace just off the line, suggesting e.g. corner of ο   6 ι[, the stroke is very near the break: I am not sure that ink joined to the right of the upright which I have taken as ι would be seen   8 . [, bit of an upright   9].., traces rubbed: cα might fit   10 a horizontal crossing the top of an upright and joined at its right end to a stroke descending more or less vertically, seemingly split into 2 ends at top

fr. 57   2.2 × 3.5 cm

```
               .       .
          ]λογος[
          ]. ιεντη. [
          ]. υτ'οсιμ[
          ]α·κλεαρ[
     5    ]. τινιδ[
          ]ονạδ[
          ]. βαсιс. [
          ].. [
               .       .
```

1 λ shows a short stroke projecting to right of right-hand diagonal, perhaps accidental; through the first ο there is a diagonal line (top left to bottom right)—also perhaps accidental   2]., tail of diagonal from left seemingly joined near base by a lower stroke from left: α suggested   . [, smudged: the traces suggest an upright coalescing with a half-circle: κ or c might be read   3]., trace at mid-level   5]., top of small upright turning to left at top   6 ạ, a more angular and open loop than other specimens; the letter is anomalous, having a small tick to the left from top of left diagonal   7 . [, a vertical with stroke to right at top, i.e. π or χ

3 τ]ρῦτ' end of lemma, ὁ Cιμ[beginning of comment? A Simalos occurs in An. 88 (*PMG* 386).

4]α· Κλέαρ[χοc (cf. Athen. 14. 639A) or Κλεαρ[ίcτη? (Cockle refers to Theoc. 5. 88), or Κλεάρ[ιcτοc? (Thgn. 511, 514).

6]ρναδ[looks more like]ονδδ[.

7]ν βάcιc?

fr. 58   0.8 × 3 cm

```
        .    .    .
      ]. [
      ]υ. []. [
      ]μο[
      ]ε. [
   5  ]λεο. [
      ]ικρ[
      ]. . [
        .    .    .
```

1 Loop of α or ω   2 .[, trace at mid-level   .[, trace level with top of υ   4 .[, trace just below mid-level   5 .[, foot (of diagonal ascending right?) on or below the line

fr. 59   1.4 × 1.8 cm

```
        .    .    .
      ]. [
      ]θαπυ. [
      ]ηενχ[
      ]ητηc[
   5  ]. π[]. ς[
        .    .    .
```

2 .[, trace on line

fr. 60   0.5 × 1.4 cm

```
        .    .    .
      ]π[
      ]ητ[
      ]αμ[
      ]. . [
        .    .    .
```

4 .[, apex of λ or α

fr. 61   1.2 × 0.7 cm

```
        .    .    .
      ]. [
      ]παυ. [
        .    .
```

1 Foot of upright   2 .[, left end of a horizontal level with tops of letters

fr. 62   1.5 × 1.3 cm

```
        .    .    .
      ]α[
      ]ιωδεο. [
        .    .    .
```

2 .[, foot of (I think) a stroke slanting rather to the right

fr. 63   0.7 × 1.5 cm

```
        .    .    .
      ]διο[
      ]ψιν[
        .    .    .
```

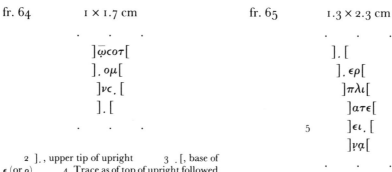

fr. 64   1 × 1.7 cm

```
          ·       ·
        ]ω̄cοτ[
        ].οµ[
        ]νc.[
        ].[
          ·       ·
```

2]., upper tip of upright   3 .[, base of
ε (or ο)   4 Trace as of top of upright followed
by a speck at the same level

fr. 65   1.3 × 2.3 cm

```
          ·     ·     ·
        ].[
        ].ερ[
        ]πλι[
        ]ατε[
   5    ]ει.[
        ]να[
          ·           ·
```

1 Diagonal ascending from left, curling over
to right at top   2]., upright with suggestion
of a stroke descending to left from top   5 .[,
speck perhaps not of ink, on line

fr. 66   1.5 × 1.5 cm

```
          ·     ·
        ]ιδ.[
        ]εc[
        ].οτ.[
          ·     ·     ·
```

fr. 67   1 × 1.7 cm

```
          ·       ·     ·
        ]α[
        ]..α[
        ]..[
        ].ε.[
   5    ]ε.[
          ·           ·
```

4 .[, bit of an upright   5 .[, upper part
of upright

fr. 68   1.1 × 1.9 cm

```
          ·     ·     ·
        ]ντ.[
        ]εcλ.[
        ]ων.[
        ]ν ει[
   5    ]c.[
          ·     ·     ·
```

2 .[, speck level with tops of letters   3 .[, a speck off the line   5 .[, trace suitable for top of ε

fr. 69   1.2 × 2.5 cm

.   .   .

]o[
].μ[.].[
].α[.].[
]τ[]ν[
5   ].o[
]τ[

.   .   .

2].μ[, two specks slightly suggestive of an acute accent over the letter before μ   3].[, foot of an upright hooked to right at base

fr. 70   2.3 × 4.6 cm

.   .   .

]...[
].ψαη..[
]..αcτηc[
]..π.θρ[
5   ].εκυρτ.[
].των.[.].[
].o.εν[
]ε.τα[
]ερον [

.   .   .

2]., speck level with tops of letters; for ψ, possibly read φ   3]., faint traces of a horizontal at mid-level and a speck above: ε might be read   4]..π, room for one or 2 letters; the first trace is a horizontal level with tops of letters   5]., lower half of an upright, perhaps to be connected with the end of a stroke which touches the back of ε, off the line   .[, left side of a circle   7]., foot of an upright 8 ε., perhaps ν is to be read, though it would be rather a sprawling specimen

5]τε κυρτο[: cf. *Anacreontea* 57. 27 W. χορὸc ἰχθύων τε κυρτόc.

fr. 71   1.3 × 3.3 cm

```
              ·        ·      ·
        1     ].ϛϛ[
       2a     ]και [
        2     ]εκ.[
              ].αι[
              ].ο[
        5     ]πι.[
              ].ϲ.ọ..[
              ]αϲ...[
              ]..[
              ·        ·      ·
```

1]., lower right part of a circle; of ϛϛ, only base visible   2a rather smaller, inserted between ll. 1 and 2   2 .[, trace suggests a crossbar, i.e. τ   3]., trace level with tops of letters   4]., a small loop rather below the level of ο, perhaps lower part of β   5 .[, γ or π   6 .[, an upright 7 ...[, room for 2 or 3 letters; the final trace is an upright   8 bits of 2 uprights, then a hook facing right

fr. 72   2.5 × 3.6 cm

space of about 4 lines blank

```
             ]τϛωϛ[
             ]    [
              ·        ·      ·
```

fr. 73   5.1 × 5.3 cm

```
         ·      ·       ·    ·
                 ].[
               ]μ...[
               ]υναιξι.[
               ].ϛαχαμ.[
        5      ]       [
               ]τọναγ.[
         ]θεν[...]ϲη[.].[..].οϲ[
```

This piece is very worm-eaten and rubbed   1 Speck on line   2 ...[, a stroke leaning slightly to right of vertical and curving to right at top; then a small loop at mid-level (ο or ρ); then a rather larger circle, possibly with a tail-stroke to the right (ο, β, or poorly made α?)   3 .[, foot of upright   6 .[, apex of a triangle, from right side of which a short diagonal rises towards the right   7].ο, bit of a crossbar

].. ϲε...ω[]δ̄αθλ.[

]..[.]ε̣ν̣τεωο̣ι̣κ[]ηϲ[].ντ.[

10   ]ε̣ι[..].περιαν̣α̣κρεοντοϲ[

]..τουαιολου ε̣τ[.]ν̣ο̣[

]ο̣νκτ.[..]..[.].γκ[

]εμα[   ].α[

9].ν, trace of horizontal at mid-level   .[, perhaps ω   11].., upright with trace of a crossbar
at mid-level, then another upright (η or ει might fit)   12 τ.[, top of upright   13]., crossbar
level with top of α

3 γ]υναιξίν? cf. An. 82. 12 (*PMG* 388).
8]..ϲ ἐν Τέῳ δ ᾱθλα[: perhaps νική]ϲα̣ϲ? sc. Anacreon?
9 τω[rather than τα̣[or το[: ἐν Τέῳ οἰκηϲάντῳ[ν?
11 αἰόλου or Αἰόλου?

fr. 74   2 × 7.1 cm

]ω[

]τ[

]θ[

]..[

5   ]..[

]ε̣.κα[

]..[]ο̣[

]..[

]ϲα̣[

10   ]νφ[]ο.[

].ν[]κ[

]ο...[

]πολ.ϲε[

]α[]π...[

15   ].[.]...[

]ε̣.[

4]..[, speck level with tops of letters, then lower left part of a circle   5]..[, speck off the line, then
an upright slanting rather to the right, joined at the centre by a stroke from the right   8]., possibly ω,
but perhaps parts of 2 letters   14 π., a faint short upright

fr. 75   1.4 × 2.5 cm

.   .   .

]α.[

].ιτα.[

].[.]ϲκ.[

] [.]ν.[

5   ]νμ[

].δ.[

.   .   .

1 .[, foot of a stroke descending a little below the line   2]., part of a broad diagonal descending to the right, with a speck on the line below   .[, speck on line   3 κ.[, trace above the general level 4 .[, a long stroke arching over the right side of ν, descending to the line, then hooked to right   6]., tip of a diagonal ascending from left   For δ, possibly α

fr. 76   2.3 × 1.8 cm

.   .   .

]κα[

]..[]πρα[

]παραϲο[

].[

.   .   .

Very dim and rubbed   4].[, part of a diagonal ascending to the right

fr. 77   1.7 × 4.5 cm

.   .   .

].λυε[

]ανηϲ[

].θειτ[

]ερηαθ[

5   ].ω τ.[

].ατωλ[

]νε[]ρϲυπ[

]...ε.[

].κν[

.   .   .

5]., χ or τ+ι, or π   .[, trace above general level   8 .[, upright seemingly turning to right at top   9]., foot of upright, preceded by a speck off the line

fr. 78   2.4 × 5.5 cm

·   ·

```
                ]ετ.[
                ]ν.να.[
                ]....μν.[
                ].[.]ει[].[].[
   5            ].α[
                  ].η[
                ].[]ν[.]φ[
                ]ρα[]γα[
                ].ια α[
  10            ]...[
                ]...[
```

·   ·   ·

1 .[, a triangular letter, λ rather than α   2 After]ν, a trace level with top of letters, then an upright hooked to left at top   3 second letter α or possibly ε   6]., end of a crossbar   9]., apex of a triangle

fr. 79   3.8 × 3.4 cm

·   ·   ·   ·

```
            ].[.....]...[
            ].[].[].[...]αο[
          ].ολ[.]π[..].[...]..[
          ].[.]ν περιβ[...]..[
   5      ].[]θαι το.[.].[...].[
          ].ναε.[..]ν.[...]κ[
                ]πε.[...].[
```

·   ·   ·   ·

3]., lower half of upright   5].[(fin.), longish upright

fr. 80   2.8 × 5.1 cm

．　　　　．

].[

].[...]..μ[

]...[...]ηϲη[

]...[..].[...].. α[

5   ].κ[.]ρα[.].κιδι..[

]..β[]α[.]ϲαρ.[

].δυ.λ[

].ϲ[].ϲχ[

]δι[.]τοϲυ[

10   ]μοϲ[

].μ[]β.[

．　　　．　　　．

6 βα[ϲ]ϲαρι[or βα[ϲ]ϲαρη[seem possible, cf. An. 33. 6 (*PMG* 356a) and An. 32 (*PMG* 411b) (Cockle).

fr. 81   5.2 × 5.5 cm

．　　．　　　．　　．

].[

]..[.]ϲα .[

]..τ[].θ.[.]με.[.]ει.[

]...[..].χ...[..]..[

5   ].........[.]η.ει [

].[..]..αιϲ[.]....ϲω[

]..[.].[]..[..]ε...τ [

][...].δ..ι.. [

][....].[..].[.].[

．　　　．　　　．　　　．

Extremely rubbed and worm-eaten; the decipherment is largely uncertain   2]..[, upright hooked to right at base, then after a short gap what seems to be a small circle   3].θ, upright hooked left and down at top   ε.[, corner of a triangle, α or δ

fr. 82 4.6 × 10.3 cm

. . .

]cκ . ν϶τ[

]϶λληϲιαι϶[

] . [.]νπ[[^εῡ]]πλον[

4   ]ειν[[τ . . . π]][

5a   ]τοχ

5   ] . . . . . . θιδ[

]νϙ[. . .]νκ . . . [

] . . [. . .]ειπε[.]ντ[

]ι . . . . ιθ[.]ων . [

] . . [. .] . ρ[. .]ρεπ϶[]ιτον . [

10   ]϶ια . [.] . τ . . νχιαν . ϙ[

]ομ . . [.] . . . ονδα . [

]϶ . κ . . . [. . . .]ν[.] . . [

]τ[. .] . . . [.] . [. . .]νει[]το[

]α[.]τϙν πιθ[.]νϙνη[

15   ]ναικ[]α·϶κ϶ι[.] . χαρ[

] . ρι϶τη . χ϶ . [

]ϙν϶ρωτ[

] . ετιγαλα[

] . . οωϲιν[

20   ]και[

]϶ϲ[

] . [

. . . .

1 κ . , room for one or two letters   5 In fourth space, an upright hooked to right at top   6 . . [, λ or lower half of χ, then lower half of an upright   8 . . ι, right side of a circle, then λ or α   . [, upright intersected by another stroke at top   9 ν . [, π or γ   10 α . [, short thick upright turning to left at base, and rising from the line at a shallow angle, followed shortly by a speck on line; but ω is not suggested. τ . . , 2 triangular letters, e.g. αλ; though between the second of these letters and the following ν is a dot level with the tops of letters—accidental?   11 . . [, diagonal ascending to right, followed by another, flatter one   12 ϵ . , left side of a circle dimly visible   κ . . . , speck off the line, bits of 2 uprights   ] . . [, 2 uprights   15] . , a speck level with top of χ, possibly to be connected with it, making τ   16] . , speck level with tops of letters   η . , a speck on line and horizontal at mid-level: γ? ϵ? ϲ?

2 Ἕλληϲι, or Ἀπ]ελλῆϲ (see on fr. 6. 2 above).

3 βαθ]υ-, ταν]υ-, or ϵ]ὐπέπλου (Cockle), or a perfect form of πλουτεῖν?

14 πιθ[α]νοῦ?

15 γυ]ναῖκα· ἐκεί[ν]η γάρ?
16] τριετῆ ϲχεδ[ὸν χρόνον?
17]ον ἔρωτ[α?
18 γαλα[: a form of γαλαθηνόϲ?, cf. An. 28 (*PMG* 408).

fr. 83   3.9 × 3.9 cm

top of column?

] [ ] [
]. δηκωϲ. ακ.. [
]ταυρουϲη... [
]. ạịρọị. αυτου·ου[
]την.. υε̣. [
5   ]. οι. [
]ṛτọ[

.   .   .   .

     1]., trace off the line   ϲ. α, I am not sure whether this is a space left between words, perhaps with a point of punctuation, or whether a letter has been lost to view; by the upper left part of α is a spot of ink which could represent the end of a crossbar   .. [, dispersed traces of 2 or 3 letters on or just above the line   2–3 the right-hand part of these lines is badly rubbed   2 η... [, after η, possibly ν (the upright in the right-hand part of this space can be seen, and the rest of the letter, though very shadowy, is definitely suggested); then trace of a cusp, and perhaps the loop—of α?—in ligature with an ι descending well below the line   3]., a horizontal trace off the line: could be a low-set τ   4 ν.., an upright curved to the left as it descends, and thickened with a blob of ink at top—then lower left section of a circle?   . [, ε (perhaps crossed out) is ligatured to a horizontal at mid-level   5]., trace level with tops of letters   . [, the traces resemble a small apostrophe, then small γ.

     1]. δ̣ likely: ἀ̣δηκώϲ? But the trace does not suggest]α.

fr. 84   3 × 4 cm

.   .   .   .

]. [......]μ. [
]. ντροπονεπ. [
]. α. []. νοινọṿτ[
]μεχρịτων ῑ [
5   ].. αιπρọπ.. ε̣. [
]. ọ[.]. [   ].. [

.   .   .   .

     1]. [, a cusp   2]., a curved letter: ο or ω   . [, diagonal ascending to the right   3]. ν, two specks at mid-level   5 . [, trace of vertical descending well below the line   6]. ọ, speck level with top of ο   ].. [, a crossbar, then a speck on the line

     4 μέχρι τῶν ῑ [: the numeral 10?

fr. 85   1.5 × 3.2 cm   fr. 86   1.5 × 2 cm

                 .   .   .   .   .   .

                ]υκ . [   ] . ω[
                ]ν[   ]τον[
                ]τραπ[   ] . ολ[
                ] . ταιδ[   ]πο̣ι[
5   ]ητ[5   ] . . [
                ]τ[.   .   .
                ] . ς[

                 .   .   .

4] . , tip of a diagonal descending to the right

1] . , speck on line, and above, a horizontal
joining the left horn of ω   3] . , an upright
5] . . [, an upright intersected at top by a stroke
from the left, and in centre by one from the right

fr. 87   1.7 × 8.2 cm

                 .   .   .

                ]ει . δ[
                ]ντι . [
                ]θωϲ [
                ]μο̣ϲγαρ[
5   ]ποδου[
                ] . . . δι[
                ]   [
8   ]θαλ [
9a   ] . .
9   ]υα̣ . ι [
10   ]φανο̄ [
                ]ερων [
                ]εφα [
                ] . αλε^(μ[) [
                ]νον . [
15   ] . αι . []η . [
                ]τ[   ] . [

                 .   .   .

1 ι . , a stroke beginning below line, ascending steeply towards right   2 . [, dot on line, I think a
point of punctuation   6] . . . , first a diagonal ascending to right and turning into vertical (right-hand
half of μ?); then λι or ν   9a interlinear letters, or possibly offsets   9 α̣ . , scattered traces which I
cannot co-ordinate   13] . , level with the top of α, the end of a stroke from left   Above the end of the
line is what resembles an enlarged capital μ—or possibly λλ . [16] . [, a diagonal ascending to the right

fr. 88   3 × 4.5 cm

<pre>
            ·   ·
           ]ι. [
        ]...ητ[
        ]ειϲυδα[
        ]..τετρ[
    5   ].ο..ιμοδ[
        ]..ρ.φοινου [
        ]..τ[..]..ν.[
        ].[..].κρ.[
        ]..λολ[
    10   ].. [
         ·   ·   ·
</pre>

2]., lower part of ο or ω   3 for ϲυ, possibly ου   5 ο.., arc open to right, from which short diagonal ascends to right (ε?); then dot on line and trace of upright (ν?)   6]., foot of an upright descending below line   7]., upright   ]., crossbar   .[, hook facing up and right   9].., upright, part of stroke beginning as diagonal ascending to right, becoming more upright

3-4 may be another quotation of Hes. *Op.* 596 (see above fr. 15 ii 8–10); if so, fr. 90. 6 may be part of the same line: τρὶϲ ὕδατοϲ προχέειν, τὸ δὲ τέτρατον ἱέμεν οἴνου. In fr. 88 the quotation would give a line of between 19 and 22 letters as against 28–9 letters attested for fr. 17; it may have been interspersed with paraphrase or comment.

fr. 89   1.5 × 3.6 cm

<pre>
            ·   ·
    1   ]ϲ.[
   2a   ]..ϲτ[
    2   ]νε..[
           ].η.π[
           ].[..]..[
    5   ]π[
           ].[
           ].[
         ·   ·   ·
</pre>

2a].., trace level with tops of letters, the upright perhaps intersected at top by stroke from left   2 ..[, ε ligatured to next letter (I think not ι), then a little χ at mid-level   3]., upright   η., little hook, then 2 traces higher to the right   4]., small circle   6 a stroke leaning slightly right of vertical   7 a small circle open at top right

fr. 90 3.2 × 5.6 cm

```
              .      .      .
                  ] . [
        ] . [ . . . . . ]οτι[
          ] . . ο[ . ] . . []α . [
        ] . [ . . ] . [ . . ] . . ι[
   5    ] . [ . . . ]βοια[
        ] . [ . . . ]χεειντ . [
           ] . [ . ]νεια[
             ] . ορ . . [
            ] . α[ . ] . []:[
   10   ] . . [ . . . . ]τν[ . ] . [
             ] . . . . [
          .      .      .      .
```

3 .ο, speck on line and horizontal trace level with top of ο   4] . ., speck level with tops of letters, crossbar hooked up at left end   8] ., hook level with top of ο facing down and left   . .[, diagonal ascending to right; bit of an upright   9] . [, bit of an upright

6 See on fr. 88. 3–4.

fr. 91   2 × 2.2 cm

```
         .      .      .
    ] . [ . ]ερ . [ . ] . [
    ] . . . . [
         ] [
         .      .      .
```

1 ρ . [, an upright

fr. 92   0.4 × 1.2 cm

```
         .      .      .
         ]τι[
         ]ερ[
         ] . [
         .      .      .
```

fr. 93   0.9 × 3.2 cm   fr. 94   0.8 × 2 cm

     .   .   .   .   .

      ]θος[   ]ει[

      ].δ.[   ]   [

      ]α.[   ]ω.[

      ]υρο[   ].[

5   ].α.[

      ]μ[

1 ς[or ω[2 .[, an upright   3 .[,
apex of a triangle   5]., upright hooked to
left at top   .[, apparently there was an interlinear letter above this letter

fr. 95   1.3 × 1.5 cm   fr. 96   0.9 × 1.6 cm

] ρωτ[   ]γω.[

] ...[   ]....[

1 .[, upright, curved to left at foot, and
possibly to right at top   2 this line is very
rubbed: the penultimate letter is perhaps upsilon

fr. 97   0.8 × 4.4 cm   fr. 98   1.2 × 2.2 cm

top of column?

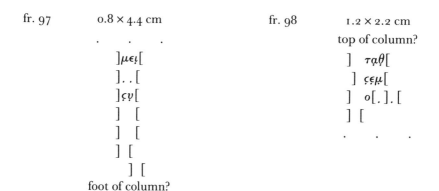

]μει[   ] ταθ[

]..[   ] ςεμ[

]ςν[   ] ο[.].[

] [   ] [

] [

] [

      ] [

foot of column?

fr. 99   1.7 × 2 cm   fr. 100   1 × 1.2 cm

```
        ]  [                               ]. [
       ]. ι  [                            ]πι[
      ]οτε  [                              ]. . [
     ]. cμο. [
     ]. . [
```

3 . [, at first sight top of ξ, or possibly left
arm and part of upright of υ

fr. 101   1 × 1.4 cm   fr. 102   1.7 × 4 cm

```
      ]. . . [                           ]α[
      ]. ν[                               ]ηοποτ[
      ]. . [                              ]ρωτικ. [
                                         ]οναφροδ[
                                    5     ]γαμει. [
                                         ]λενμ[
fr. 103          0.7 × 1.6 cm             ]. μ. . [
                                         ]χω[
      ]. . [
      ]τι[
      ]νψ[
      ]. το[
```

2 ο is enlarged   3 . [, the foot of an
upright linked to the lower arm of κ   7]. , the
bits of an upright curved a little to right at
top   . [, traces perhaps of 2 letters: short horizontal at mid-level, a speck at a slightly higher
level, an upright with a mark above middle as of
intersecting stroke from the right

fr. 104   1 × 1.4 cm   fr. 105   2.6 × 2.3 cm

    .   .   .   .

    ]α[   ].[
    ]καδ[   ].[..].[..].[
    ]ατε[   ]αοτ..ν.[

  .   .   .   ].c.[.]ον..[

5   ]..[.]νπρος[

                       ]αρ[

fr. 106   2 × 2 cm   .   .   .

    .   .   .   3 .ν, apex of triangle   .[, ν or λ   4].,

] α.[top of diagonal ascending from left
] θημ[.].[
] τῶν.[
].αρατ[

  .   .   .

1 .[, stroke beginning below the line and
rising steeply towards the right   4]., top of
an angular circle: ρ?

fr. 107   1.9 × 2.8 cm   fr. 108   1 × 2 cm

    .   .   .   .   .   .

    ]..[   ].ρ[
    ].οτι[   ]αθ[
    ]υ επι.[   ]ειν.[
    ]γαρ π.[   ]ϱcτ[

5   ]ερε[5   ].[

    .   .   .   .   .   .

4 π untypical—the crossbar projects beyond   1]., lower part of a diagonal descending
right upright; faint traces then suggest τ   from left   3 .[, end of diagonal descending
                                    from left   5 hook facing down and left

fr. 109   1 × 1.1 cm

           ].β̣ε[
          ]ακω[
           ]..[

fr. 110   1.8 × 2.6 cm

           ]πο..[..].[
           ]ακυ[
           ].υ...[
           ]....[
    5   ].[

3]., ρ or ο   4]., top half of χ or κ

fr. 111   1.2 × 2 cm

           ]πο̣α[
           ]κα̣τ[
           ]π..[
           ].[
    5   ].[

fr. 112   2.1 × 1.6 cm

          ]..ω.[]μο̣[
          ].α..αι'[
           ].ποτ[

2 First 3 or 4 letters blotted (or deleted?)

fr. 113   2 × 2 cm

           ]υευ[
          ].ε.υ.[
          ]..[].ει[
          ]..[

1]υ, or perhaps]λι   3 .[, λ or α   ].ε, a crossbar

3723. Elegy

44 5B.61/H(12-15)b   9.8 × 7.6 cm   Second century

Remains of two columns to full height, written across the fibres, on the back of an account of artabas which mentions a 14th year. At least one column is missing on the right (since the last surviving line is a hexameter); this makes it more likely that we are dealing with a roll, rather than a detached piece. But it was a roll of eccentrically small format: 7.6 cm high, with a column height of *c.* 5.5. (This is all the more marked in comparison with the recto: the document had a lower margin of 4.5 cm; that suggests a tall roll, from whose lower edge this narrow strip was cut to be reused for **3723.**) Pocket rolls of poetry do occur in the early Roman period (see E. G. Turner, *GMAW* 21, 39, 41); but the smallest of these has a height of 12 cm. We know only one roll smaller, BKT V i p. 75 (Pack² 1598), reconstructed height 4–5 cm; this contains erotic epigrams, and the editors comment: 'wir lernen ein Format kennen, geeignet für ein Poesiebuch, das eine elegante Dame rasch in dem Busen verbergen konnte'.

A sheet-join is visible on the recto, *c.* 1.5 cm in from the left-hand edge. The other edge of the overlap can just be seen at the right-hand edge of the verso; it seems that the papyrus broke along the join.

The script is a small informal one, with strong cursive tendencies: thus beta and epsilon appear in the cursive as well as the formal shape; final sigma may have its flat top prolonged to the right; ligature, e.g. of epsilon, is common. We would assign both the hand of the recto and the hand of the verso (whose general effect is like that of the BM Herodas, though not so regular and pleasing to the eye) to ii AD.

There are no accents or punctuation; there is often a slight space at word-end (and in 1 a larger space at clause-end). The scribe writes iota adscript in 15 (the only word which requires it), inorganic diaeresis in 13 (but not in 19 θρηικοс, which needs it). *Scriptio plena* in 1, unmarked elision in 9, 15(?), 18, 21. 1 ζβ for cβ is a phonetic spelling, 9 θηκ for θηχ betrays weakening of the aspirate.

The poem, in elegiacs, concerns gods and their boy-loves: 3–10 Apollo and Hyacinthus, 11–16 Dionysus and 'the Indian', 17–22 Heracles and Hylas. We might think of a simple catalogue, like Phanocles' *Erotes*;[1] there was ample material, to judge from the list in Ps.-Clem. *Hom.* 5. 15. 2. But the narratives of **3723** are so short that they more suggest a group of *exempla*. They could then illustrate a general theme, say (i) 'Gods too fall in love' (see Gow on Theoc. 8. 59 f.; Petron. 83. 1–6, citing Ganymede, Hylas, and Hyacinthus[2]), or (ii) 'Gods too fall in love with boys' (Thgn. 1345 f.; Theoc. 13. 5 f., Ganymede and Hylas), or a more particular one, say (iii) 'The favourites of the gods die young' (true at least for Hylas and Hyacinthus) or (iv) 'The gods loved these boys; but X is more handsome than any' (*AP* 12. 128 = Mel. *HE* 4470, Daphnis and Hyacinthus).

---

[1] Powell, *Coll. Alex.* pp. 106–9 (the actual title attested only for fr. 2). Notice fr. 3, Dionysus and Adonis.
[2] We owe the reference to Professor Konrad Müller.

Line 23 contains a verb in the first person singular; it is at least possible that the application of the exempla began here, but nothing unambiguous remains.

The format, script, and spelling of the manuscript suggest an amateur copyist. The style of the poem might well suggest an amateur poet: he commands the erotic argot (1, 15, 19f.) and attains a certain neatness (16, 20), but his flat sluggish composition contrasts with his ambitious vocabulary; 21 δαθεις, if it really represents δαείς, is a notable piece of levelling. He has four words new to the dictionaries, two routine (ἀμφιπυκάζειν, cυνορχηcτήc), two of rarer formation (δρυμοχόρος, εὐπάταγος); he shares ἀφρότοκος (-τόκος) with Nonnus. As a metrician, he falls short of post-Callimachean niceties: he allows word-end after the 'second trochee' in a pentameter (20; Maas, *Greek Metre* §95) and after the 'fourth spondee' in a hexameter (1; ibid. §92); in 12 a short-vowel syllable stands before the caesura of the pentameter (ibid. §22; Gow–Page, *GP* i p. xli). But we see no special treatment of the accent at caesura or line-end. Style and subject alike show that these verses are Hellenistic or later (indeed, the poet may have read Theocritus: 17 and 21 nn.); the vocabulary seems to us to point to the Roman period. Thus poet and copyist might well be contemporaries; and in fact we would assume that **3723** is the poet's own copy of his own work. We proceed on this assumption. But clearly the eccentricity of the copy constitutes the only solid evidence; we cannot exclude the possibility that this is a private transcript of an earlier (Hellenistic?) poem.

Such an amateur poet would surely have a model. Such a model, at Oxyrhynchus, in the second century AD, would surely have been Greek; imitation of Latin, though not impossible (cf. PBon. 4; POxy. L p. 60), is much less likely at this date. This model, as reflected in **3723,** has some speculative interest for literary historians. An elegy of at least twenty-four lines presents a series of mythological *exempla*, followed by a first person singular verb. That first person may or may not (23 n.) stand outside the narratives, that is, refer to the narrator; the narrator may or may not be the poet himself. If the poet speaks, and if he applies the *exempla* as argument or illustration in his personal affairs, the parallel is plainly with Roman rather than Greek elegy; we recognize the procedure, and indeed a basic element in the *exempla*, the *servitium amoris*, from Tibullus and Propertius. It has been much disputed whether the Latin love poets imitated a Hellenistic original now lost, or welded disparate Greek strains into a new creation. No such original has so far turned up. **3723** by itself is too limited and too ambiguous to settle the question. But it may be worth asking whether the presumed model of our poet, and the presumed model of Propertius, belonged to the same lost genre.

This text was the subject of a seminar at the University of Amsterdam in April 1984. We are grateful to staff and students in Amsterdam, and to a smaller group from Utrecht, for comment and discussion; in particular, Professor C. J. Ruijgh has allowed us to quote some suggestions. At a later stage, colleagues in Berne analysed the text; we owe to them clarification both of the detail and of the general bearing of the poem.

HE and *GP* refer to A. S. F. Gow and D. L. Page, *Hellenistic Epigrams* and *The Garland of Philip*.

col. i		col. ii

col. i

```
              ]ϲ ζβεϲϲεδεεονπυρ
       ]..[].φροτοκοιϲ
       ].ν...οναμφιπυκαϲϲαϲ
       ]....ντριποδα
  5    ]...ονηνυποϲηκων
       ].μενοϲϲτοματι
       ]..ριονουτιναχρηνμọ.
       ].α.ουπαθεοϲ
       ]παρạιποϲιθηκυακινθου
  10   ]ωνικε.ηρịạδοϲ
          ]τμ...οιοτ...ε.αν
```

col. ii

```
       .δεκιθαιρωνοϲδρυμοχορου[
       μυϲτιϲιϲυνβακχαιϲωνϊα[
       ηχηϲευπαταγουπροϲποδα[
  15   ινδωιϲκυλονερωτοϲεθηκα.[
       παιδιϲυνορχηϲτηνθυρϲονε[
       ναιμηναλκμηνηϲκρατεροϲ[
       ηδελεοντειηνωϲποτεναιρε.[
       ηυκομουθρηικοϲυλακατετη.[
  20   αθλονερωταλαβωνπροϲδε.[
       πανταδαθειϲχωρονμαλελẹ[
       ρυϲαϲθαιχαλεπωνθυμονε[
       ψυχηπροϲτιναμυθονεχωκα.[
```

2].φ, descending oblique, back of α, λ, or the like   3 ν..., second perhaps γ or ϲ, third ι
5]..., second probably right-hand side of ο   7].., point on the edge at two-thirds height; then 2 uprights, the second shorter and with remains of crossbar projecting to the left, i.e. η?   8]., probably the
branches, and the foot of the upright, of κ   10 ε., γ or τ   11 μ.., second a triangular top as of α,
δ, λ, right side of μ   τ.., second, lower part of upright, then another strongly curved at foot, together η or
π?   12 .δ, an upright descending well below the line, point of ink just to the right on damaged
surface   15 .[, short upright with horizontal projecting to the left at the top; damage above?
18 .[, upright on the edge   19 .[, upright on the edge   20 .[, upright curving to right at foot;
further trace to right at mid-height   23 .[, remains of upright on the edge

1   ] c ζβέϲϲε δ' ἐὸν πῦρ   ἠδὲ Κιθαιρῶνος δρυμοχόρου[

       ]. . [] ἀφροτόκοις   μύϲτιϲι ϲὺν βάκχαις ων ἰα[

       ].ν. . .ον ἀμφιπυκάϲϲας   ἠχῆϲ εὐπατάγου πρὸς πόδα[

       ]. . . .ν τρίποδα   15   Ἰνδῶι ϲκύλον ἔρωτος ἔθηκα.[

5   ]. . .ονην ὑπὸ ϲηκῶν   παιδὶ ϲυνορχηϲτὴν θύρϲον ε[

       ].μενος ϲτόματι   ναὶ μὴν Ἀλκμήνης κρατερὸς [

       ]..ριον οὔτιναχρηνμο.   ἠδὲ λεοντείην ὥϲ ποτ' ἔναιρε β[ίην

       ].α.ου πάθεος   ἠϋκόμου Θρήϊκος Ὕλα κατετη.[

       ] παραὶ ποϲὶ θῆχ' Ὑακίνθου   20   ἆθλον ἔρωτα λαβὼν πρὸς δεκ[

10   ]ων ἱκετηριάδος   πάντα δαθεὶϲ χῶρον μάλ' ελε[

         ] Τμώλοιό τε πέζαν   ῥύϲαϲθαι χαλεπῶν θυμὸν ε[

                                        ψυχή, πρὸς τίνα μῦθον ἔχω κα.[

1 ζβέϲϲε. Zeta represents a voiced sigma. This spelling occurs in Attic inscriptions from the mid 4th c. BC, but remains rare except in ζμύρνα, ζμάραγδος (Threatte, *Gramm. Att. Inscr.* i 547). It occurs also in papyri of the Ptolemaic period, especially in the 3rd c. (Mayser, *Gramm* I i² 177), and commonly in the Roman period (Gignac, *Gramm.* i 121).

Before zeta is a space, and before that a sigma with its flat top extended to the right; both suggest that the writer understood ζβέϲϲε as a new word, and discourage the restoration ἔ]ϲζβέϲϲε which Professor C. J. Ruijgh suggests (for the spelling see Mayser loc. cit.) to avoid the breach of Callimachean rules (word-end after the fourth spondee).

2 ἀφροτόκοις. The compound might be active (-τόκος) or passive (-τοκος). For the first cf. Nonn. *D.* 45. 156 ἀφροτόκοι κενεῶνες . . . θαλάϲϲης (the only instance quoted by LSJ); A. W. James, *Studies in the Language of Oppian of Cilicia* 30. The second would parallel ἀφρογενής (epithet of Aphrodite).

1-2 Fire and foam, ἀφρο- and Aphrodite. 'Fire' might, in this context, be the fire of love; an easy conceit contrasts the fire of Eros with the sea in which he was born (*AP* 9. 420 = Antip. Thess. *GP* 349). We should then look for a supplement like κύμα]ϲιν ἀφροτόκοις (the miserable traces do not exclude this). Alternatively, we could look for the same pattern as in the three *exempla* which follow: a god humbles himself and his special powers before a boy. Fiery gods might be Zeus, Helios, Hephaestus; strict parallelism requires a watery (sea or river?) youth, and one who came to a bad end, like Hyacinthus and Hylas. Chrysippus (*PMG* 751) and Ganymede (Zeus) and Peleus (Hephaestus, 'Clem.', *Hom.* 5. 15. 3) seem not to qualify, though Chrysippus at least, in the more usual form of the story, killed himself. By extension, the boy himself might have drowned; we find nothing there either (Dr Rea thinks of Antinous; that would give the whole poem a different drift). Alternatively again, the subject might be a Phaethon, whose fire ended in water; but how to make that relevant?

3-10 Line 9 refers to Hyacinthus, 4 to the tripod: thus this episode concerns Apollo, and (assuming that the poet would not change subject in mid-couplet) ll. 3 and 10 also belong to it. The story of Hyacinthus is commonly told; verse narratives Nic. *Ther.* 902 ff., Ov. *Met.* 10. 162 ff., Nonn. *D.* 3. 155 ff. In what remains here nothing touches on his death (the discus, the intervention of Zephyrus); but 15 f. (assuming that the Indian boy did die) and 21 f. (which just hint at Hylas' fate) are equally reticent.

Lines 4–7 list symbols or functions of Apollo: tripod, temple, oracle(?). One can imagine various ways in which these would lead up to his beloved: e.g. (i) 'The great god who speaks through the oracle of Delphi . . . humbles himself to Hyacinthus'; or (ii) 'The great god no longer speaks through the oracle of Delphi . . . but goes off to Sparta and courts Hyacinthus' (the same motif in the same story, Ov. *Met.* 10. 167–70; cf. 10. 529–31). Either might take the form of a string of participles (ll. 3, 6) leading up to the main verb in l. 9; the second would require a negative, cf. l. 7.

3 ἀμφιπυκάccαc or ἀμφὶ πυκάccαc. The compound seems more likely; it is new, but not objectionable (cf. ἀμφικαλύπτειν; περιπυκάζειν quoted from Ach. Tat. 1. 15; ἀμφιπεδᾶν and ἀμφί . . . πτύccεcθαι first and only found in Opp. *Hal.*). The simple verb is commonly used of garlands (Page, *Epigrams of Rufinus* 73); if Apollo here crowns himself (rather than wreathes the tripod) with laurel, the line should include a dative (δάφνηι) and an accusative (κροτάφουc) on the lines of κάρη cτεφάνοιc πυκάcανταc, Oracle ap. Dem. 21. 52; his name might not be stated (in fact, it would be a virtue not to state it), since his functions make it clear. The difficulty lies in]. ν . . . ον. The dotted nu is itself anomalous (the join of the crossbar unusually high); then a splodge of ink, from which V-like branches project at the top on to a damaged area; then a point of ink, with remains of a horizontal at mid-height leading rightwards to join a taller vertical. The metre suggests that this vertical was iota; then before it νγ, νc (e.g. Δ]ιονύcιον? but hypsilon would be cramped and misshaped)? or (if one discounts the ink at the upper left) θ (fatter than usual) or ω (a bit cramped?)? The context might suggest an epithet for 'head', but we can read nothing suitable.

4] . . . . ν: ερον likely, τὸν ζ]άθερον (M. A. Harder) possible, not δαιδ]άλεον (*AP* 6. 344. 4).

5] . . . : perhaps]. ον, but the nu would be unusually large and flourished; or]. ονι, with the iota added above the line (Rea)?

-ονην, -ον ἦν (ἤν, ἤν) ὑπὸ cηκῶν. In context, cηκοί presumably means 'shrine'; compound ὑπόcηκοc is not attested or likely in itself (Buck–Petersen cite only ἀντίcηκοc, 'equivalent in weight'). ὑπό 'from out of' (e.g. 'uttering oracles from within his temple')? or simply 'in'?

6 Say, φθεγγ]όμενοc (as *AP* 7. 641. 2 = Antiphil. *GP* 884) or μελπ]όμενοc (as Bianor, *AP* 9. 273. 2 = *GP* 1708)? With e.g. ἀψευδεῖ before?

7] . . ριον: a point of ink on the edge, at two-thirds height; then apparently an eta with its crossbar damaged; a point of ink above the rho may be accidental, or a deletion mark. If the poet intended χρηcμόν, one could think (say) of cω]τήριον to agree with it. But the articulation -ριονου τινα is also available.

χρηνμο . . (i) We have tried χρῆν μοι; with this reading the dative must depend on an infinitive now lost, and the first person (unless it refers to the poet) must belong to direct speech introduced by l. 6. But the final iota, though possible in itself, leaves further ink to the right unaccounted for. (ii) Our only other idea involves emendation: read χρηνμον for χρηcμόν. But the final nu is not satisfactory: its right-hand side would show an unexpected curl to the left at the top. ιc instead would explain the curl; but then we should expect to see more of the flat top of sigma to the right.

8 κα. ου likely; κακοῦ more likely than καλοῦ. πάθεοc might refer to the sufferings of the god (or the poet); or, if l. 7 mentions oracles, to their content (οὔτε καλοῦ φήμην οὔτε] κακοῦ πάθεοc, or the like).

9 παραὶ ποcί at this place *Il.* 15. 280 παραὶ ποcὶ κάππεcε θυμόc. Apollo 'laid at his feet' something, presumably a symbol of his power: lyre, laurels, or bow (for this see *AP* 16. 214. 5 = *GP* 3400)? Suppliants, worshippers, and the vanquished grovel (C. Sittl, *Die Gebärden d. Griechen und Römer* 164, 178); all these would have their irony here (for supplication cf. 10, for victory 15; god becomes worshipper); but it is also the usage of the *servitium amoris*, as Tibullus grovels before Marathus (1. 9. 30). But we have found it more difficult to parallel the gesture of placing something at some one's feet.

10 ἱκετηριάδοc. Tau might be gamma; the final letter, though blotted and perhaps corrected, seems identified as sigma by its long cross-stroke. If the reading is right, we have an otherwise unattested feminine to ἱκετήριοc (ἱκετρίc three times in the Orphic Hymns). For such formations see P. Chantraine, *La Formation des noms en grec* 355. They seem to proliferate in late poetry: λυτηριάc (*Orph. H.*), γενεθλιάc (Nonn.), etc.

The word preceding must then be a monosyllable (ὤν, ὦν, ζ]ῶν, c]ῶν, τ]ῶν, etc.), or an elided disyllable (ὦνα?).

The idea 'suppliant' has a surface relevance: Apollo approaches the boy in supplication. But the feminine genitive needs to be explained. Perhaps the poet presented the paradox in concrete form: Apollo, normally approached by suppliants who carry laurel branches, now carries his own laurel as suppliant to Hyacinthus, αὐτοφόροc (if such a word can be invented) δάφνηc] ὦν ἱκετηριάδοc.

11–16 Dionysus. As before, 11–14 may identify him (without naming him) from his normal haunts and activities; or say that he neglects them.

11 πέζαν. The meaning 'border' of a garment extends to 'coast-line' (e.g. *Suppl. Hell.* 429. 20; Livrea on AR 4. 46), 'skirts' of wood (*AP* 9. 669. 10), 'edge' of constellation (Call. fr. 748), 'surround' of fountain (*Suppl. Hell.* 978. 7). Of a mountain, it might mean 'foothills'; LSJ quotes DP 535 Πελινναίου ὑπὸ πέζαν. Here no doubt just an ornamental paraphrase, as often in Nonnus.

12 δρυμοχόρου or δρυμοχόρου[c; at the end e.g. cκοπιάc (Nonn. *D.* 40. 273). The adjective is not in LSJ or *Suppl.*; and none of the -χορος compounds in Buck–Petersen 336 is comparable in sense. Homer has δρῦμά

only (hence Nonn. *D.* 21. 190; δρῦμά later, e.g. Opp. *Cyn.* 2. 82); but δρυμός normally has the long hypsilon.

13 ϊα- should begin a word, to judge from the diaeresis; and the iota must be long. If it was ὦν, not ὤν, we look for a verb; if a past tense is acceptable, something like ὦν ἴα[χε κύμβαλα καινά (Ruijgh, cf. *HH* 14. 3), -ν εὔιος αὐδή.

14 εὐπατάγου: new; compare εὐκέλαδος. (Compounds of παταγ- are very rare: πολύπαταξ; μουσοπάταγος a rejected conjecture at Cic. *QF* 2. 9. 1.) The root noun 'never of the human voice (exc. in late Greek)' (LSJ) (it may refer to birds and grasshoppers, Gow–Page on *HE* 2088f.); here presumably it indicates the sound of the drums and cymbals (as e.g. Nonn. *D.* 39. 58).

If πρὸς πόδα(ς) means 'at (his) heels', and if ἠχῆς is not governed from the line before, we look for a participle to complete a genitive absolute, say πρὸς πόδας ὀρνυμένης (Ruijgh), ἐρχομένης (cf. *AP* 9. 229. 8).

15 Ἰνδῶι. This might be a name; but the shadowy mythological figures so called have no clear relevance to Dionysus. It might be an adjective attached more or less closely to 16 παιδί; in which case we need a boy-love of Dionysus who could be called 'Indian', or at least 'Oriental' (see e.g. Phld. *AP* 5. 132. 8, 'Indian' Andromeda). Ps.-Clem. *Hom.* 5. 12. 2 gives a convenient list—Achilles, Adonis, Ampelus, Hermaphroditus, Hymenaeus; other sources add Prosymnus and Staphylus. Three of these have special qualifications, and two take part in Dionysus' Indian campaign as Nonnus describes it. (i) Ampelus: Dionysus loved him as Apollo loved Hyacinthus (Nonn. *D.* 10. 250ff.); he meets an accidental death, and Dionysus puts a thyrsus in the dead hand (11. 238; cf. l. 16). Nonnus' account is set in Lydia, Ovid's (*Fast.* 3. 407) in Thrace. (ii) Hymenaeus commands the Boeotians (13. 83), and is compared with Hyacinthus (29. 95). (iii) Staphylus, king of Assyria, is also compared with Hyacinthus (19. 105) after his death (18. 329); he does not figure in Nonnus as D.'s beloved, but a Thasian Staphylus is so called by Tzetzes on Aristoph. *Plu.* 1021. Ampelus is clearly most eligible, except that there is the least excuse for calling him Indian.

ϲκῦλον. The conquering god is conquered by the boy. For 'spoils' cf. *AP* 16. 214 (Secundus) and *AP* 16. 215 (Philip) (*GP* 3118ff., 3396ff.), where the Erotes count among their spoils the thyrsus of Dionysus, as well as the thunder of Zeus, the bow and quiver of Apollo, the club of Heracles, and the like; similarly *AP* 16. 103 (Geminus), *AP* 16. 104 (Philip) (*GP* 2372, 3090), Heracles stripped by Eros. In *AP* 6. 71 (Paul. Sil.) Lais receives as spoils the tokens of Anaxagoras' passion (i.e. of his fall from philosophy). More literally, the dominant mistress claims monetary spoils (Prop. 3. 13. 12, Ov. *Am.* 1. 10. 29), the conquering lover celebrates his booty (Ov. *AA* 2. 744).

ἔθηκα. [: probably ἔθηκ' α. [; the last letter perhaps nu or pi (not ἐθήκατ[ο).

16 ϲυνορχηϲτήν: not in LSJ; compare ὑπ- (a conjecture at *CGL* iii 240. 11 for the transmitted πορκιϲτής).
ϵ[: one construction would be a participle on the lines of ἐ[πιϲχόμενος, 'presenting'.

17 ναὶ μήν is a 'mark of transition or progress' (Gow on Theoc. 27. 27), i.e. it corresponds to καὶ μήν as marking 'a new item in a series' (Denniston 352). ναί has a discontinuous history in such combinations. Homer has ναὶ δή, AR ναὶ μέν. Of ναὶ μήν there is an isolated early example in Empedocles 31 B 76. 2 DK; the MSS of Plutarch, who cites the lines twice, are unanimous, but editors normally accept the conjecture of Xylander, καὶ μήν. But from the 3rd c. BC this, and the strengthened ναὶ μὴν καί, become very popular, especially in catalogue poems:

ναὶ μήν	ναὶ μὴν καί
Theoc. 27. 27	Arat. 450 (var. καί)
Damag. *AP* 7. 541. 5	Mel. *AP* 4. 1. 43, 47 (proem)
Nicander (*Ther.*, 5×, *Al.*, 4×)	Nicander (*Ther.*, 5×)
Suppl. Hell. 455. 5	Dion. Perieg. 1123
Opp. *Cyn.* (12×)	Opp. *Hal.* (6×)
DL *AP* 7. 124 (first words of poem)	Orph. *Arg.* 216
	Kaibel, *Epigr. Gr.* 916. 3

Notice that the Oppians make different choices!

κρατερός requires a noun, say [γόνος or [πάϊς. The rest of the line, to judge from ἠδέ in 18, should refer to another triumph of Heracles. The short space might accommodate (i) an accusative dependent on ἔναιρε, or (ii) a verb coordinate with ἔναιρε, and its object; the accusative under (i) might be noun or adjective (to parallel λεοντείην), and might or might not be introduced by a conjunction (to parallel ὡς). If we assume that this was a killing, and a killing from the canonical twelve labours, the choice is limited: Hydra, Geryones, Hippolyta, Stymphalian birds, the Dragon of the Hesperides? So for example (i) ὥς ποτ' ἐχίδνην or (as Dr Holford-Strevens suggests) ὡς ὀφιῆτιν; (ii) ὡς κτάνεν ὕδρην.

Theoc. 13. 5 ff. ἀλλὰ καὶ Ἀμφιτρύωνος ὁ χαλκεοκάρδιος υἱός,/ ὃς τὸν λῖν ὑπέμεινε τὸν ἄγριον, ἤρατο παιδός,/ τοῦ χαρίεντος Ὕλα, τοῦ τὰν πλοκαμῖδα φορεῦντος.

18 β[ίην: the trace allows beta (and several other letters); the supplement is recommended by *AP* 9. 221. 2 (Argentarius, *GP* 1496), Ἔρωτα/ χερσὶ λεοντείαν ἀνιοχεῦντα βίαν.

19 Θρήϊκος. In Homer the iota is always short; long iota is attested first in Hellenistic poets; from then on short and long alternate. (See Livrea on AR 4. 905, and Colluthus 212.) This scansion at this place in the line: AR 1. 24, Call. fr. 1. 13, fr. 104, *H.* 3. 114, *AP* 10. 24. 3 (Crin. *GP* 1967), Dion. Perieg. 323, Triphiod. 30.

AR 1. 1213 makes Hylas' father Theiodamas a Dryopian; Hyg. *Fab.* 14. 11 describes Hylas as *ex Oechalia, alii aiunt ex Argis*. The difference of opinion may simply reflect the migration of the Dryopians, who traditionally lived in the area of Oeta before being driven into the Peloponnese by Heracles. Neither location justifies 'Thracian'; nor does his disappearance, which AR places near Cius in Mysia.

κατετήκ[ετο κάλλει or the like?

20 The poet clearly wants to say 'love was Heracles' greatest labour'; thus *AP* 16. 103. 6 (*GP* 2377) εἰς βαρὺς ἆθλος, Ἔρως. δεκ[can be read, with the suggestion that the conceit was put in numerical form. Twelve labours is the canonical number (hints of a ten-labour cycle, *RE Suppl.* iii 1021): πρὸς δέκ[α τοῦτο τρίτον, πρὸς δεκ[άτῳ τρίτατον?

21 The story of Heracles and Hylas is told in Greek by AR 1. 1207 ff. and Theoc. 13; in describing Heracles' search, Apollonius (1. 1248) writes ἀμφὶ δὲ χῶρον φοίτα κεκληγώς, Theocritus (13. 65) πολὺν δ' ἐπελάμβανε χῶρον. Our poet may have imitated these phrases (as he draws on Theoc. 13. 5 f. above); if so, he meant δαθείς (we see no other way of articulating the letters) to mean 'having searched', 'traversed' or the like. We have not found this participle elsewhere; our only guess is that it represents δαείς adapted to the common model in -θ- (cf. Schwyzer i 759). Even then the sense, 'come to know', 'experience', is unexpectedly oblique. Another doubt is the asyndeton. But if we write πάντα δ', what to make of αθεις?

ελε[. Something is needed to govern the infinitive in 22; since space there is limited, once a noun is supplied to agree with χαλεπῶν, we might expect a verb-form in 21, either a participle (if asyndeton is to be avoided) or a main verb (with asyndeton if need be); a main verb seems more likely, since this is a new stage of the narrative. ελε[would suit a past tense (e.g. ἐλε[ίπετο]); but if the verb is to govern the infinitive we can think of nothing better than ἐλίπτετο, ἐλίσσετο spelled itacistically. μάλ' in itself might suggest that an adjective or adverb followed; but for its use with verbs see Gow on Theoc. 25. 60, 124.

22 ε[. On the likeliest pattern, χαλεπῶν is answered by πόθων, παθέων, ἀνιῶν, or the like at line-end. We can think of no single word to fill the whole gap (ἐ[πηλυσιῶν? Lloyd-Jones); if then ε[belongs to a different word, the possibilities include (i) a participle governing the infinitive ('longing'), (ii) an adjective for θυμόν. We can think of nothing for (i); under (ii) nothing better than ἐ[όν.

23 ψυχή must be vocative: endearment (as Juv. 6. 195), or self-address (as at *AP* 5. 131. 1 (Phld. *GP* 3224) ὦ ψυχή, φλέξει σε, 9. 411. 5 (Maccius, *GP* 2486) εἴκωμεν, ψυχή· πεπαλαίσμεθα; cf. **3724** vi 19)? In what follows, we have considered two constructions: (i) μῦθον with τίνα, (ii) μῦθον with ἔχω. If (i), ἔχω might be intransitive, 'relate to', 'aim at' (KG i 92); or it might have been completed, in the second part of the line, by an accusative (equivalent to τὸν νοῦν?) or an infinitive (on the lines of τρέπεσθαι, 'to what can I' or 'must I turn?') or even a participle (to make a periphrastic perfect). If (ii), μῦθον ἔχω might simply represent μυθοῦμαι, though we have found no example of the phrase on its own (*Od.* 15. 445 ἔχετ' ἐν φρεσὶ μῦθον, *AP* 7. 92. 3 μῦθον . . . ἐνὶ στομάτεσσιν ἔχοντα), or μῦθον might depend on an infinitive now lost; or, as Professor Schäublin points out, there is a quite different range of possibilities suggested by ἐχεμυθεῖν 'keep silent' (cf. e.g. *Od.* 19. 502 ἀλλ' ἔχε σιγῇ μῦθον).

These grammatical uncertainties tangle with contextual ambiguities. ἔχω, first person singular, seems unavoidable. Who then is the first person? He might be (1) Heracles, or (2) a narrator; if (2), either (*a*) a character in the poem, or (*b*) the poet in his own person or *persona*. We do not see how to exclude (1), which would imply a speech of protest ('He begged the gods to end his pain, (saying) "To whom can I appeal?" '). But it would carry this episode to rather greater length than the two which precede; for that reason we prefer (2). If that is right, something still depends on the sense of μῦθον: 'speech' in general? or (after three *exempla*) 'myth'? Suppose, for example, that the *exempla* were intended to persuade a boy to yield, or a girl to behave (cf. Prop. 2.4), or a critic to condone pederasty, then the narrator might say 'To whom am I speaking? They will not listen' or 'To what story can I turn, if these have not persuaded you?'

If the narrator is the poet, and if the *exempla* relate, as ornament or as argument, to his personal situation, we must reckon with 'personal love-elegy' of the Roman type; see the introduction.

3724. LIST OF EPIGRAMS

75/2   fr. 1 29.8 × 20.2 cm   Later first century

The main fragment shows a heavy sheet-join just before the line-ends of col. i, and another at the extreme right; the central kollema was at least 25 cm wide, with an overlap at the right of at least 2.5 cm. At the left the line-beginnings are lost, and other columns may have preceded (one at least, if fr. 2 cannot be placed in col. i); on the right, the papyrus looks to have broken down the further edge of the join, but there is no sign that text is missing. Given the miscellaneous content, we may be dealing with a part of a roll, torn or broken off and used independently.

Three different hands contributed text. Hand A was responsible for col. i, and frr. 2–3; his is a sloppy, ugly half-cursive, comparable with such documentary scripts as XXXIV **2725** (AD 71), PSI 459 (Norsa, *Scritt. Doc.* pl. 14) (AD 72) and PSI XIII 1319 (Pintaudi, *Papiri greci e latini a Firenze* pl. 14), second hand (AD 76); a date in the later first century would suit. Hand B, a 'slow writer' in awkward upright capitals, added, some 5 cm to the right of col. i, a recipe for cough-mixture. This has been crossed out. To the left of it, below it, and to the right, hand C, a good rapid cursive, has added five columns of text, of which the last ends short; and on the back, across the fibres, more or less at mid-point (with blanks of *c.* 9 cm to left and to right), a further column and a half. C could be dated to the second century; but his script is much less distinctive than A's, and gives no good reason to deny that A and C were contemporary.

Neither A nor C writes accents, breathings, punctuation, or elision-marks; there is no example of *scriptio plena*. C generally omits iota adscript (but viii 3 εν ταυτη τηι νυκτι), and represents long iota by ει (but viii 11 λιτον ~ iv 4 λειτην). C abbreviates, on two different systems. (i) At line-ends he cuts short a word, and writes the last remaining letter above the line (e.g. iv 17 προλ^{ε} for προλεγει); this is the system of suspension normal in documentary texts. The raised letters are often written with a flourish; sometimes it is only the context, not the formal shape, which shows what letter was intended (ii 3 n.). In places he forgets to raise, and we have to infer abbreviation from the sense (e.g. ii 19 μελα for μελανευca). (ii) Much more rarely he uses signs which belong to the 'scholiastic' system: / for ἐcτι, κ for καί (see *RE* s.v. Siglae 2294; K. McNamee, *Abbreviations in Greek Literary Papyri and Ostraca* 27, 45).

Cough-mixture apart, the text seems to represent a collection of Greek epigrams. Col. i (hand A) has one epigram copied in full (15–20), and probably another after it (21 ff.); on the other hand, 1–14 are all hexameters, and it is not clear whether we are dealing with one, or more, continuous poems (not epigrams), or with a series of individual incipits (which might be epigrams). In cols. ii–viii (hand C), there is no doubt: these are epigram incipits, and indeed the first words only, not the whole first verse, of each poem. A similar, but much shorter, list of epigrams appears in *Suppl. Hell.* 976 (ii BC), and a list of lyric poems in PMich. inv. 3498R (*ZPE* 12 (1973) 86; *SLG* S 286) (ii BC); but the obvious comparison is with the very extensive epigram-list of iii

BC in PVindob. G 40611, partly published by H. Harrauer in *Proc. XVI Int. Congr. Pap.* (1981) 49.

3724 mentions about 175 epigrams. Of these only 31 have been identified elsewhere. One (ii 2) is an 'oracle' already recorded by Chamaeleon; thirty reappear in *AP*. Of these one is anonymous; two are ascribed to Asclepiades, two to Philodemus or another, and twenty-five to Philodemus without demur. The table gives the detail:

i 15–20	*AP* 5. 145	Asclepiades (again vi 18)
ii	2		'Oracle'
	5	11. 34	Philodemus
	14	11. 41	Philodemus
	18	5. 126	Philodemus
	19	5. 121	Philodemus
	21	?10. 103	Philodemus (again iv 16)
	28	12. 103	ἄδηλον
iii	7	11. 30	Philodemus (deleted, again v 31 ?)
iv	4	11. 44	Philodemus
	7	9. 570	Philodemus
	10	5. 4	Philodemus
	16	10. 103	Philodemus
	17	5. 24	Philodemus
	18	7. 222	Philodemus
	19	6. 349	Philodemus
	28	5. 150	Asclepiades
	31	5. 80	'Plato' or Philodemus
v	3	?5. 123	Philodemus
	11	5. 112	Philodemus
	13	5. 306	Philodemus
	14	5. 131	Philodemus
	20	5. 132	Philodemus
	31	?11. 30	Philodemus
vi	4	5. 308	Antiphilus or Philodemus
	18	5. 145	Asclepiades
vii	7	5. 115	Philodemus
	13	5. 107	Philodemus
	15	5. 46	Philodemus
	17	11. 35	Philodemus
	21	9. 412	Philodemus
	25	?5. 13	Philodemus
viii	2	10. 21	Philodemus
	9	5. 120	Philodemus

Philodemus clearly takes a special place. The compiler included twenty-five of the thirty poems that we know from *AP* (including 5. 24, which Jacobs, and Gow-Page after him, transferred to Meleager); in such a context, we might reasonably guess that he (or his source) found 5. 80 (col. iv 31) and 5. 308 (vi 4) ascribed to Philodemus rather than to 'Plato' and to Antiphilus. I have not identified incipits of the other five (*AP* 5. 25, 5. 124, 11. 318, 12. 173, 16. 234).

Of the new epigrams, one probably mentions Philodemus, and may be by him (ii 12); so possibly ii 15. iii 15 makes a pair with ii 19 (Philodemus); ii 8, iv 1, and iv 21 do or may have names (Antigenes, Xanthion, Demo) which recur in Philodemean poems. Other incipits mention Roman names, places or institutions: iv 14f. Naples, iv 25 *Caesar?*, v 29 *palliolum*, vii 23 Μουκιάς?, viii 4 Ῥωμαίης (cf. v 7, vi 2?). We must therefore reckon with some, and could reckon with many, unknown epigrams of Philodemus himself.

Asclepiades, and the anonymous *AP* 12. 103, had figured in Meleager's anthology, compiled (it is thought) early in the first century BC; Philodemus came in the anthology of Philip, datable to the early Empire (Gaius, on normal assumptions; Cameron, *GRBS* 21 (1980) 43 ff. argues for Claudius or even Nero). **3724,** copied not much later than Philip, shows little overlap with either. The question arises, what kind of text it represents.

Evidence of one kind could be provided by the physical format of the list. Hand C organized his material in different ways. (i) Occasional blank lines and paragraphi break up the sequence. But the blanks may be casual; and the groups set off by paragraphi seem to be of no standard length. (ii) Some items are deleted, and reappear later (ii 4 and 24; iii 7f. and v 31 f.); others stand twice (ii 15 and vii 4, ii 21 and iv 16(?), vi 7 and vii 14). (iii) Some items, or sequences of items, are marked by check marks in the margin. (iv) In v 5 ff. consecutive incipits are numbered from 1 to 10 and apparently beyond (but not consecutively, if the numeral to l. 16 is rightly read '21'); at l. 19 a new sequence begins, which goes no further than line 23 (the numerals in 21–3 struck out, or covered by check-marks). The group of ten in iii 9–19 has no numeration; three of the sequences with check-marks number five lines each.

Evidence of another kind comes from the list itself. Its main characteristics are:

(i) Chronological range. ii 2 was known already in the fourth century; v 19 may appear in PVindob., of the third century; ii 28 survives in a Meleagrean sequence of *AP*. Other poems, see above, cannot antedate the late Republic. iv 8 perhaps replies to a poem of Callimachus, v 28 may imitate Asclepiades and vi 12 Meleager.

(ii) Overall subject. There is a clear preponderance of erotic (including homosexual) and sympotic themes. Of the thirty known poems, all come in *AP* 5, 11, and 12 except six; of these six, only two (iv 16, *AP* 10. 103; iv 19, *AP* 6. 349) are not immediately relevant to love and wine; even the 'oracle', ii 2, advises drinking in the shade. Among the new poems there are perhaps forty whose subject could, with all proper reserve, be inferred; almost all look to wine and love (iv 8, iv 25, v 18, v 32 are the most obviously alien).

(iii) Grouping. (*a*) By author? No clear pattern emerges from the Philodemean epigrams: two consecutive in ii 18f., four in iv 16–19, two in v 13f. (*b*) By subject? Occasional pairings may be observable: ii 15f. (πρότερον), iv 3f. (dinners?), 10f. (witnesses to love?), 14f. (Naples), v 16f. (parties?), vi 8f. (harping). But these are not many; and, as Professor Cameron notes, there are striking failures—thus *AP* 12. 103 (ii 28) is a long way from Philodemus' adaptation (vii 13), and 5. 121 (ii 19) from its complement (iii 15). (*c*) Alphabetically? iv 28 and 31, where Philodemus follows so close on Asclepiades, exclude that.

(iv) Other anthologies. From iv 28 to vii 15 all the known epigrams except one reappear in *AP* 5. *AP* 5. 131 and 132 appear in that order at v 14 and 20. That is, coincidence of ordering is as small as overlapping of content.

A third question is much more difficult: the relation between hand A and hand C. Certainly they have something in common. C included the incipit of one poem (vi 18), which A copied complete; this poem, and its successor in A, were epigrams, and indeed sympotic epigrams. There may be other overlaps between fr. 2, presumably an earlier column of A, and C, but not enough remains to prove them (fr. 2. 4, 7 (very doubtful), 13; fr. 1 iii 18, iii 19, ii 9). On the other hand, if it was A's habit to copy poems complete, then fr. 1 i 1 ff. and (if the paragraphi are rightly read) fr. 2. 4–8 were not epigrams in the narrow sense; whereas C has, apart from ii 2, only epigrams. Overall, we could consider two lines of approach. (i) C indexed the collection of poems which A had copied in the earlier (now largely lost) part of the roll. This is the suggestion of Mr Mark Caponigro, who will develop it elsewhere. (ii) A, B, and C all used this roll (or sheet) for their memoranda. A copied some epigrams, or at least some poems including epigrams. C listed epigrams in bulk; he could have done this (*a*) by indexing a single collection, or (*b*) by selecting from such a collection (as in PVindob.), or (*c*) by selecting or collecting epigrams, individually or in groups, from various sources, which might themselves have been the work of individual poets or of anthologists. **3724** has so much the look of working papers that I incline to (ii). C intended an anthology of erotic and sympotic epigrams. He listed them in short form, perhaps from more than one source (hence the duplications and deletions); the next stage would be to copy the substantive texts; perhaps the check marks indicate that the text had been located, or copied (and similarly in PVindob., if εν can be interpreted εὑ(ρέθη) or the like). But clearly this does not explain the role of A.

A diplomatic transcript follows; suggestions for the interpretation are made in the notes. The cursive hand of cols. ii–viii presents the usual difficulties, and more, since there is no continuous context to control the decipherment. The readings should be viewed with caution.

In the notes, 'PVindob.' refers to the Vienna papyrus (pp. 65f.); *HE*, *GP*, and *FGE* to the three parts of Gow and Page's edition.

A draft of this piece was read and discussed by Professor Alan Cameron and his colleagues in New York. I am greatly indebted to them for the suggestions quoted, and for general clarification of the issues.

fr. 1

<table>
<tr><td colspan="2" align="center">col. i</td><td colspan="2" align="center">col. ii</td><td align="center">col. iii</td></tr>
</table>

col. i

```
     ]. κα. [. ]ακροτερονπροι. ωϲαν
     ]. αρ. [. ]ωνεπεκειϥα
     ]. ραϲ. [. ]. εϲεμειζον
     ]φορο. []. εμε. αυτηϲ
5    ]. κοπ[]ωναϲαπαντας
     ]ϲακρ[. ]μνουϲτεναπαϲτϲ
     ]οιρουϲελεφαντας
     ]. . δαρϲ. ϲαϲελαϲων
     ]ϲικεϲα. [. . . ]. ρωϲας
10   ]λακαϲτεμεταλλα
     ]ουϲνεφελαϲδροϲονομβρουϲ
     ]. ϲτων. ελοϲοιϲειϲ
     ]. οπαρδηϲτελοϲοιϲειϲ
     ]υϲφθιμενουϲτελοϲοιϲειϲ
15   ]ϲιταιϲδεκρεμαϲτοι
     ]. . . . [. . ]ϲοι
     ]αϲαρ[. ]. ματερωϲ. ων
     ]τεθυ[. ]ηϲ
     ]. τον[]ωϲανεκειϲου[]
20   ]α
     ]. ιϲτεφανου. . α. [ ]
     ]. ην
     ]. κα. περιμουϲα.
           ]
25        ]. . ζην
           ]
           ]
             ]
           ]ϲ
30          ].
             ]
             ]
             ]
     .    .    .    .
```

col. ii

```
     κεκρηγεινετι
     εικοϲιταϲπροκ^υ
     ουκοιδαπροφ‿
     ⟦ειμηταϲουπω⟧
5    λευκοινουϲ
     ηδηλουϲαμενη
     ηνελαβονπρωην
     μουϲωναντιϲεν^ο
     ουτοϲοτα^μ.ορφαϲ
10   μυριατηϲπαφιηϲ
     μαινεταιειβαλλει
     ιξευεινφιλοδ^η
     αψευδηϲωλυχνε
     επτατριηκοντεϲϲιν
15   μηπρο. ερονφιλ^ο
         vac.
     οπροτερουϲτ. . ϲ
     / νηφεινμεπλου
     / πεντεδιδωϲιν
     / μικκηκαιμελα
20   / οχλη  ρη
     / τηνπροτερον
       κᾱμηδειϲϲεκαλη
     / . . . . και. . . .
     / ειμηταϲουπω
     / ειμεθυεινχειω
25   / ειμεθυεινχειω
     / ουματονηδυνερωτα
     / ηϲειμητοπροϲω
     / οιδαφιλειϲινφιλεονταϲ
     τα. αϲ. τρικινα. . . ϲ
30                    ].
     .    .    .    .
```

col. iii

```
     ⟦ΑΡΤΗΡΙΑΚΗϹϹΚΕΥΗ
     ΚΡΟΚΟΥ                    ϛ
     ΤΡΑΓΑ⟦. ⟧ΚΑΝΘΗϹ   ϛ Α
     ϹΤΡΟΒΕΙΛΙΩΝ          ϛ Α
5    Ω⟦. ⟧ΟΝ                 ΕΝ
     ΜΕΛΙΤΙΟ⟦Ν⟧Υ      ⌡ ⟧


     ⟦οπρινεϲωκαιπεντε
       αιϲωπουτιναι⟧

     ατρωτοϲτϲ. . ‿
10   / τιϲμειϲειτονερω
     ⟦μηδει. ⟧
     / μητηρκαιθ^υ
     / τουϲπλοκαμουϲ
     / οκτωκαιδεχετιν
15   / λευκηκαιμακρη
     / . . . . . . ϲμαλα
     / ειμενμηκαλη
     / χρημαϲινουπλ^ο
     / φωνω ϲινωϲκου
20   ευδειϲκαλλικρ^α
     ειτιϲμ. . φιλοϲε.
     τρει. εκ. . ε. κα. ον
     ϲκλαπλαπαντο. ^ε
                      ^δ
              ]. . . . .
     .    .    .    .
```

col. iv	col. v	col. vi

col. iv

```
  .ανθιογουκηδει.
  τονφιλοναιςχυνη
  ωνηςαιγλυκερων
  αυριονεισλειτην.ε
5 ημετεραςμουςας
  ουτεφιλειςαλλοντιν
  ξανθωκηροπλαστε
  ουμειςεωτοποημᵃ
  ηδηςοιτριτονειπα
10 τονςειγωνταφιλαινι
  εισανεμουςκαι...ρ
  τιςταμακροκεοντα
  τονπρωτον⟦φ⟧ραφιη
  παρθενοπηςανα..
15 παρθενοπηςπ..
  τηνπροτερονθυμ.ᵉ
  ───────
  / ψυχημοιπρολᵉ
  / ενθαδετηςτρυφˇ
  / εὐνουςωμελικερ
20 / ζωροποτηνωρ.
  / δημ..τις..
  νηονςυληςαςας
  / τεςςαρεςεις.ραι
  ατθιδοςωπαφιη
25 / οι..τικαιςαρ
  τεςςαρακυπριδος/
  πτωχονεχουςα
  ωμολογηςηξειν
  αυταιτα.χρυςεου
30 εκτετονημαιερως
  / μηλονεγωπεμ
  ωςφυραικεφαλης
  θυετετηνεμε
```

col. v

```
         τονκρονιᵟ
         τογραψαιπο
         νυκτερι
         δευθωδ
5  α χθιζος
     ειχενδημᵒ
   γ πειθιμαρει
   δ αμφοτεροιπιθˇ
   ε παιδαπολυτρ^η
10 ς ουκεαθηλυ
   ζ ηραςθηντιςδρ
   η τρεισκυαθους
   θ δ⟦ρ⟧ακρυεις
   ι ψαλμοικαιλαλιη
15 . ηρεςεμοικομψη
   κα ναρδωκ´ςμυ.νη
   . αγροςκ´ςτεφˇ
     πρωτεοςφαρε
   α πα⟦ν⟧ρθενιος
20 β ωποδος
   . νικαρετηπειθει
   . μεισωκαιςτεφˇ
   . τουςφερεκαιπˇ
   / αιδεινκ´ψαλλειν
25 / ουδεπωεμβεβλ^η
   / μελλειμοι
   / γεινωςκωταλε.εγν
   / ηδυθερευςελκει
     τηναποπαλλιολου
30 / ηδηπολλακις
   / οπρινεγωκ´
   / αιςωπουτινα
```

col. vi

```
  / μη..ιφαρμακα[
  / ....ληκαιτη
  .αυςαικυριε
  ηκομψη
5 / ..καιεμηκα.ω
  / τιςςεκελευςε
  ορχεισθεγλαφᵘ·
  ψαλλεκατα.
  / ψαλλεινικαρε
10 οινοςκαιροδινοι.
  εκθεςεδωκεν
  ιξονεχειςτον
  ταυτα.οθε.
  ηνικαμεν...[
15 ουκελε.ουν..[]
  παυεφιληλακατη[
  ......ραι....
  α..[  ].οιςτεφα
  αρχομεθαψυχη
```

Col. i. 1–14 I do not know what to make of these lines. 15–20 contain an elegiac epigram, and 21 ff. (probably) another; cols. ii–viii consist of epigram-incipits. The first thought, then, is of epigrams; and, since 1–14 are all hexameters, of another series of incipits. But Professor Cameron and his colleagues argue reasonably (i) that these are complete lines, unlike the truncated beginnings in col. ii ff.; (ii) that complete poems follow in 15 ff., so that we should expect a complete poem (or poems) here. The question then arises, what sort of text would accommodate these rather eccentric line-ends. Professor Cameron thinks of an oracle; Dr R. Janko of a hymn to a god who is sovereign over nature (the hymn-style would explain the repetition in 12–14), perhaps Hermes, cf. 14 (Janko) or Dionysus, cf. 7 (R. Tannenbaum).

1]. καὶ [μ]ακρότερον προΐτωϲαν. The first trace, vestigial, suggests the foot of an upright. The dotted iota is a sloping upright, which in itself might represent the beginning of kappa, mu, nu, pi; but καμμακρο alone would be short for the space. The form of imperative hardly limits the date of composition: in Attic inscriptions not earlier than *c*.300 BC, but already in Eur. *Ion* 1131, *IT* 1480 (see Schwyzer i 802).

2]. αρ. [.]ων ἐπεκεινα. The first trace is a point at line-level; the second an upright which curves heavily to the left at the foot (in this irregular hand γ η ι κ λ μ ν π might all be considered). ἄρκ[τ]ων (Rea) could be read. At the end ἐπ' ἐκεῖνα or ἐπέκεινα seems likely.

3]. ραυ. [.]. εγε μεῖζον. First trace is the right side of eta or pi; after hypsilon (which might be a badly-made tau) apparently a small sigma; before the first epsilon, and joining it, a curved foot as of α κ λ μ. At the end, the articulation is uncertain; if this scribe allows himself to write ει for short iota (hand C does so only for long iota), ἐγέμιζον (Cameron) could be considered.

4]φορο. []. εμε. αυτηϲ. The first trace is a short upright curving left at the foot, with perhaps a junction with an oblique at the top (i.e. μ, ν?).]. , the end of a horizontal joining epsilon just above the level of its crossbar. After με, what might be a badly formed hypsilon; but tau too is possible. If we exclude (ἐ)μεν αὐτῆϲ (ἐμοὶ αὐτῷ *Od.* 9. 421), we have μετ' αὐτῆϲ or (-)με ταύτηϲ at the end; -φορον τε would suit space and trace before.

5]. κοπ[ρ]ῶναϲ ἅπανταϲ (or ἀπαντᾶϲ?). The initial traces look like the right-hand extremities of kappa or eta, or possibly sigma. LSJ gives no meaning for κοπρών except 'privy' (cf. *CGL* iii 313. 36 *latrina*). But I have not found another reading. If an epigram, presumably satirical.

6]εα κρ[η]μνούϲ τε νάπαϲ τε. In the epigram, 'crags' are wild and dangerous, *AP* 5. 25. 3 (*GP* 3176), 5. 168. 2 (*HE* 3659), haunted by Pan, 9. 142, 337; 'glades' are delightful, 9. 669, in the spring, 9. 374, haunted by huntsmen, 7. 717, 9. 300, and grasshoppers, 9. 373. At the beginning, perhaps ἔα, 'let them alone'; cf. 7. 50. 6 (*FGE* 82) rather than e.g. θ]εά (where we might expect -ή?). That could be addressed (say) to a hunter, or to Pan himself, cf. 7. 535 (*HE* 4700), or Dionysus?

7]οιρουϲ ἐλέφανταϲ. A spot of ink above the first omicron is probably stray. One might restore χ]οίρουϲ (part of an asyndetic string, as in 11); or -μ]οίρουϲ. εὔμ]οίρουϲ might mean 'happy' (elephants were proverbially moral and long-lived); or, as Dr Rea suggests, 'dead' and reduced to ivory.

8]. δαριων ἀγελαίων? The first traces suggest the right-hand tips of η κ π ϲ χ (ζ?); then before δ a well-preserved but anomalous letter which I can only see as a poor epsilon. But]. εδαριων is excluded by the metre; πεδαρίων for παιδαρίων would assume a phonetic spelling which, however common, does not occur elsewhere in this papyrus. Perhaps, as Dr Rea suggests, the high spot of ink to the right of ε was intended to delete it.

9]γικεϲα. [. . .]. ρωναϲ. Before rho the feet of two uprights, e.g. pi; possibly further ink to the right, but perhaps illusory.

10]λακαϲ τε μεταλλα. Possible traces before the first lambda just stray ink? μετάλλα (*AP* 16. 183) rather than μετ' ἄλλα or μέταλλα? At the beginning φύ]λακαϲ or φυ]λακάϲ, and much else.

11]ουϲ νεφελὰϲ δρόϲον ὄμβρουϲ. ὑετ]ούϲ? Lloyd-Jones.

12]. ντων τέλοϲ οἴϲειϲ. Of vowels, only alpha or possibly epsilon suits the first trace. π]άντων, 'You (Death? Time?) will bring the end of all'?

13]. οπαρδηϲ τέλοϲ οἴϲειϲ. The first letter had a flat top, with an oblique descender; zeta, (xi?), tau? A short oblique drawn through the apex of the delta may be meant to delete it.

14]υϲ φθιμένουϲ τέλοϲ οἴϲειϲ.

15–20 *AP* 5. 145 (Asclep. *HE* 860) copied in full (the incipit only, below vi 18).

16]. . . . [. .]νοι. τιναϲϲόμενοι codd. But τιν]αϲϲο[με]νοι (the expected spacing) is not especially suited to the traces, and the first sigma would be positively unlikely (the trace is a flat base, with a stroke rising at an acute angle from the left, as in the left-hand angle of a rounded delta).

17 κάτομβρ]α γὰρ [ὄ]μματ' ἐρώντων. So, rightly, C Pl: ἐρώτ- P.

18 ἴδη]τε θύ[ρ]ηϲ.

19 ὑ]ϲτὸν ὡϲ ἂν ἐκείνου. ὡϲ ἂν ἄμεινον codd. Editors generally have suspected ἄμεινον (though S. L. Taran, *Art of Variation in the Hellenistic Epigram* (1979) 75 thinks that 'the text is sound and emendation worse than unnecessary'): Ἀμύντα Wilamowitz (*Hermes* 14 (1879) 166), ἐκείνου Schneidewin. It seems that Schneidewin was right, despite Gow-Page's objections.

20 τἀμὰ πίη δάκρυ]α. So codd.: δάκρυα τἀμὰ πίη Dorville.

21-4 The alternation of long and short lines suggests another epigram copied in full. How far did it extend? 25 is short, but would not scan as a pentameter, therefore hexameter; after that nothing visible except 29, a final letter on a turned-over scrap reattached here, and 30, a messy trace which might be accidental. 29 from its length should be a pentameter; but an alternating count from 25 would make it a hexameter. Therefore either (*a*) 29 *was* a hexameter (it is only three letters shorter than 25), or (*b*) the line-space varied, as is indeed quite likely, or (*c*) an epigram ended with 26, 27 was a single first line, 28-9 the first couplet of a poem (but in that case why do we see nothing of 27?). The amount of blank in itself suggests that the text here was of different character from the upper part of the column (and therefore that fr. 2 does *not* belong to this column).

21]. ι ϲτεφάνουϲ γάρ? (γάρ read by Dr Rea). The first trace is a strongly curved right side, as of lambda: κ]αί? 'Garlands' continues the subject of 15-20.

22]. ην. Oblique tail, as of lambda etc.

23]. καὶ περὶ μοῦϲαν (μουϲᾶν). καί?

25].. ζην. Foot of upright, then perhaps part of a lower left arc: e.g.]π[ι], or]. α,]. ϲ,]. ρ.

Col. ii. 1 κεκρήγειν ἔτι? I can find no other reading, nor explain this one, except as an ionic form of (ἐ)κεκράγειν, cf. κέκληγα/κέκλαγα. κράζω occurs in *AP* only at 5. 86. 2 (Rufin. xxxi Page), κέκρᾱγεν (false quantity, unless corrupt).

2 εἴκοϲι τὰϲ πρὸ κυ(νός). Professor Cameron identified this as the 'Pythian oracle' registered by Chamaeleon (fr. 11 Wehrli) ap. Athen. 22 E and derided by Oenomaus of Gadara (fr. 10 Mullach) ap. Euseb. *PE* 5. 30: εἴκοϲι τὰϲ πρὸ κυνὸϲ καὶ εἴκοϲι τὰϲ μετέπειτα/ οἴκῳ ἐνὶ ϲκιερῷ Διονύϲῳ χρῆϲθαι ἰητρῷ (Parke-Wormell, *History of the Delphic Oracle* ii 167, no. 414; Fontenrose, *Delphic Oracle* 392, no. L 103). Clearly the verses already circulated in the fourth century, when the medical use of wine was a matter of serious discussion (Mnesitheus ap. Athen. 22 E, 36 B; J. Bertier, *Mnésithée et Dieuchès* (1972) 57 ff.); at some stage they were attributed to Hesiod (Plin. *NH* 23. 43, Hes. fr. 371 MW), who had himself recommended wine and shade for the high summer (*Op*. 589, 592f.).

3 οὐκ οἶδα προφα(   ) or οὐκ οἶδ' ἀπροφα(   ), unless οὐκ οἶδ' ἄ (or Doric ἁ) should be considered. The raised letter at the end might be taken as a flat-based omega; but, metrical difficulties apart, final omega elsewhere has the double-looped form. I therefore take it as alpha. A similar shape—a shallow cup with its right-hand side prolonged—certainly represents alpha at v 17 and 22; a narrower cup probably represents alpha at v 8 (and 23?). *AP* 7. 398 (Ant. Thess. *GP* 423), 9. 109 (Diocl. *GP* 2090) begin οὐκ οἶδ'; οὐκ οἶδᾶ, with lengthening before mute and liquid, seems less likely, though hardly impossible (see *HE* 4151 n.; *GP* i, pp. xxxviiif.). For what follows, the possibilities include (ἀ)προφανής, πρόφαϲιϲ, ἀπροφάϲιϲτοϲ (to LSJ add *AP* 7. 721. 3 (Chaeremon, *HE* 1369), 5. 250. 3), ἀπρόφατοϲ.

4 Deleted here, recurs at 24.

5 λευκοίνουϲ. *AP* 11. 34 (Phld. *GP* 3288).

6 ἤδη λουϲαμένη. A real bather, or a work of art?

7 ἣν ἔλαβον πρῴην.

8 μουϲῶν Ἀντιγένο(υϲ)? unless ἀντὶ γενο(   ). The omicron is written high, as if to end the word; but a further horizontal trace, higher still and to the right, may also belong, to give γενου(   )? Various persons called Antigenes appear in *AP*. The dithyrambic poet, 13. 28 (*FGE* 38), might be too early; the dead friend of Philodemus, 9. 412 (*GP* 3286), could be relevant.

9 οὗτοϲ ὁ τὰϲ μορφάϲ, if rightly read: after τα, it seems, a psi altered from or to an angular letter open at the right, with mu added above; then a loop open at the top altered from or to an upright. Fr. 2. 13, ουτοϲοτ[, might be the same line; but οὗτοϲ ὁ is a very common beginning (thirteen examples in *AP*; cf. *FGE* p. 316). μορφή may refer to bodily appearance in general, e.g. *AP* 5. 139. 5 (Mel. *HE* 4150), or in the context of painting or sculpture, 9. 594, 604, 687. 1 (μορφὰϲ ὁ γράψαϲ).

10 μυρία τῆϲ Παφίηϲ. Παφίη 'often stands alone for Aphrodite from Asclepiades onwards' (*FGE* p. 167); here of course a noun might follow. Ten thousand names, wiles, kisses, pleasures? *AP* 10. 123. 1f. μυρία γάρ ϲευ/ λυγρά (Life). Cf. iv 26.

11 μαίνεται εἰ βάλλει.

12 ἰξεύειν Φιλόδη(μ   ). The verb does not occur in *AP*; but the noun ἰξευτής does, of the fowler who uses bird-lime (*HE* 2144 n.). 'Bird-lime' may be literal; or denote the adhesive charm of Love or the Beloved, see *HE* 3209 n., *FGE* 1057 n. (and vi 12 below). For what follows, only a form of φιλόδημος seems possible, and the adjective much less likely than the name. If this is the epigrammatist, the poem comes from an acquaintance, or from himself; if the second, perhaps Φιλόδη(με), but *AP* 5. 115. 5, 11. 35. 3 (*GP* 3200, 3298) show that other cases might fit.

13 ἀψευδής, ὦ λύχνε (or ἀψευδῆ c',). Lovers address lamps, *AP* 5. 7. 1 (Asclep. *HE* 846), 5. 8. 1, 5. 166. 7 (Mel. *HE* 4353, 4266), 6. 333. 1 (Argentarius, *GP* 1365), and characteristically as witnesses, which may be the point of ἀψευδής.

14 ἑπτὰ τριηκόντεσσιν. *AP* 11. 41 (Phld. *GP* 3260).

15 μὴ πρότερον φιλο(   ). Again vii 4, with φιλ(   ). The possibilities include φιλό(της) (nominative or, as Dr Holford-Strevens suggests, vocative) and φιλο(τητ   ), and compound names and adjectives, among them Φιλό(δημ   ), cf. 12 above.

16 ὁ πρότερον στ . . γ: the third word probably στύγῳ (Rea), though γ might also be read as η. For epigrams on impotence, see *GP* 1517 ff. n.; the one by Phld. (below iii 7, ?v 31) begins ὁ πρίν.

17 νήφειν μεπλου. Apparently π, not γ; the final hypsilon takes a form (top arc with a long tail attached below) different from the V-shape normal to this hand, but I do not see how to take it as iota with a suspended letter above; it is not visibly raised, but then the scribe does from time to time end an abbreviated word at normal line-level. Articulate μ' ἐπλου(   ), με πλου(   )? Nothing much offers except πλοῦτος (πλουτεῖν), Πλούτων: sobriety puts money in your pocket? death drives one to drink, or drink leads to death, e.g. *AP* 7. 660. 2 (Theoc. *HE* 3427)?

18 πέντε δίδωσιν. *AP* 5. 126 (Phld. *GP* 3314).

19 μικκὴ καὶ μελα(νεῦσα). *AP* 5. 121 (Phld. *GP* 3206). Cf. iii 15.

20 ὀχληρή. The word, not attested in *AP*, may apply to persons or to things.

21 τὴν πρότερον. Possibly *AP* 10. 103 (Phld. *GP* 3310); but that comes in fuller form below, iv 16.

22 κἂν μηδείς σε καλῇ (verb?) or σε, καλή (vocative)? But the suprascript nu has an unexpected extra flourish at the top right.

23 . . . . και . . . . . The first two letters might be kappa epsilon, or together omega; the fourth nu. If it was . . . γ καί, ᾠῶν is the only metrical reading that occurs to me.

24 εἰ μὴ τὰς οὔπω. The same beginning, deleted, above l. 4.

25 εἰ μεθύειν Χίῳ. A Chian (even Homer)? or Chian wine, the best (*HE* 1454 n.), which Philodemus, for example, regards as a luxury to deny himself and Piso, *AP* 11. 34, 44 (*GP* 3288, 3302)?

26 οὐ μὰ τὸν ἡδὺν Ἔρωτα. Compare, for example, *AP* 5. 110. 3 f. (Argentarius, *GP* 1335) οὐ μὰ τὸν ἡδύν/ Βάκχον; 9. 260. 3 (Secundus, *GP* 3388) οὐ μὰ Κύπριν. ἡδὺν Ἔρωτα at the same place in the line, *AP* 12. 2. 5 (Strato), cf. *Orph. H.* 58. 1.

27 ἡ σιμὴ τὸ πρόσω(πον)? The last letter is not raised, so that the simple πρόσω could also be considered. The lady was old or ugly or African? But the point might be that her lover saw her differently: Lucr. 4. 1169 (after Pl. *Rep.* 474 D; Philaenis may have mediated the motif, as XXXIX **2891** fr. 3 shows) *simula Silena ac Saturast*.

28 οἶδα φιλεῖν φιλέοντας. *AP* 12. 103 (ἄδηλον, *HE* 3900), where the editors note: 'This sententious couplet is from the long Meleagrian section in *AP* 12, but it is not visibly paederastic or even erotic in content . . . The lines should be with Phocylides among the *Protreptica* of Book 10, and they may very well be pre-Hellenistic.' Philodemus converts this proverbial wisdom to erotic ends, *AP* 5. 107 (*GP* 3188) = vii 13 below.

29 ταύτας ὁ τρικίναιδος? But there are palaeographic difficulties: the reading αγτ assumes that hypsilon has virtually disappeared in the tail of the alpha before and the top of tau following; the reading ιδ̥ρ, satisfactory in itself, does not explain an oblique descending from the top of the supposed iota. τρικίναιδος would be new; the simple word does not appear in *AP*.

30 Only the raised final letter shows. Two more lines may be lost, if the foot of this column ranged with that of col. v.

Col. iii. 1–6 'Preparation of remedy for affections of the wind-pipe. Saffron, 3 ob. Tragacanth, 1 dr. Pine-cones, 1 dr. One egg. Honey, 3 ob.'

Recipes for arteriacs were many and various. See Gal. xiii 1 ff. Kühn; Scrib. Larg. 74–5.

7–8, the former *AP* 11. 30 (Phld. *GP* 3328), have been crossed through, and reappear at col. v 31–2. Then a blank line, and a fresh start in 9.

9 ἄτρωτος το . . . (   ). The suspended letter is a curve, such as elsewhere represents alpha, but with a flat extension to the right, which might suggest a careless omega. Before it two narrow letters (the second might be epsilon?) or one broad (mu?). μα(χ-) might be relevant.

ἄτρωτος may be literal, or amatory as *AP* 12. 101. 1 (Mel. *HE* 4540), 12. 8. 3 (Strato).

10 τίς μιϲεῖ τὸν ἔρω(τα) or ἐρῶ(ντα).

11 μηδει, then a trace like a high point to the right (accidental?); crossed through. I cannot identify this beginning in the rest of the papyrus.

12 μήτηρ καὶ θυ(γάτηρ?). Theta would at first sight be taken for omicron; but that seems intractable, and a small trace of the crossbar can perhaps be seen on a damaged patch half way down. *AP* 5. 127 (Argentarius *GP* 1355) gives one possible context.

13 τοὺς πλοκάμους.

14 ὀκτωκαιδεχέτιν. The word *AP* 7. 167. 5 (Diosc. *HE* 1717); the point there is premature death (similarly the masculine at *AP* 7. 466. 3 (Leonidas, *HE* 2405), 7. 468. 2 (Mel. *HE* 4691)). The aspiration of ἔτος is too common in the Koine to be called a mistake; see e.g. Crönert, *Memoria Graeca Herculanensis* 151.

15 λευκὴ καὶ μακρή. Both might be applied to hair, *AP* 5. 103. 3, 7. 485. 3, or life, 6. 278. 4, 7. 650. 2, or, presumably, a person: Professor Cameron suggests, very plausibly, that this epigram made a pair with its contrary ii 19 (Philodemus).

16 . . . . . . νμαλα: the second trace looks like hypsilon or perhaps kappa or chi, then perhaps tau omega sigma, then a small trace at mid-height (omicron?). ὀκτὼ ϲόν, οὕτω ϲόν or οὕτωϲ ὄν may be possible; but there is ink too far left to belong to the supposed initial omicron (and too far right to belong to the marginal check-mark).

17 εἰ μὲν μὴ καλή.

18 χρήμαϲιν οὐ πλο(   ), e.g. πλο(υτῶ), πλο(ῦτος)? True riches are the riches of the spirit, *AP* 9. 234 (Crin. *GP* 2054), 10. 41? Cf. fr. 2. 4.

19 φωνῶ γινώϲκου, or γινώϲκου(ϲα) or the like? (The last letter is not raised; but the scribe does not always so mark his abbreviations.) The second word might begin direct speech, cf. *AP* 9. 552. 3 (Ant. Thess. *GP* 301); but Professor David Sider's elegant suggestion, φωνῶ γινώϲκου(ϲι) (Pindar, *Ol.* 2. 85 φωνάεντα ϲυνετοῖϲιν) has clear advantages. Cf. fr. 2. 7.

20 εὕδεις Καλλικρα(   ). *AP* offers a beloved Callicrates, 12. 95 (Mel. *HE* 4398), and two Callicrateias, both dead, one a new Alcestis, 7. 691, the other a mother of twenty-nine, 7. 224 (anon.), related to 7. 743, Ant. Thess. *GP* 433. Similar beginnings e.g. 5. 174 (Mel. *HE* 4186), sleeping lover; 7. 29 (Ant. Sid. *HE* 270), dead poet.

21 εἴ τις μ . . φίλος ἐϲ(τί)? The final sigma would be plausible in itself; but above it stands a long rising oblique unlike any other suspended letter in this piece (and certainly not suggesting tau). Perhaps, as Dr Rea suggests, the scribe wavered between the suspension εϲ᾽ and the full-blown symbol / (which he uses below, iv 26 and vii 21). In μ . ., neither μοι nor μη seems to account for all the ink.

22 τρει¹εκ²³ε⁴κα⁵ον. The ink is reasonably clear. (1) might be gamma, pi, sigma; (2) apparently theta, and (3) perhaps the continuation of its crossbar (the spacing is confused by a split in the papyrus); (4) gamma or sigma; (5) probably delta, but with an unexplained extra flourish at the top left. Perhaps, as Dr Rea suggests, τρεῖς ἔκθες κάδον (cf. v 12); ἔκθες the verb, unless for ἐχθές (cf. vi 11).

23 ϲκλαπλαπαντο . ε(   ). The initial sigma, apparently corrected or overwritten, stands a little indented, but there is no trace of ink before it; the dotted lambda might at a pinch be tau, the dotted pi, tau iota; the penultimate letter looks most like mu, but could be lambda or nu. If the scribe intended ὀκταπλᾶ (Rea), it becomes difficult to reconstruct a hexameter; if the end was παντομέ(δων) or the like, I can do nothing with the beginning.

24 Two lines lost below this, if the last line ranged with that of col. v.

Col. iv. 1 ξάνθιον οὐκ ἤδειν (οὐ κήδειν)? The first letter has a short high horizontal (unlikely, since this is the first line of the column, to be a paragraphus), with a squiggle below. If it is rightly taken as xi, we could think of the herb, or the town Xanthus, or the proper names Ξάνθιος, Ξάνθιον. Philodemus calls his Xanthippe 'Xantho' and 'Xantharion', *AP* 5. 306 (*GP* 3240); cf. l. 7 below; 'Xanthion' might belong in a similar context.

2 τὸν φίλον αἰϲχύνῃ: the verb seems most likely, but the nominative or dative of the noun remain in play (or the personification, *AP* 7. 450. 4 (Diosc. *HE* 1632)).

3 ὤνηϲαι γλυκερῶν. The final nu, if rightly read, has been corrected. Preparation for a dinner, as in *AP* 5. 181 (Asclep. *HE* 920) and similar pieces (*HE* ii p. 132)? Another dinner in the next line.

4 αὔριον εἰς λειτήν δε. *AP* 11. 44 (Phld. *GP* 3302). The last word should be cε; the scribe apparently wrote delta for sigma, though there is unexplained ink which might belong to a correction.

5 ἡμετέρας μούсας. The Muses, or the poetry they inspire, e.g. *AP* 5. 215. 2 (Mel. *HE* 4273).

6 οὔτε φιλεῖς (οὔτ' ἐφίλεις) ἄλλον τιν'.

7 Ξανθὼ κηρόπλαστε. *AP* 9. 570 (Phld. *GP* 3240). The papyrus confirms Huschke's certain correction: ξανθοκηρόπλαστε cod.

8 οὐ μισέω τὸ πόημα. Parallel in structure (and in fact an answer to?) *AP* 12. 43 (Call. *HE* 1041) ἐχθαίρω τὸ ποίημα τὸ κυκλικόν . . . μισέω (Brunck: μιсῶ cod.) καὶ περίφοιτον ἐρώμενον.

9 ἤδη coι τρίτον εἶπα.

10 τὸν сιγῶντα, Φιλαινί. *AP* 5. 4 (Phld. *GP* 3160).

11 εἰς ἀνέμους και . . . ρ( ). The doubtful letters look most like ιδε. The first words suggest the familiar figure of 'casting to the winds', *AP* 7. 468. 8 (Mel. *HE* 4697), 5. 133. 4 (Maccius, *GP* 2497) ὅρκους δ' εἰς ἀνέμους τίθεμαι, Gow on Theoc. 22. 167.

12 τίс τἀμὰ κροκεοντα. Metre seems to exclude other articulations of ταμα. If τα is rightly read, it would be tempting to correct to κροκόεντα. Cf. vii 10.

13 τὸν πρῶτον Παφίη.

14 Παρθενόπης ἀνα . . . Above the second trace a suprascript letter, perhaps delta. The reference is presumably to the Siren or to her foundation Naples (as commonly in the Latin poets).

15 Παρθενόπη π . . ( ). The suspended letter looks most like an h-shaped eta. πλη( ) would be possible.

16 τὴν πρότερον θυμε( ). *AP* 10. 103 (Phld. *GP* 3310). P and Pl have θυμέλην. Gow–Page reject the word as corrupt; but it seems almost certain that the papyrus had it.

17 ψυχή μοι προλέ(γει). *AP* 5. 24, attributed to Philodemus in P and indirectly in Pl (τοῦ αὐτοῦ), but transferred to Meleager by Jacobs, whom Gow–Page follow (*HE* 4218). The papyrus strengthens Philodemus' claim, since the poems before and after are his.

18 ἐνθάδε τῆς τρυφε(ρῆς). *AP* 7. 222 (Phld. *GP* 3320). The raised final letter looks much more like hypsilon (as e.g. in ii 2) than epsilon.

19 Ἰνοῦς ὦ Μελικέρ(τα). *AP* 6. 349 (Phld. *GP* 3274). The scribe wrote εννους; iota was added (by another hand?) above the hypsilon.

20 ζωροπότην ωρη or ωρη( ) (not -ποτειν, less probably ωραι). The noun Hedylus, *HE* 1843 (and *AP* 5. 226); the verb *AP* 9. 300. 6 (Adaeus, *GP* 32), 11. 25. 4 (Apollonid. *GP* 1282), 12. 49. 1 (Mel. *HE* 4598) (and v.l. at Call. *Aet.* fr. 178. 12). ὥρη or ὤρη?

21 δημ . . τιс . . . After mu, perhaps a lopsided omega; at the end apparently tau and eta. One interpretation would be Δημώ τιс τῇ; various Demos appear in *AP*, hetaerae especially, and the name appealed especially to Philo-demus, *AP* 5. 115 (*GP* 3196), cf. 12. 173 (*GP* 3254) Δημώ με κτείνει, which cannot be read here.

22 νηὸν cυλήсαcαс( ). The writing rises at the end; it is not clear whether the final sigma was meant to be suspended.

23 τέссαρες εις ραι. The doubtful letter looks most like alpha; if so, εἰςᾶραι? εἰς' Ἀραί (a deliberate sophistication of the usual trio)? Not omega (ὧραι); not εἰсιν ἀγῶνες or ἔρωτες (*AP* 9. 357, 585).

24 Ἀτθίδος ὦ Παφίη. Aphrodite rivals Athena (*AP* 16. 169. 3)? Aphrodite sculpted by the Athenian Praxiteles? But in *AP* 6. 17 (Lucianus) a hetaera named Atthis makes a dedication to Aphrodite.

25 οι . . τικαιсαρ. The first trace looks most like lambda, but traces of ink below would allow delta; then probably omicron, with a linking stroke to the right, rather than alpha. οἶδ' ὅτι Καῖсαρ (or Καῖсαρ( )?), perhaps, 'Caesar' nominative or vocative. But e.g. καὶ Cάρ(δεις) (suggested by Dr Holford-Strevens) is not excluded.

26 τέссαρα Κύπριδός (ἐсτι). Among many possibilities, the four Erotes (*AP* 9. 585) or the four Graces (e.g. *AP* 5. 95) might be relevant.

27 πτωχὸν ἔχουсα.

28 ὡμολόγης' ἥξειν. *AP* 5. 150 (Asclep. *HE* 850). The ascription was added in P by the corrector (Pl does not have the epigram).

29 αὗται (αὐταὶ) τὰς χρυсέου. The first sigma is damaged, but not iota.

30 ἐκτετόνημαι, Ἔρως. I cannot see another reading; but no verb ἐκτονέω is attested, and the adjective ἔκτονος, from which it would be formed, is itself rare and dubious (Clem. *Strom.* 2. 2, p. 180. 4; suspect reading at PRossGeorg V 14.11). The norm is ἐκτενής. If the form is allowed, it might mean 'I am tense'

(psychologically, or, like ἐντέτασαι *AP* 12. 232. 2, physiologically) or 'I am floored', e.g. *AP* 9. 441. 4 (Palladas); Eros as wrestler, *HE* ii, p. 13.

31 μῆλον ἐγὼ πεμ. Two epigrams begin μῆλον ἐγώ, and in both it is the apple which speaks: 6. 252 (Antiphil. *GP* 791), 5. 80 (*FGE* 594). The second is ascribed by implication (τοῦ αὐτοῦ) to Plato in P, to Philodemus in Pl (and its pair, *AP* 5. 79, to Plato in P, to no one in Pl); it reads μῆλον ἐγώ· βάλλει με φιλῶν cέ τις· ἀλλ' ἐπίνευcον,/ Ξανθίππη· κἀγὼ καὶ cὺ μαραινόμεθα. There is at least some chance that the papyrus has this epigram, with πέμπει for βάλλει; that would strengthen Philodemus' claim (I have not identified this incipit elsewhere in the papyrus); the argument (*FGE* p. 163) that his Xanthippe (*AP* 5. 131 = *GP* 3225) was misidentified as Socrates' wife would explain the transfer. The chance becomes a certainty when it is observed (by Professor Cameron) that the translator of *Epigr. Bob.* 32 (the next oldest witness) found πέμπει in his text: *malum ego: mittit me quidam tibi munus amator.*

32 ὦ cφῦραι κεφαλῆc. Cf. v 20 (Philodemus)

33 θύετε τῇ Νεμέ(cει)? A cult act (say, at Rhamnus, *AP* 16. 221-2)? or an apotropaic gesture? This was probably the foot of the column (a line higher than col. v). No ink can be seen below 33; it is true that the surface is damaged, but, since some ink from 33 strays on to it, the damage must be ancient.

Col. v. 1 τὸν Κρονίδ(ην), -δ(αο), -δ(η). Zeus, less often Poseidon or Hades.

2 τὸ γράψαι πο( ).

3 νυκτερι(νή). *AP* 5. 123 (Phld. *GP* 3212)? But even among known epigrams one other, *AP* 12. 250 (Strato), begins with the same letters.

4 δεῦθ' ὦδ'. This combination does not occur in *AP*, nor does δεῦρ' ὦδε.

5 χθιζόc.

6 εἶχεν δημο( ). A name like Demophilus most likely? There is no sign of β in the left margin, although the surface is reasonably preserved.

7 πειθιμαρει. (*a*) πεῖθ(ε). But then what? (*b*) πεῖθι for πῖθι. *AP* 11. 56 and 12. 50 (Asclep. *HE* 880) similarly begin πῖν(ε); πῖθ' is a likely correction at 9. 315. 2 (Nic. *HE* 2772). But then what? Μαρεῖ(νε)? Μαρει(ώτην)? Mareotic wine would suit πῖθι; the adjective seems normally to be Μαρεώτηc, but Μαρει- is attested by Steph. Byz. s.v. Ἀζειῶται (I owe the reference to Professor Lloyd-Jones). This was a clear, light wine (Strab. 17. 1. 14); but, being Egyptian, might appear in more sinister contexts (Hor. *C.* 1. 37. 14).

8 ἀμφότεροι πιθα( ). The suspended letter, a flattened V-shape, occurs again in 17 and 22, where context shows that it represents alpha. πιθανόc, -ῶc in erotic contexts *HE* 824 and n., 'plausible'; at *AP* 11. 4. 1, Parmenion, *GP* 2612, apparently 'complaisant'.

9 παῖδα πολυτρη( ). πολυτρήρων, πολύτρητοc are available; the latter, in *AP*, applies to rocks, sieves, pan-pipes, and honeycombs.

10 οὐκ ἔα θῆλυ, θηλυ(τερ)? For the short alpha—if this articulation is correct—see Pfeiffer on Call. fr. 384. 32.

11 ἠράcθην, τίc δ' ο(ὐχί); *AP* 5. 112 (Phld. *GP* 3268). It seems odd (a sign of incomprehension?) that the scribe chose to end with the first vowel of a diphthong. There is in fact some damage to the papyrus surface above; but no sign of ink emerging from it, such as a suspended letter would normally leave.

12 τρεῖc κυάθουc. Toasts at a party, as e.g. *AP* 5. 110 (Argentarius, *GP* 1333). Anacr. *PMG* 383 οἰνοχόει . . . τρικύαθον κελέβην ἔχουcα; Alexis fr. 111. 3 K τοὺc τρεῖc δ' ἔρωτοc (κυάθουc), quoted by Kiessling–Heinze on Hor. *C.* 3. 19. 11f. *tribus . . . cyathis.*

13 δακρύειc. *AP* 5. 306 (Phld. *GP* 3236) is the only epigram in *AP* that begins so.

14 ψαλμοὶ καὶ λαλιή. *AP* 5. 131 (Phld. *GP* 3224): ψαλμόc codd. For the plural cf. 9. 409. 2 (Antiphan. *GP* 754).

15 ἤρεcέ μοι κομψή. For the first word cf. *AP* 11. 132. 2 (Lucillius); for κομψή 5. 308. 1 (Antiphilus or Philodemus, *GP* 865) = vi 4 (the only use of the word in *AP*).

16 νάρδῳ κ(αὶ) cμύρνη. Both unguents: for nard see *HE* 3968n. (the perfumed oil sent to a lady, *AP* 6. 250. 6 (*GP* 788); offered to Isis, 6. 231. 5 (*GP* 2777)); on myrrh, *GP* 3288-9n. (one of the delights of the high life). The marginal numeral: κα is certainly suggested (Rea); not ιβ.

17 ἀγρὸν καὶ cτεφα(ν). 'Farm' and 'country' are the usual meanings: provides garlands (and other things for the party)? contrasts with the urban luxury of 16?

18 Πρωτέοc Φάρε. The genitive in -έοc is epic (*Od.* 4. 365, QS 3. 303, scanned as a dactyl); but it will not scan in a hexameter, even if contracted to a spondee, given that the first syllable of Pharos is always short. Probably the poet had written Πρωτῆοc, cf. *AP* 7. 78. 6 (Dionys. *HE* 1446). Epigrams on the Pharos by

Posidippus (*HE* 3100), and Diodorus (*AP* 9. 60 = *GP* 2184); but the island may be relevant in other contexts (*AP* 7. 169 = *FGE* 1360).

19 παρθένιος, the rho corrected from nu rather than the other way about. Noun, *AP* 7. 384. 7 (*GP* 1475), adjective, 9. 706. 3 (*GP* 523), or name (the only examples in *AP* may or do refer to the poet). One of the Vienna epigrams began Παρθένιός μοι κομψὸς ἀπ' Ἀρκαδίης (P Vindob. 4).

20 ὦ ποδός. *AP* 5. 132 (Phld. *GP* 3228).

21 Νικαρέτη πείθει. *AP* 5. 153 (Asclep. *HE* 820) begins Νικαρέτης; there and 6. 285. 2 (*HE* 2738) a hetaera, 7. 166 (*HE* 1707) a respectable mother. *AP* 5. 38 (Nicarchus II) begins εὐμεγέθης πείθει με καλὴ γυνή. The marginal number may be γ, crossed though or covered by a check-mark; in 22 and 23 too there seems to be more ink than required by simple check-marks, but I cannot recognize δ and ε.

22 μισῶ καὶ στεφά(νους). The poet gives up parties, like Philodemus (*AP* 11. 34. 1-4 = *GP* 3288)?

23 τοὺς φέρε καὶ πα( ). If this articulation is right, the 'ear' may be literal, as in Hipp. fr. 118. 5 W. τοὺς μοι παράσχες, Plat. *Rep.* 531 A παραβάλλοντες τὰ ὦτα, or edible, as in the dinner-party scene, *AP* 5. 181. 8 (Asclep. *HE* 927), rendered 'sea-urchin' or 'sow's ear' (only one here, a meagre provision). But τούς is also available: Dr Holford-Strevens suggests e.g. τοὺς φέρε καὶ πά(λι) ⟨τούς⟩.

24 ἀιδειν κ(αὶ) ψάλλειν. Cf. *AP* 5. 131. 1 (Phld. *GP* 3224) ψαλμὸς καὶ . . . ὠιδή; 7. 221. 3f. μετ' ἀοιδῆς/ ψαλμός (an accomplished hetaera).

25 οὐδέπω ἐμβεβλη( ). -(κα), -(μαι) etc.

26 μέλλει μοι.

27 γεινώσκω (γείνωσκ' ω) ταλε, εγν. For the first word cf. vii 13 below; after λε, gamma or tau (or corrected iota)? ν, or possibly eta?

28 ἡδὺ θέρευς ἕλκει. Similarly Asclep. *AP* 5. 169. 1 (*HE* 812), ἡδὺ θέρους διψῶντι χιὼν ποτόν. ἕλκει seems more likely to be the verb than the noun.

29 τὴν ἀπὸ παλλιόλου. *Pallium* and *palliolum* are not attested in literary Greek elsewhere; but they were current in the normal speech of the Roman period, as the Fathers (Lampe, *PGL* παλ(λ)ίον) and the papyrus documents (Daris, *Lessico latino* παλλιόλιον, παλλίολον, πάλλιον) make clear. Latin writers, at least, associate this Greek garment with Greek practices—comedy, philosophy, immorality; only in Christian usage does it become respectable. One approach is suggested by Mart. 9. 32. 1 *hanc volo, quae facilis, quae palliolata vagatur*; Philodemus may have treated the theme, see Hor. *Serm.* 1. 2. 119 ff.

30 ἤδη πολλάκις.

31 ὁ πρὶν ἐγὼ κ(αί). *AP* 11. 30 (Phld. *GP* 3328)? But the same first words in 7. 172 (Ant. Sid. *HE* 312). At iii 7 above, a deleted entry, the scribe adds πέντε, which makes it certainly Philodemus.

32 Αἰςώπου τινά. Also at iii 8, deleted. Αἰςώπου τινὰ ⟨μῦθον⟩, as Dr Holford-Strevens suggests? No mention of Aesop in *AP*, except 16. 332 (Agathias), on a statue of him by Lysippus. This was probably the foot of the column; the papyrus below is broken, but line-ends would show, unless the lines were exceptionally short.

Col. vi. 1 μή μοι φάρμακα? *AP* 5. 225. 4 ἤπιά μοι πάσσει φάρμακα. The epigrammatists deal much in drugs against grief (5. 130) and love (5. 113, 116, 221).

2 . . . . λη καὶ τη. At first sight the beginning looks like ρονλλη (but then horizontal ink to the right of the supposed rho must be explained as an (uncharacteristic) linking-stroke) or βονλλη (but one might expect to see more of the lower loop); in either case we should have to think of Latin (*rulla* is very rare, and I find no example of *Rulla; bulla* or *Bulla*, as place- or personal name, might serve). I have tried to persuade myself that εἰ καλή could be read; but, though the initial epsilon is not impossible, the other dotted letters would all be anomalous.

3 . αυσαι κύριε. If the alpha is rightly read, the obvious possibilities are καῦσαι, παῦσαι, ψαῦσαι (κλ-, θρ- probably too long). The third seems excluded by the trace; the first is better than the second, since (*a*) there seems to be ink extending to the right at mid-height and (*b*) the cap of pi would be expected to show. κύριος occurs only once in the classical epigrams of *AP* (9. 334. 4 = *HE* 2894), and then not in the vocative.

4 ἡ κομψή. *AP* 5. 308 (*GP* 865). Disputed attribution: P has τοῦ αὐτοῦ (Antiphilus) [C] ἢ μᾶλλον Φιλοδήμου, Pl τοῦ αὐτοῦ (Philodemus).

5 . . καιεμηκα. ω. The first letter apparently epsilon, overwritten with heavy ink rising well above the line; the second letter might be taken for a florid kappa, or a corrected iota (but the tail is short) sigma: εἰς corrected to οἰς (Rea) or ης? Then καὶ ἐμὴ (ἐμῆ) καίω or (perhaps better) κἀγώ.

6 τίς c' ἐκέλευσε.

7 ὀρχεῖcθε γλαφυ(ρ). See vii 14. Hypsilon is written directly above phi; therefore a heavy trace to its right, on the edge, must be accident, not a suspended letter.

8 ψάλλε (ψάλλ' ε-) κατα. ( ). The last letter most suggests a very cursive pi, though nu (no example of this form elsewhere) and sigma (normally less flattened) could be considered as well; it is not raised, so that the word could, but need not, end here.

9 ψάλλειν Ἴκαρε. AP 16. 107–8 are epigrams by Julian of Egypt on a statue of Icarus; otherwise it is rare as a personal name. The island, *cunctis Baccho iucundior hospes/ Icarus* (Tib. 3. 7. 9), might be relevant to festive music.

10 οἶνος καὶ ῥοδινοι. . -οι not -αι, it seems; the ink following, a heavy descending oblique, seems not to be a letter. In *AP* only Asclepiades uses ῥόδινος (ῥόδεος is commoner), 5. 185. 5 (*HE* 936), 5. 181. 2 (*HE* 921) πέντε cτεφάνους τῶν ῥοδίνων. Hedylus begins similarly *AP* 5. 199 (*HE* 1831), οἶνος καὶ προπόcεις. The best parties have wine and roses: Hor. *C.* 1. 36. 15 etc., Mart. 3. 68. 5 *deposito post vina rosasque pudore*.

11 ἐκθὲς ἔδωκεν. Kappa for chi before another aspirate: Gignac i 88 gives a few examples from documents of the Roman period; Crönert, *Memoria Graeca Herculanensis* 88f. found similar spellings in the papyrus of Philodemus, *de ira*.

12 ἰξὸν ἔχεις τόν (ἔχει cτον-?). Mel. *AP* 5. 96. 1 (*HE* 4296) begins ἰξὸν ἔχεις τὸ φίλημα. See ii 12 n. on lime and love.

13 ταῦτα. οθε. . ταῦτα rather than ταῦτ' ἀ-, since the extended tail of the second alpha suggests a word-break. After that I had tried ποθεν (πόθεν), but pi seems excluded by a horizontal trace which crosses it at mid-height.

14 ἡνίκα μεν. . . [. Philip *AP* 11. 36 (*GP* 3027) begins ἡνίκα μὲν καλὸς ἧς; μέν is no doubt likely here, but καλ[does not suit the remains at the line-end.

15 οὐκ ἔλεγον ν. . []? Gamma might be tau. Rufin. *AP* 5. 21 (vii Page) begins οὐκ ἔλεγον, Προδίκη, γηράcκομεν; But the second word might be a noun. At the end, perhaps parts of two letters: hypsilon, and then e.g. sigma? or eta, and then what?

16 παῦε φιληλακατη[. φιληλάκατος is attested for Antip. Sid. *AP* 6. 160. 5 (*HE* 186), καὶ τόνδε φιληλάκατον καλαθίcκον. But the feminine termination points rather to φίλ'ἠλακάτη[.

17 . . . . . . ραι. . . . . The first letter perhaps epsilon, then a high horizontal and part of vertical as of tau. After the iota, probably kappa; then one wide or two normal letters, then at the end perhaps a straggling nu (but e.g. omega also possible?).

18 αὖτ[οῦ] μοι cτέφα(νοι). *AP* 5. 145 (Asclep. *HE* 860). Copied in full in i 15–20.

19 ἀρχόμεθα ψυχή (or ψυχῇ?). Lucill. *AP* 11. 134 begins ἀρχόμεθ', Ἡλιόδωρε; ποιήματα παίζομεν οὕτω . . . ; ψυχή might be nominative (with stop before); or vocative, as Philodemus *AP* 5. 131. 2f. (*GP* 3225) πῦρ ἄρτι καταρχόμενον,/ ὦ ψυχή, φλέξει cε, Maccius, *AP* 9. 411. 5 (*GP* 2486) εἴκωμεν, ψυχή, πεπαλαίcμεθα, cf. **3723** 23.

Back

col. vii

μηπ. . νη. εινου
ηδη. . πεμπτον
ωλεταπανθρωπων
μηπροτερονφι^λ
5 μειcωπανταιει
οιδοτι καιτοπρο^c
ηραcθηνδημους
νυνοψωνηcαι
μην. π. .
10 ουματε. κροκεοντα

col. viii

ηνψηχηπιθαν. c
κυπριγαληναιη
ενταυτητηινυκτι
ενχειρ. . αιης
5 εγλεγομαικαλα
ηδυλιονπεφιληκα
οιδαcτονθυ. κο.
ειπωχαιρεκα
καινυκτοcμεcατης
10 ω. . . . . εcτι

```
      ειτιποτενθν. . αι. . .                        λιτονϲοιτουτα. . . ϲ
      χρυϲηκερ[ ]. . . ϲχϙ.                         κυπριδικαι. . . . . με
      γεινω. . [. ]χαριεϲϲα
      ορχειϲθε. λαφυρ. ϲ
 15   χαιρεϲ. [   ]. . . . . . .
      πεμπτηϲ. . τιϝμοι
      κραμβηϝαρτεμι
      νικ. . . . υϲιπ. ωϲ.
      μημε. . μημε. α
 20   ευχαριϲεϲτιφιλιν. .
      ηδηκαιροδον/
      εξηδεινηδη.
      μουκιαδα
      ειμεφιλοι. . . . ηϲ
 25   εξηξονṭα. . . .
```

Col. vii. 1 μὴ π. . ϝη γείνϙϋ? But if this articulation is right, I can make nothing of the second word: possibly a rho after the pi (not πόρνη or πϙινή): Πρόγνη could be considered, but not Πρόκνη. (Another phonetic spelling, cf. Gignac, *Grammar* i 76 ff? Even in Latin there seems to be no substantive evidence for *Progna*, see Housman, *Classical Papers* iii 1144 ff.). γίνεο three times in *AP*, but not γίνου.

2 ἤδη . . . πέμπτον. μη looks likely, but I doubt whether μϙι is excluded (in which case 'fifth' may be part of the writer's or subject's age, as e.g. *AP* 7. 601).

3 ὤλετ' ἀπ' ἀνθρώπϙϋν (ἀπανθρώπϙϋν). *AP* 7. 403. 1–3 (Argentarius, *GP* 1477) ψύλλος . . . ἐνθάδε κεῖται/ αἰϲχρὸν ἀπ' ἀνθρώπων μιϲθὸν ἐνεγκάμενος.

4 μὴ πρότερον φιλ( ). See ii 15.

5 μιϲῶ πάντ' αἰϙί.

6 οἶδ' ὅτι καὶ τὸ πρός(ωπον?). The same first foot in *AP* 12. 148 (Call. *HE* 1071), 9. 577 (Ptol. *FGE* 466), as well as iv 25 above.

7 ἠράϲθην Δημοῦϲ. *AP* 5. 115 (Phld. *GP* 3196).

8 νῦν ὀψωνῆϲαι. The infinitive, that is, rather than the optative (or the middle imperative)? Another dinner, as in iv 3?

9 μην. π. . . . After nu, perhaps omega (rather than iota nu or even eta sigma); after pi, apparently omicron. μὴ νώ, μὴ νῷ, μὴν ω- do not promise much; Professor Lloyd-Jones suggests a form of μηνωπός (new, but cf. ἀϲτερωπός, ἠλιωπός).

10 οὐ μὰ ṭεὰ κροκϙεοντα? ii 26 and two epigrams in *AP* begin with the negative oath. For the last word see iv 12; again a miswriting of κροκόεντα? If the oath invokes a god, it might be Dionysus or Priapus, crowned with ivy, *AP* 13. 29. 6, 9. 338. 3 (*HE* 2716, where see n., 3474), or Dawn κροκόπεπλος.

11 εἴ τί ποτ' ἐν θνηταῖϲϊν? The first iota looks short (but apparently not εϲτι). Since theta nu seems secure, choice in what follows is limited; but the dotted letters are all dubious readings. ἐν θνητοῖϲι at this place *AP* 7. 148. 3.

12 χρυϲηκερ[ ]. . . ϲχϙ. . At the end sigma or (if ink further right is not accidental) nu? That looks like word-end; among limited possibilities, μόϲχϙϋ would suit the earlier traces. Since the letters before rho suggest kappa epsilon, χρυϲόϙκερϝ μόϲχϙϋ is very tempting: *AP* 6. 231. 8 (Philip, *GP* 2780) has χρυϲόκερων κεμάδα of a sacrificial victim (see n.). But, if the accusative in -ω is legitimate, given normal variations within the Attic declension, there is the palaeographic difficulty: the letter before κ was very probably eta, certainly not omicron.

13 γεινώϲκ[ω], χαρίεϲϲα. *AP* 5. 107 (Phld. *GP* 3188). (Ascribed to Philodemus in P: Pl ἄδηλον.)

14 ὀρχεῖϲθε γλαφυρ. c. Already vi 7, where the second word is abbreviated; here the penultimate letter, V-shaped, looks most like υ; of grammatically more plausible vowels, ο (open-topped, as often, but anomalously angular) is easier to read than α or ω. A smooth performer, a beardless boy (*AP* 11. 168. 4 = *GP* 768), a hollow lyre (*Od.* 17. 262) might be relevant; or the piper Glaphyrus, celebrated by Antip. Thess. *AP* 9. 266, 517 (*GP* 93, 681).

15 χαῖρε ϲύ. καὶ ϲύ γε? *AP* 5. 46 (Phld. *GP* 3180). Since the first two words are pretty certainly read, and the rest well suits the remains, the identification seems likely. The difficulty is in the spacing: before καὶ there must have been a blank (it would fall on an area of fibres already damaged in ancient times; but elsewhere the scribe seems to write on regardless) — ideal to punctuate the dialogue, but the scribe normally takes no note of such things.

16 πέμπτης ἐϲτίν μοι? A good reading, but clearly the metrical awkwardness makes it suspect. The fifth hour *AP* 5. 183. 6 (*HE* 3099), 9. 640; the fifth day — and so on.

17 κράμβην Ἀρτεμί(δωρος). *AP* 11. 35 (Phld. *GP* 3296).

18 νικ. . . .νϲιπ. ωϲ. After kappa, straggly remains; omicron or omega, then nu? Then possibly chi rho, but not Χρύϲιππϲς.

19 μὴ μέγα, μὴ μέγα or μεγα(λ   )? The gammas could be taus.

20 εὔχαρίς ἐϲτι Φίλιννα? Φίλιννα (Rea) suits the remains better than Φιλίνος. The name may be vocative, as in the similar beginning *AP* 5. 258 (Paulus Silentiarius), πρόκριτός ἐϲτι, Φίλιννα, τεὴ ῥυτὶς ἢ ὀπὸς ἥβης/ πάϲης. εὔχαρις occurs only once in *AP*, of Eros, 9. 666. 1 οὐ μέγας . . . ἀλλ᾽ εὔχαρις.

21 ἤδη καὶ ῥόδον (ἐϲτί). *AP* 9. 412 (Phld. *GP* 3280).

22 ἐξήδεινήδη. . ἐξ-, ἔξ, ᾔδει ν-, ᾔδειν (first or third person?), ᾔδειν, ἡ δεῖν᾽, and much else. The last letter looks most like nu, or possibly lambda omicron (omicron raised); the latter would allow e.g. ἢ δῆλο(ν), ἡ Δῆλο(ϲ).

23 μουκιαδα. I can do nothing with this, unless it represents a Greek adjective (cf. *Appias, Daunias*) or patronymic (cf. *Memmiades* etc.) to the Roman name Mucius.

24 εἴ με φιλοι. . . .ης. The first of the doubtful letters is nu or possibly mu; the iota before it is dim, but certainly ink (that excludes φιλομμειδής, where in any case delta does not suit). φίλοι? φιλοιν- (φίλοινον, φίλοινε)? At the end, eta rather than epsilon iota.

25 ἐξήξοντα. . . . . *AP* 5. 13 (Phld. *GP* 3166)? The second xi is not a typical phonetic error; I assume it is simple carelessness. But there is the added difficulty of the traces at the end; what little remains does not suit τελεῖ particularly: just offsets?

Col. viii. 1 ἦν ψήχῃ πιθαν. c. πιθανάϲ looks the likeliest reading, but -ῶϲ may not be excluded; for the word see on v 8. 'Stroke'?

2 Κύπρι γαληναίη. *AP* 10. 21 (Phld. *GP* 3246).

3 ἐν ταύτῃ τῆι νυκτί. Ink above the first letter, which I have taken, doubtfully, as a paragraphus.

4 ἔγχει Ῥωμαίης? Unexplained ink in the left margin. Four epigrams in *AP* begin ἔγχει; the name of the toast may follow in the genitive (see *HE* ii p. 631), *AP* 5. 110, Argentarius (*GP* 1333), ἔγχει Λυσιδίκης κυάθους δέκα, Mel. 5. 137 (*HE* 4228). Rhomaia might be a name; or a name or noun may follow.

5 ἐγλέγομαι καλά. 'I pick out for myself' (Plat. *Symp.* 198 D τὰ κάλλιστα ἐκλεγομένους)? *AP* 9. 72. 4 (*GP* 612) (Heracles), ἐν θύος ἐκλέγεται, 5. 18. 1 (Rufin. v Page).

6 Ἡδύλιον πεφίληκα. Hedylium is one of Ballio's girls, Plaut. *Pseud.* 188; Maccius finds her irresistible, *AP* 5. 133 (*GP* 2494).

7 οἶδας τὸν (οἶδ᾽, οἶδ᾽, ἀϲτόν) θυ. κο. . The strokes at the end most suggest ου; but that seems to exclude any metrical reading. Best then to assume that they represent a nu with an additional flourish at the lower left, i.e. read τόν θ᾽ υἱκόν (Rea).

8 εἴπω Χαῖρε κα(λή?); Thus, deliberative subjunctive, as e.g. *AP* 5. 108. 1 (*HE* 1841), rather than εἴ πω? Cf. vii 15, and Page on Rufin. x 1.

9 καὶ νυκτὸς μεϲάτης. *AP* 5. 120 (Phld. *GP* 3202).

10 ω. . . . .εϲτι. ω. . . c μ᾽ ἐϲτι would be possible.

11 λιτόν ϲοι τοῦτ᾽ α. . . .ϲ. αὗτιϲ perhaps (not -τ̣ϲ), but hypsilon and tau are not very satisfactory as readings; my only other idea is α⟨ὖ⟩θιϲ. 'Humble' gifts *AP* 6. 230. 5 (*GP* 3362), 190. 2 (*FGE* 182); cf. iv 4.

12 Κύπριδι καὶ ..... με? Assuming this to be a dedication (cf. Argentarius, *AP* 6. 248 (*GP* 1419), beginning with the same word), and if με is rightly read and interpreted as the object of dedication, the word between should be another dative. I have tried Χάρισιν; the first four letters certainly suit the remains, but the other three would be rather cramped.

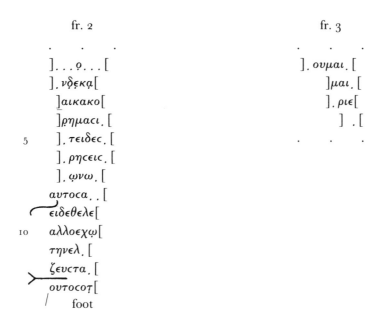

fr. 2

.   .   .
]...ọ...[
].νδεκα̣[
]αικακο[
]ρημασι.[
5   ].τειδεϲ.[
].ρηϲειϲ.[
].ωνω.[
αυτοϲα..[
⌒ειδεθελε[
10 αλλοεχω[
τηνελ.[
≻ζευϲτα.[
ουτοϲοτ[
/   foot

fr. 3

.   .   .
].ουμαι.[
]μαι.[
].ριε[
] .[
.   .   .

Fr. 2

1]...ọ..[: second and third traces perhaps tau iota; after omicron, lower left quadrant of oval (sigma etc.); then remains of horizontal at line-level, and foot of upright.

2].: point on edge, just below the tops of letters, e.g. ϲνδεκα[.

3 ν]αὶ κακο[or the like? Below the first alpha the end of a paragraphus?

4 .[: upright, with oblique crossing at the top (nu?). χ]ρημασιν[? cf. fr. 1 iii 18.

5].: upright. .[: left side of gamma or pi (rather than tau?).

6].: short rising oblique, as of hypsilon, damage below (so that e.g. kappa, chi not excluded?), e.g. ϲ]ϋρηϲει(ϲ). .[: left side of chi?

7].: point on the edge, above the tops of letters: letter, or paragraphus? .[: gamma-shaped, but with further ink joining on right, i.e. a narrow pi? Fr. 1 iii 19 has the incipit φωνω γινωϲκον; that is perhaps possible, but phi would not suit the first trace (if it is a letter), and gamma iota is less suited to the last. κωνωπ[would be possible.

8 ..[: lambda, then an upright on the edge? or simply nu? If the second, note *AP* 9. 403. 1 (*GP* 2530), αὐτὸς ἄναξ κτλ; the author, Maecius/Maccius, was apparently early enough to be included in Philip's *Garland*.

9-12 Four lines set off by paragraphi: a group of incipits, or one poem?

9 εἰ δέ? The conjunction at first sight does not suit the beginning of a poem; perhaps the wispy paragraphus, by contrast with the forked one below, simply marks a section (Hes. *Op*. 106 εἰ δ' ἐθέλεις, ἕτερον ...). Or εἶδε or the like?

10 ἄλλο (ἀλλ' ὅ) ἔχω[: the reading is certain; and I cannot find an articulation which would remove the hiatus. If ἄλλο has strayed in from a heading, we have still to explain εχω[.

11 .[: first part of gamma or pi. τὴν ἐλπ[?

12 *Ζεῦ, Ζεύς.* .[: probably the left hand part of mu.
13 *οὗτος ὁ τ*[? Cf. fr. 1 ii 9 above. But similar beginnings are common, see *FGE* p. 316.

Fr. 3
1].: curving right-hand side, as of alpha, lambda, mu. .[: epsilon or theta.
2 .[: left-hand arc, omicron, sigma, or omega.
3].: two high traces, suggesting the upper extremities of hypsilon or chi, but rather close together, and another below touching the tail of rho. If hypsilon (*κ*]*υριε*, cf. fr. 1 vi 3), the tail must curl to the right. Below the descender of rho, a horizontal trace, not part of the descender? and yet too far in to belong to a paragraphus?
4].[: upper left of hypsilon or chi? Before it space for one letter, where the papyrus is intact in the upper half of the line but stripped below.

3725. EPIGRAMS

38 3B.86/D(1) + K(2)a   Fr. 1 6.2 × 11 cm   First–second century

Three fragments, written across the fibres; on the other side, along the fibres and upside-down in relation to **3725**, are scrappy remains of an account or register. The script, smaller in frr. 2–3 than in fr. 1, belongs to the type exemplified by *GLH* 11a (Ninus Romance, before *c.*100 AD) and by Schubart, *Pal.* fig. 81 (later than AD 81); it is approximately bilinear, and without serifs; characteristic letters are the pear-shaped theta, and epsilon with the crossbar detached and ligatured to the next stroke. I should assign it to the late first, or early second, century. The scribe uses no lectional signs.

The text, so far as can be seen, consists of epigrams. Two are identifiable: *AP* 5. 40, 11. 241 appear consecutively in fr. 1 ii 1–12. Each epigram has a heading, either (i) *ἐπὶ* . . . or (ii) *ὁμοίως*. (i) clearly refers to subject-matter; similar headings have been restored in an epigram papyrus of iii BC, *Suppl. Hell.* 985; it is a question how far the lemmata of *AP* derive from such early practice (A. S. F. Gow, *The Greek Anthology: Sources and Ascriptions* (1958) 17 f.). In this context (ii) must mean 'on a similar theme', not 'by the same author'; papyri more usually have *ἄλλο* in this sense (*Suppl. Hell.* 973. 8–11 n.), but *ὁμοίως* recurs (rarely) in *AP* (Gow, op. cit. 29).

Since **3725** has subject-headings, not author-headings like those in IV **662**, we could infer that it represents, not an anthology, but a single epigrammatist: so PKöln V 204 (Mnasalces) and XLVII **3324** (Meleager). *AP* assigns 11. 241 directly, and 5. 40 indirectly (*τοῦ αὐτοῦ*), to 'Nicarchus', that is, on the normal assumption that the one name covers two different poets, to Nicarchus II (*HE* ii p. 425). This Nicarchus imitates Lucillius; Lucillius dedicated his second book to Nero (*AP* 9. 572), probably early in the reign (Cichorius, *Römische Studien* 372–4; disputed by L. Robert, *Entretiens de la Fondation Hardt* 14 (1967) 208f.). Nicarchus II therefore worked no earlier than the second half of the first century; **3725** shows that he worked not much later. His poems reached Oxyrhynchus quite quickly; that does not prove the theory that he was himself Egyptian (Keydell in *Kl. Paul.* iv 100), for books could move with speed (LII **3685** introd.), but may support it.

fr. 1

col. i   col. ii

    ·   ·   ·

].   [

]   [

].ϲαι   .[π[αντα λιθον κινει ϲαυτην τρεφε και γραφε προϲ με

].   ει..[εις π[οιην ακτην ευφροϲυνον γεγονας

5].ϲ   ευτ.[ευτα[κτειν πειρω το δ ενοικιον ην τι περιϲϲον

]   .εινηταικα.[γεινηται και [εμοι φροντιϲον ηματιον

]   αν..γαϲτρι[αν εν γαϲτρι [λαβηϲ τεκε ναι τεκε μη θορυβηθηϲ

]   ευρηϲειπο.[ευρηϲει ποθ[εν εϲτ ελθον εϲ ηλικιην

]   επιϲα.[επι ϲα.[

10]   τοϲτομ.χω.[το ϲτομα χωπ[ρωκτοϲ ταυτον Θεοδωρε ϲου οζει

]   ωϲτε[..]..[ωϲτε [δι]αχ[νωναι τοιϲ φυϲικοιϲ καλον ην

]   ηγρα[η γρα[ψαι ϲε εδει ποιον ϲτομα ποιον ο πρωκτοϲ

]   νυν.[νυν δ[ε λαλουντοϲ ϲου

]   [

15]   αλλω[

].. [

    ·   ·   ·

fr. 2   fr. 3

  ·   ·   ·   ·   ·   ·

].εω.[   ]π...η....πτερυ[

].νω.[   ]φε.εγδη.ωνε.[

]μοιωϲ [   ].μ.δηνφ......[

].ονδιοκληνα.[   ]κενεβαλλεγολη[

5].ενδημωνω[   ]   ομοιωϲ [

]ϲχεδιαϲοδε[   ].θυϲιαδαμω[..].[

].ενοϲπαρατω.[·   ·   ·

]   επιϲφιγγ[

]αι.ρ.νακεϲω[

10].νουτουν.[

  ·   ·   ·

Fr. 1

Col. i. 1]. , overhang of sigma?

3]. , point (top of upright?) level with tops of letters

4]. , lower right-hand quadrant of small circle (omicron, rho, omega)?

5]. , upright, probably iota.

Col. ii. 3-8 *AP* 5. 40. 5-10 (τοῦ αὐτοῦ, sc. Νικάρχου). In 7 the papyrus has ἄν, the MSS ἤν; MSS have ἄν (ἤν Jacobs) in 5 above, where the papyrus is not preserved.

9 The heading of the next poem. . [, if the trace is not delusory, is an upright on the edge. Given the subject, there are temptations in ἐπὶ caπ[ροcτόμου, although LSJ cites the word only from [Arist.] *Chreiai* as quoted at Stob. 3. 5. 42. If the heading was centred on l. 8, it might need to be a little longer (add τινος?).

14 Heading.

15 αλλω[, αλμ[cannot be altogether excluded.

16]. . [, perhaps the oblique and right side of nu, then a sloping top as of alpha, lambda, delta, mu.

Fr. 2

1 . [, left-hand arc, as of sigma omicron omega.

2]. , point at line level; more ink to the left, but on stripped underlayer of fibres. . [, apparently left-hand curve of omega: i.e. -νωω[before the caesura of the pentameter?

3 Heading o]μοιωc.

4 . [, pi? (less likely gamma, with a trace of a junction at the right). If the heading is approximately centred, we should end in mid-hexameter, say –◡◡] . ον Διοκλῆ ναπ[, Διοκλῆν απ[(for the form of accusative see *HE* ii p. 256). Various Diocles appear in *AP*.

5 -εν (ἐν) δήμῳ (δήμων), ἐνδημῶ, -ῶν. A slight space after the second nu perhaps suggests that the word-break fell there; otherwise Δημώ also possible.

6 –◡◡–] cχεδίαc· ὁ δε[---]μενος? cχεδίηc at pent. end *AP* 6. 341. 2 (*FGE* 697), of Darius' bridge of boats.

7]. , upright with curving link from base to back of epsilon, mu likely. . [, part of curving back as of sigma etc.? On the face of it, παρὰ τώ, τῷ. For the article before the diaeresis, see Gow–Page on *HE* 913; *GP* i p. xlv (only three examples in Philip's authors); most examples have καί (ἤ in *GP* 3337, Philodemus) before the article; παρά in *HE* 913 (Asclepiades), 1090 (Callimachus).

8 Title. If ἐπί is to be taken separately, cφιγγ[óc is a possibility (*AP* has nothing relevant, except a passing reference to Oedipus' Sphinx, 7. 429. 8, and a copy of her riddle, 14. 64; a local epigram on the Egyptian Sphinx, Bernand, *Inscr. Metr.* no. 129). (But sphinx and cφιγγίον may also describe a kind of ape.) If this title centred approximately under that in 3, it must have been short; which tells against cφιγγ[ομένου (or the like) plus noun.

9 Apparently]αιηρηνακεcω[. I do not see how plausibly to divide this.

10]. , upright with ink to the left, eta or nu? . [, lambda or first part of mu? or an anomalous alpha?

Fr. 3

2 After the first epsilon, apparently rho; at the end perhaps the back and lower oblique of kappa.]φερεγ δη- (if the accommodation is acceptable in a MS of this period), φερ' εγδη. ω νεκ[, εγδη. ων εκ[? Since 4 must be a pentameter, so is this; the succession of long syllables shows that the caesura falls after ω/ων.

3]ομαδην (-δρ]ομάδην) possible.

4 ου]κ ενεβαλλεν ολη[(ου κ]εν εβαλλεν)? The first, not the second, half of the pentameter, to judge from 2.

5 Title.

6]. , remains of upright on the edge. Proper names (Damo, Damon) are among the possibilities.

3726. Epigrams

32 4B.7/H(1)a   Fr. 1 3.5 × 19 cm   Second–third century

These scraps from a fine manuscript (fr. 1 has a lower margin of 5 cm), written in a handsome upright Severe Style, include one identifiable text, the epigram *AP* 9. 434 (fr. 1. 25–6). This epigram was probably composed for an edition of Theocritus' works (see Gow, *Theocritus* ii p. 549); it appears also in the Prolegomena of the Theocritus Scholia, preceded by *AP* 9. 205 (Artemid. *FGE* 113) (p. 6. 11 ff. Wendel; cf. pp. 9. 30, 10. 29). In principle, then, **3726** might be (i) a prose work, in which the epigram was cited; (ii) a text of Theocritus, to which the epigram was appended; or (iii) an independent anthology of epigrams. Hints of metre, and dialect forms in fr. 2. 2, 5, seem to exclude (i); no line of Theocritus has been identified, which excludes (ii); (iii) therefore remains, and certainly what little survives can be reconciled with elegiac couplets. There is no trace of *AP* 9. 205.

The back is blank.

	fr. 1	fr. 2
	. . .	. . .
	]δαϲφ[	]φα. [
	]ε. . [	]. αιηϲμητη[
	]κρ. . [	]. α. . . . νε. [
	]. . . [	]. ομαϲέμεπ. [
5	] [	]. φιλευνκαι. [
	] [	]αδιουϲπωϲ. . . [
	] [	]ντ[.]μεν[
	]. [	]. τουτοϲϲη[
	] [	]. χρη. [
10	] [	]. . [
	] [	. . .

Fr. 1

2 . . [, upright and then, on vertical fibres, rising oblique, together κ? then perhaps beginning of high horizontal as of τ   3 κ rather than χ   . . [, top of upright, with hook to right (ε, ϲ?); trace high in the line, perhaps beginning of ω?   4–14 Largely stripped; even the number of lines is uncertain

Fr. 2

1 . [, upright   2]. , low trace running into the nose of α   3]. , perhaps parts of the top and right side of π   α. . . . , first, perhaps upright (rather short), and top of loop, of ρ; last, upper right arc of small circle (ο? ω?)   . [, point at line-level   4]. , upright crossed at foot by stroke from left (ν?)   5]. , gently rising stroke at mid-height, joining loop of φ   . [, upright, perhaps join at top (γ? π?)   6 . . . [, short upper curve of ε, ϲ?, upper arc of circle (ο?), top of upright   8]. , tip of horizontal at two-thirds height, projecting below the left-hand horizontal of τ, crossbar of ε?   9]. , part of upright on edge, stripped above   . [, high horizontal as of τ?   10]. , upper trunk and right-hand branch of υ?

].[
].[
].[
15].ε..[
].αϲτ[
]θυπε[
]αμ.[.]α[
]ηϲκ[.].π.[
20]μυθο[.]ψευ.[
].εγ..ϲε κα[
].νηϲφθ[
]επικρηνω[
].ρωποιϲουκεφ[
25].εθεοκριτοϲτ.[
].ωνειμιϲυρ[

fr. 3

. . .
].[
]καια[
]ϲφορτ[
].. [
. . .

ἄλλος ὁ Χῖος· ἐγώ] δὲ Θεόκριτος ⟨ὃς⟩ τά[δ' ἔγραψα
εἶς ἀπὸ τῶν πολ]λῶν εἰμὶ Ϲυρ[ακοϲίων

Fr. 1

13].[, ρ? 15]., right-hand branches of χ rather than κ? ..[, foot of upright; foot of long descender (ρ υ φ ψ, ?τ) 16]., upright on the edge, apparently reaching only to half height (i.e. ω?) 18 μ., upright, perhaps with rightward extension near the top (i.e. η?) 19]., loop of ρ rather than ο? .[, upper left arc of circle (ο?) 21]., point on the edge at line-level ν.., lower left arc with heavy ink at centre, stripped above (ο, with a gap where its component strokes should join at bottom right?); two uprights (η? ν?) 22]., upright 24]., tip of horizontal at two-thirds height

Fr. 1

19 ff. Assuming that these are elegiacs, and given that in 25 f. the caesura falls towards the left of the preserved portion, possible readings might be:

19 hex.]ηϲ κ[α]ρπọ[(not *AP* 7. 331. 6, 9. 79. 1). 20 pent. –⏑⏑–] μυθο[.] ψευδ[. 21 hex. –⏑⏑–⏑]. εγọγ ϲε κα[(but the first trace does not suggest μ); the scribe left a space after ϲε, which suggests word-end. 22 pent.]. νηϲ φθ[. 23 hex. –⏑⏑–⏑] ἐπὶ κρηνῷ[ν? But it is at least unexpected that a word-group should bridge the third-foot caesura. 24 pent. –⏑⏑ αν]θρώποιϲ οὐκ ἐφ[, οὐ κεφ[.

Fr. 2

If 4 is rightly guessed to be the central part of a hexameter, possible readings might be:

2 hex. –⏑⏑–]. αιηϲ μητη[(μήτη[ρ?) 4 hex. –⏑⏑ ω]νόμαϲέν με π.[. Cf. *AP* 9. 684. 2. 5 pent. –⏑⏑–] ἐφίλευν καὶ.[. 6 hex. –⏑⏑–]αδιọυϲ πῶϲ ϲọι.[. 8 hex. –⏑⏑–⏑]ϵτον τοϲϲη[.

Fr. 3

3]ϲ φορτ[.

II. OFFICIAL DOCUMENTS

3727. DECLARATION TO THE LOGISTES FROM AN
ἐπιμελητὴς ἐργατῶν Μέμφεως

22 3B.16/K (3–4) b   13 × 17.5 cm   303

This fragmentary document is primarily of interest for providing the earliest attestation of the office of logistes, previously unattested before 304; cf. J. Lallemand, *L'Administration civile* 108, and see the note below on l. 4.

An ἐπιμελητὴς ἐργατῶν Μέμφεως swears to the logistes apparently that he has taken charge of a total of 45 persons, levied from various villages to provide compulsory labour in Memphis. See further 7 n.

Written along the fibres. No kollesis survives. The back is blank.

$$\begin{array}{ll}
 & [\dot{\epsilon}\pi\dot{\iota}\ \dot{\upsilon}]\pi\acute{a}\tau\omega\nu\ \tau\hat{\omega}[\nu]\ \kappa[\upsilon]\rho\acute{\iota}\omega\nu\ \dot{\eta}\mu\hat{\omega}\nu\ A[\dot{\upsilon}\tau\upsilon\kappa\rho\alpha\tau\acute{o}\rho\omega\nu] \\
 & \Delta\iota\upsilon\kappa\lambda\eta\tau\iota\alpha\upsilon\hat{\upsilon}\ \tau\grave{o}\ \eta//\ \kappa\alpha\grave{\iota}\ M\alpha\xi\iota\mu\iota\alpha\underaccent{.}{\upsilon}[\hat{\upsilon}\ \tau\grave{o}\ \zeta//] \\
 & C\epsilon\beta\alpha\sigma\tau\hat{\omega}\nu. \\
 & A\dot{\upsilon}\rho\eta\lambda\acute{\iota}\omega\ C\epsilon\dot{\upsilon}\theta\eta\ \tau\hat{\omega}\ \kappa\alpha\grave{\iota}\ {}^{\varsigma}\Omega\rho\acute{\iota}\omega\nu\iota\ \lambda\upsilon\gamma\iota\sigma\tau\hat{\eta}\ {}^{\varsigma}O\xi[\upsilon\rho\upsilon\gamma\chi\acute{\iota}\tau\upsilon\upsilon] \\
5 & [\pi]\alpha\rho\grave{a}\ A\dot{\upsilon}\rho\eta\lambda\acute{\iota}\upsilon\upsilon\ \mathring{A}\pi\phi\upsilon\hat{\upsilon}\tau\upsilon\sigma\ \upsilon\acute{\iota}\upsilon\hat{\upsilon}\ C\alpha\rho\alpha\pi\acute{\iota}\omega\nu\upsilon\sigma\ [\quad\quad c.\ 10\quad\quad] \\
 & \gamma[\epsilon]\underaccent{.}{\rho}\upsilon\mu\acute{\epsilon}\nu[\upsilon\upsilon]\ .\ [\ .\ ]()\ [\tau\hat{\eta}\sigma]\ \lambda\alpha\mu(\pi\rho\hat{a}\sigma)\ \kappa\alpha\grave{\iota}\ \lambda\alpha\mu(\pi\rho\upsilon\tau\acute{a}\tau\eta\sigma) \\
 & \quad\quad\quad\quad\quad\quad\quad\quad\quad {}^{\varsigma}O\xi\upsilon\rho\upsilon\gamma\chi\iota\tau\hat{\omega}[\nu\ \pi\acute{o}\lambda\epsilon\omega\sigma] \\
 & \dot{\epsilon}\pi\iota\mu\epsilon\lambda\eta\tau\upsilon\hat{\upsilon}\ \dot{\epsilon}\rho\gamma\alpha\tau\hat{\omega}\nu\ M\acute{\epsilon}\mu\phi\epsilon\omega\sigma.\ \dot{\upsilon}\mu\nu\acute{\upsilon}[\omega\ \tau\grave{\eta}\nu\ \tau\hat{\omega}\nu\ \kappa\upsilon\rho\acute{\iota}\omega\nu] \\
 & \dot{\eta}\mu\hat{\omega}\nu\ A\dot{\upsilon}\tau\upsilon\kappa\rho\alpha\tau\acute{o}\rho\omega\nu\ \Delta\iota\upsilon\kappa\lambda\eta\tau\iota\alpha\upsilon\hat{\upsilon}\ \kappa\alpha\grave{\iota}\ M[\alpha\xi\iota\mu\iota\alpha\upsilon\upsilon\hat{\upsilon}] \\
 & C\epsilon\beta\alpha\sigma\tau\hat{\omega}\nu\ \kappa\alpha\grave{\iota}\ K\omega\nu\sigma\tau\alpha\nu\tau\acute{\iota}\upsilon\upsilon\ \kappa\alpha\grave{\iota}\ M\alpha\xi\iota\mu\iota\alpha\upsilon\upsilon\hat{\upsilon}\ \tau[\hat{\omega}\nu\ \dot{\epsilon}\pi\iota\phi\alpha\nu\epsilon\sigma\tau\acute{a}\tau\omega\nu] \\
10 & \underaccent{.}{K}\alpha\iota\sigma\acute{a}\rho\omega\nu\ C\epsilon\beta\alpha\sigma[\tau\hat{\omega}]\underaccent{.}{\nu}\ [\tau\acute{\upsilon}]\chi\eta\nu\ \pi\alpha\rho\epsilon\iota\lambda\eta\phi[\acute{\epsilon}\nu\alpha\iota\ \pi\alpha\rho\grave{a}\ \tau\hat{\omega}\nu] \\
 & \kappa\omega\mu\alpha\rho\chi\hat{\omega}\nu\ \tau\hat{\omega}\nu\ \dot{\epsilon}\xi\hat{\eta}[\sigma]\ \gamma\epsilon\gamma\rho\alpha\mu\mu\acute{\epsilon}\nu\omega[\nu\ \kappa\omega\mu\hat{\omega}\nu\quad c.\ 6\quad] \\
 & \dot{a}\rho\iota\theta\mu\hat{\omega}\ [\![\ .\ ]\!]\ (\text{added, m. 2})\ \tau\rho\iota\acute{a}\kappa\upsilon\nu\tau\alpha\ \pi\acute{\epsilon}\nu\tau\epsilon\ (\text{m. 1})\ \kappa\alpha\grave{\iota}\ \dot{\epsilon}\pi[\quad c.\ 6\quad] \\
 & \dot{a}\rho\iota\theta\mu\hat{\omega}\ (\text{added, m. 2})\ \delta\acute{\epsilon}\kappa\alpha\ (\text{m. 1})\ \dot{\upsilon}\mu\upsilon\hat{\upsilon}\ [\quad \text{up to } c.\ 12\quad] \\
 & .\ [\quad\quad\quad\quad\quad\quad].\ [\\
15 & .\ [\\
 & .\ [
\end{array}$$

·   ·   ·   ·   ·

'Under the consuls our lords Imperatores Diocletianus for the 8th time and Maximianus for the 7th time, Augusti.

'To Aurelius Seuthes alias Horion, *curator* of the Oxyrhynchite, from Aurelius Apphous son of Sarapion . . . former . . . of the illustrious and most illustrious city of the Oxyrhynchites, supervisor of the workmen of

Memphis. I swear by the fortune of our lords Imperatores Diocletianus and Maximianus Augusti and Constantius and Maximianus most noble Caesares, Augusti, that I have received from the comarchs of the following villages . . . in number' (added, m. 2) 'thirty-five' (m. 1) 'and . . . in number' (added, m. 2) 'ten', (m. 1) 'together . . .'

1–3 For the form of the consular date-clause cf. P.Wisc. II 61. 1–2, and R. S. Bagnall and K. A. Worp, *The Chronological Systems of Byzantine Egypt* 105.

3 The month and day will probably have been given at the foot after ὑπατείας τῆς αὐτῆς *vel sim.*

4 For Aurelius Seuthes alias Horion and the chronology of the Oxyrhynchite logistae from 303 to 346, see Appendix I below. This document provides a new earliest date for Seuthes, who is the earliest known logistes.

6 For ἐπιμεληταί as drawn from the councillor class see F. Oertel, *Die Liturgie* 219; J. Lallemand, *L'Administration* 215.

7 ἐπιμελητοῦ ἐργατῶν Μέμφεως. For ἐπιμεληταί see Oertel, *op. cit.* 214–21, and also 84 n. 2; N. Lewis, *The Compulsory Public Services of Roman Egypt* (= Pap. Flor. XI) 27–8. For levies in respect of workmen at Memphis cf. P. Sak. 22. 23 ff. and 23; for Alexandria likewise, CPR VI 5. 1–9 (with R. S. Bagnall, *Bull. Soc. Arch. Copte* 24 (1979–82) 115); also P. Sak. 25. 1–11, 24 ff. The language here (παρειληφέναι, 10, with 12–13) suggests that, unusually, it is human labour which is being levied here. For παρειληφέναι cf. e.g. XLVII **3346** 11–12. Wording lost in the lacuna in 11 may nevertheless have converted the 'men' into a payment in lieu.

9 τ[. Or ϵ[? For omission of τῶν before ἐπιφανεστάτων cf. e.g. VIII **1104** 19.

10 For repeated Σεβαστῶν cf. P. Col. VII 136. 3 with 1–4 n.

11 The document presumably continued with a list of the individual villages with the number of men levied from each.

12 After ἀριθμῷ, a short curved upright, partially erased: not the remnant of a more substantial erasure, but simply due to the second hand's at first beginning τριάκοντα (the stroke being the vertical of τ) too far to the left?

3728. APPLICATION TO THE LOGISTES

A 7.B4/1 (H)   11.2 × 7.7 cm   Feb./Mar. 306

This fragmentary document provides the second attestation (see 4 n.) of the ὀνομάγγωνες, here shown as forming a guild. The guild makes application to the logistes but the nature of that application is unclear; it is not a declaration of prices like **3731** etc. It may share the same format as the even more fragmentary **3730**.

Of prosopographical interest, besides the logistes (Aurelius Seuthes alias Horion: see Appendix I below), is a mention of the prefect Clodius Culcianus; see 7 n. **3728** falls within the known term of office of both.

The back is blank.

ἐ[πὶ ὑ]π[άτ]ων τῶν κυρίων ἡμ[ῶν] Αὐ[τοκρατόρων Κωνσταντίου]
    καὶ Μαξιμιανοῦ Σεβαστῷ[ν τὸ ϛ′.]
Αὐρηλίῳ Ϲευθῃ τῷ καὶ Ὡρίωνι λογ[ιστῇ Ὀξυρυγχίτου]
παρὰ τοῦ [κοι]νοῦ τῶν ὀνομανγώνω[ν τῆς αὐτῆς πόλεως]
5   δι' ἐμοῦ Αὐρηλίου Ἀμμωνίου Ἀπολλωνίου. αἰ[τοῦντί]
    ϲοι ἀκο[λούθ]ως τοῖϲ κελευϲ[θεῖ]ϲι ὑπὸ το[ῦ κυρίου ἡμῶν]

4 l. ὀνομαγγώνων

Κλωδίου [Κ]ουλικιανοῦ τὴν τιμὴν . [　　　　c. 14　　　　　]

cυνωγ[η]μένων καὶ πρας . . μέν[ων?　　c. 13　　　　　]

τῆς λ΄ [το]ῦ ὄντος μηνὸc Φαμενὼ[θ　　c. 14　　　　　]

10　　[　c. 6　] κυρίῳ[ν] ἡμῶν Αὐτοκρ[ατόρων　　c. 10　　]

· · · · ·

7 l. *Κουλκιανοῦ*　　8 πρας . . μέν[ων?: uncertain letters obscured by a correction

'Under the consuls our lords Imperatores Constantius and Maximianus, Augusti, for the 6th time.

'To Aurelius Seuthes alias Horion, *curator* of the Oxyrhynchite, from the guild of the donkey-sellers of the same city through me Aurelius Ammonius son of Apollonius. At your request in accordance with the orders of our lord Clodius Culcianus . . .'

1-2 For the consular formula cf. R. S. Bagnall and K. A. Worp, *The Chronological Systems of Byzantine Egypt* 105. The length of the final lacuna in 1 and the plural Cεβαcτῷ[ν in 2 are important factors in controlling the choice. Note that though *Μαξιμιανοῦ* features in the formulae from 302 to 306, 306 is the only one of those years in which the consuls are both Augustus but do not carry different consular numbers.

4 ὀνομανγώνω[ν. Cf. XLIV 3192 10 (9 May 307). Their formation in a κοινόν attested here accords well with the situation in 3192.

7 Clodius Culcianus. See XLVI 3304; and C. Vandersleyen, *Chronologie des préfets* 12 and J. Lallemand, *L'Administration civile* 238, with the amendments tabulated in XLIII 3120 8-9n.; and T. D. Barnes, *The New Empire of Diocletian and Constantine* 149. He is attested as prefect from 6 June 301 until 4 February 307.

3729. DOCTOR'S REPORT

39 3B.76/F(1-2)c　　　　　　　11.4 × 12.3 cm　　　　　　　4 May 307

A public doctor reports to the logistes Aurelius Seuthes alias Horion that as instructed he has examined a man who has been wounded, perhaps on the buttocks. For such reports cf. XLIV 3195 and LI 3620 17-18n. The victim is styled κράτιcτοc δουκηνάριοc. The text provides the latest attestation for Seuthes in office as logistes: cf. Appendix I below.

A large blot of ink partially obscures the centre-right of the text. Traces of ink at the extreme left margin (level with 10-12) may be only further blots; at any rate the appearance of the left edge of the papyrus suggests that we have the original margin of the document.

There is no kollesis. The back is blank.

]. .

[ἐπὶ ὑπάτων τῶν κυρίω]ν ἡμῶ[ν]

[Αὐτο]κρ[άτοροc Cεουήρου C]εβαcτο[ῦ]

καὶ Μαξιμ[ίνου τοῦ ἐπι]φ[α]νεcτάτου

5　　　　　　[Καί]cαροc.

Αὐρηλίῳ Ζεύθει τῷ καὶ Ὡρίωνι λογιcτῇ Ὀξ(υρυγχίτου) διὰ Αὐρηλίου Ἀνθεcτίου ἐξη-
γητοῦ διαδόχου
παρὰ Αὐρηλίου Ἥρωνοc Ἥρωνοc τοῦ

10   καὶ Διονυcίου ἀπὸ τῆc λαμ(πρᾶc) καὶ λαμ(προτάτηc)
Ὀξ(υρυγχιτῶν)

πόλεωc δημοcίου ἰατροῦ. ἐπεcτά-
λην ὑπὸ coῦ τῇ ἐνεcτώcῃ ἡμέρᾳ
ἥτιc ἐcτὶν Παχὼν θ— ἐκ βιβλιδίων
ἐπιδοθέντων coι ὑπὸ Αὐρηλίου Ἰcιδώ-

15   ρου κρατίcτου δουκηναρίου ἐφιδεῖν
τὴν περὶ αὐτὸν διάθεcιν καὶ ἐνγρά-
φωc coι προcφωνῆcαι· ὅθεν ἐφῖδον
τὸν προκίμενον Ἰcίδωρον ἔχοντα
ἐπὶ ἀρ[ιcτερο]ῦ ἰθῶνοc τραῦμα καὶ

20   [c. 16   ].[..].. καὶ ἐπὶ του

. . . . . .

7 οξ′   10 λαμʃ, λαμʃοξ′   14 ὗπο   15 l. ἐπιδεῖν   16–17 l. ἐγγράφωc
17 l. ἐπεῖδον .   18 l. προκείμενον

'Under the consuls our lords Imperator Severus Augustus and Maximinus the most noble Caesar.

'To Aurelius Seuthes alias Horion, *curator* of the Oxyrhynchite, through Aurelius Anthestius exegetes, deputy.

'From Aurelius Heron, son of Heron alias Dionysius, from the illustrious and most illustrious city of the Oxyrhynchites, public doctor. I was instructed by you today which is the 9th of Pachon, consequent on a petition presented to you by Aurelius Isidorus, *vir egregius*, *ducenarius*, to examine his condition and report to you in writing. Wherefore I examined the aforesaid Isidorus, who has a wound on the left buttock(?) and . . .'

1 The traces may be accidental. If not, they are likely to be from a docket rather than a column or item number, for which they would be set rather far to the right.

2–5 For this version of the consular formula cf. P. Mil. II 55. 1–3 (R. S. Bagnall and K. A. Worp, *The Chronological Systems of Byzantine Egypt* 105).

7–8 In XVIII **2187** 2, 5 the logistes (presumably Seuthes again, cf. Appendix I below) is likewise represented by a διάδοχοc; likewise there the διάδοχοc is an exegetes.

9–10 Can this be the same Aurelius Heron who is a δημόcιοc ἰατρόc in 316 (VI **896** 24) and 331 (XLIV **3195** 29)? Cf. **3195** 28 ff. n. The remains of the patronymic in **896** 24 are too damaged for a photograph to be conclusive, but the space is perhaps insufficient to admit the patronymic with alias attested by **3729**.

11 A vertical stroke begins below μ of δημοcίου and reaches down to 13; it is presumably accidental. Another similar stroke to the right begins lower and reaches to 14, and there is a further stroke to the right of that.

15 κρατίcτου δουκηναρίου. Cf. J.-M. Carrié, *ZPE* 35 (1979) 217–18 and C. Foss, ibid. 283. For the debasement of this and other equestrian categories see also F. Millar, *JRS* 73 (1983) 90 ff.

19 ἰθῶνοc is uncertain. I am very doubtful about]ν preceding it. The only alternative culled from P. Kretschmer and E. Locker, *Rückl. Wörterb.* (pp. 188, 191) is ῥ]ώθωνοc, 'nostril', which would require a shorter word in front of it. ἰθών would be an addendum to the papyrological lexica.

3730. APPLICATION TO THE LOGISTES

A 21/6 (25.4.67)   4.8 × 8.2 cm   *c.*308–12

A fragment from the top or from near the top of an application to the logistes Valerius Heron alias Sarapion, whose term of office known from elsewhere supplies an approximate dating (see Appendix I below). The format of the document (which is not a declaration of prices) may be similar to **3728**; see 7 n.

The back is blank.

.   .   .   .   .   .

[Οὐ]α[λε]ρ[ίῳ] Ἥρωνι τῷ [καὶ Cαραπίωνι λογ(ιcτῇ)]
          ᾿Οξυρυ[γχίτου]
    παρὰ τοῦ κοινοῦ τῶν ς[*c.* 12   τῆc]
    [λαμ(πρᾶc)] καὶ λαμ(προτάτηc) ᾿Οξυρυγχιτ[ῶν πόλεωc διὰ *c.* 4]
5   [. . .] μηνιαρχῶν Α[ὐρ(ηλίων)   *c.* 13   ]
    καὶ Cαρμάτου Ἀρτεμιδώ[ρου ἀμφοτέρων(?) ἀπὸ τῆc]
    [αὐ]τῆc πόλεωc. αἰτο[ύμεθα?   *c.* 9   ]
    [*c.* 4] . [

.   .   .   .   .   .

4 λαμ/

'To Valerius Heron alias Sarapion, *curator* of the Oxyrhynchite, from the guild of the . . . of the illustrious and most illustrious city of the Oxyrhynchites, through . . . monthly presidents Aurelii . . . son of . . . and Sarmates son of Artemidorus, both from the same city. We request(?) . . .'

1 The slightly wider gap above this line indicates that it may be the first of the document. On the other hand the consular date is expected, although cf. e.g. **3742**, a price-declaration where the consular date follows the body of the declaration.

3 The guild can hardly be identified. If sigma is correct, then the cταγματοπῶλαι (**3748**) and cτιπποχειριcταί (**3753**) are likely only to be two of several possibilities. For what it is worth, the μηνιάρχαι in **3730** are different from those in **3748** and **3753**.

4–5 After πόλεωc, perhaps δι᾽ ἡμῶν] |⁵[τῶν]?

5–6 There is no change of hand indicating insertion of the names of the μηνιάρχαι.

7 αἰτο[recalls **3728** 5–6 αἰ[τοῦντί] coι and the two texts may be parallel. Or should we compare VIII **1104** 6 and XLIV **3193** 2 and reconstruct αἰτο[ύμεθα ἐπιcταλῆναι?

3731. DECLARATION OF PRICES

A 10.B5/2   8 × 14 cm   *c.*310–11

A fragment from a declaration of prices by the guild of μυροπῶλαι, perfume-sellers: cf. **3733** and XXXI **2570** iii = **3766** v, and also **3765** 32–40. As in the two former texts, the items declared here were set out in two columns: we lack the right-hand column but the left column contains the same items in the same order as **2570** = **3766**. Commentary on the items will be found under **3766**.

An approximate date is provided by the mention of the prefect Sossianus Hierocles, for whom see XLIII **3120** 8–9 n. and P. Coll. Youtie II 79; also now in P. Heid. IV 323. The addressee in 1 will at this date presumably be the logistes Valerius Heron alias Sarapion, for whom see Appendix I below.

There are scanty remains of a crude four-layer kollesis at the left edge, with a few illegible line-ends; this suggests that the papyrus was a τόμος ϲυγκολλήϲιμος, unusual among these declarations (cf. **3742**?). The back is blank.

Previously published declarations of prices are I **85** (re-ed. *ZPE* 39 (1980) 115–23), PSI III 202 (see ibid. 124–5), P. Harr. 73 (re-ed. *ZPE* 37 (1980) 229–36), XXXI **2570** republished here as **3766**, and LI **3624–6**. The type is surveyed in the *ZPE* articles and in **3624–6** introd. Note also P. Ant. I 38 (AD 300), republished as SB X 10257, with the comments of M. H. Crawford and J. M. Reynolds, *ZPE* 34 (1979) 164, and J. R. Rea in LI **3628** 10 n.; on this text see now especially R. S. Bagnall, *Currency and Inflation in Fourth Century Egypt* (*BASP* suppl. 5 (1985)) 63.

Declarations of this type generally exhibit signs of advance drafting, sometimes obvious, sometimes less so. I discussed this bureaucratic procedure in *ZPE* 39 (1980) 115. The draft was prepared by copying from an exemplar, most probably the roll of declarations from the previous month since the guilds had to make these declarations every month. A gap was left for the name(s) of the μηνιάρχαι, while the items declared and the units of measurement and of currency (talents or denarii) were all filled in in advance; thus the names of the μηνιάρχαι and the actual price-figures are expected to show signs of later insertion, even if sometimes this is by the same hand (**3731** does not entirely accord, see 4 n. and 9 ff. n.). The use of the previous month's roll to copy from would obviously help to keep the ready written currency units up to date. The subscriptions too were additions, of course. The date was already written; the day where preserved is always the 30th of the month. This does not imply that the drafts were actually prepared on that day or that they were necessarily filled in on that day.

.   .   .   .   .   .

Οὐ̣[αλερίῳ

[

παρὰ τοῦ κοιν[ο]ῦ τῶν μυ[ροπωλῶν

Αὐρηλίου . . . ει[. .] Διογένους ἀ[πὸ

5   χιτῶν πόλεως. ἀκολού[θωϲ

ὑπὸ τοῦ διαϲημοτάτου Ϲοϲ[ϲιανοῦ Ἱεροκλέουϲ

τιμήματι προϲφωνῶ τὴ[ν

τιμὴν ὧν χιρίζω ὠνί[ων

	πιπέρεωс	λί(τρας) α	τάλ(αντον) α
10	λιβάνου	λί(τρας) α	(δηνάρια) c
	μαλα`βά΄θρου	λί(τρας) α	τάλ(αντον) α
	сτύρακος ὑ[ψ]ηλοῦ	λί(τρας) α [	
	сτύρακος ἐλα[φροῦ		
	κόсτου	λί(τρας) α	. [
15	μαστίκης	λί(τρας) α	(δηνάρια) φ[
	ἀμώμου	λί(τρας) α	(δηνάρια) Ἀcκ[ε?
	βδέλλης	λί(τρας) α	(δηνάρια) το[ε?
	κασίας	λί(τρας) α	(δηνάρια) το[ε?
	κασάμου	λί(τρας) α	(δηνάρια) το[ε?

9 λ, ταλ′   10 ✱: so in 15-19   11 First α of μαλαβάθρου rewritten or corrected   ταλ′

4 After Αὐρηλίου, the first name may be Ἑρμεί[ου]; the second name at least appears to have been inserted by a different hand, and runs into α of ἀ[πό by the first hand.

4-5 The order here is surprising, with the representative's name preceding the reference to Oxyrhynchus.

9 ff. The prices are in the same hand as the main text, with no evidence of insertion.

16 The reading is not Ἀcν, i.e. 1,250 den. Ἀcκ[ε] (1,225) is perhaps a more likely figure than just Ἀcκ (1,220), cf. 3732 13-15 n.

17-19 375 den. = ¼ tal. and therefore is a likely figure.

3732. DECLARATION OF PRICES

70/16 bis (a)   (31.5 × 25.5 cm)   25 May 312
+71/51 (b)

This and the three following items are consecutive declarations of prices on a continuous if much broken and damaged roll. Little survives of this first one, the ends of lines only; for the layout and restorations cf. 3734. Comparisons with 3733 (or 3735), where the layout is much wider, are not apt. The column here must have begun at a higher level than 3733. The guild-name ends in -π]ωλῶν (6); this is not helpful except inasmuch as it indicates that the guild-order here differs from XXXI 2570 = 3766, where the μυροπῶλαι (3733 here) are preceded by the κεραμεῖc.

The texts fall within the known limits of tenure of the *curator* Valerius Heron alias Sarapion: see Appendix I below.

The main hand of the declarations is the same in 3732-5; here in 3732 there is a proxy subscription which may be in a different hand, different therefore (the name is lost) from the proxy subscription in 3733 which was written by Aurelius Nilus the main hand of 3732-5 (see 3733 introd.).

There is a kollesis between **3733** and **3734**; the roll is not a τόμος ϲυγκολλήϲιμοϲ. The declarations are written along the fibres. On the back, along the fibres, is part of a roll of reports of proceedings, published here as **3764**.

[ὑπατείαϲ τῶν δεϲποτῶν ἡμῶν]
[Φλαυίου Οὐαλερίου Κωνϲταντίνο]υ
[καὶ Λικινιανοῦ Λικινίου Ϲεβαϲτῶν τ]ὸ β′.
[Οὐαλερίῳ Ἥρωνι τῷ καὶ Ϲαραπίω]νι
5   [λογιϲτῇ Ὀξυρυγχίτου]
[παρὰ τοῦ κοινοῦ τῶν   ?- π]ωλῶν
[τῆϲ αὐτῆϲ πόλεωϲ διὰ   ]ϝοϲ καὶ Ω. . . . .
[ἀκολούθωϲ τοῖϲ κελευ]ϲθ(εῖϲιν) ἰδίῳ
[τιμήματι προϲφωνοῦμεν] τὴν ἑξῆϲ
10   [τιμὴν ὧν χειρίζομεν] ὠνίων καὶ
[ὀμνύομεν τὸν θεῖον] ὅρκον μὴ
[διεψεῦϲθαι. ἔϲτι δ]έ·
[   ] (δηνάρια) Ꜣ
[   ] (δηνάρια) χκε
15 [   ] (δηνάρια) ιγ
[ὑπατείαϲ τῆϲ αὐτῆ]ϲ,
       [Παχὼν λ′.]
(m. 2)   [Αὐρήλιοι . . . καὶ . . . προϲφωνοῦ]μεν ὡϲ (πρόκειται).
[Αὐρήλιοϲ . . . ἔγραψα ὑπὲρ αὐτῶν] γρ(άμματα) μὴ εἰδότ(ων).

18 ωϲ)?   19 γρ∫, ειδο^τ

3 For the order of the names cf. **3733–4**.

6 κοινοῦ probably abbreviated, cf. the two following declarations.

6 ff. Space-assessment and restoration in this and the following lines are very uncertain. It is not absolutely certain that there were two declarants, the readings in 7 and 18 being very doubtful. With only one declarant of course the verb-forms in 9, 10, and 11 as well as 18 must be adjusted to the singular.

13–15 We cannot exclude the possibility that a sum in talents preceded the denarii. The figure of 13 denarii in 15 is surprising, not only because it is so low (unless a sum in talents preceded it); denarius-sums are normally multiples of twenty-five, as witness **3733**.

18 The very cursive remaining traces are very uncertainly read.

18–19 Perhaps Αὐρ(ήλιοι) and Αὐρ(ήλιοϲ), and the lost part of 19 may have had further abbreviations.

3733. Declaration of Prices

70/16 bis (a)   (31.5 × 25.5 cm)   25 May 312
+ 71/51 (b)

This is the second in the sequence of declarations **3732–5**; for some general comments on the tattered roll that preserves them, see **3732** introd. This item is of special interest for its economic information: it supplies a third declaration by the guild of μυροπῶλαι, perfume-sellers, to add to **3731** (*c*.310–11) and XXXI **2570** iii = **3766** v (27 October 329); cf. too **3765** 32–40 of *c*.327. The items declared are arranged in two columns as in the parallels, and follow the same order. Commentary on the items will be found under **3766**. Comparisons with **3766** indicate that seven items have been omitted here between lines 18 and 19.

Distribution of hands is not totally clear. I think the whole of this declaration, including the names in 5, the prices and the subscription, is by the same hand; i.e. Aurelius Nilus (32) will have been a scribe in the logistes' bureau who was hired to act as ὑπογραφεύς in this case. More disturbingly, I see no clear evidence of the later insertion of names and prices, unless perhaps the pre-drafted entry only listed the items, and the quantity-unit (λί(τρας) α) and price-unit (talents/denarii) were inserted along with the figures. The crisper ink for some of these entries (especially clear in 24–8) may indicate this.

ὑπατείας τῶν δεςπ[ο]τῶν ἡμῶν Φλαυίου Οὐαλερίου
Κωνςταντίνου καὶ Λ[ι]κινιανοῦ Λικινίου Cεβαςτῶν τὸ β΄.
Οὐαλερίῳ Ἥρωνι τῷ καὶ Cαραπίωνι λογ(ιςτῇ) Ὀξυρυγχίτου
παρὰ τοῦ κοι(νοῦ) τῶν μυροπωλῶν τῆς αὐτῆς πόλεως
5   διὰ Ἰςιδώρου Cαραπίωνος. ἀκολ(ούθως) τοῖς κελευςθεῖςιν
ἰδίῳ τιμήματι προςφωνῶ τὴν ἑξῆς τιμὴν ὧν χειρίζω
ὠνίων, καὶ ὀμνύω τὸν θεῖον ὅρκον μὴ [διε]ψεῦςθα[ι. ἔςτ]ι δέ·

πιπέρεως	λί(τρας) α	(τάλαντον) α
λιβάνου	λί(τρας) α	(δηνάρια) c
10 μαλα⟨βά⟩θρου	λί(τρας) α	(τάλαντα) β
ςτύρακος ὑψηλοῦ	λί(τρας) α	(δηνάρια) Ἄςν
ςτύρακος ἐλαφροῦ	λί(τρας) α	(δηνάρια) ψν
κόςμου	λί(τρας) α	(τάλαντον?) ạ
μαςτίκης	λί(τρας) α [	
15 ἀμώμ[ο]υ	λί(τρας) ạ	(δηνάρια?) . .

1 Part of beginning of line obscured by ink-blot   4 κοι   5 ακο^λ   13 l. κόςτου
14 l. μαςτίχης

βδέλλη[ς   λί(τρας)] ą   (δηνάρια) ςν

κασίας   λί(τρας) α   (δηνάρια) φ

κασάμου   λί(τρας) α   (δηνάρια) υν

πατήματος   λί(τρας) α   (δηνάρια) ςν

20 ἀςφαλανθί[ο]υ   λί(τρας) α   (δηνάρια) ϙε

ἀρνą[3-4] . . . . [

λί(τρας) α   (δηνάρια) ρν

(Ll. 23–30 to right of ll. 8–22)

ςαςέλεως   λί(τρας) α   (δηνάρια) ρε

ςφαγνίου   [λί(τρας)] ą   (δηνάρια) οε

25 εἰρωνων   λί(τρας) α   (δηνάρια) ρν

ἐλενιδίων   λί(τρας) [α]   (δηνάρια) ροε

ἀλκεωτίδων   λί(τρας) α   (δηνάρια) ϙε

ὀνυχίων   λί(τρας) α   (δηνάρια) ς

ξυλομαςτίκη[ς]   λί(τρας) α   (δηνάρια) οε

30 αλιμαςτου   λί(τρας) α   (δηνάρια) οε

(At foot, below ll. 1–22)

ὑπατείας τῆς α(ὐτῆς), Παχὼν λ‾.

[Αὐρ(ήλιος) Ἰς]ίδωρος προςφ(ωνῶ) ᾧ[ς] πρόκ(ειται). Α[ὐρ](ήλιος)

Νεῖλος ἔγρ(αψα) ὑ(πὲρ) αὐτοῦ

[μὴ εἰδ]ότ(ος) γρ(άμματα).

20 l. ἀςπαλάθου?   27 ϙε: less probably ρε   31 α‾   32 προςᶠ, προᴷα[υρ]´, εγρʃυ) 33 ειδ]οᵀγρʃ

'In the consulship of our masters Flavius Valerius Constantinus and Licinianus Licinius Augusti, for the 2nd time.

'To Valerius Heron alias Sarapion, *curator* of the Oxyrhynchite, from the guild of the perfume-sellers of the same city, through Isidorus son of Sarapion. In accordance with orders, at my own risk I declare the price below for the goods which I handle, and I swear the divine oath that I have not been deceitful. As follows:

Pepper	1 lb.	tal. 1
Incense	1 lb.	den. 200
Malabathrum	1 lb.	tal. 2
Storax, tall	1 lb.	den. 1250
Storax, dwarf	1 lb.	den. 750
Costmary	1 lb.	tal. 1(?)
Mastic	1 lb.	[ ]
Amomum	1 lb.	den.? –
Bdellium	1 lb.	den. 250
Cassia	1 lb.	den. 500
Cassamum	1 lb.	den. 450
Pounded spice(?)	1 lb.	den. 250

Camel's thorn(?)	1 lb.	den. 75
Zedoary	1 lb.	den. 150
Hartwort	1 lb.	den. 105
Sphagnium	1 lb.	den. 75
?	1 lb.	den. 150
Elecampane	1 lb.	den. 175
?	1 lb.	den. 75
?	1 lb.	den. 200
Mastic wood	1 lb.	den. 75
?	1 lb.	den. 75

'The same consulship, Pachon 30.

'I, Aurelius Isidorus, make my declaration as aforesaid. I, Aurelius Nilus, wrote on his behalf because he is illiterate.'

2 Λ[ι]κινιανοῦ Λικινίου. Cf. **3734** 3. The order is correct, see *PLRE* i 509, and regular in the papyri, cf. the examples in R. S. Bagnall and K. A. Worp, *The Chronological Systems of Byzantine Egypt* 106, where the presentation of the formula as Λικινίου Λικινιανοῦ is incorrect.

3 Ductus of abbreviation of λογ(ιστῇ) not clear.

12 Or possibly φν (550), but 750 den. (half a talent) is a more likely quantity (though note 450 den. in 18).

21 Cf. **3766** 104. The traces here are too scanty to provide help with the textual uncertainty at this point in **3766**. The entry here occupies two lines because the item-description is both long and written generously large.

23 The price is an unexpected figure. Is this an error for ρκε (125) or ροε (175)? The reading is certain.

32 Νεῖλος. I cannot exclude Μέλας.

3734. DECLARATION OF PRICES

70/16 bis (a)   (31.5 × 25.5 cm)   25 May 312
+71/51 (b)

The third in the sequence of declarations **3732–5** (for general comments on the roll that preserves the four see **3732** introd.) is that of the ἁλοπῶλαι, the salt-merchants. They turn up again in a declaration of 319, **3750** below, where the price of salt—250 denarii per artaba—has not changed. The guild-order there—the ἁλοπῶλαι are bracketed by γαροπῶλαι (**3749**) and ἐριοπῶλαι (**3751**)—is different from here.

ὑπατείας τῶ[ν δεc]π[ο]τῶν ἡμῶν
Φλαυίου Οὐαλερίου Κωνcταντίνου
καὶ Λικινιανοῦ Λικινίου Cεβαcτῶν τὸ β'.
Οὐαλερίῳ Ἥρωνι τῷ καὶ Cαραπίωνι
5   λογιcτῇ Ὀξυρυγχίτου
παρὰ τοῦ κοι(νοῦ) τῶν ἁλοπωλῶν τῆc
αὐτῆc π[ό]λ(εωc) διὰ Πτολεμαίου Λουκίου
μηνιάρχο[υ]. ἀκ[ο]λ(ούθωc) [το]ῖc κελευcθ(εῖcιν) ἰδίῳ

6 κοι̅   7 πο^λ?   8 ακο^λ?, κελευc^θ

τιμήματι προϲφωνῶ τὴν ἑξῆϲ τιμὴν

10   ὧν χει[ρ]ίζω ὠνίων, καὶ ὀμνύω
τὸν θεῖον ὅρκον μὴ δι-
εψεῦϲ[θ]αι.

[ἔϲ]τι δέ·

ἁλὸϲ   [(ἀρτάβηϲ)] α   (δηνάρια) cν.

15   ὑπατείαϲ τῆϲ αὐτῆϲ,
Παχὼν λ‾.

(m. 2)   Αὐρήλι[οϲ] Πτολεμαῖοϲ προϲφωνῶ
ὡϲ πρ[όκει]ται.

13 Enlarged letters with a long filler-stroke at end

'In the consulship of our masters Flavius Valerius Constantinus and Licinianus Licinius Augusti, for the 2nd time.

'To Valerius Heron alias Sarapion, *curator* of the Oxyrhynchite, from the guild of the salt-merchants of the same city, through Ptolemaeus son of Lucius, monthly president. In accordance with orders, at my own risk I declare the price below for the goods which I handle, and I swear the divine oath that I have not been deceitful. As follows:

'Salt   1 art.   den. 250.
'The same consulship, Pachon 30.'
(2nd hand) 'I, Aurelius Ptolemaeus, make my declaration as aforesaid.'

8 For the guild μηνιάρχαι—one acts as declarant in the present instance, but sometimes more do so, six in I **85** iii (re-ed. *ZPE* 39 (1980) 118)—see XLIII **3126** i 19 n. and XLIV **3195** 6–7 n. **3743** and **3752** attest the same persons as μηνιάρχαι (of the guild of λευκανταί) in two successive consular years.

14 For salt note LI **3628** 17 n.; A. Lucas, *Anc. Egyptian Materials and Industries*, 4th edn. rev. J. R. Harris (1962), 268–9.

3735. DECLARATION OF PRICES

70/16 bis (a)   (31.5 × 25.5 cm)   25 May 312
+71/51 (b)

Only scanty remains survive of the fourth and last-preserved declaration of the **3732–5** sequence (for general comments on this roll, see **3732** introd.). The guild is unidentified and the remains contribute nothing except a possible example of a layout unusual in these declarations, and they are really transcribed only for completeness' sake. What survives is sufficient to show that we have a wide format with the consular date on two lines (1–2), cf. **3733** above, the declaration of the μυροπῶλαι. It is not clear whether the items here declared occupied two columns as there. I do not know as yet of any guild that used this format except the μυροπῶλαι, for whom it was regular.

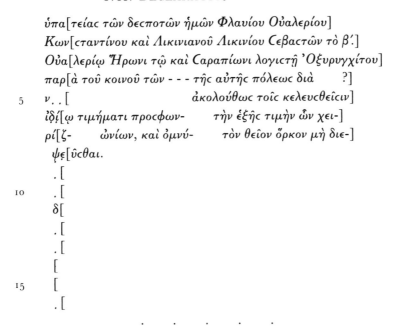

ὑπα[τείας τῶν δεσποτῶν ἡμῶν Φλαυίου Οὐαλερίου]
Κων[σταντίνου καὶ Λικινιανοῦ Λικινίου Σεβαστῶν τὸ β΄.]
Οὐα[λερίῳ Ἥρωνι τῷ καὶ Σαραπίωνι λογιστῇ Ὀξυρυγχίτου]
παρ[ὰ τοῦ κοινοῦ τῶν - - - τῆς αὐτῆς πόλεως διὰ   ?]
5   ν . . [ἀκολούθως τοῖς κελευσθεῖσιν]
ἰδί[ῳ τιμήματι προσφων-   τὴν ἑξῆς τιμὴν ὧν χει-]
ρί[ζ-   ὠνίων, καὶ ὀμνύ-   τὸν θεῖον ὅρκον μὴ διε-]
ψε[ῦσθαι.
. [
10   . [
δ[
. [
. [
[
15   [
. [

            .   .   .   .   .

4–7 The uncertainty over identification of the guild, the presence or otherwise of abbreviations, and the number of declarants make accurate reconstruction of these lines impossible.

3736. DECLARATIONS OF PRICES?

13 1B.212–213/A h(i) and (ii)   h(i) 10 × 21 cm.   27 September(?) 312
                                         h(ii) 10 × 17 cm.

These tattered fragments preserve the foot (on h(ii) = col. i) and the top (on h(i) = col. ii) of what presumably were declarations of prices. On the back of fragment h(ii) are **3758** 221–8 and on the back of h(i) are **3758** 214–20. Lines 181–213 of **3758** are on the back of the price-declaration sequence **3737–40** below, dated 27 September 312. The year in **3736** col. ii is certainly 312, though month and day have not survived, while the addressee Valerius Heron (alias Sarapion, *curator* of the Oxyrhynchite) is shared with the **3737–40** sequence (**3738** inadvertently omits him), and the inventory numbers are sequential, so that the circumstantial evidence for unity is strong.

The declarations are written along the fibres. From the foot of col. i scanty ink traces of only two or three lines remain, which we do not transcribe. The last line begins Αὐρή[λιος. There was a blank lower margin of perhaps up to 8 cm. Of col. ii we transcribe the first five lines; occasional traces survive below this on a tangled mass of loose (and mostly vertical) fibres, extending about 18 cm. below l. 5.

ὑπατείας τῶ[ν] δεςποτ[ῶ]ν
ἡμῶν Φλαυίου Οὐαλερίου
Κωνςταντίνου καὶ Λικιννια[νο]ῦ
Λικινίου Cεβαςτῶν τὸ β[ſ".]
5   Οὐαλερίῳ Ἥρων[ι] τ[ῷ

2 φλαυϊου

3737. DECLARATION OF PRICES

13 1B.212–213/A (h)   Height 25 cm   27 September 312

This price-declaration addressed to the logistes by the guild of κεμιοπῶλαι (see 7–8 n.) is the first of a sequence of four of the same date occupying part (39 cm long) of the other side of **3758**. The three items that follow it are published below as **3738–40**. The sequence of these three (ἐλαιουργοί, ἀρτυματοπῶλαι, κάπηλοι) is echoed in the declarations **3760–2**, perhaps of 326. **3737** is more or less complete except for the loss of part of the right centre, but the loose and shredded nature of the surface fibres renders transcription hazardous. Considerable stray ink (offsets?) adds to the difficulties. There appears to have been a strengthening-strip (for **3758** presumably) attached down the left side of the document, which must itself have been inscribed; traces of its fibres remain, with ink visible through them.

The sequence greatly extends the known span of office of the logistes Valerius Heron alias Sarapion and provides the latest known date for him. See Appendix I below.

The main hand of all four texts **3737–40** is the same. See **3731** introd. for the practice of drafting the common form of such declarations in advance. **3738** bears an autograph signature by the declarant; the other three are signed by a ὑπογραφεύς, Sarmates in **3737**,]ion in **3739**, and Horion (the ὑπογραφεύς in **3739**?) in **3740**. Horion, in a hand clearly different from the main hand, also inserted the prices and the names of the μηνιάρχαι in **3740**. Authorship of the insertions in **3737–9** is uncertain; they may all be in the same hand, or the ὑπογραφεῖς may have made them in **3737** and **3739** respectively, and there are other possibilities obviously. If they are all in the same hand, the writer may be Sarmates, the ὑπογραφεύς of **3737**. His handwriting is hardly to be distinguished from the main hand of all four texts **3737–40**, although that may be due to the poor surface condition of the papyrus. It is conceivable that Sarmates, like Aurelius Leontius in P. Harr. 73 (see R. A. Coles, *ZPE* 37 (1980) 230), was a scribe in the logistes' bureau and in that capacity drafted the main texts, made the insertions in a number of them and was commissioned by the μηνιάρχης in one instance to write the subscription. See Appendix IV below. Such a man would be in a position to insert the missing details of nomenclature and price in a document for which another man was ὑπογραφεύς.

There is a kollesis to the right of **3740**, just before the edge of this particular offcut scrap of papyrus, but elsewhere the extreme surface damage and decomposition makes the presence of these joins very hard to discern.

ὑπατεία[ς] τῶν δεσποτῶν
ἡμῶν Φλαυίου Οὐαλερίου
Κωνσταντίνου καὶ Λικιννιανοῦ
Λικινίου Σεβαστῶν τὸ βϛ′ ′.

5 Οὐαλερίῳ Ἥρωνι τῷ καὶ Σαρα-
  [πίω]νι λογιστῇ Ὀξυρυγχίτου
  [παρὰ τοῦ κο]ι̣[νο]ῦ̣ τῶ̣ν κεμι̣ο-
  πωλῶν τῆς αὐτῆς πόλε[ως]
  [1–2?] . . . . Αὐρηλίου Ἱερακᾶ[τος?]

10 [ἀ]κ̣ολούθως τοῖς κελευσθ(εῖσιν) [ἰδίῳ]
   [τι]μήματι προσφωνῶ τὴν
   ἑξῆς τιμὴν ὧν [χιρίζω]
   [ὠνί]ω̣ν κα̣[ὶ ὀμνύω τὸν θεῖον]
   [ὅρκον] μὴ ἐψεῦς̣θαι. ἔ[στι δέ·]

15	[2–3] . [.]ο̣υ̣	(ἀρτάβης) α	τάλ(αντον)	(added; m. 2?)	α
(m. 1)	[φ]α̣ς̣ήλου	(ἀρτάβης) α	τάλ(αντον)	(added; m. 2?)	α
(m. 1)	[ἐρ]εβίνθου	(ἀρτάβης) α	τάλ(αντον)	(added; m. 2?)	α̣
(m. 1)	τήλεως	(ἀρτάβης) α	(δηνάρια)	(added; m. 2?)	ψν
(m. 1)	ὀρόβου	(ἀρτάβης) α	(δηνάρια)	(added; m. 2?)	Ⱥ
(m. 1)	ὑπατείας τῆς αὐτῆς, Θὼθ λ′.				
(m. 2?)	Αὐρήλιος Ἱερακᾶς προσφω[νῶ ὡς πρόκειται.]				

22 Αὐρ(ήλιος) Σαρμάτη[ς] ἔγρ(αψα) ὑ(πὲρ) αὐτοῦ γρ(άμματα)
                          μὴ [εἰδότος.]

---

2 φλαυϊου Last o of Οὐαλερίου rewritten   9 ϊερακα[10 κελευς^θ?   16 ταλ′ So in 15, 17?   21 ϊερακας   22 αυρ′, εγρ/υ)   Form of abbreviation of γρ(άμματα) not discernible

'In the consulship of our masters Flavius Valerius Constantinus and Licinianus Licinius Augusti, for the 2nd time.

'To Valerius Heron alias Sarapion, *curator* of the Oxyrhynchite, from the guild of the seed-vegetable merchants of the same city', (m. 2?) 'through me(?) Aurelius Hieracas'. (m. 1) 'In accordance with orders, at my own risk I declare the price below for the goods which I handle, and I swear the divine oath that I have not been deceitful. As follows:

[ ]	1 art.	tal.'	(added; m. 2?) '1'
(m. 1) 'Calavance	1 art.	tal.'	(added; m. 2?) '1'
(m. 1) 'Chick-pea	1 art.	tal.'	(added; m. 2?) '1(?)'

    (m. 1) 'Fenugreek   1 art.   den.' (added; m. 2?) '750'
    (m. 1) 'Vetch   1 art.   den.' (added; m. 2?) '1000'
(m. 1) 'The same consulship, Thoth 30'.
    (m. 2?) 'I, Aurelius Hieracas, make my declaration as aforesaid. I, Aurelius Sarmates, wrote on his behalf as he is illiterate.'

7–8 κεμιοπῶλαι recur in two other texts in this volume, **3744** and **3755**. Neither of those texts contributes to our knowledge of the meaning of the word. The most recent treatment is that of Z. Borkowski, *Une descr. topogr. des immeubles à Panopolis* (Warsaw 1975) 71. Now that we know four of the items handled by the κεμιοπῶλαι (16–19), we may more firmly reject the translation 'marchand de gomme' than Borkowski was able to do. If the κεμιοπῶλαι were concerned with chickens, then here they would have to be declaring the prices of the foodstuffs they bought. Borkowski's third possibility, based on κέμιον = some type of vegetable, is more acceptable and suits the nature of the items declared here in **3737**. For κέμιον see P. Ryl. IV 627, 629–30, 639 freq., esp. 627. 192 n., CPR VIII 85. 5 n. and P. J. Sijpesteijn and K. A. Worp, *ZPE* 29 (1978) 269. The association κεμίων καὶ θυδράκων (*vel sim.*), and κεμοράφανος, both frequent in P. Ryl. IV, provide added weight for the vegetable-based interpretation. A common characteristic of the vegetables handled here (16–19) is that they are all leguminous vegetables cultivated for their seeds; hence I opt for the translation 'seed-vegetable merchants'.

9 One expects δι' ἐμοῦ at the beginning of the line but I have failed to read it. An insertion or change of hand for the name of the declarant is expected but is not palaeographically clear. There are at any rate script similarities in the words recurring in 21. Ἱερακᾶς (cf. 21) is not in F. Preisigke, *Namenbuch* or D. Foraboschi, *Onomasticon* or in Pape–Benseler or in F. Dornseiff and B. Hansen, *Rückl. Wörterbuch*. The short genitive Ἱερακᾶ is also possible, see F. T. Gignac, *Grammar* ii 16–18.

12–14 χιρίζω . . . ὅρκον. The wording is restored on the basis of the other items in this series but the papyrus is so damaged and the traces in 13 so uncertain that the distribution of words between lines is very conjectural.

15–19 The amounts of money are expected to be in a different hand or at least to have been added in; that they have at least been added in is apparent from the amounts in talents not being quite in alignment with the indication ταλ῀.

16–19 For the items here (that in 15 remains undetermined) see M. Schnebel, *Die Landwirtschaft* 189–91, 193–5. φάσηλος, ἐρέβινθος and ὄροβος recur together in P. Cair. Isid. 71. 7 and 72 introd. For φάσηλος cf. BGU XV 2496 introd. On fenugreek (τῆλις) see also D. Crawford, *Kerkeosiris* 112–13. For ὄροβος see O. Lund 1. 2 n.; R. Pintaudi, *Aeg.* 61 (1981) 99, discusses ὀρβαρ- variants. Note the unfortunately incomplete price-declaration of the ὀρβιοπῶλαι, **3745** with 7–8 n.

17 The reading of the price is very uncertain; the surface is disfigured by offsets.

21 The use of the indicative of προσφωνῶ, without ἐπιδέδωκα, is not in accord with the later practice, but is consistent through this sequence except for the curious double subscription in **3738**. πρόκειται probably abbreviated.

21–2 A change of hand is expected but is not palaeographically clear. Surface damage helps to obscure the individuality of the handwriting. Cf. the introd. above.

22 εἰδότος probably abbreviated.

3738. DECLARATION OF PRICES

13 1B.212–213/A (h)   Height 25 cm   27 September 312

    This declaration by the oil-workers of Oxyrhynchus is the second in the sequence of four contemporary declarations **3737–40**, for which cf. **3737** introd. This one has suffered some loss from a diagonal break across the centre. The writer has omitted the address to the logistes, thus depriving τῆς αὐτῆς πόλεως in 6 of any point of reference. Another curiosity is the repeated subscription (here not by a ὑπογραφεύς but in the declarant's autograph). For the various handwritings of the four-document sequence, see **3737** introd.

For the ἐλαιουργοί and the oil they declare cf. **3760**, and see 5–6 n. below.

ὑπατείας τῶν δεσποτῶ[ν]
ἡμῶν Φλαυίου Οὐαλερίο[υ]
Κωνσταντίνου καὶ Λικινν[ιανοῦ]
Λικινίου Cεβαcτῶν τὸ β[ʃ΄.]
5   παρὰ τ[ο]ῦ κοινοῦ τ[ῶ]ν [ἐλαι-]
ουργῶν τῆc αὐτῆc [πόλεωc]
δι' [ἐμο]ῦ Αὐρηλίου

(added, m. 2?)   [Πετ]τίρις Πα . . . [
(m. 1)   [ἀκο]λούθωc τοῖc [κελευcθεῖcιν]
10   [c. 11   ] . [c. 7   ] . .
[c. 19   ] ὠνί-
[ων καὶ ὀμνύω] τὸν θεῖον ὅρκον
[μὴ ἐψεῦcθαι. ἔ]cτι δέ·
14   [λαχανο]cπέρμου   (ἀρτάβης) α   τάλ(αντα)   (added; m. 2?) β
                                             (δηνάρια) cν.

(m. 1)   [ὑπατείας] τῆc αὐτῆc, Θὼθ λ΄.
(m. 3)   [Αὐρή]λιος Πεττῖρις προcφω-
[νῶ] ὡc πρόκειται.
[Α]ὐρήλιος Πεττῖρις ἐπιδέδωκα προcφωνῶν
20   ὡc πρ⟨όκειται⟩.

1 ὑπατειας?   2 φλαυϊου   8 l. Πεττίριος   14 ⌐, ταλ΄, ✗   14–15 Parts of this line and the next appear to have been re-inked   16 First τ of Πεττῖρις added   18 πετ'τιρις

'In the consulship of our masters Flavius Valerius Constantinus and Licinianus Licinius Augusti, for the 2nd time.

'From the guild of the oil-workers of the same city, through me Aurelius' (added; m. 2?) 'Pettiris son of Pa . . .' (m. 1) 'In accordance with orders, [at my own risk I declare the price below for the] goods [which I handle], and I swear the divine oath that I have not been deceitful. As follows:

         'Vegetable-seed   1 art.   tal.' (added; m. 2?) '2, den. 250'

(m. 1) 'The same consulship, Thoth 30.'

(m. 3) 'I, Aurelius Pettiris, declare as aforesaid. I, Aurelius Pettiris, presented this, making my declaration as aforesaid.'

5–6 ἐλαιουργοί are discussed briefly by Z. Borkowski, *Une descr. topogr. des immeubles à Panopolis* (Warsaw 1975) 71–2. That the oil they handled was not olive oil is clear from λαχανοcπέρμου in 14 here (partly restored) and in **3760** 12 (cf. n.). (Olive oil is discussed by A. Wittenburg, *ZPE* 38 (1980) 185–9, and also posited by

A. M. Tromp, *Stud. Pap.* 21 (1982) 39–40. On olive cultivation in Egypt see A. Lucas, *Anc. Egyptian Materials and Industries* (4th edn. rev. J. R. Harris) 333–5.)

7 For the prior classification of the guild's representative as an Aurelius cf. J. G. Keenan, *ZPE* 53 (1983) 245–50, esp. 246. Filler-stroke at the end of the line; whether it is by the first or the second hand is not clear.

10–11 Unless there were abbreviations (e.g. κελευcθ(εῖcιν) in 9, cf. **3737** 10), space is tight for restoring the formula as in **3739**. Did the writer omit ἐγγεγραμμένην as in **3737** and **3740**?

14 [λαχανο]ϲπέρμου. Cf. **3760** 12.

16–20 Cf. **3737** 21 n.

20 The sentence was never finished; only the loop of rho was written.

3739. Declaration of Prices

13 1B.212–213/A (g)   Height 25 cm   27 September 312

This declaration by the condiment-sellers of Oxyrhynchus (cf. **3761**) is the third in the contemporary sequence **3737–40** (see **3737** introd.) and is mostly preserved or restorable except for the items declared, ll. 15–23 (see n.).

For a discussion of the handwritings of the four-document sequence, see **3737** introd.

```
        [ὑπατείας τῶν δεc]ποτῶν ἡμῶν
        [Φλαουίου Οὐα]λερίου Κωνcταντίνου
        καὶ [Λικιν]γιανοῦ Λικινίου
        [Cεβα]cτῶν τὸ βϛ΄.
   5    [Οὐα]λερ[ίῳ] Ἥρωνι τῷ καὶ Cαραπίωνι
            [λογιcτῇ Ὀ]ξυρυγχίτου
        [παρὰ τοῦ] κοινοῦ τῶν ἀρτυματοπω-
        [λῶν τῆc] αὐτῆc πόλεωc (added; m. 2?) δι(ὰ) Εὐ-
        [αγγέλου? . .]. ωνοc. (m. 1) ἀκολούθωc
  10    [τοῖc κελευc]θεῖcιν ἰδίῳ τιμήματι
        [προcφω]ν[ῶ] τὴν ἑξῆc ἐνγε-
        [γραμμένη]ν τιμὴν ὧν χιρίζω
        [ὠνίων κ]αὶ ὀμνύ[ω] τὸν θεῖον
        [ὅρκον μ]ὴ ἐψεῦcθαι. ἔcτ[ι δ]έ·
  15    .[ . . . . . ]ου        (ἀρτάβηc) α [
        [              ]  (ἀρτάβηc) α  τάλ(αντον)  (added; m. 2?) α (δηνάρια) ψ
(m. 1)  .[          ].  (ἀρτάβηc) α΄  (δηνάρια)  (added; m. 2?) ψν
(m. 1)  μ.[      ]. . . . .ϛ  δεcμ(ιδίου) α΄ (δηνάρια)  (added; m. 2?) κε
```

8 δι΄   11–12 l. ἐγγεγραμμένην   12 l. χειρίζω   15 ff. ⸕   16 ταλ΄ So in 22, 23
⸕ So in 17–21, 23   18 δεcμ΄

(m. 1)	κ[	].	(ἀρτάβης) α	(δηνάρια)	(added; m. 2?) Ἀϲν
(m. 1)	. . . . [	]	(ἀρτάβης) α	(δηνάρια)	(added; m. 2?) Ἀϲν
(m. 1)	. [	]. ϲ	(ἀρτάβης) α	(δηνάρια)	(added; m. 2?) Ἀϛν
(m. 1)	. [	].	(ἀρτάβης?) α	τάλ(αντον)	(added; m. 2?) α
(m. 1)	[	]	(ἀρτάβης) α	τάλ(αντον)	(added; m. 2?) α
					(δηνάρια) ψγ

(m. 1)   [ὑπατείας τῆ]ϲ αὐτῆϲ, Θὼθ λ´.

(m. 3?)   Α[ὐρήλιος Εὐάγ]γελος προϲφωνῶ ὡϲ πρόκ(ειται).

26   [Αὐρήλιος ?ʾΩρ]ίων ἔ[γρ](αψα) ὑ(πὲρ) αὐτοῦ γρ(άμματα) μὴ
                 εἰδ(ότος).

25 προᵏ?   26 εγρ/υ), γρ/, ει^δ

'In the consulship of our masters Flavius Valerius Constantinus and Licinianus Licinius Augusti, for the 2nd time.

'To Valerius Heron alias Sarapion, *curator* of the Oxyrhynchite, from the guild of the condiment-sellers of the same city, through' (added; m. 2?) 'Evangelus son of -on.' (m. 1) 'In accordance with orders, at my own risk I declare the price entered below for the goods which I handle, and I swear the divine oath that I have not been deceitful. As follows:

. . .	1 art. [		
. . .	1 art.	tal.' (added; m. 2?) '1, den. 750'	
(m. 1) '. . .	1 art.	den.' (added; m. 2?) '750'	
(m. 1) '. . .	1 bundle	den.' (added; m. 2?) '25'	
(m. 1) '. . .	1 art.	den.' (added; m. 2?) '1250'	
(m. 1) '. . .	1 art.	den.' (added; m. 2?) '1250'	
(m. 1) '. . .	1 art.	den.' (added; m. 2?) '1250'	
(m. 1) '. . .	1 art.(?)	tal.' (added; m. 2?) '1'	
(m. 1) '. . .	1 art.	tal.' (added; m. 2?) '1, den. 750'	

(m. 1) 'The same consulship, Thoth 30.'

(m. 3?) 'I, Aurelius Evangelus, make my declaration as aforesaid. I, Aurelius Horion(?), wrote on his behalf as he is illiterate.'

15-23 The items here should be identical with those declared in **3761** 6-14. The number of items is the same. Unfortunately, comparing **3739** 18-19 with **3761** 9-10 (the fourth and fifth items in each case) makes it clear that the order in the two lists must be different (surprisingly, contrasting the regularity, say, in the lists submitted by the μυροπῶλαι), thus making it impossible to supplement the items. Equally]. ϲ here from the seventh item (l. 21) will not square with the seventh item in **3761** 12, κνήκου.

18 For the δεϲμίδιον as a unit of measurement cf. **3765** 9.

26 For the restoration of Horion's name see **3740** introd., and Appendix IV below.

3740. DECLARATION OF PRICES

13 1B.212-213/A (g)   Height 25 cm   27 September 312

     This declaration of prices to the logistes by the guild of tavern-keepers (cf. **3762**) is the fourth (and final one to have survived) in the contemporary sequence **3737-40** (see **3737** introd.).

For a discussion of the handwritings of the four-document sequence see **3737** introd. It is not clear whether the ὑπογραφεύς Aurelius Horion, who clearly also inserted the prices and the names of the μηνιάρχαι, might not also be identified with the ὑπογραφεύς of **3739**. Apparent differences in the script could perhaps be attributed to use of a different pen. For Horion see Appendix IV below.

The document was drafted in expectation of one declarant. For the scribal havoc created by two declarants turning up, see the app. crit. on 8 and 13 and 8–10, 12, 14nn.

$$
\begin{array}{ll}
& \text{ὑπατείας } [τῶ]ν \text{ δεσποτῶν} \\
& \text{ἡμῶν Φλαυίου Οὐαλερίου} \\
& \text{Κωνσταντίνου καὶ Λικιννιαν}[ο]ῦ \\
& \text{Λικινίου Cεβαcτῶν τὸ βſ ′ ′.} \\
5 & \text{Οὐαλερίῳ Ἥ}[ρ]ωνι τῷ καὶ Capα-} \\
& \text{πίωνι λογιcτῇ Ὀξυρυγχ(ίτου)} \\
& \text{παρὰ } [τοῦ] \text{ κοινοῦ τῶν καπήλων} \\
& \text{τῆc } [αὐτῆc] \text{ πόλεωc δι(ὰ) (m. 2) ἡμῶν} \\
& \text{Θεοδ}[ώρου] \text{ Capαπίωνοc καὶ} \\
10 & \text{Διο}[δώρου] \text{ Διονυcίου μη(νιαρχῶν). (m. 1) ἀκολού-} \\
& \text{θω}[c τοῖc κελευ]cθεῖcιν ἰδ[ί]ῳ τι-} \\
& \text{μήμα}[τι προcφωνο]ῦμεν τὴν ἑ-} \\
& \text{ξῆ}[c τιμὴν ὧν] \text{ χιρίζομεν ὠνίων} \\
& \text{κ}[αὶ ὀμνύομεν τὸ]ν θεῖον ὅρκον μὴ} \\
15 & \text{ἐψε}[ῦcθαι.] \qquad \text{ἔcτι δέ·} \\
& \text{οἴν}[ου Ὀα]cιτικοῦ ξ(έcτου) α \quad (δηνάρια) (m. 2) oε \\
\text{(m. 1)} & \text{κνι}[δίου Θ]ηβαϊκοῦ ξ(έcτου) α \quad (δηνάρια) (m. 2) oε \\
\text{(m. 1)} & \text{ὑπατε}[ίαc τῆ]c αὐτῆc, Θὼθ λ΄.} \\
\text{(m. 2)} & \text{Αὐρή}[λι]οι Θεόδωροc καὶ Διόδωροc} \\
20 & \text{προ}[c]φωνοῦμεν ὡc πρόκειται. Αὐρ(ήλιοc) Ὠρί-} \\
& [ων \text{ ἔ}]γρ(αψα) ὑ(πὲρ) αὐτῶν γρ(άμματα) μὴ εἰδότων.
\end{array}
$$

1 υπατειαc   2 φλαυϊου   6 οξυρυγχ ?   8 δι΄; δ re-inked by m. 2   Not certain whether the second hand's heavily-inked ἡμῶν has been written over anything (ἐμοῦ?) by the first hand   10 μηſ   11 ϊδιω   13 χιρίζομεν corr. from χιρίζω; l. χειρίζομεν   17 θηβαϊκου   18 υπατειαc?   19 Horizontal mark in margin close to line-beginning, cf. 20   20 Unexplained horizontal mark before προcφωνοῦμεν, cf. 19   αυρ΄   21 εγρſ υ), γρſ

'In the consulship of our masters Flavius Valerius Constantinus and Licinianus Licinius Augusti, for the 2nd time.

'To Valerius Heron alias Sarapion, *curator* of the Oxyrhynchite, from the guild of the tavern-keepers of the same city, through' (m. 2) 'us Theodorus son of Sarapion and Diodorus son of Dionysius, monthly presidents.'

(m. 1) 'In accordance with orders, at our own risk we declare the price below for the goods which we handle, and we swear the divine oath that we have not been deceitful. As follows:

      'Oasite wine   1 sextarius   den.' (m. 2) '75'
        (m. 1) 'Theban (wine) of Cnidian type
                       1 sextarius   den.' (m. 2) '75'
   (m. 1) 'The same consulship, Thoth 30.'

   (m. 2) 'We, Aurelii Theodorus and Diodorus, make our declaration as aforesaid. I, Aurelius Horion, wrote on their behalf as they are illiterate.'

7 While κάπηλοι (= *caupo, cauponarius, tabernarius* CGL) elsewhere can indicate a different or less specific occupation, it is clear that here they are wine-merchants or rather tavern-keepers, declaring the price of two types of wine. M. San Nicolò, *Äg. Vereinswesen* (2nd edn., Munich 1972) i 133-4 discusses the development of this specialized meaning of the term. It is odd that the κάπηλοι as a class seemingly did not stock Oxyrhynchite wine, listed in **3765** 5, where it must be derived from the declaration of a different guild.

8-10 The first hand left space at the end of 8 and before ἀκολού- in the line following, sufficient for a single declarant. The second hand has squeezed in more than was planned for, and ἀκολού- printed as if ending 10 is in fact physically sandwiched by 9-10 as inserted by the second hand.

12 προcφωνο]ῦμεν. The ductus is far from clear. A correction from προcφωνῶ is expected.

13 Space precludes inclusion of ἐγγεγραμμένην before τιμήν. Cf. **3737** 12.

14 ὀμνύομεν will presumably have been corrected from ὀμνύω, cf. the app. crit. on 13.

16-17 Cf. **3762** 15-16 and **3765** 3-4. For Oasite wine cf. XLVIII **3425** 1 n. The other variety here is less straightforward. The other two occurrences assure the reading. Geographical adjectives or adjectival nouns such as κνίδιον when encountered in papyri are often taken to describe a particular style and size of jar (as indeed κνίδιον does in **3748** 15; and cf. V. Grace and J.-Y. Empereur, *BIFAO* 81 suppl. (1981) 424-5) rather than refer to genuine imported wine or other commodity; but such cannot quite be the case here. The volume is specified, namely the *sextarius*, and the addition of a second unit of volume would make no sense; in any case the measurement-units do not normally precede the item. Moreover, the provenance is given as the Thebaid, Θηβαϊκοῦ, so that we cannot have a reference to imported Cnidian wine. I believe we have to understand the description here as '"Cnidian" (wine), made in the Thebaid', or more freely 'Theban (wine) of Cnidian type'. Cf. M. Schnebel, *Die Landwirtschaft* 251-2; O. Lund. 12. 6-7 n.; also H. Cockle, *JRS* 71 (1981) 95 with the reference to H. C. Youtie, *Scriptiunculae* I 154-5 (note the *caveat* on p. 170).

The abbreviation for ξ(έcτου) is the usual one of a xi cut by an oblique stroke rising to the right at a shallow angle.

19-21 A fold on the surface as manufactured interrupts the writing in the middle of these lines, giving θ εοδωρος,]φωνο υμεν and αυ των.

3741. OFFICIAL DAYBOOK

70/16 (a)   49.7 × 15.3 cm.   2 September-7 October ?313

   3741 preserves part of an official daybook. The official concerned is nowhere clearly specified. The logistes is cited in 59, and certain sections (5-8, 39-40) record matters that fall within the sphere of his activity. Yet 62, following on 59, appears to exclude him as the official whose decisions are recorded at intervals. In both format and brevity the daybook is in contrast with the long *transversa charta* reports of hearings or series of hearings exemplified elsewhere in this volume. For other examples of daybooks cf. XLII **3072-4**. **3741** gives the lie to the statement of E. Bickermann, *Aeg.* 13 (1933) 346, that Diocletian did away with the keeping of official journals.

   The papyrus is written across the fibres and preserves the lower parts of four columns plus traces of a fifth (the occasional traces of line-beginnings of this, never more than one letter, are not transcribed). Preserved dates run from Thoth 6 (l. 13, = 3/4 September; ll. 1–12 presumably all date to Thoth 5) till Phaophi 10 (l. 63: = 7/8 October). There is a wide margin of 7 cm to the left of col. i and it is a fair assumption that this was the first column of the roll and that the roll started with Thoth 1 = 29/30 August.

A curiosity of the daybook, apart from the frequency with which the level of business transacted was οὐδέν, is the entry Διός occurring regularly every seven days (ll. 13 (Thoth 6), 18 (Thoth 13), 36 (Thoth 27), 44 (Phaophi 4)). On none of these Διός-days are transactions of any kind recorded. Διός presumably = *dies Iovis*, i.e. Thursday: cf. e.g. *CCAG* VIII. 3 p. 192. For days of the week cf. XLIV **3174** 17 n. with references (the wooden tablet referred to there is redated to 327 in place of 294 by R. S. Bagnall and K. A. Worp, *BASP* 17 (1980) 17, while a revised edition of Bickermann, *Chronology*, appeared in 1980); D. R. Jordan, *Hesp.* 54 (1985) 215. For the regular cessation of official business on Thursdays perhaps compare Caesarius of Arles, *Sermones* 13. 5 (also 19.4 and 52.2; we owe these references to Dr Holford-Strevens); there may be a hint of the practice in XXII **2343** 8–9 (29 December 287), see R. A. Coles, *ZPE* 61 (1985) 113.

The date of **3741** should probably be 313. The calculation is as follows: if Thoth 6 (l. 13 = 3/4 September) and every seventh day following was a Thursday, use of V. Grumel, *La Chronologie* 316 shows that in the early fourth century possible years are 302, 307, 313, 324, 330, and so on. 302 and 307 can be excluded because they antedate the date of the document on the front of **3741** (mid 313: see below) while 330 and later dates postdate the fall of Licinius, after which, because of Constantine's legislation on Sunday observance, we ought not to find official bureaux routinely closed on Thursdays (contrast **3759** introd. and 38 n.). 324 is theoretically possible because 3 September in that year still precedes the fall of Licinius (news of which would not have reached Oxyrhynchus by the latest date on the papyrus), but 313 is much more likely as yielding a very plausible interval after which the document on the front that came in to the logistes' bureau would have been discarded for reuse. (Intervals evidenced by these texts from the logistes' bureau range from a possible one month (**3766–7**) to possibly nearly twenty years (see **3756–8** introd.).) Perhaps this attractive interval is too short. The earliest day on **3741** would have been 29 August if the year were 313, see above. The petition on the front must fall between 28 July and 13 September 313, see below; this interval reduces to 28 July–29 August if the daybook dates to the same year. This leaves a very brief time for the petition to remain on file, and would of course have consequences, albeit very hypothetical ones, for the date of the death of Maximinus Daia and the date by which the consular change to Constantine alone was known in Egypt. Nevertheless so rapid a reuse of the back of the petition for a record starting Thoth 1 has a compact neatness which is very persuasive.

This petition on the front, from a woman to the logistes and dated 313, is extensive but too damaged to yield connected sense beyond its first four lines. It is written along the fibres upside down in relation to the daybook. The text opens as follows: [1](m. 1 or m. 3?) ὑπατία[ς τ]οῦ δεσπότου ἡμῶν Φλαυίο[υ] Οὐαλερίου Κωνσταντίνου Σεβαστο[ῦ τὸ] γ´.

²(m. 2) Οὐαλέριος Ἀμμωνιανὸς ὁ καὶ Γερόντιος λογιστὴς Ὀξυρυγχίτου Αὐρηλίῳ Cαραπίωνι πραι(ποσίτῳ) πάγου τῷ φιλτάτῳ χαίρειν. τῶν δοθέντων μοι βιβλίων ὑπὸ ⟦τοῦ⟧ τῆς ἐγγεγραμμέν⟦ου⟧ης ἴϲον ἐπιϲτέλλεταί ϲοι ὅπωϲ [³(m. 1) Οὐαλερίωι Ἀμμωνιανῷ τῷ καὶ Γεροντίῳ λογιϲτῇ Ὀξυρυγ[χίτου] ⁴παρὰ Αὐρηλίας Τεχωϲοῦτ[ο]ς τῆς καὶ Εὐδαιμονίδος θυγα[τρὸ]ς Διδύμου τοῦ καὶ Εὐδαίμονο[ς] καὶ ὡς χ[ρ]ηματίζει ἀπὸ τῆς λα[μ(πρᾶς)] καὶ λαμ(προτάτης) Ὀξυρυγχιτῶν πόλεως. ὁ ὑπ. . . . .[(much-damaged remains of ten further lines). The very wide lines were once wider still although the end of 3 suggests that not much has been lost. The last preserved line was apparently a short one, but the document probably continued below that; if not, it will have been of unusual proportions. (Comparison of ll. 14–16 (col. i) on the back with l. 17 (top of col. ii) shows that a minimum of four lines has been lost there at the top of col. ii.) The consular formula (1) is of interest since it records a stage hitherto unattested in the papyri, see R. S. Bagnall and K. A. Worp, *The Chronological Systems of Byzantine Egypt* 106–7. The month is not preserved but the date should fall between 28 July and 13 September, cf. P. Sakaon 6. 13–14 and XLIII **3144** 1–2 n. That terminal date must move earlier (into August) if the daybook on the back also dates from 313, see above. In any case the petition probably belongs nearer the beginning of the interval, since it represents a stage after it was known to omit Maximinus Daia from the formula but before the knowledge of his replacement by Licinius; while a further reason would be to maximize the petition's potential life on file, a month at most if the daybook on its reverse is to be assigned to the same year. Regardless of these refinements, the date will fall within the known limits of tenure of the logistes Valerius Ammonianus alias Gerontius, for whom see Appendix I below. The address to him (3) is pretentiously written in a large script with the words well spaced out. The smaller script of 4 ff. is presumably in the same hand. Ample space was left above the address for the insertion of the logistes' instructions by a second hand (2). It is not clear whether the consular date above that is by yet another hand or by the writer of the main text. In 4 the size of omicron and the spacing suggest the articulation ὁ ὑπ- at the end. Three kolleseis are preserved, giving visible sheet widths between them of 16 and 14.5 cm.

Col. i

. . . . . .

. [
[*c.* 7   ]. [.]. [*c.* 6   ].. [. .]. [
[ἔδ]οξ(εν) ἐπ[ὶ] τὸν ἐ[πί]τροπον τῇ[ς ζ′νο-?]
[?μία]ς ἀναπέμπεσθ[α]ι τὸ πρᾶγμα.
5   ,ἄλλο [*c.* 3   ]. Λίβυϲϲα διὰ Κάϲτοροϲ π(ερὶ) τ[οῦ]
δεῖν β. . . . . ην γυναικ( ) ξενικοῦ τῇ
ὁϲίᾳ παραδοθῆναι.

3 εδοξ′   5 π′   6 γυναικ

ἔδοξ(εν) οὕτω γίγνεϲθαι.

,ἄλλο [.]η[.].…[.]..ϲ καὶ Θεοδώρα πρ(ὸϲ?) Ἀριαν[ὸ]ν

10   π(ερὶ) οἰκίαϲ. ἔδοξ(εν) καὶ τὸν υἱωνὸ[ν]

Ἡράκλειον λαβεῖν τὴν μοῖραν τῆϲ

…… ⟦.ου⟧.

,ϛ Διόϲ.

ζ τειμῆϲ ἰχθυηρᾶϲ ἔνεκεν ἀνεδ….

15   ἁλιέων δοθέντων εἰϲ λειτουργίαν

ὡϲ κατὰ τὴν τοῦ καθολικοῦ κέλευ[ϲιν.]

Col. ii

.   .   .   .

[ιβ   οὐδέ]ν.

ιγ′   Διόϲ.

ιδ′   οὐδέν.

20   ,ιε   Ϲερῆνοϲ Διοϲκουρίδου ἠξ[ίωϲεν

καϲ ἐπιδιδοὺϲ δανίου (ταλάντων?) ι[

τῇ πόλει ὑ(πὲρ) ὀνόματοϲ Θε.[

πιδοϲ γυν(αικὸϲ) Ὠρίωνοϲ αρ.[

λαβεῖν τὰ ὑπάρχοντα.

25   ἔδοξ(εν) οὕτω γίγνεϲθαι.

ιϛ   οὐδέν.

ιζ   οὐδέν.

ιη   Μαξεντίου π(ερὶ) πιϲ.....

κ.ϛ( ) ργ Μακεδο.....

Col. iii

.   .   .   .

30   [   ]..[

,κβ   οὐδέν.

,κγ   οὐδέν.

,κδ   οὐδέν.

,κε   οὐδέν.

8 εδοξ′   9 ρ)   10 π′, εδοξ′, ϋιωνον   14 l. τιμῆϲ; ἰχθυηραϲ   21 l. δανείου   ι: or

ρ 22 ῠ)   23 γυ^ν   25 εδοξ′   28 π′   29 εϛ

35 ,κϛ οὐδέν.

   ,κζ Διός.

   ,κη οὐδέν.

   ,κθ οὐδέν.

   ,λ   π(ερὶ) λύϲεωϲ διαθήκηϲ . [. . .] . . . γαμβρᾶϲ

40   Ἀπίου παρέδρου [vac.?]

   ,Φαῶφι α′ οὐδέν.

      ,β οὐδέν.

      ,γ οὐδέν.

      ,δ Διός.

45   ,ε Ἀϲκληπιάδηϲ ἐπιμελητὴϲ ἀκμιναλίων

         ὅπου κατέθετο αἰτιώμενοϲ ὡϲ τρο-

         φῶν μὴ δοθειϲῶν ταῖϲ μρύλαιϲ.

Col. iv

.   .   .   .   .

   [   ] . [

   [   ] . [

50 [   ] . ϵι . [

         ἔδοξ(εν) ὑπερτ . [

   [date   ο]ὐδέν.

   [date] . οὐδέν.

   [date] Ϲαραπ[ί]ων [.] . αλ . . [

55 [   ] . . π . . . . . οι . . τ[

   [   ] . . . τους ἔχειν τὰϲ ἀγωγάϲ.

         ἔδοξ(εν) τὴν ἐπιϲτολὴν ἀναλημφθ(ῆναι)

         τοῖϲ ὑπομ(νήμαϲι).

   ἄλλο ὁ λογ(ιϲτὴϲ) ἠξίωϲεν . . . . . . κοταϲ

60   πληρῶϲαι τοὺϲ δανιϲτὰϲ ἐπὶ

         τριετεῖ χρόνῳ.

         ἔδοξ(εν) οὕτω γίγνεϲθαι.

   ι   π(ερὶ) ἐξετάϲεωϲ ἀπελαϲίαϲ βοόϲ

39 π′   47 ταῖϲ corr. from τοῖϲ   51 εδοξ′?   57 εδοξ′, αναλημφθ^θ   58 υπομϳ
59 λογ( ): form of abbreviation not clear because of damage to the papyrus   60 l. δανειϲτάϲ
62 εδοξ′   63 π′

Col. i 3

'Decided: to transfer the matter up to the *procurator Heptanomiae*(?).

'Another. . . . , a Libyan woman, through Castor, concerning the necessity . . . wife . . . foreigner . . . to be handed over for burial.

Decided: that this should be done.

'Another. . . . and Theodora against Arianus(?) concerning a house.

Decided: the grandson also, Heraclius, should receive the share of the . . .

'6th *dies Iovis*.

'7th On account of the value of the fishing-concession (a list?) was submitted of fishermen presented for liturgy in accordance with the order of the *rationalis*.'

Col. ii 17

'12th Nothing.

'13th *dies Iovis*.

'14th Nothing.

'15th Serenus son of Dioscurides requested . . . presenting . . . a loan of 1[?] talents(?) . . . to the city in the name of The- . . . -pis wife of Horion . . . to receive his property.

Decided: that this should be done.

'16th Nothing.

'17th Nothing.

'18th Maxentius(?) concerning . . .'

Col. iii 31

'22nd Nothing.

'23rd Nothing.

'24th Nothing.

'25th Nothing.

'26th Nothing.

'27th *dies Iovis*.

'28th Nothing.

'29th Nothing.

'30th Concerning the opening of the will of . . . sister-in-law(?) of Apius(?), assessor . . .

'Phaophi 1 Nothing.

'2nd   Nothing.

'3rd   Nothing.

'4th   *dies Iovis*.

'5th   Asclepiades, in charge of baggage-animals somewhere(?), made a deposition containing an accusation that the mules were not given their fodder.'

Col. iv 51

'Decided: . . .

[Date] Nothing.

[Date] Nothing.

[Date] Sarapion . . . to have the right of procedure.

Decided: the letter to be incorporated into the minutes.

'Another. The *curator* requested that . . . should refund the creditors over a three-year period.

Decided: that this should be done.

'10th Concerning an inquiry into the driving-off of an ox.'

1 Trace is a long diagonal, not from ϵ (= Thoth 5), not a check mark (cf. 5 etc.), not I think from ἄλλο (cf. 5, 9, etc.: if stroke were from first λ, cf. 9, more traces should be visible). Possibly cf. unexplained marks at the beginning of 10 and elsewhere, see 16 n.

3-4 For the *procurator Heptanomiae* cf. J. Lallemand, *L'Admin. civile* 261, and XLII **3031** and L **3573**. Or τῆ[ϲ πριουά-]⁴[τη]ϲ?

5-7 These lines obviously summarize a hearing regarding *apertura testamenti* or more specifically the burial arrangements that may conclude such hearings: cf., for τῇ ὁcίᾳ παραδοθῆναι, **3758** 153, 210. Cf. also 39–40 below.

6 Or Ξενικοῦ?

14 τειμῆc ἰχθυηρᾶc ἕνεκεν. The precise implications of this phrase are unclear. I take it that the absence of a number of fishermen on liturgical duties would lead to a drop in the revenues from the fishing-concession, whether rents or taxes or both, hence the interest in a list of such persons. Possibly ἀνεδ(όθη) χρ(αφή)? For ἰχθυηρᾶc cf. e.g. XLVI **3270** 6 and P. Harr. II 194; for fishing in general see the bibliography collected in XLIX **3495**.

16 In the margin an unexplained mark, similar to a cursive Latin *q*. Identical marks occur in the margin beside 29, 46–7, and 61. A damaged mark in the margin beside 10 may have been similar. Also cf. 1 n. The mark beside 40 is different, see n. There is a small further mark, different, in the margin midway between 42 and 43; this may be accidental.

17–19 Ink traces to the right of the text as printed are perhaps to be explained as offsets. More offsets interfere with 21.

21 See 17–19 n.

28 First two letters of Μαξεντίου obscured by blots, offsets or a correction. Αὐξεντίου is a possible alternative. If Μαξεντίου is correct and this person was named after Maximian's son, the latter's date of birth (*c*. 283?) becomes relevant. See T. D. Barnes, *The New Empire of Diocletian and Constantine* 34.

39–40 For hearings on *apertura testamenti* cf. **3758** 134–55 and 181–213; also 5–7 above.

40 In the margin an unexplained mark, similar to the rough-breathing sign in literary papyri. Cf. 16 n.

45 ἀκμιναλίων. Lat. *agminalium*. See *TLL* s.v. *agminalis*, with especially D. Just. 50. 4. 18. 21 *agminales . . . mulae* (μούλαιc here in 47). The Greek form seems not to have occurred before, nor is this particular variety of ἐπιμελητής attested (N. Lewis, *The Compulsory Public Services of Roman Egypt* (= Pap. Flor. XI) 27–8).

46 If ὅπου is not a substitute for the unknown name of the place where Asclepiades was active, it may be relative (meaning 'since') and the entry will then have continued into the next column.

55–6 It is difficult to assess the number of letters lost at the line beginnings because of the probability of a staggered layout, cf. 45–7 and earlier. It seems almost certain that 54–8 all belong to the same day because only four days are to be accommodated between 45–7 (Phaophi 5) and 63 (Phaophi 10), with new days definitely at 52, 53, and 54.

56 ἀγωγάc. Probably to be understood in its legal sense of *actio*. Cf. e.g. XVII **2111** 3 n.

3742. DECLARATION OF PRICES

4 1B. 76/m   10.2 × 23.9 cm   26 November 317

A declaration of the price of glass, by weight, addressed to the logistes Valerius Ammonianus alias Gerontius (for whom see Appendix I below) by the guild of glassworkers of Oxyrhynchus. For the glassworkers see P. Coll. Youtie II 81 (= XLV **3265**). 5 and n. They recur in the list PUG I 24 (ii 8). **3742** is the text referred to in P. Coll. Youtie II 81. 15 n.

On the back are the first five lines from a report of proceedings, written *transversa charta*, probably before the logistes. The date is 15 December 325, in the consulship of Paulinus and Julianus (cf. **3756** 26 n.), the location in τῷ Κορίῳ ἱερῷ (cf. **3759** 1).

Analysis of the handwriting is not totally straightforward. For the regular format cf. **3731** introd. The expected additions in 5–6 and 13 (the names in 5–6 clearly added, the price in 13 less so) are not obviously the work either of the main scribe or of Aurelius Pathermouthis who wrote the subscription.

At the extreme left edge there are traces of a four-layer kollesis (the original manufacturer's joins would be of three-layer type, see LI **3624–6** introd.). Was the roll of declarations a τόμος cυγκολλήcιμος? This would be unexpected; a possible example of this format, rare in guild declarations, is **3731**. Alternatively, the traces may be from a repair patch; or the discarded declaration-roll was cut up for reuse on the back, and **3742**—neatly cut up its left margin—had the declarations that once preceded it replaced with some other document(s), pasted on to take the report of proceedings on the back. At the extreme right edge there are remains of another kollesis, again four layers thick: this time **3742** overlaps the writing on the strip of a document attached to it, which is upside-down relative to **3742**. Clearly there is no question here of a τόμος cυγκολλήcιμος, nor is there need of a join here to extend the area for reuse on the back, since we have the beginning of the report of proceedings (written *transversa charta*) on the back, and the right edge of **3742** is the top margin of the proceedings. Probably the surviving 1.5 cm.-wide strip was all that was ever attached to **3742** and was there as a strengthening strip (for **3742** or for the proceedings). It may itself have been cut from a price-declaration, since]ταλ[is visible. Whether **3742** had been neatly cut up its right margin (as well as its left?), or whether it was conceivably the last declaration on the roll, we cannot say.

       [Οὐαλερίῳ] Ἀμμωνιαν[ῷ τῷ καὶ]
       [Γεροντί]ῳ λογιστῇ Ὀξυρυγχίτ[ου]
       [παρὰ τοῦ] κοινοῦ τῶν ὑελουργῶν
       [τῆς λ]αμ(πρᾶς) καὶ λαμ(προτάτης) Ὀξ(υρυγχιτῶν) πόλεως
    5 [δι’ ἐμο]ῦ Αὐρηλίου (m. 2) Ἀρι⟨ω⟩νος
       [. . . .] . του. (m. 1) ἀκολούθως
       [τοῖc κ]ελευcθεῖcιν ἰδίῳ τιμήμα-
       [τι προ]cφωνῶ τὴν ἑξῆς ἐνγε-
       [γ]ρ[α]μμένην τιμὴν ὧν χιρί-
    10 ζω ὠνίων καὶ ὀμνύω τὸν
       θεῖον ὅρκον μηδὲν διε-
       ψεῦcθαι. ἔcτι δέ·
       ὑέλου ὁλκῇι   κεντ(ηναρίου) α   τάλ(αντα) (m. 2) δ.
(m. 1) ὑπατείας Ὀουϊνίου Γαλλικανοῦ
    15 καὶ Καιcωνίου Βάccου τῶν
        λαμπροτάτων, Ἀθὺρ λ‾.
(m. 3) Αὐρήλιος Ἀρείων ἐπιδέδωκα
        προcφωνῶν ὡς πρόκ(ειται). Αὐρή(λιος) Παθερ-
        μοῦθις ἔγρ(αψα) ὑ(πὲρ) α[ὐ]τοῦ γρ(άμματα) μὴ εἰδότο[c].

3 ὑελουργων   4 λ]αμ/, λαμ/οξ'   5 l. Ἀρείωνος   6 First υ re-inked   8-9 l. ἐγγεγραμμένην
9-10 l. χειρίζω   13 ὑελου, κεντ', ταλ'   14 ὑπατειαcοουϊνιου   15 ν of τῶν rewritten
18 προ^κ αυρῆ‾?   19 εγρ/υ/, γρ/

'To Valerius Ammonianus alias Gerontius, *curator* of the Oxyrhynchite, from the guild of the glassworkers of the illustrious and most illustrious city of the Oxyrhynchites, through me Aurelius' (m. 2) 'Areion, son of ...' (m. 1) 'In accordance with orders, at my own risk I declare the price entered below for the goods which I handle, and I swear the divine oath that I have been deceitful in nothing. As follows:

'Glass, by weight   100 lb.   tal.' (m. 2) '4.'

'In the consulship of Ovinius Gallicanus and Caesonius Bassus, *viri clarissimi*, Hathyr 30.'   (m. 1)
I, Aurelius Areion, have presented this, making my declaration as aforesaid. I,(m.)Aurelius Pathermouthis, wrote on his behalf as he is illiterate.'

13 The price here of 4 tal./100 lb. had increased by 326, just over 8½ years later, to 22 tal./100 lb., as P. Coll. Youtie II 81 (= XLV **3265**).15 attests, an increase of 450% (not 550% as in P. Coll. Youtie II 81. 15 n.). The average annual percentage increase is 22.2%.

14-15 For the consuls see T. D. Barnes, *The New Empire of Diocletian and Constantine* 95, 101; R. S. Bagnall and K. A. Worp, *The Chronological Systems of Byzantine Egypt* 107.

3743. DECLARATION OF PRICES

A 21/6(i) (25.4.67)   7 × 23.2 cm   318

This declaration of prices to the logistes by the guild of λευκανταί, bleachers (see H. C. Youtie, *ZPE* 22 (1976) 63-4), is physically separate, but it was found in close proximity to **3744** and may, with **3745**, once have formed part of the same roll of declarations, drafted by the same hand. The year is the same throughout, but only in **3743** does a trace of the month survive and that trace is indeterminate.

3743 is of special prosopographical interest: supported by **3744** and **3745**, it attests a brief period of office as logistes for Valerius Dioscurides alias Julianus earlier than his previously known tenure and interrupting the once apparently continuous tenure of Valerius Ammonianus alias Gerontius, the result being that both officials have second periods of office. For fuller details see Appendix I below.

λευκανταί appear again in **3752** of the following year. Unfortunately the damage to **3743** prevents our knowing the effect of one year's inflation, other than that the price for the first item declared cannot have increased—if it increased at all—by more than 25 denarii, just over 1.5%.

The names of the μηνιάρχαι (9 ff.) and the prices declared (20 ff.) are expected to have been inserted by a second hand or at least added by the same hand (for the normal format cf. **3731** introd.). Here they are clearly by the same hand and it is far from obvious that they have been added. The denarius-sign in 20 is in an ink blacker than the ink generally is elsewhere in the document.

On the back, but along the fibres and thus at right angles to **3743**, are the fragmentary remains of the last two lines of a report of proceedings before a logistes. The first line was partially deleted; the second runs /ὁ λογιcτὴc εἶ(πεν)· ἀχ[θή]cονται, the rest of that line and the remaining space below being blank.

[ὑπα]τείας τῶν δεσποτῶ[ν]
[ἡμῶ]ν Λικινίου Cεβαστοῦ τὸ εʃʹ
[καὶ Κ]ρίς[που τοῦ] ἐπιφανεστάτου
[Καίς]αρ[ο]ς τ[ὸ αʃʹ.]

5 [Οὐα]λερίῳ Διοσκουρίδῃ τῷ κ[αὶ]
[Ἰου]λιανῷ λογιστῇ Ὀξυρυγχί[το]ν
[πα]ρὰ τοῦ κοινοῦ τῶν λευκαν-
[τῶ]ν τῆς λαμ(πρᾶς) καὶ λαμ(προτάτης) Ὀξ(υρυγχιτῶν) πό-
[λεω]ς δι' ἡμῶν Αὐρηλίων [Μ]α-

10 [ξί]μου Cαρμάτου καὶ Παθ[ε]ρ-
[μου]θίὀ υʹ Cα[ρ]α[π]ίωνος μ]ηνι-
[αρχῶν. ἀκολούθ]ως τοῖς
[κελευσθεῖσιν ἰδίῳ τι]μήμα-
[τι] προσφ[ωνοῦ]μεν τὴ[ν] ἑξῆς

15 [ἐγγ]εγραμμένην τιμ[ὴν ὧν]
[χειρί]ζομεν ὠνίων κα[ὶ]
[ὀμν]ύομεν τὸν θεῖον ὅρ[κο]ν
[μηδὲ]ν διεψεῦσθαι. ἔστι [δ]έ·
[λίν]ων παντοίων λευκ[ῶ]ν

20 [τοῦ] μὲν τρυφεροῦ λί(τρας) [α   τά]λ(αντον) α (δηνάρια) ρ[
[τοῦ δ]ὲ κοινοῦ   λί(τρας) [α   ]...[
[ὑποδε]εστέρων χω[ρικῶν λί(τρας) α
[ὑπατεία]ς τῆς προκ(ειμένης), .[

(m. 2) [Αὐρήλιοι] Μάξιμος κ[αὶ Παθερμούθιος]

25 [ἐπιδεδώκ]αμεν προ[σφωνοῦντες ὡς πρόκ(ειται).]
[c. 8   ] ἀξιωθεὶς ἔγρ(αψα) ὑ[(πὲρ) αὐτῶν γρ(άμματα) μὴ εἰδότων.]

8 λαμʃ, λαμʃοξʹ   20 λ?, ταλʹ, ✕   23 προᴷ   26 εγρʃ

'In the consulship of our masters Licinius Augustus for the 5th time and Crispus the most noble Caesar for the 1st time.

'To Valerius Dioscurides alias Julianus, *curator* of the Oxyrhynchite, from the guild of the bleachers of the illustrious and most illustrious city of the Oxyrhynchites, through us Aurelii Maximus son of Sarmates and Pathermuthius son of Sarapion, monthly presidents. In accordance with orders, at our own risk we declare the price entered below for the goods which we handle, and we swear the divine oath that we have been deceitful in nothing. As follows:

'All kinds of white linens:

Fine quality	1 lb.	tal. 1 den. 100[+?]	
Standard quality	1 lb.	[	]
Inferior, local	[1 lb.		]

'The aforesaid consulship, [month and day.]'

(m. 2) 'We, Aurelii Maximus and Pathermuthius, presented this, making our declaration as aforesaid. I, Aurelius . . . , on request wrote on their behalf as they are illiterate.'

1 δεϲποτῶ[ν]. The nu is obscured by a piece of extraneous papyrus glued over the upper right corner (perhaps in preparation of the roll for the text on the back?). It would be risky to remove it and since readings are not in doubt the attempt does not seem worthwhile.

9–12 The same persons were μηνιάρχαι in Phamenoth the next year, as **3752** shows; **3743** 9–12 and 24 can be restored in combination with each other and with **3752**.

11 The reading here is assured by the parallel **3752**, even though the traces are only dubiously allocated to particular letters.

12 ἀκολούθ]ωϲ. A trace remains (on mainly vertical fibres) from near the beginning of this word, it is uncertain from which letter.

19 λευκ[ῶ]ν. Like **3753**, this is another example where to suppose the guild declares the price paid for the raw material of its trade (cf. LI **3624–6** introd.) is not the ready explanation; it would seem much more obvious that here we have a service industry or better still a retail trade (since the goods are described as already λευκ[ῶ]ν) listing its prices. **3626** is another text that will not easily fit the raw-material pattern of declarations, along with **3776**. The Michigan text published by H. C. Youtie, *ZPE* 22 (1976) 63 ff. (cited in the introd. above), is evidence for dealings with λευκανταί by the λίτρα (ll. 16–18), perhaps not outright purchase (as Youtie's translation suggests) since ll. 27–8 appear to keep a fee for the work separate from any price for the actual material. The drop from 3½ lb. (ll. 17–18) to 2½ lb. (l. 26) is disconcerting. If not simply an error, had Aria taken 3½ lb. to the bleacher for bleaching, sold 1 lb. for a profit and paid him, and now she still owes him for bleaching the remaining 2½ lb.? Measurement by weight suggests that yarn and not cloth is meant.

20 τρυφεροῦ, 22 [ὑποδε]εϲτέρων. For the combination cf. *Aeg.* 54 (1974) 94, a text also concerned with textiles. The commentary on l. 5 there is invalidated by a lexicographical misunderstanding, as checking XXXI **2599** 31 n. quickly makes clear. καταδεέϲτεροϲ is the term which occurs *passim* in the textile sections of Diocletian's Price Edict. The parallel **3752** uses ὑποδεέϲτεροϲ.

22 See 20 n.

24 Cf. 9–12 n. above.

26 The ὑπογραφεύϲ may be the ubiquitous Aurelius Horion, cf. e.g. the letter-forms in **3748** 20 and see Appendix IV below. His name may have come partly in 25; Αὐρήλιοϲ is likely to have been abbreviated αυρ΄. Various of the words lost at the end of 26 are likely to have been abbreviated; ὑ(πέρ) and γρ(άμματα) almost certainly so, αὐτ(ῶν) and εἰδ(ότων) (or εἰδότ(ων)) possibly so. For ἀξιωθείϲ see H. C. Youtie, *ZPE* 17 (1975) 211 and n. 26.

3744. Declaration of Prices

A 21/6(viii) (25.4.67)   7.2 × 12 cm   318

This fragment from the beginning of a declaration of prices to the logistes by the guild of κεμιοπῶλαι (cf. **3737** 7–8 with n. and also **3755** 30) is additional evidence for the early tenure of the office of logistes by Valerius Dioscurides alias Julianus: cf. **3743** and Appendix I below. No month survives in **3744** but it is dated to the same year as **3743** (and was found in close proximity to it) and also **3745**, and all three are in the same hand and may have come from the same roll.

The papyrus is broken off at the left and below. There is no trace of a following item.

The fragmentary text on the other side (also along the fibres) may be a draft, with several corrections and interlineations. Appearance suggests it may be from a report of proceedings, written *transversa charta* and probably before the logistes, but there is no internal evidence for that.

[ὑπατείας τῶ]ν δεςποτῶν

[ἡμῶν Λι]κινίου Cεβαστοῦ τὸ εϛ′

[καὶ Κρίςπ]ου τοῦ ἐπιφανεςτάτου

[Καίςαρος τ]ὸ αϛ′.

5 [Οὐαλερίῳ Δι]οςκουρίδῃ τῷ καὶ

['Ιουλιανῷ λ]ογιςτῇ 'Οξυρυγχίτου

[παρὰ τοῦ κο]ινοῦ τῶν κεμιο-

[πωλῶν τῆς λαμ(πρᾶς)] καὶ λαμ(προτάτης) Ὀ[ξ(υρυγχιτῶν)]

[πόλεως δι' ἐμ]οῦ Αὐρηλίου

10 [*c.* 14   ]...[.]..[*c.* 2]

[ἀκολούθως τοῖς κ]ελευςθε[ῖςιν]

. . . . .

8 λαμϛ

'In the consulship of our masters Licinius Augustus for the 5th time and Crispus the most noble Caesar for the 1st time.

'To Valerius Dioscurides alias Julianus, *curator* of the Oxyrhynchite, from the guild of the seed-vegetable merchants of the illustrious and most illustrious city of the Oxyrhynchites, through me Aurelius . . . In accordance with orders, . . . '

9 Papyrus broken after *Αὐρηλίου*; space (for about three letters) probably left blank.

10 The scanty traces are insufficient to show whether a second hand entered the names here.

3745. DECLARATION OF PRICES

11 1B.145/G (c)   13 × 22 cm   318

Details of the item(s) declared, and the subscription, are lost from this price-declaration by the vetch-sellers which otherwise poses no problems, despite its condition, except for the name of the μηνιάρχης in 10. Lines 5–6 provide further supporting evidence for the brief first tenure of the office of logistes by Valerius Dioscurides alias Julianus in 318: cf. **3743–4** and Appendix I below. We do not know in which month **3745** was written. It is in the same hand as the declarations **3743–4** and all three may have come from the same roll.

Written along the fibres. The tattered condition of areas of the text renders the measurements approximate only. There are scanty traces of the beginnings of lines of a following column, which are not transcribed. On the back, *transversa charta* along the fibres, are the remains probably of proceedings, in all likelihood before the logistes. There are parts of nine damaged and heavily corrected lines.

ὑπατείας τῶν δεσποτῶν
[ἡμῶ]ν Λικινίου Cεβαστοῦ τὸ εſ
καὶ Κρίcπου τοῦ ἐπιφανεcτάτου
[Καίcαρος τὸ] αſ.

5   [Οὐαλερίῳ Δ]ιοcκουρίδῃ τῷ καὶ
       ['Ιουλιαν]ῷ λογιcτῇ 'Οξυρυγχίτου
       [παρὰ τοῦ] κοινοῦ τῶν ὀρβιο-
       [πωλῶ]ν τῆc λαμ(πρᾶc) καὶ λαμ(προτάτηc) 'Οξ(υρυγχιτῶν)

9   [πόλεω]c δι' ἐμοῦ Αὐρηλίου
(m. 2) [c. 5-6   ]δου Ἄμμωνοc.
(m. 1) [ἀκολο]ύθωc τοῖc κελευcθεῖ-
       [cιν ἰδί]ῳ τιμήματι προc-
       [φωνῶ] τὴν ἑξῆc ἐνγε-
       [γραμμέ]νην τιμὴν ὧν

15   [χειρίζ]ῳ ὠνίων καὶ
       [ὀμνύω] τὸν θεῖον ὅρκον
       [μηδὲν δι]εψεῦcθαι. [
       [   ]. . . . [
·   ·   ·   ·   ·

8 λαμſ, λαμſοξ'   13 l. ἐνγε-

'In the consulship of our masters Licinius Augustus for the 5th time and Crispus the most noble Caesar for the 1st time.

'To Valerius Dioscurides alias Julianus, *curator* of the Oxyrhynchite, from the guild of the vetch-sellers of the illustrious and most illustrious city of the Oxyrhynchites, through me Aurelius' (m. 2) '. . . son of Ammon.' (m. 1) 'In accordance with orders, at my own risk I declare the price entered below for the goods which I handle, and I swear the divine oath that I have been deceitful in nothing. . . .'

7-8 This is the only surviving declaration of the ὀρβιοπῶλαι, regrettably broken away before giving us the object of their declaration. Supposedly they will have declared the price of ὄροβος (**3737** 16-19 n.). ὄροβος is one of four (at least, and probably five) leguminous vegetables declared by the κεμιοπῶλαι (**3737**); how the two guilds stood in relation to one another, we can only guess.

3746. UNDERTAKINGS ON OATH

70/24 bis (a)   24 × 24.5 cm   23-5(?) March 319

This text is of prosopographical interest: it provides the earliest evidence for the second period of tenure of the office of logistes by Valerius Ammonianus alias Gerontius, and describes him as logistes (47) in contrast with the rest of the evidence for this second tenure which describes him as διοικῶν τὴν λογιcτείαν. I have not yet seen the solution to this disagreement. See Appendix I below. The papyrus falls within the known limits of tenure of the *praeses Herculiae* Valerius Ziper (cf. J. Lallemand, *L'Administration civile* 255, and now especially CPR V 7. 2 n.).

It is a τόμος cυγκολλήcιμος preserving two sworn declarations (preceded by a more fragmentary third) addressed to the logistes of the Oxyrhynchite by persons who bind themselves to guard named individuals and present them at the headquarters of the *praeses*. The dates are not quite certain but the declarations may have been submitted on three successive days. All three have been drafted by the same hand, with different subscription hands. For the type of document cf. XLIII **3127** and L **3576**. Note also P. Harr. I 65 and the somewhat different SB VI 9192.

A kollesis belonging to the original manufacture (and of the expected three-layer type, cf. LI **3624-6** introd.) runs down col. iii, two-thirds the way along its lines. The joins made in creating the τόμος obscure the line-beginnings in cols. ii-iii; this has only occasionally caused reading problems, and elsewhere the transcript treats the obscured letters as if they were fully visible.

On the back, across the fibres, are two columns of a list of names, followed by scantier remains of a third. The purpose of the list is uncertain. All entries are masculine; the usual format is name plus father's name only. There is no alphabetical arrangement, no date, and no heading. There is a sub-heading (11) beginning τάξεως. In 38-9 occur Ἀττίων Εὐποτίου καὶ Ἀφθ[ό]νιος ἀδελφός. The unusual combination of the first two names recalls the homonym (Εὐπόθιος, correctly, for Εὐπότιος) in XXII **2347** 15 and elsewhere (see P. Oxy. XLV p. xvi) and may therefore provide an approximate date for the back of *c.* 360. On Ἀττίων Εὐποθίου see also S. Daris, *Aeg.* 63 (1983) 150-6, esp. 153. An Attion recurs in **3776** below of 24 July 343. On this side can be seen the remains of a kollesis where a fourth item was attached to the right of **3746** col. iii. The τόμος-kolleseis are readily visible on this side and coarsely made compared with the one due to the original manufacture of its roll.

. . . . .

Col. i

[	*c.* 11-13	] . . [	*c.* 12-14	]
[	*c.* 11-13	] . . . . . [	*c.* 9-11	]
[	*c.* 11-13	] . . . . . . [	*c.* 8-10	]
[	*c.* 14-16	] . . . [. .] . [	*c.* 5-7	]
5 [	*c.* 14-16	] . . . . [	*c.* 0-2	]
[	*c.* 12-14	] ἐπὶ τῷ με τὴν ταύτης		

[τήρηcιν καὶ παραφ]υλακὴν ποιήcαc-
[θαι νύκτωρ τε καὶ] μεθ' ἡμέραc ἄχριc
[ἂν αὐτὴν παραcτήc]ω τῇ τάξι τοῦ

9 l. τάξει

10 [διαϲημ(οτάτου) ἡγ(εμόνοϲ) Οὐαλερίου Ζίπε]ροϲ καὶ τῆϲ παρα-
[ϲτάϲεωϲ γρ(άμματα) ἐποίϲειν εἰϲ τὸ] ἐν μηδενὶ
[μεμφθῆναι ἢ ἔνοχοϲ] εἴην τῷ θίῳ
[ὅρκῳ. ὑπατείαϲ τῆϲ α(ὐτῆϲ), Φαμε]νὼθ κζ′.

(m. 2)   [Αὐρήλιοϲ   name   ]ϲ
15 [father's name παρείληφα τὸ] πρό-
[ϲωπον καὶ παραϲτήϲω] ὡϲ
[πρόκειται.]

Col. ii

(m. 1)   ὑπα[τείαϲ τῶν δεϲ]ποτ[ῶ]ν ἡμῶν Κωνϲταν[τίνου]
Ϲεβαϲ[τοῦ τὸ εϲ̄]′ καὶ Λικινίου τοῦ ἐπιφανε[ϲτάτου]
20 Καίϲαρ[οϲ τὸ αϲ̄]′.
[Οὐαλ]ερίῳ [Ἀμμ]ωνιανῷ τῷ καὶ Γεροντίῳ
λογ(ιϲτῃ) διὰ Ἑρμίνου διαδεχ(ομένου) ϲτρ(ατηγίαν) Ὀξ(υρυγχίτου)
παρὰ Αὐρη[λ]ίων Ὡρίωνοϲ Ἀλεξάνδρου
ἀπὸ Ὀξ[υρύγχων) πόλ[εωϲ κ]αὶ Ἀμμωνᾶ Παὸλ ἀπὸ κώ-
25 μηϲ Δωϲειθέου η πάγου. ὁ[[ ].]μολο-
γοῦμεν {ομολ} ὀμνύντεϲ τὸν ϲεβάϲμιον
[θ]ῖον ὅρκον τῶν δεϲποτῶν ἡμῶν
Αὐτοκρατόρων καὶ Καιϲάρων παριληφέναι Κ. . . . υμον ἐγγυητὴν Χαρι-
30 . .νηϲ δούληϲ Πλουτίωνοϲ ἐπὶ τῷ ἡμᾶϲ
τὴν τούτου τήρηϲειν καὶ παραφυλα-
κὴν ποιήϲαϲθαι νύκτωρ δε καὶ μεθ' ἡμέ-
ραϲ ἄχριϲ ἂν αὐτὸν παραϲτήϲωμε(ν)
τῇ τάξι τοῦ διαϲημ(οτάτου) ἡγ(εμόνοϲ) Οὐαλερίου
35 Ζίπεροϲ κ[α]ὶ τῆϲ παραϲτάϲεωϲ γρ(άμματα)
ἐποίϲειν εἰϲ τὸ ἐν μηδενὶ μεμφθῆναι
ἢ ἔνοχοι εἴημεν τῷ θείῳ ὅρκῳ.
ὑπατίαϲ τῆϲ α(ὐτῆϲ), Φαμενὼθ κη′.

---

12 l. θείῳ   14 ϲ extended as filler-stroke   22 λογ¹? διαδεχ´ϲτρʃοξ′   24 οξ′
25 l. Δωϲιθέου   26 ϲεβαϲμιο̄?   27 l. θεῖον   28-9 l. παρειληφέναι   29 εγ´γυητην
31 τούτου corr. from αὐτοῦ; l. τήρηϲιν   32 δε = τε   33 παραϲτηϲωμε̄?   34 διαϲημʃηγ¹
35 γρʃ   36 ἐποίϲειν partly rewritten   38 l. ὑπατείαϲ; αʃ

(m. 3)   Αὐρήλιοι Ὡρίων καὶ Ἀμμωνᾶς

40   παρειλήφαμεν τὸ πρόσωπο(ν)

    καὶ παραστήσομεν ὡς πρόκειται.

    Αὐρ(ήλιος) Ὡρίων ἔγρα⟨ψα⟩ ὑπὲρ τοῦ ἄλλου

    γράμματα μὴ εἰδότος.

Col. iii

(m. 1)   [ὑπατείας τ]ῶν δεσποτῶν ἡμῶν Κωνσταντίνου

45   [Σεβαστοῦ] τὸ εϛ′′ καὶ Λικινίου τοῦ ἐπιφανεστάτου

    [Καίσαρος τὸ] αϛ′′.

    [Οὐαλε]ρίῳ Ἀμμωνιανῷ τῷ καὶ Γεροντίῳ λογ(ιστῇ)

    διὰ Ἑρμίνου διαδεχ(ομένου) στρ(ατηγίαν) Ὀξ(υρυγχίτου)

    παρὰ Αὐρηλίου Φιλουμένου Θωνίου

50   ἀπὸ τῆς λαμ(πρᾶς) καὶ λαμ(προτάτης) Ὀξυρυγχιτῶν

    πόλεω[ς] προπ[ο]μποῦ. ὀμνύω

    τὸν σεβάσμιον θῖον ὅρκον τῶν δεσποτῶν

    ἡμῶν Αὐτοκρατόρων καὶ Καισάρων

    παριληφέναι Μαξίμαν γυναῖκα Ἱέρα-

55   κος υἱοῦ Κασιανοῦ γαμβροῦ Ἀγαθίνου

    ἐπὶ τῷ με τὴν ταύτης τήρησειν καὶ

    παραφυλακὴν ποιήσασθαι νύκτωρ δε

    καὶ μεθ' ἡμέρας ἄχρις ἂν αὐτὴν παρα-

    στήσω τῇ τάξι τοῦ διασημ(οτάτου) ἡγ(εμόνος) Οὐαλε[ρίου]

60   Ζίπερος καὶ τῆς παραστάσεως γρ(άμματα)

    ἐποίσειν εἰς τὸ ἐν μηδενὶ μεμφθῆ-

    ναι ἢ ἔνοχος εἴην τῷ θίῳ ὅρκῳ.

    ὑπατίας τῆς α(ὐτῆς), Φαμενὼθ κθ′.

────────────

(m. 4)   Αὐρήλιος Φιλούμεν[ος]

65   Θωνίου παρείληφα [τὸ]

    πρόσωπον καὶ πα[ρα-]

    στήσω ὡς πρόκειτ[αι.]

40 προσωπο̅   42 αυρ   47 λογ˪   48 διαδεχ′ϲτρϛοξ′   50 λαμϛ, λαμϛ   52 l. θεῖον
54 l. παρειληφέναι   54–5 ἱερακος   56 l. τήρησιν   57 δε = τε   59 l. τάξει; διασημϛηγ˪
60 γρϛ′   61 θ of μεμφθῆναι corr.?   62 l. θείῳ   63 l. ὑπατείας; ā ?

Col. i 6 ff.

'... to the end that I watch and guard her by night and day until I deliver her to the headquarters of the *praeses* Valerius Ziper, *vir perfectissimus*, and that I will produce receipts for her delivery, so as not to be blamed in any respect, or may I be liable to the penalties of the divine oath. In the same consulship, Phamenoth 27.'

(m. 2) 'I, Aurelius . . .s son of . . . , have taken charge of the person and I shall deliver her as aforesaid.'

Col. ii

(m. 1) 'In the consulship of our masters Constantinus Augustus for the 5th time and Licinius the most noble Caesar for the 1st time.

'To Valerius Ammonianus alias Gerontius, *curator*, through Herminus, administering the office of the strategus, of the Oxyrhynchite, from Aurelii Horion son of Alexander from the city of Oxyrhynchus and Ammonas son of Paol from the village of Dositheou in the 8th *pagus*. We acknowledge, swearing the august divine oath by our masters Imperatores and Caesares, that we have taken charge of C . . ymus, guarantor for Charixena(?), slave of Plution, to the end that we watch and guard him by night and day until we deliver him to the headquarters of the *praeses* Valerius Ziper, *vir perfectissimus*, and that we will produce receipts for his delivery, so as not to be blamed in any respect, or may we be liable to the penalties of the divine oath. In the same consulship, Phamenoth 28.'

(m. 3) 'We, Aurelii Horion and Ammonas, have taken charge of the person and we shall deliver him as aforesaid. I, Aurelius Horion, wrote on behalf of the other as he is illiterate.'

Col. iii

(m. 1) 'In the consulship of our masters Constantinus Augustus for the 5th time and Licinius the most noble Caesar for the 1st time.

'To Valerius Ammonianus alias Gerontius, *curator*, through Herminus, administering the office of the strategus, of the Oxyrhynchite, from Aurelius Philumenus son of Thonius from the illustrious and most illustrious city of the Oxyrhynchites, escort. I swear the august divine oath by our masters Imperatores and Caesares that I have taken charge of Maxima, wife of Hierax son of Casianus son-in-law of Agathinus, to the end that I watch and guard her by night and day until I deliver her to the headquarters of the *praeses* Valerius Ziper, *vir perfectissimus*, and that I will produce receipts for her delivery, so as not to be blamed in any respect, or may I be liable to the penalties of the divine oath. In the same consulship, Phamenoth 29(?).'

(m. 4) 'I, Aurelius Philumenus son of Thonius, have taken charge of the person and I shall deliver her as aforesaid.'

1–5 I can make nothing of these damaged lines, where the text will diverge in part from the wording preserved in cols. ii–iii. Estimates of numbers of letters can only be approximate.

10 Cf. 34–5 and 59–60 and the introd. above.

22 Cf. 48 and n.

29–30 Perhaps Χαριξένης. The beginning of 30 is hidden under the well-glued edge of the preceding item of the τόμος.

37 θείῳ ὅρκῳ was surely the intention, though it is not easy to see exactly how the reading conforms to the writing ductus. The ink is fairly well preserved.

41 Text transcribed on the basis of col. iii. In fact, virtually nothing is visible of the dotted letters; I cannot allocate occasional ink traces to particular letters.

47 Slight ink traces actually remain from the beginning of Οὐαλερίῳ; I cannot certainly assign them to letters.

48 Cf. 22. Herminus(?) is an addendum to the list of J. E. G. Whitehorne, *ZPE* 29 (1978) 184, where there is a substantial gap in the sequence at this point (note that Gerontius, no. 119, is to be deleted from the list, cf. XVII **2114** 20 n. where he is reidentified as a ὑπηρέτης στρατηγοῦ). As regards the next holder in Whitehorne's list, Aur. Hermias, no. 120, there is no evidence for his having been gymnasiarch (confirmed to me by John Whitehorne by letter dated 2 March 1984).

51 προπ[ο]μποῦ. Cf. L **3576** 6 and n.

3747–3753. Declarations of Prices

11 1B.145/G (a)   55.5 × 24 cm   26 March 319

This sequence of seven price-declarations, all dated 30 Phamenoth = 26 March 319, is not a τόμος cυγκολλήcιμος, and may all have been drafted by the same hand (with later insertions, of course: cf. *ZPE* 39 (1980) 115) although attributions to hands are not absolutely certain. For the normal format cf. **3731** introd. The declarations are not, however, drawn up with the same degree of uniformity as is present for example in I **85** (re-ed. R. A. Coles, *ZPE* 39 (1980) 115–23; note especially p. 116 on the differences between the two later columns and the rest—in the present sequence there are many differences of detail).

The sequence provides further and repeated evidence for Valerius Ammonianus alias Gerontius' second tenure of the office of logistes. Here Ammonianus is consistently described as διοικῶν the office of logistes, as in PSI V 454; contrast **3746** 47 λογ(ιcτῆ), and see Appendix I below. For the distinction between διοικῶν and διάδοχος see **3755** 28n.

The declarations come from the following guilds: **3747** μελιccουργοί?, beekeepers; **3748** cταγματοπῶλαι, aromatic-oil(?) merchants; **3749** γαροπῶλαι, fish-sauce sellers; **3750** ἁλοπῶλαι, salt-merchants; **3751** ἐριοπῶλαι, wool-merchants; **3752** λευκανταί, bleachers; and **3753** cτιππoχ[ειρι]cταί, tow-handlers.

The declarations are written along the fibres. Kollesis-positions occur near the right edge of **3748**, the left edge of **3751**, and the middle of **3753**, giving sheets approximately 19.5 cm wide by 24 cm, and 19 cm by 24 cm (visible-area measurements). All the kolleseis are of the three-layer type.

On the back, along the fibres, are proceedings before the logistes, published here as **3759**. A docket relating to that text has been written on the price-declaration side, vertically up between **3747** and **3748**: see **3759** introd.

3747. Declaration of Prices

See the general introduction to **3747–53** above. This one, at the left-hand edge of the surviving portion of the roll, is in much damaged condition; besides the loss of the very top and the beginnings of lines, the beginning is in a very poor state, and the surface of the lower part is partly stripped so that assessment of line-numbers is not absolutely certain. The guild is perhaps that of the μελιccουργοί, who recur in the last column of I **85** (re-ed. *ZPE* 39 (1980) 120); unfortunately we do not learn from either papyrus what the beekeepers were declaring.

Distribution of hands, as far as can be ascertained, follows usual patterns.

．　．　．　．　．

1-4　Scanty traces, very badly damaged

5　[παρὰ τοῦ κοινοῦ τ]ῶν μελ[ιϲϲ]ουρ-
　　[γῶν δι' ἐμοῦ Αὐρ]ηλίου

(m. 2)　[　　　c. 11　　　].τοϲ.

(m. 1)　[ἀκολούθωϲ τοῖ]ϲ κελευϲθ[ε]ῖϲι(ν)
　　[ἰδίῳ τιμήματ]ι προ[ϲ]φ[ω]νῶ

10　[τὴν ἑξῆϲ ἐγγεγ]ραμμένην
　　[τιμὴν ὧν χειρίζω] ὠνίων κ[α]ὶ [ὀ]μνύ-
　　[ω τὸν θεῖον ὅρκον μ]ηδὲν δι[εψ]ευ-
　　[ϲθαι.　　(vac.)　] ἔϲτι δέ·
　　[　　　　　　　].

15　[　　　　　　] (δηνάρια)　(m. 2) Ἄρν

(m. 1)　[　　　　　]....

(m. 3)　[Αὐρήλιοϲ c. 4]　.ϲ
　　[ἐπιδέδωκα προ]ϲφω-
　　[νῶν ὡϲ πρόκειτ]αι.

6 Final υ extended to right as filler-stroke　　7 Horizontal of ϲ extended?　　8 κελευϲθειϲι‾
15 ✳

1 Probably one more line completely lost at the top.
5-6 For beekeepers see R. D. Sullivan, *BASP* 10 (1973) 5-13.
6 For the omission of τῆϲ λαμπρᾶϲ 'Οξυρυγχιτῶν πόλεωϲ cf. e.g. **3749** (where it has been added in) and **3750**. For its inclusion, and this form of the phrase, see **3748** 7 n.
14-15 The question of what the beekeepers declared is tantalizing, and the loss here is particularly regrettable. We can at least deduce that they declared the prices of two items.
16 Presumably the repeat consular formula, month, and day (cf. **3748** 16-17) came here, though I have failed to discern it in the scanty traces.
17-19 The subscription is autograph, in heavy crude letters.

3748. DECLARATION OF PRICES

See the general introduction to **3747-53** above. This declaration, by the ϲταγματοπῶλαι, aromatic-oil(?) sellers, poses no textual problems despite some physical damage. It follows the expected pattern of distribution of hands and later insertions, see *ZPE* 39 (1980) 115 and **3731** introd.

[ὑπατείαϲ τῶ]ν δεϲποτῶν
ἡμῶν Κω[ν]ϲταντίνου Ϲεβαϲτοῦ
τὸ ϛʹ καὶ Λικιν̣ίου Καίϲαροϲ τὸ αʃ.
Οὐαλερίῳ Ἀμμωνιανῷ τῷ καὶ

5 Γεροντίῳ διοικ(οῦντι) λογ(ιστείαν) Ὀξυρυγχίτου
   παρὰ τοῦ κοιν[ο]ῦ τῶν σταγματο-
   πωλῶν τῆς λαμ(πρᾶς) Ὀξ(υρυγχιτῶν) πόλεως
   δι' ἐμοῦ Αὐρηλίου (m. 2) Ἀμμωνίου Τρύ-
   φωνος. (m. 1) ἀκολούθως τοῖς κελευ-

10 cθεῖciν ἰδ[ί]ῳ τιμήματι προcφωνῶ τὴν ἑξῆς ἐνγεγραμμένην τιμ[ὴν] ὧν χιρίζω ὠνίων καὶ ὀμν[ύ]ῳ τὸν θεῖον ὅρκον
   μηδὲν διεψεῦcθαι. ἔcτι δέ·

15   cτάγματος   τὸ κνίδ(ιον) α   (δηνάρια) (m. 2) φ⟦ . ⟧`.´
(m. 1) ὑπατείας τῆς προκ(ειμένης), Φαμε-
         νὼθ λ΄.

(m. 2)   Αὐρήλιος Ἀμμώνιος ἐπιδέ-
         δωκα προcφωνῶν ὡς πρόκ(ειται). Αὐρ(ήλιος)
20   Ὡρίων ἔγρ(αψα) ὑ(πὲρ) αὐτοῦ γρ(άμματα) μὴ εἰδότος.

---

5 διοι^κλογ∫^ι; 7 λαμ∫οξ΄; λ of λαμ(πρᾶς) corr. from ο   11 l. ἐγγεγραμμέ-   12 l. χειρίζω
15 κνι^δ; l. τοῦ κνιδ(ίου); ✗   16 προ^κ   19 προ^καυρ΄   20 εγρ∫υ), γρ∫

'In the consulship of our masters Constantinus Augustus for the 5th time and Licinius Caesar for the 1st time.

'To Valerius Ammonianus alias Gerontius, administering the office of *curator* of the Oxyrhynchite, from the guild of the aromatic-oil(?) sellers of the illustrious city of the Oxyrhynchites, through me Aurelius' (m. 2) 'Ammonius son of Tryphon.' (m. 1) 'In accordance with orders, at my own risk I declare the price entered below for the goods which I handle, and I swear the divine oath that I have been deceitful in nothing. As follows:

   'Aromatic oil(?)   1 Cnidian jar   den.' (m. 2) '500.'
(m. 1) 'The aforesaid consulship, Phamenoth 30.'
(m. 2) 'I, Aurelius Ammonius, presented this, making my declaration as aforesaid. I, Aurelius Horion, wrote on his behalf as he is illiterate.'

6–7 cταγματοπωλῶν. 'Sellers of aromatic oils', LSJ, but cτάγμα is differently explained elsewhere, 'rosewater' (cf. Stephanus; Preisigke *WB*: I 155, where it is also measured in κνίδια) or 'liquid honey' (P. Mich. III 214. 23). Cf. cτακτή, apparently a perfume, in Diocletian's Price Edict §. 34. 41 and 59 (ed. M. Giacchero), with the commentary of S. Lauffer, *Diokletians Preisedikt* 287, 288. cτάγμα is glossed *liquamen* in *CGL*, which is itself glossed γάρον, 'fish sauce', but γάρον itself appears in the adjoining declaration **3749**, at 28 den./sextarius. I do not yet see a resolution to this problem. cτάγμα should at least be a product obtained by 'dripping' in some way, e.g. a resin; but the price—500 den. for a Cnidian jar—is not exceptionally high at this period (nor, equally, notably cheap), cf. the tables in Appendix III below, so that a rare luxury commodity seems inappropriate. The price is just under half of that declared for one item by the beekeepers in the contemporary and adjoining **3747**—but, if the guilds are to declare the raw materials of their trade (cf. LI **3624–6** introd.), the beekeepers are not expected to declare the price of honey! Honey and cτάγμα are found together in I **155** cited above.

7 τῆς λαμ(πρᾶς) Ὀξ(υρυγχιτῶν) πόλεωc. The formula with single epithet is exceptional at this period, see

D. Hagedorn, *ZPE* 12 (1973) 285. The formula recurs in **3749** (inserted), **3751**, **3752** and **3753**, and also in **3760**.

14–18 The line-spacing between these lines is wider than elsewhere.

15 *cτάγματος*. See 6–7 n. The size of the *κνίδιον* is uncertain, cf. P. Oxy. LI p. 76 and **3628** 15 n.

The correction at the end: I suspect that a lower hundreds-figure has been deleted and the φ inserted to the left, not that a tens-figure has been deleted. A high trace after the deletion (itself washed out?) is of uncertain meaning.

20 For Horion see Appendix IV below.

3749. Declaration of Prices

See the general introduction above to **3747–53**. Despite some damage down the centre, this one, the declaration by the *γαροπῶλαι* or fish-sauce sellers, presents no problems of reading or interpretation. The insertions in the text are later work of the main hand; the subscription is the work of Horion whom we have already encountered in **3748** and who recurs in **3750** and elsewhere: see Appendix IV below.

ὑπατείας τῶν δεςποτῶν
ἡμῶν Κων[cτ]αντίνου Cεβαςτοῦ
τὸ εϨʹ καὶ Λικιν[ίου] Καίcαρος τὸ αϨʹ.
Οὐαλερίῳ Ἀμμ[ω]νιανῷ τῷ καὶ
5 Γεροντίῳ [δι]οικ(οῦντι) λογ(ιcτείαν) Ὀξ(υρυγχίτου)
παρὰ τοῦ κοιν[οῦ τ]ῶν γαροπω-
λῶν ʼτῆς λαμ(πρᾶς) Ὀ[ξ(υρυγχιτῶν) πόλεω]ς· διʼ ἐμ[οῦ] Αὐρηλίου
                                    (m. 1, added) Ἀρτεμι-
δώρου Διογ[έ]νους.
(m. 1) ἀκολούθως [τ]οῖc κελευcθεῖ-
10 cιν ἰδίῳ τι[μ]ήματι προcφωνῶ τὴν [ἑξῆc ἐ]νγεγραμμένη(ν)
τιμὴν ὧν [χει]ρίζω ὠνίων καὶ ὀμνύ-
ω τὸν θεῖον ὅρκον μηδὲν διεψεῦcθαι.   ἔcτι δέ·
15 γάρου   ξ(έcτου) α   (δηνάρια) (m. 1, added) κη.
(m. 1) ὑπατείας τῆς προκ(ειμένης), Φαμενὼθ λʹ.

(m. 2) Αὐρήλιος Ἀρτεμίδωρος ἐπιδέδωκα
προcφωνῶν ὡς πρόκειται. Αὐρ(ήλιος) Ὡρίων
ἔγρ(αψα) ὑ(πὲρ) αὐτοῦ γρ(άμματα) μὴ εἰδότος.

5 διοι^κλογⱡ)οξʹ   7 λαμⱡ   10 ἰδιω   11 ε]νγεγραμμενη̄; l. ἐγγ-   15 ✕   16 προ^κ   18 αυρʹ   19 εγρⱡυ), γρⱡ

'In the consulship of our masters Constantinus Augustus for the 5th time and Licinius Caesar for the 1st time.

'To Valerius Ammonianus alias Gerontius, administering the office of *curator* of the Oxyrhynchite, from the guild of the fish-sauce sellers of the illustrious city of the Oxyrhynchites, through me Aurelius' (m. 1, added) 'Artemidorus, son of Diogenes.' (m. 1) 'In accordance with orders, at my own risk I declare the price entered below for the goods which I handle, and I swear the divine oath that I have been deceitful in nothing. As follows:

    'Fish sauce   1 sextarius   den.' (m. 1, added) '28.'
    (m. 1) 'The aforesaid consulship, Phamenoth 30.'
    (m. 2) 'I, Aurelius Artemidorus, presented this, making my declaration as aforesaid. I, Aurelius Horion, wrote on his behalf as he is illiterate.'

7-8 The agent's name is in the same hand as the body of the text, but to judge from the space at the end of 8 (sigma has an extraordinarily long finial stroke reaching right to the next column = **3750**) the name was written into the ready-prepared text.

14-17 The spaces between these lines are wider than in the text elsewhere.

3750. DECLARATION OF PRICES

See the general introduction above to **3747–53**. This example, the declaration by the ἁλοπῶλαι = salt-merchants, is well preserved and presents no problems. Later insertions by a second hand follow the expected pattern, and are here clearly the work of Horion, who wrote the subscription (cf. **3748–9**).

Cf. **3734**, another declaration by the ἁλοπῶλαι, from 312; the price seven years later in **3750**—250 denarii per artaba—is still the same.

ὑπατείας τῶν δεσποτῶν
ἡμῶν Κωνσταντίνου Σεβαστοῦ
τὸ εϛ′ καὶ Λικινίου Καίσαρος τὸ αϛ′.
Οὐαλερίῳ Ἀμμωνιανῷ τῷ καὶ
5   Γεροντίῳ διοικ(οῦντι) λογιστείαν Ὀξ(υρυγχίτου)
παρὰ τοῦ κοινοῦ τῶν ἁλοπωλῶν
δι' ἐμοῦ Αὐρηλίου (m. 2) Παησίου Σαπρί-
ωνος. (m. 1) ἀκολούθως τοῖς
κελευσθεῖσιν ἰδίῳ τιμήματι
10 προσφωνῶ τὴν ἑξῆς ἐνγεγραμμένην τιμὴν ὧν χιρίζω
ὠνίων καὶ ὀμνύω τὸν θεῖον
ὅρκον μηδὲν διεψεῦσθαι. ἔστι δέ·

. 5 διοι^κ, οξ′   7 l. Παήσιος   9 ἴδιω   10 l. ἐγγ-   11 l. χειρίζω

14 ἁλὸς (ἀρτάβης) α (δηνάρια) (m. 2) cν.

(m. 1) ὑπατείας τῆς προκ(ειμένης), Φαμενὼθ λ′.

)

(m. 2) Αὐρήλιος Παῆσις ἐπιδέδωκα

   προσφωνῶν ὡς πρόκειται.

   Αὐρ(ήλιος) Ὠρίων ἔγρ(αψα) ὑ(πὲρ) αὐτοῦ γρ(άμματα) μὴ εἰδ(ότος).

14 ⲻ, ✕ 15 προ^κ 18 αυρ′, εγρ/υ), γρ/ Ductus and method of abbreviation in μη ειδ( ) not clear.

'In the consulship of our masters Constantinus Augustus for the 5th time and Licinius Caesar for the 1st time.

'To Valerius Ammonianus alias Gerontius, administering the office of *curator* of the Oxyrhynchite, from the guild of the salt-merchants, through me Aurelius' (m. 2) 'Paesis son of Saprion.' (m. 1) 'In accordance with orders, at my own risk I declare the price entered below for the goods which I handle, and I swear the divine oath that I have been deceitful in nothing. As follows:

  'Salt   1 art.   den.' (m. 2) '250.'

(m. 1) 'The aforesaid consulship, Phamenoth 30.'

(m. 2) 'I, Aurelius Paesis, presented this, making my declaration as aforesaid. I, Aurelius Horion, wrote on his behalf as he is illiterate.'

6 Note the omission of τῆς λαμ(πρᾶς) Ὀξ(υρυγχιτῶν) πόλεως. Cf. **3749**, where it was omitted and then inserted later. The phrase is present in the other declarations in this set except **3747**.

13-16 Cf. **3749** 14-17 n.

3751. DECLARATION OF PRICES

See the general introduction above to **3747–53**. This one, the declaration of the wool-merchants, ἐριοπῶλαι, has been much broken but offers no serious textual problems. Later insertions occur in the expected places, but there is some uncertainty over the allocation of hands. Apparently Aurelius Pecyllus wrote his own subscription, but his script is scarcely distinguishable from that of Horion (**3750**) on one side of him or that of Aurelius Sarmates on the other (**3752**). I have assigned the other insertions to a different hand less on palaeographical grounds than on the basis that the subscriber would be less likely to have filled in these details himself. Palaeographically I could not say whether the name inserted in 8 was written by Pecyllus (**3751** 19), Horion (**3750** 18), Sarmates (**3752** 23–4), or another person altogether.

   ὑπατείας τῶν δεσποτῶν ἡμῶν

   [Κ]ωνςταντίν[ο]υ Cεβ[α]ςτο[ῦ τὸ εϛ′] καὶ

   [Λ]ικινίου Καίςαρος τὸ αϛ′.

   Οὐαλερίῳ Ἀμμωνιανῷ τῷ καὶ Γερον-

5   τίῳ διοικοῦντι λογιστείαν Ὀξυρυγχ(ίτου)

π[α]ρὰ τοῦ κοινοῦ τῶν ἐριοπωλῶν

τῆς λαμ(πρᾶς) Ὀξ(υρυγχιτῶν) πόλεως δι᾽ ἐμοῦ Αὐρη-

λίου (m. 2) Πεκύλλου Στεφάνου. (m. 1) ἀκολού-

θως τοῖς κελευςθεῖςιν ἰδίῳ τιμή-

10   ματι προσφωνῶ τὴν ἑξῆς ἐν-

γεγραμμένην τιμὴν ᾧ[ν] χιρί-

ζω ὠνίων κ[α]ὶ ὀμνύω τὸν θεῖ[ο](ν)

ὅρκον μηδὲ[ν δ]ιεψεῦςθαι.

ἔςτι δέ·

15   ἐρίου λευκοῦ ἐντ(οπίου) λί(τρας) α   (δηνάρια) (m. 2) ρν.

(m. 1)   ἰδιοχρώμων καὶ ἄλλων

       χρωμάτων   λί(τρας) α   (δηνάρια) (m. 2) ροε.

(m. 1)   ὑπατείας τῆς προκ(ειμένης), Φαμενὼθ λ΄.

(m. 3)   Αὐρήλιος Πεκύλλος ἐπι-

20   δέδωκα προσφωνῶν

      ὡς προκ(ειται).

---

5 Ὀξυρυγχ(ίτου). No sign of abbreviation other than a slightly extended diagonal (up to the right) of χ   7 λαμ/οξ΄   9 ϊδιω   10–11 l. ἐγγ   12 θεϊ[ο]   15 εν^τλ, ✕   Apparently ρ̄ν pap.   16 ϊδιο-?   17 λ, ✕   17–18 Wider space between these lines   18 προ^κ   21 προ^κ

'In the consulship of our masters Constantinus Augustus for the 5th time and Licinius Caesar for the 1st time.

'To Valerius Ammonianus alias Gerontius, administering the office of *curator* of the Oxyrhynchite, from the guild of the wool-merchants of the illustrious city of the Oxyrhynchites, through me Aurelius' (m. 2) 'Pecyllus son of Stephanus.' (m. 1) 'In accordance with orders, at my own risk I declare the price entered below for the goods which I handle, and I swear the divine oath that I have been deceitful in nothing. As follows:

     'Wool, white, local   1 lb.   den.' (m. 2) '150.'

     (m. 1) 'Natural and

     other colours   1 lb.   den.' (m. 2) '175.'

     (m. 1) 'The aforesaid consulship, Phamenoth 30.'

     (m. 3) 'I, Aurelius Pecyllus, presented this, making my declaration as aforesaid.'

15 On the Price Edict's section on wool note J. Reynolds, *ZPE* 42 (1981) 283–4. It is perhaps surprising that white wool is less expensive, at least than natural-coloured wool. The papyrus is cracked across the price in 17, but I do not think ρκε can be read.

3752. Declaration of Prices

See the general introduction above to **3747–53**. This example, the declaration of the bleachers, λευκανταί (cf. **3743**), is badly shredded at the top but presents no problems in reading. Allocation of hands is another matter, since insertions in the text appear not to follow expected patterns: see 8 n. The guild's monthly presidents are the same persons as in **3743**, of an uncertain month in the previous year. The items declared are the same too; damage precludes comparisons of price except that the price of the best grade has increased, if at all, by no more than 25 denarii.

ὑπατ[είας τῶν δεσποτῶν ἡμ]ῶν

Κωνϲτ[αντίνου Ϲεβαστοῦ τὸ εϚ′] καὶ

Λικιν[ίου Καίϲαροϲ τὸ αϚ′ .]

Οὐαλερίῳ Ἀμμωνιανῷ τῷ καὶ

5   Γεροντίῳ δι[οι]κοῦντι λογ(ιϲτείαν) Ὀξ(υρυγχίτου)

παρὰ τ[ο]ῦ κοινοῦ τ[ῶν] λευκαντῶν τῆϲ

  λαμ(πρᾶϲ) Ὀξ(υρυγχιτῶν) πόλεωϲ δι᾿ ἡμῶν Αὐρηλί-

ων Μαξίμου Ϲαρμάτου καὶ Παθερ-

μουθίου Ϲαραπίωνοϲ μηνιαρ-

10   χῶν. ἀκολούθωϲ τοῖϲ κελευϲθεῖ-

ϲιν ἰδίῳ τιμήματι προϲφωνοῦ-

μεν τὴν ἑξῆϲ ἐνγεγραμμένη(ν)

τιμὴν ὧν χιρίζομεν ὠνίων καὶ

ὀμνύομεν τὸν θεῖον ὅρκον μη-

15   δὲν διεψεῦϲθαι. ἔϲτι δέ·

λίνων παντοίων λευκ(ῶν) τοῦ μὲν

    τρυφεροῦ λί(τραϲ) α τάλ(αντον) (m. 2) α (δηνάρια) ρκε.

(m. 1)   τοῦ δὲ κοινοῦ λί(τραϲ) α (δηνάρια) (m. 2) ωοε.

(m. 1) ὑποδεεϲτέρ(ων) χωρικ(ῶν) λί(τραϲ) α (δηνάρια) (m. 2) φ.

(m. 1) ὑπατείαϲ τῆϲ προκ(ειμένηϲ), Φαμενὼθ λ′.

)

(m. 3)   Αὐρήλιοι Μάξιμοϲ καὶ Παθερ-

22   μοῦθιϲ ἐπιδεδώκαμεν προϲ-

φωνοῦντεϲ ὡϲ πρόκ(ειται). Αὐρ(ήλιοϲ) Ϲαρμά-

τηϲ ἔγρ(αψα) ὑ(πὲρ) αὐτῶν γρ(άμματα) μὴ εἰδ(ότων).

5 λογ^ιοξ′   7 λαμϚοξ′   12 ενγεγραμμενη ; l. ἐγγ-   13 l. χειρίζομεν   16 λευ^κ

17 λ, ταλ, ✳   18 λ, ✳   19 υποδεεϲτερ/χωρι^κλ, ✳   20 προ^κ   23 προ^κ αυρ′

24 εγρϚυ), γρϚ, ει^δ

'In the consulship of our masters Constantinus Augustus for the 5th time and Licinius Caesar for the 1st time.

'To Valerius Ammonianus alias Gerontius, administering the office of *curator* of the Oxyrhynchite, from the guild of the bleachers of the illustrious city of the Oxyrhynchites, through us Aurelii Maximus son of Sarmates and Pathermuthius son of Sarapion, monthly presidents. In accordance with orders, at our own risk we declare the price entered below for the goods which we handle, and we swear the divine oath that we have been deceitful in nothing. As follows:

'Linens, all kinds, white:

Fine quality	1 lb.	tal.' (m. 2)	'1, den. 125.'
(m. 1) 'Standard quality (varieties)	1 lb.	den.' (m. 2)	'875.'
(m. 1) 'Inferior, local	1 lb.	den.' (m. 2)	'500.'

(m. 1) 'The aforesaid consulship, Phamenoth 30.'

(m. 3?) 'We, Aurelii Maximus and Pathermuthis, presented this, making our declaration as aforesaid. I, Aurelius Sarmates, wrote on their behalf as they are illiterate.'

1–3 Considerable traces do actually survive of the letters in the lacunae indicated in these lines, but on a tangled mass of separated fibres whose correct positions could only be established with great difficulty. The supplements, however, are not in any doubt, the date obviously being the same as in the declarations that precede and follow on this same papyrus (**3751** and preceding, **3753**).

8 Unexpectedly (for the normal format cf. **3731** introd.) there is no evidence of change of hand or even later insertion at this point. The latter is surely excluded by the exact fit before ἀκολούθως in 10—indeed, μηνιαρχῶν is ligatured to ἀκολούθως. The same applies, excepting the ligature, if a resumption were sought at μηνιαρχῶν.

3753. DECLARATION OF PRICES

See the general introduction above to **3747–53**. This, the last survivor of the sequence, is the declaration of the tow-handlers, cτιπποχειριcταί. The right edge is partly lost but there are no textual problems beyond an incomplete personal name (10–11). Allocation of hands is another matter, as in **3752**: the pattern and problems are much the same in the two texts, see **3752** 8n. and **3753** 8–11 n.

```
        ὑπατείας [τῶν δεσποτῶν ἡμῶν]
        Κωνσταντ[ίνου Cεβαστοῦ τὸ εʃ′ καὶ]
        Λικινίου Καίςαρ[ος τὸ αʃ′.]
        Οὐαλερίῳ Ἀμμ[ω]νιανῷ [τῷ] καὶ Γ[ερον-
    5   τίῳ διοικοῦ[ν]τι λογ(ιστείαν) Ὀξ[υρυγ]χ[ίτου]
        παρὰ τοῦ κοινοῦ τῶν cτιπποχ[ειρι-
        cτῶν τῆς λαμ(πρᾶς) Ὀξ(υρυγχιτῶν) πόλεως δι' ἡμῶ[ν]
        Αὐρηλίων Ὡρίωνος Εὐδαίμ[ονος]
        καὶ Ἑρμεία Ὡρίωνος καὶ {καὶ} Ἀλε[ξάν-
    10  δρου Ἀντωνίου καὶ Χαιρήμονος [  c. 5   ]
```

5 λογ^ι   7 λαμʃοξ′

μόνος μηνιαρχῶν. ἀκολούθω[ς τοῖς]
κελευςθεῖςιν ἰδίῳ τιμήματ[ι προς-]
φωνοῦμεν τὴν ἑξῆς ἐνγεγραμ[μέ-]
νην τιμὴν ὧν χιρίζομεν ὠν[ίων]
15   καὶ ὀμνύομεν τὸν θεῖον [ὅρκον]
μηδὲν διεψεῦςθαι. ἔςτι δέ·
ςτιππίου κεχιριςμένου τοῦ
μὲν τρυφεροῦ   λί(τρας) α   (δηνάρια) (m. 2) υν.

(m. 1)   τοῦ δὲ κοινοῦ   λί(τρας) α   (δηνάρια) (m. 2) ρξβ.

(m. 1)   ὑποδεεςτέρω(ν) χωρικ(ῶν) λί(τρας) α (δηνάρια) (m. 2) ρ.

(m. 1)   ὑπατείας τῆς προκ(ειμένης), Φαμενὼθ λ['.]

(m. 3)   Αὐρ(ήλιοι) Ὡρίων καὶ Χαιρήμων καὶ Ἑρμίας καὶ Ἀλέ-
ξανδρος δι' ἐμοῦ τοῦ προκ(ειμένου) Ὡρίωνος ἐπ[ιδε-]
δώκ(αμεν) προςφ[ω]νοῦντες ὡς πρόκει[ται.]

13 l. ἐγγ-   14 l. χειρίζομεν   17 l. κεχειριςμένου   18 τρυφυρου written?   λ, ✕
19 λ, ✕   20 Traces of washed-out writing before the beginning of this line   υποδεεςτερω simply?
χωρι^κλ, ✕   21 προ^κ   22 αυρ̄   23 προ^κ   23–4 επ[ιδε]δωκ'

'In the consulship of our masters Constantinus Augustus for the 5th time and Licinius Caesar for the 1st time.

'To Valerius Ammonianus alias Gerontius, administering the office of *curator* of the Oxyrhynchite, from the guild of the tow-handlers of the illustrious city of the Oxyrhynchites, through us Aurelii Horion son of Eudaemon and Hermias son of Horion and Alexander son of Antonius and Chaeremon son of ...mon, monthly presidents. In accordance with orders, at our own risk we declare the price entered below for the goods which we handle, and we swear the divine oath that we have been deceitful in nothing. As follows:

'Tow, worked: fine quality   1 lb.   den.' (m. 2) '450.'
(m. 1) 'Ordinary quality   1 lb.   den.' (m. 2) '162.'
(m. 1) 'Inferior, local (varieties)   1 lb.   den.' (m. 2) '100.'
(m. 1) 'The aforesaid consulship, Phamenoth 30.'
(m. 3) 'We, Aurelii Horion and Chaeremon and Hermias and Alexander, through me the aforesaid Horion, presented this, making our declaration as aforesaid.'

8–11 Cf. **3752** 8 n.; the same considerations apply here.

9 For genitive Ἑρμεία cf. F. T. Gignac, *Grammar*, ii p. 13.

17 ςτιππίου. See P. Mich. XIV 680. 3 n.; also, on the variant forms of the word and its derivatives, P. J. Sijpesteijn, *ZPE* 24 (1977) 101 and n. 31. With the grades declared in 17–20, cf. **3765** 9–11?

23 Aurelius Horion is not the same as the writer of the subscriptions of **3748–50**. It is clear that he did not add the denarius-amounts in 18–20.

3754. APPLICATION FOR REGISTRATION OF A CHILD

71/62 (b)   8.3 × 9 cm   320

The upper left corner from an application for registration of a child addressed to Valerius Ammonianus alias Gerontius, acting *curator civitatis*, for whom see Appendix I. This document falls in his last year of office and might be our latest evidence for him but month and day are lacking.

Aurelia Taÿris seeks to register the birth of her grandson, if we understand the text rightly, on behalf of her son Aurelius(?) Theodorus, who is now a recruit. No indication survives of the current age of the child. The most recently published example of this type of document is P. Upps. Frid. 6 (AD 273), where the comparable texts are listed. There are now several parallels from Oxyrhynchus from the last decades of the third century. This is the first example from the fourth century. It has other unusual features: the declaration comes from the grandmother (cf. III **479**), and is made to the (acting) logistes when the parallels would lead us to expect to find the systates as addressee.

Written along the fibres; the back is blank. There is a kollesis down the right edge, of the expected three-layer type (see P. Harr. II 212 introd., and LI **3624–6** introd.); the papyrus has fractured down the right edge of the overlap.

ὑπατείας τῶν δεσποτῶν ἡμῶν Κων[σταντίνου Cεβαστοῦ τὸ ϛ ΄]
καὶ Κωνσταντίνου τοῦ ἐπιφανεστάτου [Καίσαρος τὸ α΄, month and day?]
Οὐαλερίῳ Ἀμμωνιανῷ τῷ καὶ Γερο[ντίῳ διοικοῦντι τὴν]
λογιστίαν Ὀξυρυγχείτου
5   παρὰ Αὐρηλίας Ταΰριος Ὡρίων[ος   c. 22   ]
ἀπὸ τῆς λαμπρᾶς καὶ λαμπροτάτης Ὀ[ξυρυγχιτῶν πόλεως. βούλομαι]
πρώτως ἀναγραφῆναι τὸν γενόμε[νον τῷ ἡμετέρῳ υἱῷ Αὐρηλίῳ(?)]
Θεοδώρῳ ἐν στρατίᾳ ἐξεταζομέν[ῳ υἱὸν   c. 18   ]
μου τοῦ καὶ Ἡρακλάμμωνος ἀπὸ τ[ῆς αὐτῆς πόλεως ἐφ᾽ ἧς ἔχει(?)]
10   ὁ ἡμέτερος υἱὸς τοῦ δὲ υἱωνοῦ μ[ου πατήρ   c. 6   οἰκίας(?)ἐπὶ]
ἀμφόδου Παμμέν[ου]ς Παραδίζου . [c. 22   ]
Ὡρι[–?   c. 10   ]. . . . . . τος[c. 22   ]
. . . . . [

.   .   .   .   .

4 l. λογιστείαν; οξυρυγ᾽χειτου/   5 ταϋριος   8 l. στρατείᾳ   10 ϋιος?   ϋιωνου
11 l. Παραδείσου

'In the consulship of our masters Constantinus Augustus for the 6th time and Constantinus the most noble Caesar for the 1st time, [month and day?]

'To Valerius Ammonianus alias Gerontius, administering the office of *curator* of the Oxyrhynchite, from Aurelia Taÿris daughter of Horion . . . from the illustrious and most illustrious city of the Oxyrhynchites. I wish to have registered for the first time the son X born to me by my son Aurelius(?) Theodorus who is being passed for military service [and his wife X daughter of?] -mus(?) alias Heraclammon from the same city, in the house which my son the father of my grandson has . . . in the quarter of Pammenes' garden . . .'

3 For the distinction between διοικῶν and διάδοχος see **3755** 28 n.

7 Αὐρηλίῳ. Theodorus might at this date have been allocated the *gentilicium* Valerius as a soldier, see J. G. Keenan, *ZPE* 11 (1973) 46, but since at this moment he was in process of enlistment (cf. 8 and n.), he may still have had the name Aurelius. For recruits as Flavii at a later date, cf. Keenan, ibid. 50 and n. 77.

8 ἐν στρατίᾳ ἐξεταζομέν[ῳ. Theodorus is a recruit in the process of formal enlistment, cf. the *CGL*: ἐν στρατείᾳ ἐξητασμένος = *militia probatus*; P. Mich. VIII 467. 22, *antequam me probarem in militiam*. The lacuna perhaps mentioned his wife, daughter of X alias Heraclammon in 9, after the name of the child followed by μητρός.

11 Παραδίζου: for the change from c to ζ cf. F. T. Gignac, *Grammar* i p. 123. For the district see A. Calderini, *Diz. dei nomi geogr.* iv 1, p. 32.

3755. DECLARATION OF PRICES

11 1B.151²/F (b)　　　　　　8.5 × 14.5 cm　　　　　　27 September 320

Parts of three items from a roll of declarations of prices addressed to the logistes. Only scanty remains survive of the first and third items; the middle one, from the κεμιοπῶλαι (see 30 n.), has lost its top and lower part but is otherwise well preserved.

The text provides the earliest attestation of the second period of tenure of the office of logistes by Valerius Dioscurides alias Julianus. For his first period see **3743** above, and see Appendix I below. A reference apparently to his son is tantalizing, see 27–8 n.

The back is blank.

col. ii

. . . .

col. i		
. . .	20	[ἡ]μῶν Κ[ωνσταντίνου]
]ν		Σεβαστοῦ τὸ ςϛ′ κ[α]ὶ
].		Κωνσταντίνου τοῦ
].		ἐπιφανεστάτου
'Οκτω]βρ(ίων)		Καίσαρος τὸ αϛ′, πρὸ ε′
5　Διοσκο]υρί-	25	Καλανδῶν 'Οκτωβρ(ίων).
'Ιουλια]νῷ		Οὐαλερίῳ Διοσκουρί-
διὰ] 'Ιου-		δῃ τῷ καὶ 'Ιουλιανῷ
διαδόχ]ου		λογιστῇ διὰ 'Ιουλι-
κοινο]ῦ		ανοῦ υἱο̣[ῦ] διαδόχ[ο]υ
		παρὰ τοῦ κοινοῦ

4]βρ′　　7 ϊου　　24 οκτωβρ′　　26 ϊουλιανω　　27 ϊουλι　　28 υϊου?

10   ]ν   30   τῶν κεμιοπωλῶν

         ].   τῆς λαμ(πρᾶς) καὶ λαμ(προτάτης) Ὀξ(υρυγχιτῶν)

         ].   πόλεως δι' ἐμοῦ

        ]λει   Αὐρηλίου (m. 2) Cελεύκου

         ].   34   Ἡρακλίου.

15   ].   (m. 1)   ἀκολούθως τοῖς

         ].   κελευ[c]θεῖcιν ἰδίῳ

         ].   τιμήματι προc-

         ].   φωνῶ τὴν ἑξῆc

     .   .   .   ἐ[γγε]γρ[αμμένην

                        .   .   .   .

col. iii

                   .   .   .

40   . [

       παρ[ὰ τοῦ κοινοῦ]

       τῶ[ν

       τῆc [

       πόλ[εως

            .   .   .   .

31 λαμ/, λαμ/οξ´   36 ϊδιω

Col. ii

'[In the consulship] of our [masters] Constantinus Augustus for the 6th time and Constantinus the most noble Caesar for the 1st time, on the 5th day before the Kalends of October.

'To Valerius Dioscurides alias Julianus, *curator*, through his son Julianus, deputy, from the guild of the seed-vegetable merchants of the illustrious and most illustrious city of the Oxyrhynchites, through me Aurelius' (m. 2) 'Seleucus son of Heraclius.' (m. 1) 'In accordance with orders, at my own risk I declare the (price) entered below . . .'

1 The highest trace remaining from col. i is level with the third preserved line (= 21) of the better-preserved col. ii.

13]λει. Spacing-comparisons with col. ii suggest that this will be part of the name of the μηνιάρχης, e.g. Ἡρακ]λεί-¹⁴[δου.

23–4 The Roman month-and-day formula is unusual. Perhaps the customary Egyptian version (the equivalent would be Thoth 30) came lower down between the items declared and the subscription.

27–8 Julianus. If the reading υἱὸ[ῦ] is correct, this is the third generation of this family to be known to us; clearly he was following in his father's official footsteps. He is almost certainly to be identified with the Flavius Julianus known as *curator* of the Oxyrhynchite a decade later (for whom see Appendix I below).

28 διαδόχ[ο]υ. Clearly this implies a different (and lower) level of responsibility from διοικῶν τὴν λογιcτείαν (**3748–53** and elsewhere). Here the post of διάδοχος is held by a young man near the beginning of a long career in public office, who would himself be *curator* later on (cf. the preceding note), and whose capacity here will perhaps be as an assistant rather than as a deputy. Elsewhere an ἔκδικος serves as διάδοχος (e.g. PSI

VII 767), and the διάδοχος is always associated with a full λογιστής. Valerius Ammonianus alias Gerontius is διοικῶν τὴν λογιστείαν, supposedly without there being a λογιστής as such in office, near the end (he was dead fifteen years later) of a presumably distinguished career of which the only other detail so far known to us is that he had himself already been *curator* not long before. Cf. Appendix I below.

30 κεμιοπωλῶν. Cf. **3737** 7–8 with n., and **3744** 7–8.

40 The highest surviving trace of col. iii is level with col. ii 29.

42 The sequence **3737–8** suggests that this might be the guild of ἐλαιουργοί.

3756–3758

The complicated physical relationships of **3756–8** are best presented in a diagram of each side of the papyrus on which they stand:

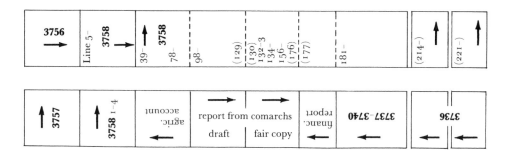

The arrows indicate fibre-direction, the publication numbers the direction in which the particular text is to be read.

It is clear that **3758** 39–228, containing records of cases heard by the logistes, were written on a roll specially made up by pasting together out-of-date documents which had been sent in to the logistes, five of which are published above as **3736–40**. No attention was paid to the orientation of the documents. It was enough if they were of the right height and if their blank backs could be joined to give a continuous roll. The proceedings are written in a single column, the writing running along the fibres of the backs of the documents. At the head of this column there was attached a separate piece, otherwise unused, containing similar proceedings on the same side (**3758** 5–38) and a title on the back (**3758** 1–4). It is not possible to say whether this was added when the roll was first made up or at a later stage, but perhaps the former is more likely, the object being to provide the roll with an outside cover containing only the title. The final stage was to add at the top, above **3758** 5, yet another separate piece containing on the front an earlier document (**3756**) relating to one of the cases within, on the back of which a fair copy (**3757**) of the record of that case (**3758** 78–97) was later written out.

The agricultural accounts, the report from comarchs to the logistes (AD 305) in draft and fair copy, and the fragment of a financial report are not published in the present volume. The datable reused documents date to 305 and 312, up to twenty years earlier. I am not sure how long the 305 text (the report from comarchs) would have remained on file; the declarations of 312 (= **3736–40**) would have had a very short life, as is clear from **3766** with **3767**, and will have been stored as waste paper for many years.

3756. Acknowledgement of Receipt of Property

7 1B.212/11   46.3 × 25 cm   Jan./Feb. 325

This document, more or less complete, concerning the estate being held in trust for a girl minor, has the long *transversa charta* format roll of proceedings **3758** attached to its right edge, and has the single report of proceedings **3757**—which is a fair copy of **3758** 78–97—written out on its back. The explanation of this structure may be that Philammon—most likely, as the recipient of **3756**—obtained the proceedings-roll **3758** and attached it to his primary document, then had copied out on the back of the latter the only actually relevant section of **3758**. All the cases in **3758** are dated in the month following **3756**; the interval before they were attached to **3756** may have been much longer. How, and indeed why, Philammon obtained the whole roll remains a mystery.

The principals in **3756** come from Alexandria or from the so-called territory of the Mastitae in the Mareotic nome. There is no reason to suppose that this is not an Alexandrian document; see below, **3757** introd., for the Oxyrhynchite connection.

Aurelius Ammonius in his will had appointed as guardian for his daughter Isis a certain Boccas. Shortly before the date of **3756** this Boccas had also died, leaving children of whom the eldest, Philammon, was still a minor. In these circumstances by the intervention of Isidorus, apparently then *praeses Ioviae* (see 7 n. and cf. LI **3619**), the duty of guardianship passed to Aurelius Aeithales. Aeithales then petitioned the prefect Flavius Magnus (see 9 n.) for the retrieval of the property of Isis which was being detained by Philammon and his brothers (cf. **3757** 8), the sons of Boccas. In the present document Aeithales now acknowledges to Philammon and his brothers the receipt of all the property, both money and goods, belonging to the girl Isis, with the exception of specified money and goods retained in connection with the funeral of Boccas and the girl's mother's childbirth expenses. This apparent complete discharge (see the terms of ll. 23–5) had a flaw in it; the following month we find Aeithales at Oxyrhynchus in court before the *curator civitatis* demanding from Philammon the repayment of a residual 50 talents, see **3757**.

The data on *praeses* and prefect mentioned above (see 7 n., 9 n.) are of wider historical importance, and help to confirm the conclusions of J. R. Rea (LI **3619** introd.) that there was no official in Egypt with overriding authority in the decade preceding the date of this text.

The measurements given above are those of the piece with **3756** before **3758** was attached to it. There are two manufacturer's joins in **3756**, in l. 2 through ω of Ἥρωνος and ω of οἰκῶν, so that we can see one complete sheet of the original roll with a writing surface of 22.5 × 25 cm.

(m. 2) ἀ(ντίγραφον).

(m. 1)   Αὐρήλιος Ἀειθάλης Ἥρωνος τοῦ Ἱέρακος ἀπὸ τῆς λαμπροτάτης πόλεως
           τῶν Ἀλεξανδρέων οἰκῶν ἐν τῷ εἶ γράματος πρὸς τόπῳ καλουμέ[ν]ου
           Cίγματος

           [ἐ]ν τοῖς Καςίου κληρονόμου Βότκα ἀπὸ χώρας Ματιτῶν τοῦ Μαρεώτου
           νομοῦ διὰ τοῦ πρεσβυτέρου ἀδελφοῦ Αὐρηλίου Φιλάμμωνος μετ’
           εὐδοκήσεως

           Αὐρηλίου Cύρου Ἀπολλων[ί]ου ἀπὸ τῆς αὐτῆς χώρας Ματιςτῶν πρὸ
           τούτου καταςταθέντος κουράτορος αὐτῷ Φιλάμμωνι χαίρειν. ἐπιδὴ
           ὁ προδηλού-

5   [μ]ενος ὑμῶν πατὴρ Βόκκας κατὰ διαθήκας Αὐρηλίου Ἀμμωνίου Cύρου
           ἀπὸ τῆς αὐτῆς χώρας Μαςτιτῶν ἐπίτρο⟨πο⟩ς ἐτύγχανεν καταςταθεὶς
           τῆς τοῦ
           αὐτοῦ Ἀμμ[ωνίου] θυγατρὸς Εἴςιτος τοῖς ὑπ’ αὐτοῦ κληρονόμου μόνης
           ἀποληφθείςης, τὸν δὲ βίον μεταλλάξαντος τοῦ αὐτοῦ πατρὸς ὑμῶν
           κατε{ς}-
           ςτάθην ἐγὼ κατὰ πρόςταγμα τοῦ κυρίου μου Ἰςιδώρου τοῦ διακοςμήςαντος
           τὸν θρόνον τῆς ἡγεμονίας τῆς αὐτῆς Ἀλεξανδρίας ἐπίτροπος τῇ
           παιδὶ ἀκολούθως τοῖς περὶ τούτου γενομένοις ὑπομνήμαςι καὶ τῆς τῶν
           πραγμάτων τῆς αὐτῆς παιδὸς ἀποκαταςτάςεως ἕνεκεν ἐντυχείαν
           πεποίημαι τῷ κυρίῳ μου τῷ διαςημοτάτῳ ἐπάρχῳ τῆς Αἰγύπτου Φλαουίῳ
           Μάγνου καὶ ἐκέλευς[εν] ἀποδοθῆναι, κατὰ ⟨τα⟩ῦτα παραγενόμενος

10   ἐνταῦθα περι.[c. 9   ]τηρ[c. 6   ]...[.δ]εδέχθαι παρ’ ὑμῶν τῶν
           τοῦ Β[ό]κκα κληρονόμων τοῦ π.........ν παιδὸς ἐπιτρόπου
           πάντα
           τὰ διαφέροντα τῇ ἐπιτροπευ[ομένῃ] ὑπ’ ἐμοῦ παιδὶ τῇ αὐτῇ Εἴςιτι
           ἀκολούθως τῇ τοῦ πατρὸς αὐτῆς Ἀμμωνίου [δι]αθήκῃ ἐ[φ’] οἷς
           περιέχει δικαίοις

2 ἱερακος; l. γράμματι   3 l. κληρονόμοις, Βόκκα, Μαςτιτῶν   4 l. Μαςτιτῶν, ἐπειδή   5 ῡμων
6 l. Ἴςιτος τῆς; ῡπ, ῡμων   7 ἱςιδωρου; l. Ἀλεξανδρείας   8 l. ἐντυχίαν   9 l. Μάγνῳ   10 ῡμων
11 l. Ἴςιτι

πᾶςι καὶ παριληφέναι τὰ ἐγκύρο[ντ]α τῇ αὐτῇ β[ο]υλήςει πάντα τη . . . . .
μέχρι ἀσσαρίου ἑνὸς χωρὶς μ[ό]νης τῆς ὀθόνης διὰ τὸ καιχωρῆςθαι εἰς
περιςτολὴν καὶ κηδίαν τοῦ Βόκκα, προςεπὶ δὲ τῶν ἀπὸ τιμῆς τῶν
διαπραθέντων ὑπαρχόντων ἀκολούθως τῇ αὐτῇ διαθήκῃ ὄντων ἐπὶ τὸ
αὐτὸ ἀργυρίου
ταλάντων ὀκτα[κ]οσίων μετὰ ⟨τὰ⟩ κουφιςθέντα [ὑ]φ' ἡμῶν εἰς λόγον κατὰ
τὰ διαταγέντα τῷ μὲν πατρὶ ὑμ[ῶ]ν Βόκκα ταλάντων ἑκατὸν καὶ εἰς
κηδίαν
15 αὐτ[ο]ῦ κατὰ τὴν ἰδ[ί]αν βούλησιν [τά]λαντα ἐνενή[κο]ντα αἴτι τὲ καὶ εἰς
λόγον λοχιῶν τῆ[ς] τοῦ Ἀμμωνίου γυναικὸ[ς] μητρὸς τῆς παιδὸς
διαταγέντα ὁμοίως
τάλαντα τριάκον[τ]α τὰ λοιπὰ τά[λα]ντα πεντακόσια [ὀ]γδοήκοντα πρὸς
οἷς ἀπὸ τιμῆς ὄνου τάλαντα δέκα καὶ ἀπὸ [.]..χυρου Μηνᾶ
κ..[.]...ἀποδοθέντος
ἀργυ[ρί]ου τάλαντα δεκ[α]τέσσαρα ὧν [ἡ] ἀπαρίθμηςίς [μο]ι ἐκ πλήρους
τετέλ[ε]ςται· οὗ ἀργυρ[ί]ου τῆς προκιμένης {τῆς} ποςότητος τὸ
πρόςεργον τοῦ ἀνέκαθεν
χρ[ό]νου μέχρι τῆς ἐνεστώς[ης] ἡμέρας ὑπελ[ογή]θη ἀντὶ τῶν τροφίων καὶ
ἀναλωμάτων τῶν γενομένω[ν] ε[ἰ]ς τὴν ὀρφανὴν τὰ δὲ ἀπὸ τῶν
προςέργων
με[τὰ] τὰ λογιςθέντα τοῦ παντὸς ἀν[α]λώματος εν...[..]τα ἐν ὑμεῖν
εἶνα[ι] τάλαντα ἐνενήκοντα ἓξ ὁμοίως ὑπεδε[ξά]μην, ὡς εἶναι ἐπὶ τ[ὸ]
αὐτὸ ἀπαριθμηθέντα
20 μοι ἀ[ρ]γυρίου τάλαντ[α] ἑπτακόσια. π.[.].. δὲ ὁ αὐτὸς Ἀμμώνιος ἐν τῇ
ἑαυτοῦ διαθήκῃ ἐντολ[ὴ]ν παρέσχετο τῷ αὐτ[ῷ π]ατρὶ ἡμῶν Βόκκα
δικάςαςθαι πρὸς Ἀκύλαν
[c. 19   ]....[.]ης..[..].ως περὶ υ..[.].των περὶ
κώμης.καβε εξου......ως καὶ τοῦ διαν.[.]..αι ἐπεδεξάμην παρ'
ὑμῶν καὶ εἰς τότε
[c. 17   ]υ λίτρας τέσσαρ[ας π]ερὶ τῆς ὑ[μῶ]ν ὑποδοχὴν τοῦ τε
ἀργυρίου καὶ ἀσήμου αἴτι τὲ καὶ χρυςίο[υ κ]αὶ χαλκωματίου καὶ
αἱρεᾶς ἐςθῆτος

12 l. παρειληφέναι, ἐγκύροντα, κεχωρῆςθαι   13 l. κηδείαν   14 [ὑ]φ' ἡμῶν: l. ὑφ' ὑμῶν; ὑμ[ω]ν;
l. τάλαντα ἑκατόν, κηδείαν   15 l. ἔτι δέ, λοχειῶν   17 απαριθ'μηςις; l. προκειμένης, θ of ἀνέκαθεν corr.
from τ   18 υ of χρ[ό]νου corr. from ν; ὑπελογηθη; l. τροφείων   19 ὑμειν: l. ὑμῖν; απαριθ'μηθεντα?
20 l. ὑμῶν; second α of δικάςαςθαι corr. from ε (or vice versa)   21 After περί, ϋ; ϋμων   22 l. ἔτι δέ,
χαλκωματίων, ἐρεᾶς

καὶ τῶν ἄλλων [πάν]των μέχρι ἀςςαρίου ἑνὸς χ[ωρὶ]ς ὀθόνης μόνης
ἐπερωτηθὶς ὡμολ[όγ]ηςα παρειληφέν[α]ι ἐκ πλήρους ἀκολούθως τῇ
διαθήκῃ καὶ ἐν-
τε[ῦ]θεν μηδένα [λόγον] ἔχειν πρὸς ὑ[μᾶς πε]ρὶ τῆ[ς διοική]ςεως τῆς
γενομένης ὑπὸ τοῦ πατ[ρὸ]ς ὑμῶν τῶν ὀρφανικῶν [χρ]ημάτων καὶ
περὶ ὧν ἐνεχείρηςεν ὑπαρχόντω(ν)

25 πά[ν]των ἀπαξαπ[λῶς] κατὰ μηδένα τρόπ[ον] μηδὲν ἐγκ[αλεῖν μ]ηδὲ
ἐνκαλέςιν προφά[ςε]ι ἡτινιοῦν [καὶ] ἀπ[ο]χὴν ταύτην τριςςὴ[ν] ὑμεῖν
ἐκςεδόμην ἀποτελεςτικὴν ἣν ἐξές-
ται [ὑ]μεῖν δημ[οςιῶςα]ι περὶ πάντων ... [.]. των ἀρχει[.. ἐ]περωτηθὶς
ὡμολό[γης]α. ὑπατίας Πρόκλ[ου καὶ] Παυλίνου, Μεχεὶρ [   ].

(m. 2 or m. 3?)   ειςτε.....

23 l. ἐπερωτηθείς; first ε of παρειληφέναι corr. from α   24 υπαρχοντω̄   25 l. ἐγκαλεῖν,
ἐγκαλέςειν; ὑμειν; l. ὑμῖν, ἐξεδόμην; ἀποτελεςτικήν: first τ corr. from λ, λ corr. from ς   26 l. ὑμῖν,
ἐπερωτηθείς, ὑπατείας

(m. 2) 'Copy.'
(m. 1) 'Aurelius Aeithales, son of Heron and grandson of Hierax, from the most illustrious city of the
Alexandrians, residing in the Epsilon district in the locality of the so-called Sigma, in the house of Casius, to the
heirs of Boccas from the territory of the Mastitae in the Mareotic nome, through the elder brother Aurelius
Philammon, with the consent of Aurelius Syrus son of Apollonius from the same territory of the Mastitae,
previously appointed as guardian for the said Philammon, greetings. Since your aforementioned father Boccas,
in accordance with the testament of Aurelius Ammonius son of Syrus from the same territory of the Mastitae,
became appointed guardian of Isis the daughter of the said Ammonius, who had been left by him as sole
heiress, and on your aforementioned father's death I was appointed guardian for the child following an order
of my lord Isidorus, who then adorned the throne of the praesidiate of the said Alexandria, in accordance with
the minutes which were made concerning this matter, and for the sake of the recovery of the estate of the said
child I made a petition to my lord the prefect of Egypt Flavius Magnus, *vir perfectissimus*, and he ordered (her
estate) to be given back, accordingly being present here ... received from you the heirs of Boccas, the guardian
of ... child, everything belonging to the girl in my guardianship, namely the said Isis, in accordance with the
testament of her father Ammonius upon all the legal conditions which it contains, and to have received back
everything pertaining to the said will ... down to the last penny, excepting alone the linen on account of its
being allocated to the laying-out and funeral of Boccas; and in addition from the moneys from the price for the
possessions sold in accordance with the said testament, totalling eight hundred silver talents, I have received
(after deductions by you on account in accordance with what was bequeathed, namely one hundred talents for
your father Boccas and ninety talents for his funeral in accordance with his own will, and a further thirty
talents similarly bequeathed on account of the childbirth of Ammonius' wife the mother of the girl) the
remaining five hundred and eighty talents, plus ten talents from the price for a donkey and fourteen silver
talents from the ... sold to Menas ..., of which the counting out to me has been fully completed. The interest
on the aforesaid quantity of money, from the first up to the present day, has been offset against the maintenance
and expenses incurred with regard to the orphan; but I have likewise received the ninety-six talents remaining
of the interest after the amounts reckoned for all expenses had been credited(?) to you. Thus in total seven
hundred silver talents have been counted out to me. ... the aforesaid Ammonius in his own testament gave
instructions to your said father Boccas to go to law against Aquila ... I have received from you and ... four
pounds of ... Questioned in respect of your stewardship of the money and uncoined silver and also the gold
and bronze objects and woollen clothing and everything else down to the last penny, excepting only the linen, I
have acknowledged full receipt in accordance with the testament, and from henceforth I shall have no case
against you regarding your father's management of the orphan's money, and in general as far as concerns all

the property he took in hand in no way do I make any charge against you nor shall I do so on any pretext whatever. I have issued this final receipt to you in triplicate, which you may register . . . in answer to the question I have given my assent. In the consulship of Proculus and Paulinus, Mecheir [   ].'

(m. 2 or m. 3?) ' . . . '

1 ἀ(ντίγραφον). Alpha is bisected by a diagonal from lower left (cf. LI **3611** 22 n.). There were three copies, cf. 25. The printed transcript does not show the correct location of this marginal notation, which is halfway along the sheet above πόλεως in 2.

2 Ἀεϊθάλης. The name appears as Ἀϊθάλης in **3757** 15 and **3758** 81 and Ἀειθάλης in **3758** 89, 95. **3757** 21 inadvertently omits initial letters, thus ⟨Ἀε⟩ιθάλης. These are the only appearances so far in papyri of this rare name. Spelling Ἀει but above all the diaeresis in **3757** 15 and **3758** 81 indicate that the name was not trisyllabic but tetrasyllabic.

ἐν τῷ εἶ γράματος (l. γράμματι). For the five γράμματα, divisions of Alexandria, see Calderini, *Diz. geogr.* i 1. 79–80; P. M. Fraser, *Ptolemaic Alexandria* i 34–5. XLVI **3271** 6 now provides a reference to the Gamma district, and the present papyrus appears to be our first reference to the Epsilon district.

Cίγματος. This appears to be previously unrecorded. Given our limited knowledge of Alexandrian topography, there can be no justification for supposing this to be a misspelt reference to the tomb of Alexander, see Calderini, op. cit. i 1. 149–51, s.v. cῶμα, cῆμα. A semicircular portico, cf. LSJ?

3 [ἐ]ν τοῖς Κασίου. Cf. XLI **2980** 14, delivery instructions εἰς τὰ Θέωνο(ς) on the back of a letter.

Βότκα. Elsewhere in this volume the name is consistently spelt Βοκκ-, and is written uniformly Βοκκα in the oblique cases; there is one nominative example (l. 5 here) where the name appears as Βόκκας. This name found no entry in the *NB* but is now well attested: P. Bour. 42. 572, SB V 7515. 295, 305, 309, X 10615. 3. There is some chance that another example exists in XIV **1728** 10, where Grenfell and Hunt read Βόκκου (or Βοκκα( ), see their n.); from a photograph Βόκκα may be the right reading. See now also *ZIE* 66 (1986) 90.

Ματιτῶν. Cf. 4 Ματιστῶν, and ultimately the right spelling Μαστιτῶν in 5. For the territory of the Mastitae see A. Calderini and S. Daris, *Diz. geogr.* iii 3. 241. Note also XLVI **3292**.

τοῦ Μαρεώτου νομοῦ. See Calderini-Daris, op. cit. iii 3. 234; also M. Rodziewicz, *Graeco-Arabica* 2 (1983) 199–216.

4 κουράτορος. Cf. 5 ἐπίτρο⟨πο⟩ς (also 7, 10 and ἐπιτροπευομένη in 11 and **3757** 6–7). For the fading distinction between these terms see *Aeg.* 61 (1981) 109 n. 15; R. Taubenschlag, *Law²* 180.

7 For Isidorus, *praes* of *Aegyptus Iovia*, see LI **3619**. The description τῆς ἡγεμονίας . . . Ἀλεξανδρείας adds welcome confirmation of his sphere of authority. We cannot fix the date at which Isidorus was in office, without knowing the date of the death of Boccas, but nevertheless the events of **3756** suggest only a brief time-lapse between involvement of *praeses* and involvement of prefect, and Isidorus may have been the last holder of the office of *praeses Ioviae*. A *terminus post quem* for the end of the tenure of the last holder would be supplied by the last attested date for Sabinianus as *praeses Mercurianae* (AD 324), cf. 9 n., as well as by the abdication of Licinius (September 324), see **3619** introd. For *Mercuriana* as Sabinianus' area of authority see J. D. Thomas, *BASP* 21 (1984) 225–34.

τοῦ διακοσμήσαντος τὸν θρόνον τῆς ἡγεμονίας. Cf. **3758** 7–8 (Sabinianus, *praeses Mercurianae*); also P. Sak. 32. 18–19, Septimius Apollonius κοσμήσαντος τὴν διοίκησιν.

9 Flavius Magnus is an addition to the known prefects of Egypt (J. Lallemand, *L'Admin. civile* 241). He is attested several times in the texts in this volume; this is the earliest reference, the papyrus being dated Jan./Feb. 325, and he is still in office at the date of **3759**, 2 Oct. 325. In between come **3757** (13 Mar. 325, but the reference is probably to the same action as in **3756** 9) and **3758** 10 and 15 (and 80–1 and 93 which = **3757**). Can we say how much earlier than Jan./Feb. 325 Magnus may have been in office? Sabinianus (see **3758** 8 n.) is still attested as *praeses Mercurianae* in 324. It is possible that Iovia could have been put in the hands of a prefect while Mercuriana and Herculia each continued under a praeses, but it is much more likely that the three subdivisions were amalgamated and brought under the control of a prefect simultaneously, after September 324 (**3619** introd.). It is possible then that Magnus was the first prefect after the decade without one. His successor may have been Ti. Flavius Laetus, attested for 2 Feb. 326 by LI **3620**. The next certain prefect was Septimius Zenius, Oct./Nov. 327, P. Harr. II 215 recto. See now also *BASP* 22 (1985) 25–7.

10 π. . . . . ν. I cannot ascertain the reading over this much damaged section. The general sense is clear enough however. The probable initial π excludes reading τῆς Ἀμμωνίου. προδηλουμένου (cf. 4–5) ⟨τῆς⟩?

12 μέχρι ἀσσαρίου ἑνός. Cf. 23, and P. Köln III 155. 16–17 (ἕως ἀσσαρίου ἑνός) and SB VI 9403. 14 (revised *ZPE* 35 (1979) 140), ἄχρι ἀς⟨σ⟩αρίου ἑνός; also **3758** 11, 30, 38. West-Johnson, *Currency* 121.

13 κηδίαν. See CPR VI (pt. 1) 1. 14 n.

προϲεπί very doubtful. Of the first five letters virtually nothing remains, but a horizontal suggests π and a small loop following is consistent with ρ. πι is certain. If προϲεπί were right, this would appear to be an earlier adverbial use of a word frequent in later Byzantine papyri in usages of the type προϲεπὶ τούτοιϲ (though some commentators would divide πρὸϲ ἐπί and take πρόϲ adverbially, cf. P. Lond. V 1660. 33 n.). Or did our writer intend προϲέτι?

15 λοχιῶν. The child Isis was born before her father's death, cf. 6 where she is left his heir; since there is no mention of a second child of Ammonius', this deduction of 30 talents must be to meet obligations Ammonius incurred towards Boccas and his family in connection with Isis' birth.

16 For early fourth-century donkey prices cf. *ZPE* 6 (1970) 181; *Aeg.* 54 (1974) 61–2; XLIII **3143** 13 n., **3145** 11 n., and *ZPE* 24 (1977) 116–17; and, most recently, R. S. Bagnall, *Currency and Inflation in Fourth Century Egypt* (= BASP Suppl. 5 (1985)) 67–8. Ten talents for the donkey here may be only a partial price.

[.]. . χυρου. Space and much-damaged traces could suggest [ἐ]ν̣εχύρου̣; the space might possibly admit of [το]ῦ̣ ἀχύρου̣, which is more easily comprehended with ἀποδοθέντοϲ (and the donkey has already provided an agricultural context), but first υ is difficult.

After Μηνᾶ, a damaged patronymic? A construction with genitive Μηνᾶ is also conceivable.

19 Reading after ἀν[α]λώματοϲ is baffling. ϲ could be read as χ, if its supposed centre bar were in reality the extended finial of preceding ϲ. ν is almost certain. I had initially thought of γνωϲθ[έν]τα, but the supposed right loop of would-be ω seems rather to consist of a vertical (with an awkward low trace) and centre horizontal; these might suggest eta, but then the left loop is unexplained. A verb implying 'credited' or the like seems to be wanted. For the periphrastic construction see F. Blass, A. Debrunner, and F. Rehkopf, *Grammatik des neutestamentlichen Griechisch* (1979) §355; cf. too εἶναι . . . ἀπαριθμηθέντα at the end of this same line.

20 π. [.]. . . We might expect περιών but it seems too wide for the space.

δικάϲαϲθαι πρὸϲ Ἀκύλαν. There is no further mention of this lawsuit in the archive. Presumably it was pending when Ammonius drew up his will (this is curious; was the lawsuit one which would arise on Ammonius' death?), now past with Boccas' death. The damaged next line may have elaborated on the case.

21 ̣καβε. The name of the village probably lurks here. No village that will fit the traces is recorded, but this is not surprising.

22 τῆϲ. I do not think τήν can be read. Therefore correct to τήν, or alternatively correct ὑποδοχήν (ν certain) to ὑποδοχῆϲ. For ἄϲημον = uncoined silver see *CE* 48 (1973) 372–4.

25 ἀποτελεϲτικήν. Cf. the app. crit. The writer wrote απολεϲ before realizing and correcting his error.

26 For δημοϲίωϲιϲ see M. Hässler, *Die Bedeutung der Kyria-Klausel* 77 ff., and H. J. Wolff, *Das Recht der griechischen Papyri Ägyptens* (Handb. d. Altertumswissenschaft X 5. 2) 129 ff.

For the consular formula cf. XLIII **3125** 9 n. The proceedings referred to in the first paragraph of that note, with dates by Proculus and Paulinus for 3 and 17 March 325, are **3758** below, which adjoins the right edge of this text. The dating by Paulinus and Julianus for 13 March 325 is in **3757** on the back of this text. A further example of Proculus and Paulinus may be in VI **889** 11–12, see T. D. Barnes, *ZPE* 21 (1976) 279–81. This article wrongly reports the day of the month in **889** 12 as Pachon 24 (= 19 May, not 18 May) when the papyrus (and *ed. pr.*) clearly has Pachon 29 (= 24 May). This is uncomfortably but of course not impossibly close to the dating by Paulinus and Julianus in XIV **1626** 23 (Pauni 1 = 26 May). **889** was independently and concurrently discussed by J. D. Thomas, *Anc. Soc.* 7 (1976) 301–8 (with pl. VI), but without suggesting Proculus and Paulinus as the consuls in 11–12. **889** was further discussed by T. D. Barnes, *The New Empire of Diocletian and Constantine* 234–7, and by T. D. Barnes and K. A. Worp, *ZPE* 53 (1983) 276–8.

27 Full transcription of the docket has so far escaped me. The transcript does not accurately record its location; it begins at the mid-point of the full line-length, 1.5 cm below l. 26. There are some scattered ink-marks both before and after it, but insufficient remains to show whether they are other than mere blots.

3757. Proceedings before the Logistes

7 1B.212/11   Width 25 cm   13 March 325

This report, more or less complete if somewhat shredded, is written along the fibres *transversa charta* on the back of **3756**, which is dated the previous month and documents an earlier stage of the same affair; **3757** is itself a fair copy of the cancelled ll. 78–97 of **3758** which is attached to the right edge of **3756**. For the chronology and explanation of this composition see **3756** introd.

In Jan./Feb. 325 Aeithales had given Philammon and his brothers a complete discharge (= **3756**) regarding their involvement with the property of the child Isis in his (Aeithales') guardianship. All was apparently not well, however: here in the following month we find the two parties in dispute before the *curator civitatis* in Oxyrhynchus over the allegedly unpaid sum of 50 talents. **3758** 78–97 = **3757** records this hearing. Aeithales adduces an order of the prefect, probably the same instructions as are referred to in **3756** 9, which required Philammon and his brothers to release the property in dispute; and he also claims to have a document in which Philammon acknowledges the residual debt of 50 talents. Philammon for his part produces the discharge document (presumably **3756** itself) in which Aeithales declares all Philammon's obligations have been cleared. The *curator*, bound to see that the prefect's order is complied with, while faced with incompatible documentation, takes the easy way out and elects to assert the terms of **3756** which had satisfied Aeithales and still of course satisfied Philammon; he ignores Aeithales' document concerning the 50 talents, and instructs him to initiate a new process for the reclamation of this sum. There is no further reference to this document of Aeithales' in the archive, so that we do not know the outcome of the affair. For the time being **3758** 78–97 = **3757** exonerated Philammon, thus providing the more reason for him (see **3756** introd.) to attach the roll with the rough copy of the proceedings to **3756** and then have the revised version copied out on **3756**'s back.

The Oxyrhynchite connection of this sequence is puzzling, since both Aeithales and Philammon came from Alexandria or its environs. Had Philammon between Jan./Feb. 325 (**3756**) and 13 March 325 (**3758** 78–97 = **3757**) moved to Oxyrhynchus, taking **3756** with him, and had Aeithales pursued him there?

3757 and **3758** 78–97 help to supplement each other in the damaged or missing passages, except in **3757** 12, which is absent from the rough copy, and in the lacuna in **3757** 14, which contained something absent from the rough copy. The opening with the consular formula in **3757** 1–2 is also different from every example of the consular formula in **3758**; **3757** was clearly copied not from the rough copy **3758** 78–97 but from some other exemplar, and copied after the consular change (see **3756** 26 n.).

$$[(\H{\epsilon}\tau o v c)] \; \iota[\theta\varsigma]\,'\H{\epsilon}\nu\acute{\alpha}\tau[o]\nu, \; \Phi\alpha\mu\epsilon\nu\grave{\omega}\theta \; \iota\zeta. \; \H{\upsilon}\pi\alpha\tau\epsilon\acute{\iota}\alpha c \; \Pi\alpha\upsilon\lambda\acute{\iota}\nu o v \; \kappa\alpha\grave{\iota}$$
$$'I o v\lambda\iota\alpha\nu o\hat{v} \; \tau\hat{\omega}\nu \; \lambda\alpha\mu\pi\rho o\tau[\acute{\alpha}\tau\omega\nu.]$$
$$\pi\rho\grave{o}c \; \tau\hat{\omega} \; K\alpha\pi\iota\tau\omega\lambda\acute{\iota}\omega. \; \H{\epsilon}\pi\grave{\iota} \; \pi\alpha\rho\acute{o}\nu\tau\omega\nu \; '\Omega\rho\acute{\iota}\omega\nu o c \; \kappa\alpha\grave{\iota} \; 'H\rho\hat{\alpha} \; \H{\upsilon}\pi\eta\rho[\epsilon\tau\hat{\omega}\nu]$$
$$\kappa\alpha\grave{\iota} \; E\H{\upsilon}\lambda o\gamma\acute{\iota}o v \; \pi\alpha\rho\acute{\epsilon}\delta\rho o v. \; \grave{o} \; \lambda o\gamma\iota(c\tau\grave{\eta}c) \; \epsilon\hat{\iota}(\pi\epsilon\nu)\cdot \; \pi\rho\acute{o}c\tau\alpha\gamma\mu\alpha \; \tau o\hat{v} \; \kappa v\rho\acute{\iota}o v \; \mu o v \; \tau o\hat{v}$$
$$\delta\iota\alpha c\eta\mu[o\tau\acute{\alpha}\tau o v \; \H{\epsilon}\pi\acute{\alpha}\rho\chi o v]$$

4 λογι ει; so in 17   Final supplement cramped or abbreviated

5   τῆς Αἰγύπτο[υ] Φλ[αουίο]υ Μάγνου ἐπήνεγκεν τῇ ἐμῇ με[τρ]ι[ότητι
                                                 Ἀειθάληc]

    ἀπὸ χώρας Μαcτι[τῶν περὶ πραγμάτων διαφερόντων τῇ ἐπιτρο-]

    πευομένῃ ὑπ' αὐτοῦ παιδὶ Ἴcιτι καὶ διακατεχομένων ὑπὸ τοῦ παρ[όν-]

    τος Φιλάμμωνος καὶ τῶν ἀδελφῶν αὐτοῦ κληρονόμων Βόκκα. ἐν cτ[έρ-]

    νοιc τοίνυν ἔχων τὸν . . . τῆς ἀνδρείας φόβον τοῦ τηλικούτου ἄρχο[ντος]

10   μεταδέδ[ωκα μὲν τοῖc ἀντιδικοῦcι τὰ προcτεταγμένα, ἐνήγα-]

    γον δὲ αὐτοὺς ἵνα γνῶμεν τίνα ἐcτὶν ἃ διεπράξαντ[ο] πρὸ[c αὐτοὺc]

    ὑπὲρ τοῦ παν . . . . . τὸ τηλικοῦτο πληροῦcθαι πρόcταγμα. Φιλά[μμων]

    ἀπεκρ(ίνατο)· διελύθημεν καὶ ἔχω γραμματεῖον περὶ τ[ούτου. ὁ λογι(cτὴc)
                                                    εἶ(πεν)· ἀναγνωcθή-]

    τω. καὶ ἀνεγνώcθη οὕτωc ὡc π[ε]ριε[χει] . [2-3] . [.] . [2-3] . [.] . [*c.*6
                                                       μετὰ τὴν]

15   ἀνάγνωcιν, Ἀϊθάληc ἀπεκρ(ίνατο)· ἀπὸ τούτων τῶν πραγμάτων ἐνωφ[εί-]

    λησεν ⟦μοι⟧ ἀργ(υρίου) (τάλαντα) ν΄, ὧν καὶ ἐγράψατο εἴcω προθεcμίαc
                                                          ἀποδώc[ειν,]

    καὶ ἔχω τὸ γραμματεῖον τῆς ὀφειλῆς. ὁ λογι(cτὴc) εἶ(πεν)· τὸ πρόcταγμα
                                                         τοῦ κυρίου

    μου τοῦ διαcημοτάτου ἐπάρχου [τ]ῆc Αἰγύπτου Φλαουίου Μάγνου ἐπὶ πέραc

    ἤχθη· τὸ γὰρ γραμματεῖον τῆς μεταξὺ γενομένῃς [δ]ια[λύcεωc]

20   διελέγχει πεπῖcθαι ἀμφότερα τὰ μέρη. ὅθεν ἀναχωρήcειτε ἐ⟦πι⟧'πι' τ[οῖc]

    γενομένοιc ὑφ' ὑμῶν cυμφώνοιc. περὶ δέ γε οὗ φηcιν ὁ ⟨Ἀε⟩ιθάλη[c]

    γραμματείου τοῦ χρέουc τῶν (ταλάντων) ν΄, κατὰ κ[αι]ρὸν [μετελεύcεται]

    τὸν χρεώcτην περὶ τῆς ἐνκειμένη[c ὀ]φειλῆc.

---

7 διακατεχομένων: κατ rewritten; ων corr. (cf. **3758** 83)?   8 First μ of Φιλάμμωνος corr. from ν
12 αι of πληροῦcθαι rewritten   13 απεκρ( ): see 13n.   15 αϊθαληc: l. Ἀειθάληc   16 l. ἅ
17 ο of first τό rewritten   20 l. πεπεῖcθαι; χ of ἀναχωρήcειτε corr.? l. ἀναχωρήcετε   21 ϊθαληc

'Year 19 and nine, Phamenoth 17. In the consulship of Paulinus and Julianus, *viri clarissimi.*

'At the Capitolium, in the presence of Horion and Heras, assistants, and Eulogius, assessor. The *curator* said, "An order of my lord the prefect of Egypt, Flavius Magnus, *vir perfectissimus*, has been brought before my humble self by Aeithales from the territory of the Mastitae, concerning property belonging to the child Isis, who is in his guardianship, which is being detained by Philammon, here present, and his brothers, heirs of Boccas. So, keeping in my heart the fear of the Nobility of so great an official, I have communicated his orders to the parties in the case, and I have brought them in so that we may know what mutual arrangements they have come to for the . . . fulfilment of so great an order." Philammon answered, "We made an agreement, and I have a document about this." The *curator* said, "Let it be read." And it was read as follows . . . After the reading, Aeithales answered, "Out of this property he owed 50 silver talents, which he wrote that he would repay within the appointed time, and I have the document attesting the debt." The *curator* said, "The order of my lord the prefect of Egypt, Flavius Magnus, *vir perfectissimus*, has been carried out; the document of discharge between you shows both sides to be in agreement. Wherefore you will depart, abiding by the conditions of the agreements made between you. As regards the document which Aeithales mentions concerning the debt of 50 talents, at the proper time he is to sue the debtor regarding the obligation contained therein."'

1 For the avoidance of θ in regnal-year dating see J. D. Thomas, *ZPE* 24 (1977) 241–3; P. Mich. XV 724. 8 n. For the consuls cf. **3756** 26 n.

3 Καπιτωλίῳ. See A. Calderini and S. Daris, *Diz. geogr.* iii 68; G. Ronchi, *Lex. Theonymon* iii 570. For its use for court hearings cf. **3758** 156. Other locations for hearings before the logistes: Ἀδριανίῳ (**3758** 134, **3767** 1, **3764** 14, P. Harr. 160. 2 as re-ed. *ZPE* 37 (1980) 237); γυμνασίῳ (**3758** 181); Κορίῳ ἱερῷ (**3759** 1 and **3742** back), and λογιϲτηρίῳ (**3758** 98). ἐπὶ παρόντων: see **3758** 156–8 n.

Horion and Heras recur elsewhere: Horion in **3758** 79 (the duplicate of this passage), 98, 137, 157, and 184; Heras in **3758** 79 (the duplicate passage) and 99.

4 Εὐλογίου παρέδρου. He recurs several times in **3758**: 79 (the duplicate of this passage), 99, 157, 184, 221. Could this Eulogius conceivably be the later logistes (AD 341: see Appendix I below)?

5 Flavius Magnus, *praefectus Aegypti*. See **3756** 9 n. τῇ ἐμῇ με[τρ]ι[ότητι: see **3758** 81 n.

6 ἀπὸ χώραϲ Μαϲτι[τῶν. Cf. **3758** 81. Aeithales describes himself as an Alexandrian in **3756** 2. Scattered traces are visible in the indicated lacuna, but I cannot allocate them to individual letters; the reading is restored from the cancelled copy. Similarly in 10.

8–9 ἐν ϲτέρνοιϲ κτλ. Cf. M. *Chr.* 77. 6 (= P. Lips. 36) and 78. 5.

9 Possibly four letters between τόν and τῆϲ. Presumably a preposition came here, but I have not been able to establish which one, in the broken state of the papyrus. Cf. **3758** 85.

ἀνδρείαϲ: cf. **3758** 10 and see CPR V 7. 9 n. These new examples applied to the prefect amplify the pattern outlined in the note in CPR V and show that the title was resumed by the prefect when the post was restored after the defeat of Licinius; it continued to be used by the *praeses Thebaidos*.

13 ἀπεκρ(ίνατο) is marked as abbreviated by a horizontal cutting the descender of rho; so also in 15 and frequently in proceedings in this volume and elsewhere.

17–19 τὸ πρόϲταγμα . . . ἐπὶ πέραϲ ἤχθη. Cf. M. *Chr.* 78. 4.

3758. PROCEEDINGS BEFORE THE LOGISTES

7 1B.212/11 +
13 1B.212–213/A(a–h)　　　　　　25 × 290 cm　　　　　Feb.?/Mar. 325

For a general introduction to this papyrus and its physical relationship to **3756–7** and other texts in this volume, see the general introduction to **3756–8** above; further comments are in the introductions to **3756** and **3757**. Lines 39 to the end of **3758**, covering at least seven different hearings with dates from Phamenoth 7–22, are on one roll 246.5 cm long made up to take them, it seems, by reusing documents that had come into the logistes' bureau and been discarded. Lines 5–38, containing a report of an earlier hearing in Phamenoth, were recorded on an unused piece of papyrus, measuring 25 × 43.5 cm and blank on the back except for the title ὑπομνήματα μηνὸϲ Φαμενώθ etc. (= **3758** 1–4); this may have been the title for 5–38 simply, or it may have been written there as the title for the whole of **3758**. At any rate its location on the back of the roll makes it clear that it was written before the combined **3758** roll was affixed to **3756**. The whole of **3758** is written in *transversa charta* form. A result of its bipartite structure is that 5–38 are written across the fibres, 39 onwards along them.

On the *transversa charta* format see E. G. Turner, *The Terms Recto and Verso* (Pap. Brux. 16) 26–53, esp. 51. **3758** is the unpublished Oxyrhynchus text referred to on p. 51.

Note that it is not a τόμος ϲυγκολλήϲιμοϲ, as there stated, in the usual implication of that expression. I confirm the *transversa charta* format of XXXI **2562**, re-edited here as **3767**.

The chronological pattern of the hearings is as follows:

5–38	date lost (but it should be Phamenoth 1, 2, 3, 5, 6, or 7)
39–77	Phamenoth 7 = Wednesday, 3 March 325
78–97 98–131	Phamenoth 17 = Saturday, 13 March 325
134–155	Phamenoth 21 = Wednesday, 17 March 325
156–180	Phamenoth 22 = Thursday, 18 March 325
181–213	Phamenoth 19 = Monday, 15 March 325
214–228	date(s) lost

The date Phamenoth 19, which interrupts the sequence, must of course throw some doubt on the conclusions above and in 5 n. below on the date of ll. 5–38.

Some of the hearings have such extensive alterations (e.g. over twenty in 39–77, over a dozen in 78–97) as to give the impression of being drafts. That they are copies is clear from the gaps between the day-figures.

Why were these hearings copied out together? Clearly they do not form the total of the *curator's* activity, and they are in no way his daybook. Many of the cases concern inheritance law in some aspect or other (not, notably, the first, ll. 5–38), and the reason for the collection may lie in this direction; yet they do not obviously illustrate the Aeithales case (= **3756**) to which they were attached, except of course for ll. 78–97, which were recopied as **3757**.

Lines 5–38 are concerned with the responsibility for a quantity of compulsorily purchased military clothing now surplus to requirements. Initially a sum of money was exacted from the δημόται = παγανοί by the councillors and/or landowners. This money was then used for the purchase in Tyre of 150 ϲτιχάρια, through the agency of the prytanis Leucadius. The prefect then decreed that the παγανοί = δημόται should be refunded their money, and Leucadius is instructed to pay it back and try to recover his losses from the landowners or his fellow councillors, who had been ordered to purchase the ϲτιχάρια: if they were now willing to repurchase them, they could then sell them themselves for whatever price they wished (or could get!). Naturally, Leucadius was unhappy with this arrangement, and the dialogue is lively almost to the point of rudeness. But Leucadius loses, it seems: the logistes overrides his objections and insists on the implementation of the prefect's orders.

The case contrasts the authority of the *praeses Mercurianae* (Sabinianus, see 8 n.) with that of the *praefectus Aegypti* (Flavius Magnus, see **3756** 9 n.) in a way which probably reflects a chronological contrast: cf. LI **3619** introd., **3756** introd. and 7 n., 9 n., and note also l. 43 below, τὴν ἡγεμονίαν τὴν τότε, implying that the first of the two offices no longer existed. The apparent ability of the councillors/landowners to ignore the *praeses'* authority (16–17: implicit in εἰ μὲν βούλονται . . . καθὼϲ προϲτέτακται) is at first sight astonishing, but is presumably explicable by the *praeses*' orders having been superseded by those of the prefect.

Lines 39–77 concern conflicting claims to some gold jewellery, which appears to have been passed around various members of the family concerned in trust, and then ultimately—legitimately?—to have formed the object of a bequest by the plaintiff's mother, now deceased. Much is unclear, perhaps because of abridgement in drafting the report (either the original record of the hearing or this copy of it). The various family relationships in particular are not clear to me.

Lines 78–97 were cancelled and a revised version written out on the back of **3756**; this revised version is published here as **3757**. It differs from the cancelled version, even after the many corrections in that, at (line-numbers in brackets are those of **3757**) 78 (1–2), 86 (11), 87 (12), 89 (14), 90 (16), and 91 (16).

These lines (78–97) record a sequel to the wrangling over the property of an orphan minor in guardianship, revealed to us by **3756**. Now the child's current guardian is suing his predecessor's sons over the alleged retention of 50 talents. The *curator civitatis* avoids an impasse, temporarily, by asserting the validity of the previous document of receipt and discharge (presumably **3756** itself) supplied by the current guardian to his deceased predecessor's sons.

Detailed commentary on these lines will be found under **3757**; I provide notes here on points specific to this version of the report, along with an apparatus criticus.

Lines 98–131 are concerned with conflicting claims on some house-property left by Amois, now deceased, to his daughter; the girl had had a brother, but he had died, leaving her as sole heiress. A Libyan called Syrus has made some claim on the property, the details of which remain obscure for us.

Lines 132–3 give the consular year, closely preceding the following section but in a different hand so that the structural link is uncertain, although this is hardly of importance.

Lines 134–55 record a straightforward *apertura testamenti*. The will was made on Phamenoth 20 (16 March) and opened and read in this hearing the following day, Phamenoth 21, after the death of the *testatrix*. Lines 181–213 record a similar case, and the two usefully supplement each other where one or other is damaged. Regarding the time-lapse note M. Amelotti, *Il testamento romano* i (1966) 186. It is to be noted that the *curator* authorizes the start of preparations for burial (152–3); if this were a routine element in the procedure (cf. 209–10), it provides an obvious reason for haste. The session in 134ff. was held in the Hadrianeum, but this was a routine location for proceedings before the logistes (cf. **3767**) and need not necessarily be connected with the custom that wills should be opened in an imperial temple (see e.g. P. Mert. II 75 introd.); the session in 181ff. is held in the γυμνάϲιον.

Lines 156–80 are more damaged than the preceding sections, as the condition of the roll deteriorates the nearer it gets to its end. There is no obvious connection with inheritance law here; the case concerns a house in Oxyrhynchus belonging to a councillor apparently from some other city. Seemingly the house had been let to a certain Hermias, who had disappeared to the Oasis locking (? ὑπὸ cημάντροιc ποιήcαc αὐτήν, 162–3) the house up behind him. It appears that the owner is now trying to regain access to the property. 164–7 imply that this is the second time the case has come before the *curator*, and 170 and 173–4 suggest that the case may earlier have come before the *praeses*. The plaintiffs request that the *curator* should authorize action in their favour in accordance with his earlier instructions; prima facie this would be a judgement *in absentia*, but it is seemingly argued that Hermias is in some way under his mother's control and that since she is present in court (she is technically the defendant, see 156–8 n.) she can receive judgement on his behalf. The mother denies any responsibility for her son (her claim presumably is that the obligations of *materna potestas* have been annulled by ἀποκήρυξιc, see 169 n.); a much-damaged section follows, but at the end of the proceedings (180) the *curator* gives a decision in favour of the plaintiffs.

Lines 181–213 contain another record of *apertura testamenti* closely parallel to 134–55 above. The main 3758 roll breaks off at l. 213 before the record has quite finished (probably little is lost, cf. 134–55). The testator here is a veteran, Besarion, and the will was made in the preceding year, AD 324. Four of the original signatories are present for the opening.

The text transcribed as 3758 concludes with ll. 214–28, which are on two tattered fragments found with the rest of 3758 and presumably from the deteriorating end of the roll. The similarities between 3736 col. ii, on the front of 214–20, and 3737–40, on the front of 181–213, provide a reasonable guarantee of the connection, but it is not clear what interval there may have been between the main stretch of 3758 and these two fragments. That the only reply to the *curator* preserved (214) does not come from Poemenius (cf. 184, 197, 205) or Capitolinus (cf. 193–4) indicates that 214–19 are not a continuation of 181–213, as too does 219 if rightly read. Spacing between 219 and 220 suggests that 220 may then begin a fresh hearing; if so, 214–19 conclude a hearing separate from 181–213 and the gap between 213 and 214 will have been considerable. It is uncertain whether the hearing beginning in 220 continues in 221–8 on the last fragment, where 221 (see n.) again indicates that we are near the beginning of a report. The length measurements given at the beginning of this introduction and in the heading take no account of these potential gaps.

There are considerable variations in the script, but often the changes in style are so gradual that it is very difficult to ascertain where there are hand-changes. There is a change, perhaps only a change of pen, at 58; more abrupt changes of style occur at 79, 98, 132, and 134.

As regards sheet-joins or kolleseis, the roll exemplifies two types: (*a*) three-layer joins (see LI 3624–6 introd. and P. Harr. II 212 introd.) in the manufacture of original new rolls; (*b*) four-layer joins where pieces of scrap papyrus have been pasted together for reuse on the back, which occur *passim* in this roll, cf. the diagram in the general introduction to 3756–8 above. The kolleseis I am concerned here to pinpoint first are those of type (*a*). In **3758**, ll. 1–38 are the only section where the kolleseis relate to **3758** as the primary document. Their presence elsewhere in the roll is irrelevant here, being the concern of the commentaries on the texts on the other side; after the reuse, of course, they may lie either way round, depending on which way round the disused papyrus was laid. Establishing their location in the section with ll. 1–38 is not as easy as it should be, because of damage to the papyrus surface and because of complex fibre-structures in several areas. First, there appears to be a kollesis between 9 and 10, although this is very unclear at the right edge. There must be another one, I think, between 37 and 38 (here there appears to be an extra layer of fibres, about three-quarters of the way across). There is the possibility of a further one at 25. At one point here (seen from the back of around 22) the papyrus is six layers thick! The resulting kollema-widths are 6.5 cm (incomplete), 16.5 cm and 15 cm (if there is a kollesis at 25), and 4.5 cm (incomplete). All these kolleseis would provide 'steps down' in relation to the writing of **3758** 5–38. Strengthening strips have been laid down along the level of (and have been overwritten by) ll. 21–3. On the other side, the fibre-structure between 1 and 2 seems more complicated than is warranted by a simple attachment of **3758** to **3756**, but I cannot disentangle it.

As regards the joins of type (*b*), was the roll made up in advance, out of scrap papyrus, to take the collected reports of proceedings, or were the separate hearings recorded on separate scrap pieces and subsequently glued together? Reference to the diagram in the general introduction to **3756–8** will show where the joins occur relative to the line-numbers of **3758**, and it will readily be apparent that although at three points (39, 98, 181) the joins coincide with the gaps between hearings, three of the other hearings (78 ff., 134 ff., and 156 ff.) do not start on a separate scrap piece. Also the fragmentary sections with 214 ff. and 221 ff. were probably on the same stretch as 181 ff., cf. **3736** introd., so that only 5–38 could ever have been a completely separate record. The new joins between the scrap pieces were not consistently laid down to provide a series of 'steps down' on the new surface, as might be expected, but overlap both ways; the joins between 129 and 130 and between 176 and 177 are arranged as 'steps up'. There must have been some trimming to obtain an even width for the roll, but the extent of this is not apparent.

(Ll. 1–4 on back, along the fibres)

.⟦   *c.* 12   ⟧

ὑπομν(ήματα) μη(νὸϲ) . . . . . . [. .] . . . .
ὑπομν(ήματα) μη(νὸϲ) Φαμε[ν]ὼθ τ[ο]ῦ ιθϟ''θϟ''ἔτουϲ ἐπὶ Διοϲκουρίδου
      (vac.)   λογιϲτοῦ (π)ρ(ὸϲ) καταχωριϲμ[ό]`γ´.

2–3 υπομν⫽, form of abbreviation in μη(νόϲ) not clear   4 ρ⫽

5 .....[..].....[.]..[....].[....].ι..[..] ἐπὶ παρόντων ....
[.]..αρχο.................

προπολ(ιτευομένων) καὶ ῾Τείρωνος ῾Ηρακλείδου᾽⟨καὶ⟩ πλείστου μέρους τῶν
δημοτῶν δι(ὰ) Cαραπίων[οc] Ταυc[..]..

[.].[.] καὶ Παράμμωνος καὶ Ἄμμωνο[c]
καὶ Ἀμμωνίου καὶ ἄλλων. ὁ λογιcτὴc εἶ(πεν)· κατὰ τὴν ἀρχὴν κελ[ευ]cθέντεc
ὑπὸ τοῦ διακοcμήcαντο[c]

τὸν θρόνον τῆc ἡγεμονίαc Cαβινιανοῦ ὥcτε ἀπ[α]ιτῆcαι ειτε κτήτοραc ἢ
βουλευτὰc

παγανοὺc ἀριθμὸν χρημάτων, οὕτωc ἀπῃτήcατε [κ]α[θ]ὼc προcτέτακται. νῦν
δὲ γράμ-

10 ματα ἐκομιcάμην τῆc ἀνδρείαc τοῦ κυρίου μου τοῦ διαcημοτάτου ἐπάρχου τῆc
Αἰγύπτου Φλαουίου Μάγ[νου]

τ.............. τῶν παγαν[ῶ]ν ....θηναι ἐκ πλήρουc μέχρι
ἀccαρίου ἑνόc. ἐπεὶ ο[ὖν]

μετεκαλεcάμην ὑμᾶc τοὺc γενομένουc cυνωνητὰc τῶν cτιχαρίων ὀνομαcθένταc
καὶ πεμφθ[έν-]

ταc ὑπὸ τοῦ αὐτοῦ ἡγεμονεύcαντοc Cαβινιανοῦ ὥcτε τοὺc δημόταc λαβεῖν
αὐτῶν τὸ ἀργύριον τὸ προcταχθὲν ὑπὸ τῆc ἀρετῆc τοῦ αὐτοῦ κυρίου

15 μου τοῦ διαcημοτάτου ἐπάρχου τῆc Αἰγύπτου Φλαουίου Μάγνου 〚.〛
παραινῶ ὑμῖν ὥcτε

δοῦναι αὐτοῖc τὸ ἀργύριον καὶ εἰ μὲν βούλονται βουλευταὶ ἢ κτήτορεc καθὼc
προcτέτακται

ὑπὸ τῆc μείζονοc ἐξουcίαc cυνωνήcαcθαι τὰ cτιχάρια ἃ ἐλέγετε ἐνηνοχέναι
δύναν[ται]

πωλεῖν 〚αι...βουλον〛 οἵαc τιμῆc βο[ύ]λ[ο]ν[τ]α[ι.] Λευ[κ]άδιοc ἀπε-
[κ]ρ(ίνατο)· ὁ κύριόc μου ὁ διαcημότατοc

πρὸc τῇ ἡγεμονίᾳ γενόμενοc Cαβινιανὸc προcέταξεν ἀπαντῆcαι 〚ημ〛῾ἡμᾶc᾽
εἰc Τύρον καὶ τὴν

20 cυνωνὴν τῶν παραγαυδίων ποιήcαcθαι καὶ ἀν[έ]cτειλα ἀντ᾽ ἐμαυτοῦ τὸν
βοηθὸν κ[αὶ]

---

6 προπολ, δι᾽; ω of Cαραπίων[οc] corr.?   7 ει⟩   10 Initial μ rewritten?   τα of
διαcημοτάτου partly obscured by fold   13 c αβι νιανου: here and in several places below there are gaps
in the writing where the papyrus surface was already damaged before the text was written   18 απεκρ( ):
see 3757 13 n.   20 ο of ἐμαυτοῦ rewritten

τὴν cυνωνὴν πεποίηται ἑκάcτου cτιχαρίου (δηναρίων) (μυριάδων) ϛ Ἑ χωρὶc
τῶν ἀναλωμάτων καὶ ἠν[έ]χ[θη]

τὰ cτιχάρια καὶ ἐνταῦθά ἐcτιν καὶ εἰ μὲν βούλῃ ταῦτα ἐνέγκαι πρὸc cὲ καὶ
διαδοῦναι οἷ[c]

βούλει καὶ δὴ εἰπέ· μόνον ἀcφάλειαν θέλω ε . . [.] . . . . ρạθ . . . οὐδὲ γὰρ τὸ
ἀργύριον οι . . [0–3]

. . [*c.* 25   ] . . α . . [. .] . [. .] . . . . . . δύναμαι ἅψαcθαι.
ὁ λογι(cτὴc) εἶ(πεν)·

25   τὰ cτιχάρια οὐ λαμβάνουcι οἱ παγανοί, οὐ γὰρ ἐκελεύcθηcαν λαβεῖν, ἀλλὰ τὸ
ἀργύριον

ὅπερ καὶ παρὰ τὴν εὐχὴν δεδώκαcι. εἰ μὲν οὖν παρεκομίcατε τὰ cτιχάρια, τοῖc
cυνβουλευταῖc δύναcθε παραχωρῆcαι τοῖc κελευcθεῖcιν ὠνήcαcθαι καὶ τοῖc
κτήτορcιν

καὶ δοῦναι τὸ ἀργύριον τοῖc παγανοῖc· ποιήcατε. Λευκάδιοc πρύτ(ανιc)
εἶ(πεν)· ἐγὼ ἀλλότριόc εἰμι τῶν

παγανῶν· παραγαύδια ἠνέχθη· λάβε, δόc μοι ἀcφάλειαν καὶ δὸc οἷc βούλει. ὁ
λογι(cτὴc) εἶ(πεν)·

30   ạ . . . . [.] . . . . . [.] . . . . ἀποδοῦναι μέχρι ἀccαρείου ἑνόc.
Λευκάδιοc πρύτ(ανιc) εἶ(πεν)·

λάβε cὺ τὰ cτιχάρια καὶ πώλει ἢ ὃ θέλειc πρᾶττε· μόνον δόc μοι ἀcφάλειαν.
πίcτιν ἐγὼ

ἔcωcα. ὁ λογι(cτὴc) εἶ(πεν)· πόcα cτιχάρια ἠγάγετε τῶν (ταλάντων) Ζ
παρὰ τῶν δημοτῶν;

Λευκάδιοc πρύτ(ανιc) εἶ(πεν)· ⟦ε . .⟧ εἰc πάντα λόγον ἠνέχθη cτιχ(άρια)
ρν ἑκάcτου cτιχ(αρίου) (δηναρίων) (μυριάδων) ϛ (ἡμίcεωc)

καὶ ὑπὲρ ἀναλωμάτων (δηνάρια) Ἑ ἀνάλωται. δίδωμί cοι τὸν λόγον εἰc
ἕκαcτον κατὰ τὴ[ν]

35   κέλευcιν τοῦ κυρίου μου τοῦ διαcημοτάτ[ο]υ ἡγεμονεύcαντοc Cαβινιανọῦ.
ὁ λ[ογ]ι(cτὴc) [ε]ἶ(πεν)· δ . . . . . [.] . . . ἢ δὸc οἷc βούλει τὰ cτιχάρια οἵαc
βούλει τιμῆc. πάντωc γὰρ

δεῖ κατὰ τὴν πρόcταξιν τοῦ κυρίου μου τοῦ διαcημοτάτου ἐπάρχου [τῆc
Α]ἰ[γύπτου Φλαουίου Μάγνου]

τὸ ἀργύριον ἑαυτῶν μέχρι ἀccαρίου ἑνὸc τοὺc δημόταc ἀπολαβεῖν.

---

21 ✳∩   24 λογι   28 πρυ^τ   30 l. ἀccαρίου   31 πρατʼτε   33 cτι^χ
38 ω of ἑαυτῶν corr. from o

[(ἔτους)] ιθſ θſ Φαμενὼθ ζ΄, ὑπατείας Πρόκλου καὶ Παυλί[ν]ου.

40 [*c.* 14   ]. [*c.* 12   ].. [. . . .]φάνου παρέδρου.

Θέων ῥ(ήτωρ) εἶ(πεν)· Ϲαραπίων Ἀφυγχίου ἐπὶ παρούσῃ Ἑλένῃ γυναικὶ
αὐτοῦ. τὴν ⟦cύμβιον⟧ ʿγαμετὴνʾ
ἑαυτοῦ περιγραφομένην ʿθεωρῶν ὁ βοηθούμενοςʾ λόγῳ μὲν καὶ τῷ δοκεῖν τῇ
ἐντυχείᾳ κέχρηται ἀνενεγκὼν ἐπὶ
τὴν ἡγεμονίαν τὴν τότε, ἔργοις δὲ καὶ αὐταῖς ταῖς δυνάμιcιν ἴδιον κτῆμα
ἡγούμενος εἶναι ταῦτα τὰ εἰς τὴν γυναῖκα μεταπηδήcαντα ὁμοίως τὴν
ἐκδικείαν

45 ποιούμενος τῇ αὐτῇ ἀναφορᾷ κέχρηται. καὶ ἐξ(ῆς) λέγοντος ⟦ολο⟧ ὁ
λογι(cτὴς) εἶ(πεν)· περιττ⟦ὼς μὲν ἀνή-⟧ ʿὼς μὲν ἀνή-ʾ
νεγκεν ἐπὶ τὴν ἡγεμονίαν· ἐπειδὴ δὲ ἁπαξαπλῶς νόμος ἐcτὶν ὥcτε τοὺς
χαμαιδι-
καcτὰς ἀκοῦcαι ⟨τοιούτων⟩ τῶν πραγμάτων, δίδωμι τὴν ἀκοὴν ⟦καὶ τῷ π⟧
ʿτῷ πράγματιʾ καὶ ἀκούω τ⟦οῦ⟧ʿῆςʾ
⟦πράγματος⟧ ʿὑποθέcεωςʾ. Θέων ῥ(ήτωρ) εἶ(πεν)· ἔcτηκεν ἡ γυνὴ
. . . . [.] το[ῖc] ἀνενεχθε[ῖ]cιν καὶ τοῖς λεγομέ{ν}-
νοις ὑπὸ τοῦ ἀνδρὸς αὐτῆς. ⟦Θέων ῥ(ήτωρ) εἶ(πεν)⟧ ἐκγόνων ʿτοίνυνʾ ἰδίων
κόcμον ʿπεριʾποιηcάμενος χρύcι[ν]ο[ν]

50 παρέθετο τῇ ἑαυτοῦ γαμετῇ. ταῦτα τὰ εἴδη ἡ παῖς ὡς ἂν πρὸς πλείονα
φυλακὴν
παρέθετο τῇ μητρὶ τῇ τοῦ βοηθουμένου· ἐκείνη καλῶς ποιοῦcα ἡνίκα
. . . . [. .] . . . [.] . . βουλημάτιον cυνιcταμένη ἠθέληcεν ⟦. . . . .⟧
πάντα τὰ εἴδη
ἀποκαταcταθῆναι τῇ παιδί. καὶ ἐξ(ῆς) ʿλέγοντοςʾ ὁ λογι(cτὴς) εἶ(πεν)· ⟦ἡ
διαθή⟧ τὸ βουλημάτιον διαλέγεται παραθή-
κην εἶναι καὶ δεῖν ἀποκαταcταθῆναι τῇ παιδὶ ἢ οὔ; Θ[έων] ῥ(ήτωρ) εἶ(πεν)·
οὕτως ἔχει καὶ ἀναγεινώcκω.

55 ὁ λογι(cτὴς) εἶ(πεν)· ἀνάγνωθι. καὶ ἀνεγνώcθη· μετὰ τὴν ἀνάγνωcιν ὁ
λογι(cτὴς) εἶ(πεν)· ʿτίςʾ ἐπήνεγκεν
τῇ λογιcτείᾳ τὸ βουλημάτιον πρὸς λύcιν; Θέων ῥ(ήτωρ) εἶ(πεν)· ἡμεῖς, παρ᾽
ᾗ Δημέας οὐκ ἀντεῖπεν.

---

39 The line will have begun slightly in ecthesis   40 Occasional traces survive, on loose fibres,
besides those indicated   42 l. ἐντυχίᾳ   44 l. ἐκδικίαν   45 εξ΄, περιτˊτωc
54 l. ἀναγινώcκω   55 A space (no diagonal stroke) before the second occurrence of ὁ λογι(cτὴς) εἶ(πεν)

ἀλλ' ἐπειδὴ ἐδόκει χρόνον διατρέχειν τῆς γυναικὸς τῆς ἐχούσης τὰ εἴδη
⟦ὑπερ⟧ `τῆς παρού-´
`cης Ταπατρίνιος ὑπερ´τιθεμένης διὰ τοῦτο ἐδέησεν ἡμᾶς εἰς ἀνάγκην
ἐλθόντας καὶ τῆς ἡγεμονίας
[.].[..].................[.]........[....]... πρὸ δίκης
μὲν μηδεμί-

60 αν..ιαν γείνεϲθαι, ἀποδοθῆναι δὲ τῇ παιδὶ κατὰ τὴν βούληϲιν τῆς μητρὸς τοῦ
`βοηθου[μ]ένου τὸ´ χρυϲίον. Δημέαϲ ἀπεκρ(ίνατο)· δέδωκα. Θέων ῥ(ήτωρ)
εἶ(πεν)· ἕϲτηκεν ἡ παῖϲ, ἕϲτηκεν δὲ
καὶ ἡ τὸ χρυϲίον ἔχουϲα. λοιπὸν οὐδὲν ὑπολίπεται ἢ ἀγανακτήϲαϲαν
τὴν ϲὴν ἀγχίνοιαν ὅτι τολμᾷ τιϲ ὑπεναντίον βουλήματοϲ γεγενημένου
διαπράξαϲθαι ἀποφήναϲθαι καὶ τὴν γυναῖκα τὴν διακατέχουϲαν ἀπο-

65 δοῦναι ἡμῖν· `ϲυνορᾷ γὰρ ἡ ϲὴ ἐμμέλια ὡϲ καὶ τέκνων δικαίῳ γεγένηται τὸ
γύναιον.´ Ἀμμώνιοϲ ῥ(ήτωρ) εἶ(πεν)· ϲυνχώρηϲον
εἰπεῖν. Θέων ῥ(ήτωρ) εἶ(πεν)· παραγράφομαι
.... Ἀμμώνιοϲ ῥ(ήτωρ) εἶ(πεν)· ἐγὼ πρὸϲ τὴν ἐναγωγὴν
λέγ⟦ει⟧ `ω´. Θέων ῥ(ήτωρ) εἶ(πεν)· ⟦οὐδὲν⟧
ληρεῖ· τίϲ ἐδίδαξ⟦εν⟧ `ατο´ αὐτὸν εἰπάτω. /ὁ λογιϲτὴϲ εἶ(πεν)· τίϲ
ὢν ἀντιλέγειϲ; Ἀμ-
μώνιοϲ ῥ(ήτωρ) εἶ(πεν)· ἐγὼ ἀντιλέγω πατὴρ ὢν τῆϲ παρούϲηϲ παιδὸϲ καὶ
ὅτι αἱ ἐντολαὶ
Ἀλεξάνδραϲ ἐπληρώθηϲαν. /ὁ λογιϲτὴϲ εἶ(πεν)· πρὸ πόϲου χρόνου ἡ
Ἀλεξάνδρα

70 ἀπεγένετο; Δημέαϲ ἀπεκρ(ίνατο)· πρὸ τριῶν ἐτῶν. Ἀμμώνιοϲ ῥ(ήτωρ)
εἶ(πεν)· ἔϲτωϲαν κύριαι
αἱ διαθῆκαι. καὶ ἑξῆϲ λέγοντοϲ /ὁ λογιϲτὴϲ εἶ(πεν)· εἴτε παρὰ τῷ πατρί ἐϲτιν
τὰ εἴδη
εἴτε παρὰ τῷ ἀνδρὶ ἢ παρὰ τῇ Ταπατρίνῃ τῇ παρούϲῃ δεήϲει κατὰ τὸ βου-
λη[μα]..[....].....[.].[.]α........[....].... ταῦτα ἔχειν
[.]....ν εἰ βούλεται ἀπὸ ἰδίαϲ γνώμηϲ τῷ [ἀν]δρὶ δοῦναι, ἐξουϲίαν ἔχει

75 ⟦εἰ δὲ⟧ `]..[.].[´τῷ ἀνδρὶ μήτηρ ⟦..⟧`..´ τέκνων γεγένηται ⟦ἀποδώϲι
ἕωϲ γὰρ⟧ `ὑπὲρ τοῦ ἀπαξαπλῶϲ´

---

60 l. γίνεϲθαι; υ of final τοῦ added   62 l. ὑπολείπεται   65 l. ἐμμέλεια   67 End of
ληρεῖ corr.

⟦μήτηρ τέκνων γέγονεν ἐξέσται αὐτῇ⟧ τῶν ἰδίων ἀπολαύειν ὧν
⟦ἔλαβεν⟧ ʽδιετάχθηʼ παρὰ τῆς γαμβρᾶς αὐτῆς τῆς ἀναπαυσαμένης.

[(ἔτους)] ι[θ]∫θ∫ʹ, Φαμενὼθ ιζʹ. πρὸς τῷ Καπιτωλίῳ. ἐπὶ παρόντων
Ὡρίωνος καὶ Ἡρᾶ ὑπηρετῶν καὶ Εὐλογίου παρέδρου. /ὁ λογιστὴς εἶ(πεν)·

80 πρόσταγμα τοῦ κυρίου μου τοῦ διασημοτάτου ἐπάρχου τῆς Αἰγύπτου
Φλαυίου

μ( ) Μάγνου ἐπήνεγκεν τῇ ἐμῇ μετριότητι Ἀϊθάλης ἀπὸ χώρας Μασσιτῶν
περὶ πραγμάτων διαφερόντων τῇ ἐπιτροπευομένῃ ὑπ' αὐτοῦ
ʽπαιδὶʼ ⟦Ε⟧Ἴσιτι καὶ διακατεχομέν⟦ου⟧ʽ ωνʼ ὑπὸ τοῦ παρόντος Φιλάμμωνος
καὶ τῶν ἀδελφῶν αὐτ[ο]ῦ κληρονόμων Βόκκα. ⟦καὶ τουν⟧ ἐν στέρνοις

85 ⟦ἔχων⟧ ʽ⟦οντες⟧ʼ ʽτοίνυν ἔχωνʼ τὸν ... τῆς [ἀνδ]ρ[είας] φ[ό]β[ον τοῦ
τηλικούτου ἄ]ρχοντος μετα-
δ[έ]δ[ω]κα μὲν τοῖς ἀντιδικοῦσι τὰ προστετα[γμένα], ἐνήγαγον δὲ καὶ αὐτοὺς
ἵνα γνῶμεν τίνα ἐστὶν ἃ διεπράξαντο πρὸς αὐτούς. Φιλάμμων ἀπεκρ(ίνατο)·
διελύθημεν καὶ ἔχω γραμμάτιον περὶ τούτου. /ὁ λογιστὴς εἶ(πεν)·
ἀναγνωσθήτω.
καὶ ἀνεγνώσθη ʽοὕτως ὡς περιέχειʼ· μετὰ τὴν ἀνάγνωσιν Ἀειθάλης
ἀπεκρ(ίνατο)· ἀπὸ τούτων

90 τῶν πραγμάτων ἐνωφίλησέν μοι ἀργυρίου τάλαντα πεντήκοντα
ὧν ʽκαὶʼ ἐγράψατό μοι εἴσω προθεσμίας ἀποδώσιν· καὶ ἔχω ʽτὸʼ γραμμάτιον
τῆς ὀφιλῆς.
/ὁ λογιστὴς εἶ(πεν)· τὸ πρόσταγμα τοῦ κυρίου μου τοῦ διασημοτάτου ἐπάρχου
τῆς Αἰγύπτου
Φλαυίου Μάγνου ἐπ[ὶ π]έρας [ἤ]χθ[η]· τὸ γὰρ γραμμάτιον τῆς μεταξὺ
γενομένης
διαλύσεως διελέγχ ʽεʼι⟦ν πε⟧ʽπεʼῖσθαι ἀμφότερα τὰ μέρα. ὅθεν
ἀναχωρήσειτε

95 ἐπὶ τοῖς γενομένοις ὑφ' ὑμῶν συμφώνοις. περὶ δέ γε οὗ φ⟦α⟧ʽηʼσιν ὁ Ἀειθάλης
γραμματίου τοῦ χρέους τῶν ταλάντων πεντήκοντα, κατὰ καιρὸν μετελεύσεται τὸν χρεώστην περὶ τῆς ἐνκʽεʼιμένης ὀφειλῆς.

78–97 These lines have been cancelled by a series of diagonal lines sloping down to the right
80 φλαυϊου   81 αϊθαλης; l. Ἀειθάλης, Μασιτῶν   84 βοκ'κα   89 περιεχει''   90 l.
ἐνωφείλησεν   91 l. ἅ, ἀποδώσειν, ὀφειλῆς   93 φλαυϊου   94 l. πεπεῖσθαι, μέρη; ει of
ἀναχωρήσειτε corr. from η by a different hand: l. ἀναχωρήσετε   97 αι of μετελεύσεται corr. from ε by
a different hand; ει of ὀφειλῆς corr. or rewritten

[(ἔτους) ιθ∫θ∫´,] Φ[α]μ[ε]νὼθ ιζ´. πρὸς τῷ λ[ο]χιϲτ[ηρίῳ.] ἐ[πὶ π]αρόντων Ὠρίωνος καὶ

Ἡρ[ᾶ] ὑπηρετῶν καὶ Εὐλογίου παρέδρο[υ]. Θ[έων ῥ(ήτωρ) εἶ(πεν)·]
Ταχῶνϲιϲ Ἀμόϊτος ἀπὸ κ[ώ-]

100   μης Ἰϲίου Παγγᾶ ἐπὶ παρόντι Cύρῳ Λίβυει. πολὺ τὸ παραλλάττον καθέ-
ϲτηκεν. Λίβυ[ϲ] γὰρ ὢν πάροικος [.].[.....].ι..ον περιπαιϲὼν τῇ ἀπουϲίᾳ
τῇ[ϲ]

συνηγορουμένης ἐπελήλυ[θ]εν [οἰκοπέδῳ] διαφέροντι αὐτῇ καὶ εἰ μὲν
δεϲπότης ἐν τούτῳ δικ........[.]....... ἀπὸ καταγραφῶν ἢ ἀπ[ὸ]
διαθήκης τοῦ πατρὸς.........πα..φ..[.].[c. 17   ]

105   [....].[..]..[..]...................[c. 5] τοιοῦτον ἐπιφέρει
ἀξ[ιοῦϲα]

αὐτὸν ἀναχωρεῖν τῆς βίας [[ἣν]] ῾ἧϲ´ καθ᾿ ἡμῶν ἐργάζεται. τούτου γὰρ ἕνεκα τῇ ἡγεμονίᾳ ἐντετυχήκαμεν, καὶ ἐκδικίας τυχεῖν ἐνταῦθα πάρεϲμεν.
/ὁ λογιϲτὴς εἶ(πεν)· τί πρὸς ταῦτα λέγει Cύρος; πόθεν διακατέχεις τὸ οἰκόπεδον; Cύρος ἀπεκρ(ίνατο)· ἀπὸ διαδοχῆς τοῦ πατρός. /ὁ λογιϲτὴς εἶ(πεν)· τὰ

110   γνωρίϲματα τῆς δεϲποτίας παραϲτῆϲον. Cύρος ἀπεκρ(ίνατο)· λεγ[έτ]ω ἀπ[ὸ]
τίνος εὔχεται. Θέων ῥ(ήτωρ) εἶ(πεν)· Ταχῶνϲ[ι]ς θυγάτηρ γείνεται Ἀμόϊ.
Ἀμόϊϲ δὲ

Cύρῳ ....[..]...[.].[.]..[..]..[.]...[.]......ειλε. /ὁ λογι(ϲτὴς)
εἶ(πεν)· μή τι-

[νες ϲυνεκλη]ρ[ο]νόμηϲαν τῇ γυναικί; Ταχῶνϲιϲ ἀπεκρ(ίνατο)·
ἀδελφὸν εἶχον, ἀπέθανεν. /ὁ λογι(ϲτὴς) εἶ(πεν)· ϲὺ μόνη ἐκληρονό-

115   μηϲάς ϲου τὸν πατέρα; ἀπεκρ(ίνατο)· ναί. /ὁ λογι(ϲτὴς) εἶ(πεν)· τὸ οἰκόπεδον
τοῦτ[ο]

τίνος ἐϲτίν, μητρῷον ἢ πατρῷον; Ταχῶνϲις ἀπεκρ(ίνατο)· ἀπὸ τοῦ πάππο[υ]
ἔϲχεν ὁ πατήρ μου, ἀπὸ τοῦ πατρὸς ἐγώ. /ὁ λογι(ϲτὴς) εἶ(πεν)· μή τι ὁ
ἀδελφός ϲου

πέπρακεν περιών; Ταχῶνϲις ἀπεκρ(ίνατο)· αὐ. Θέων ῥ(ήτωρ) εἶ(πεν)·
παραϲτηϲάτω τῆς

δεϲπ[ο]τίας τὰς ἀποδίξεις ἢ ἀν[α]χωρηϲ[ά]τω. Cύρος ἀπεκρ(ίνατο)· μετὰ
τὴν

---

100 l. Λίβυϊ; παραλατ᾿τον   101 l. περιπεϲών   102 Marginal ink traces may be accidental
110 l. δεϲποτείας   111 Unexplained ink traces above ετ of εὔχεται; l. γίνεται   118 l. οὐ
119 l. δεϲποτείας, ἀποδείξεις

120 αὔριον ἐπιφέρω, οὐερεδάριος γὰρ ἐλθὼν ἤγαγέν με ἀπὸ Ἀλεξαν-
δρε[ί]ας. /ὁ λογιστὴς εἶ(πεν)· Λίβυς δὲ τῷ γένει εἶ; ἀπεκρ(ίνατο)· ναί. /ὁ
λογ(ιστὴς) εἶ(πεν)·
καὶ αὐτὸς ὁμολογεῖ ξένος εἶναι τῆς πολιτίας· καὶ μέμνημαι ὡς
τῆς γυναικὸς κέλευσιν ἐπενε[γ]κούσης τῇ ἐμῇ μετριότητι τοῦ
κυρίου μου τοῦ διακοσμήσαντος τὸν θρόνον τῆς ἡγεμονίας ζ[α]β[ιν]ιανο[ῦ]

125 .[.]..[.....].[.......].[*c.* 15   ]... κελεύειν προ[..].ςι
[....]....[..]. ἐπεὶ τοίνυν [.].[.....]... σήμερον ἐπὶ τῶν τόπ[ων]
παρακεκομίσθαι αὐτῷ τὰ βιβλία καὶ μετὰ τὴν αὔριον ἐποίσιν
τὰς ἀποδίξεις, δύναται [..]....κων δεσπόζειν κατὰ τὰ
ἐνκίμενα μέρη. εἰ δὲ μὴ περιποιῇ, ἀλλότρειός ἐστιν

130 τοῦ οἰκοπέδου τοῦ ἐλθόντος εἰς τὸ γύναιον ἀπὸ κληρονομί[ας]
[.].[*c.* 12   ]...[..]β[*c.* 9   ]ν.

ὑπατείας Πρόκλου καὶ Παυλίνου τῶν λαμπροτάτων.
{ὑπατείας}
/(ἔτους) ιθϛ θϛ΄, Φαμενὼθ κα΄. ἐν τῷ Ἀδριανίῳ. ἐπὶ παρόντων
Βερεγ[ι]κι[α]ν[ο]ῦ β[ο]ηθ(οῦ)

135 /καὶ Θεοδώρου τοῦ καὶ Ὠρίωνος καὶ Ἀμμωνᾶ καὶ Ἰσχυρίωνος Ἀνουβίωνος
/τῶν τεσσάρων σφραγιστῶν καὶ Διογένους ταβελλίωνος καὶ Ὡρ[ί]ωνος
/ὑπηρέτου. Διογένης ταβελλίων εἶ(πεν)· Τανεχ[ῶ]ντις ἐπινόσως ἔχ⟦ων⟧
ʼ[ου]ςαʼ
/μετεκαλέσατό με καὶ ἠξίωσεν γραφῆναι αὐτῇ ⟦τὸ⟧ β[ο]υλημάτιον τῆς
/....[..]. αὐτῆς [*c.* 18   ].. Ἡρακλᾶς βιβλιοφύλαξ εντο[

140 /..[....]..[.]..[..] τοῦ βίου ἀπέλθοι ..[......] πρὸς λύσιν. ἐπεὶ
τοίνυν τε-
/⟨τε⟩λεύτηκεν, σήμερον ἐπιφέρεται τὸ βουλημάτιον τῇ σῇ ἐμμελείᾳ πρὸς
/λύσιν. /ὁ λογιστὴς εἶ(πεν)· σύ, Ἡρακλᾶ, ἐνε[χειρί]σθης τὸ γραμμάτιον
ἐπενέγκαι
/πρὸς λύσιν; ἀπεκρ(ίνατο)· ναί. /ὁ λο[γισ]τὴς Διογένι εἶ(πεν)· κατὰ γνώμην
τῆς Τανε-
/χώντιδο`ς΄ συνεστήσω τὸ γραμμάτιον; ἀπεκρ(ίνατο)· ναί. /ὁ λογιστὴς
εἶ(πεν)· τί-

120 l. μοι   121 Simply λογ seemingly   122 l. πολιτείας   127 l. ἐποίσειν   128 l.
ἀποδείξεις   129 l. ἐγκείμενα, ἀλλότριος   134 l. Ἀδριανείῳ; β[ο]ηθ   135 Ἀμμωνᾶ corr.
from Ἀμμωνος   139 After αὐτῆς occasional traces survive on loose and tangled fibres   143 l.
Διογένει   144 δο of -χώντιδο`ς΄ written over ος

145 ⸍νων παρόντων; ἀπεκρ(ίνατο)· τῶν cφραγιcτῶν. /ὁ λογι(cτὴc) εἶ(πεν)·
πόcοι εἰc[ὶ]
⸍cφραγιcταί; Διογένηc εἶ(πεν)· ἑπτά, τέccαρεc δὲ πάρειcι. /ὁ λογι(cτὴc)
εἶ(πεν)· ὑπο-
⸍χ[ρ]α̣[ψάτωcαν οἱ] τ̣έ̣c̣[cα]ρ̣[ε]c ἐ̣[πεγνω]κ̣έ̣ναι ἑ̣[α]ν̣τ̣ῶ̣ν̣ τ̣ὰ̣c̣ c̣φραγῖδαc.
καὶ τῶν̣
[⸍]π̣α̣ρ̣ό̣ντ̣[ων] cφραγιcτῶν̣ ὑποcημιωcαμένων ἐπεγνωκέναι
⸍ἑ̣α̣υτῶν τὰc cφραγῖδαc, /ὁ λογι(cτὴc) εἶ(πεν)· λυθήτω τὸ γραμμάτιον
150 ⸍κ[αὶ] ἀναγνωcθήτω. καὶ γραμματίου Τανεχῶντι ᾿δ᾿οc ἀπὸ τῶν
⸍αὐτόθι λυθέντοc ᾿καὶ ἀναγνωcθέντοc᾿ κεχρονιcμένου εἰc ᾿τὴ[ν] [[αὐτὴν]]
ἐνεcτῶcαν᾿ ὑπατείαν, Φαμενὼθ κ´,
⸍μετὰ τὴν ἀνάγνωcιν /ὁ λογι(cτὴc) [ε]ἶ(πεν)· τὸ [μ]ὲν cῶμα τῆc
κ[ατο]ιχομένηc
⸍τῇ ὁcίᾳ παραδοθήcεται· οἱ δὲ ἐνγεγραμμένοι κληρονόμοι φρον-
⸍τιοῦ[c]ι τὰ ἀντίγραφα διδόντεc τ̣ο̣ῦ βουλ̣ηματίου λ[α]μβάνειν τὸ αὐθεντι-
155 [⸍κὸν] . . . . . [.] . . . . [..]. [. . .]. [. .]. μ̣ο̣ν γενέcθαι.

(ἔτουc) ιθ⌠θ⌡ϛ´, Φαμενὼθ κβ´. πρὸc τῷ Καπιτωλίῳ. ἐπὶ παρόντων
Ὠρίωνοc ὑπηρέτου καὶ Εὐλογίο̣υ παρέ̣δρου, Ἀμμώνιοc ῥ(ήτωρ) εἶ(πεν)·
Χαιρήμων
ὁ καὶ Ἰcχυρίων βουλευτὴc τῆ[c c. 7] π̣ό̣λεωc ἐπὶ παρούcῃ [[.]]Θαήcει
Ἡρακλᾶτοc ἀπὸ τῆcδε τῆc {δετηc} πόλεωc. ὑπάρχει τῷ βοηθουμένῳ
160 οἰκία ἐπὶ τῆc αὐτῆc πόλεωc ἣν . . . . ον Ἑρμείαc γεωμέτρηc
υἱὸc Παπιρίωνοc κα̣ὶ . . . . . . ο̣. .ςηc ἀλλ᾿ ἐπὶ τὴν Ὄαcιν ἐκεῖνοc διαβὰc
[c. 7] . . . . ο̣γ̣η̣ . . . . . [. . . . . .] . . .ο̣ν̣ ὑπὸ cημάντροιc ποιήcαc
αὐ-
τὴν . . . . [. .] . . . . νηνδε . . . . [.] . . . . . . ι̣α̣ν τοὺc τόπουc ἔχειν
ἀξιοῦντεc καὶ τὰ cήμαντρα [[λυθῆναι]] ᾿ἀφαιρεθῆναι᾿. προνοίᾳ τῆc cῆc
ἐμμελείαc προc-
165 τέτακται τοῦτο γείνεcθαι, καὶ ἀξιοῦμεν ἐπείπερ ἀπολίπεται cήμερον
ἐν κυρίᾳ ὁ̣ Ἑρμείαc τῆc μητρὸc παρούcηc ὅτι δὴ μάλιcτα καὶ παῖc
ὑποχίριόc ἐcτιν τὸ πρό[c]ταγμα ἐπὶ πέραc ἀχθ[ῆ]ναι. /ὁ λογιcτὴc εἶ(πεν)·

148 l. ὑποcημειωcαμένων   151 φ of Φαμενώθ corr.   153 l. ἐγγεγραμμένοι
161 αλλ· rather than ἀλλά?   164 cήμαντρα: τ rewritten above the line   165 l. γίνεcθαι, ἀπολείπεται
167 l. ὑποχείριοc

τί λέγει Θαῆcιc; π[ο]ῦ Ἑρμείαc ὁ c[ὸc] υἱόc; ἀπεκρ(ίνατο)· εἰc Ὄαcιν

         ἀ[π]ῆλθεν·

ἀπεκηρύξα ‘μεν’ αὐτόν· οὐκ ἔχω πρᾶγμα πρὸc αὐτὸν οὐδὲ ὁ πατὴρ

170 αὐτοῦ προδ[..].........των [ἀπ]επεμψά[. .]‘[μ]εθα’ αὐτὸν παρὰ τῇ

         ἡγεμονίᾳ

[*c.* 22   /ὁ λο]γι(cτὴc) εἶ(πεν)· οἱ νόμοι κελεύ-

[ουcιν ..].....ον ἀποχα...[*c.* 5].λιων. ἐπεὶ οὖν

[*c.* 6].....[.].........ἡγεμονικὴν περὶ τοῦ ἔχειν

τὴν οἰκίαν αὐτοῦ καὶ ..[*c.* 7].....ει κατὰ ἐνοίκηcιν

175 Ἑρμείαc ἠξίωcεν δὲ εξαρι.[*c.* 7]..το⟦υc τόπουc⟧‘.....’

         ἐκταγηcετ[..]

..ι...ιοc οcε..[*c.* 5]..ποιήcεται τὰ cκεύη ‘ἐκείνου’ καὶ εἰάcει ενεν[0–3]

.................[..]ον τόπουc Χαιρήμ⟦ων⟧‘ονα’.

Ἀμμ[ώνιο]c ῥ(ήτωρ) εἶ(πεν)· ἀξιο[ῦ]μεν ...[.]..[.]..[*c.* 8]ν

         δημοcι..[0–5]

[*c.* 14   ]...............ρ.[*c.* 15   ]

180 /ὁ λογι(cτὴc) εἶ(πεν)· ἐν τῇ αὔριον γενήcεται ὃ ἠξιώcατε.

(ἔτουc) ιθ∫ θ∫, Φαμενὼθ ιθ. πρὸc τῷ γυμναcίῳ. ἐπὶ παρόντων

Καπιτωλίνου ἄρξαντοc τῶν αὐτόθι καὶ Cαραπίωνοc Ἑρμείου καὶ

Ἰcίωνοc Ἥρατοc καὶ Ἀμοϊτᾶ Cιλβανοῦ καὶ Ὡρίωνοc Ὡρίωνοc τῶν δ′

cφραγιcτῶν καὶ Ὡρίωνοc ὑπηρέτου ‘καὶ Εὐλογίου παρέδρου’, Ποιμένιοc

         ῥ(ήτωρ) εἶ(πεν)· τὴν κοινὴν ‘καὶ τεταγμένην’ ἐπὶ

185 πάντων ὑπὸ τηc...[*c.* 15   ].του βίου ὑπεcτη[.]..

[....].....[.]..[*c.* 22   ]......ηcεωc τῆc ἑαυ-

[το]ῦ γνώμηc ...η.......[..].... καὶ προcκαλεcάμενοc τὸν

         αἰδεcιμώτα-

τον Καπιτωλῖνον βουλευτὴν τῆcδε τῆc πολιτίαc ἐνεχίριcεν ἐντο-

λὰc παραcχ[ό]μενοc ⟦ι.⟧ εἰ τοῦ βίου ἀπέλθοι ἐπενεγκεῖν τῇ cῇ

190 ἐντρεχίᾳ κατὰ τὸ ἔθοc πρὸc τὸ λυθῆναι καὶ γνωcθῆναι τὰ ἐν αὐτῷ

γεγραμμένα. τούτου ἕνεκα ἐνταῦθα ἀπήντηcεν τὴν ἐκίνου

γνώμην ἀποπληρῶν καὶ ἀξιοῖ τὴν λύcιν τοῦ βουλήματοc κατὰ

νόμουc γενέcθαι. /ὁ λογιcτὴc εἶ(πεν)· τί λέγει ὁ παρὼν Καπιτωλῖνοc;

cοὶ παρέθετο ὁ ἀναπαυcάμενοc τὸ γραμμάτιον τοῦτο; ἀπεκρ(ίνατο)· ναί.

176 l. ἐάcει   188 l. πολιτείαc, ἐνεχείριcεν   189 Unexplained high traces above and to right
of deletion, and above final c of preceding word   190 l. ἐντρεχείᾳ   191 l. ἐκείνου

195 [　　　　　　　　c. 40　　　　　　　　] ἑπτὰ μέν εἰσι
[　　　c. 13　　　]. . . . . . .[. .]. . . . . κυρια. /ὁ λογιστὴς εἶ(πεν)·
[τίς ἐστιν ὁ συστη]σάμενος ταβελλίων; Ποιμ[ένιος ῥ(ήτωρ)] εἶ(πεν)· ἐγώ.
　　　　　　　　　　　　　　　/ὁ λογισ[τὴς εἶ(πεν)· ἕκασ-]
τ[ο]ς τῶν παρόντων σφραγιστῶν ὑπογραψ[ά]τ[ω ἐπ]ε[γνωκέναι ἑαυ-]
τοῦ τὰ γράμματα καὶ τὴν σφραγῖδα. καὶ τῶν παρ[ό]ντων σφραγιστῶν]
200 ὑποσημιωσαμένων ἐπεγνωκέναι ἑαυτῶν [τὰς σφραγῖδας,]
/ὁ λογιστὴς εἶ(πεν)· λυθήτω καὶ ἀνα[γνωσθήτω τὸ γ]ραμμάτιον.
καὶ ἀναγνωσθέντος γραμματίου φ. . .[. .]. [. . .] Βησαρίωνος οὐετρανοῦ
καταμένοντος ἐν τῆδε τῆ πόλει [κεχρονισ]μένου εἰς ὑπατείαν τῶν
δεσπ[ο]τῶν ἡμῶν Κρίσπ[ου] κ[αὶ Κωνσταντίνο]υ τῶν ἐπιφανεστάτων
205 [Καισάρων τὸ γ΄, month and day, Πο]ι[μ]ένιος ῥ(ήτωρ) εἶ(πεν)· ἀναγνω[σ-]
θήτω καὶ τα. . . . . .ν. . . .[c. 5]. [. . .]. [. .]. τὸ γενόμενον ὑπὸ
.[.].[. . . .]. . .[. .]χρεων ἀπο[.]. . . . . . ἀξιοῦμεν δὲ τὰ
ἀντίγραφα [δ]ιδόντες λαβεῖν τὸ αὐθεντικὸν πρὸς ἀσφάλιαν
τῶν κληρονόμων. /ὁ λογιστὴ[ς εἶ(πεν)·] τὸ μὲν σῶμ[α] τοῦ κατοιχομένου
210 τῆ ὁσίᾳ παραδοθήσεται· ἀνεγνώσθη δὲ παρὰ τῆ ἐμῆ μετριότητι τὸ
γραμμάτιον τὸ γενόμενον ὑπὸ Βησαρίωνος οὐετρανοῦ καὶ δύνανται
οἱ κληρονόμοι διδόναι .[. .]. . .ι τὰ ἴδια τοῦ βουλήματος πρὸς κληρο-
[. .]. [. . . . .]. [. . . . . .]. [. . . . . .]. . . . . πρὸς ἀσφάλιαν

　　　　　　　·　　　·　　　·　　　·
　　　　　　　　·　　　·　　　·

　　　　　　　　　　　]. .[. . .]. υρος ἀπεκρ(ίνατο)· [vac.?]
215　　　　　　　　　　　]. . . . .[
　　　　　　　　　　]. α. . . . . καταγραφῆναι . . . .
　　　　　　　　　　　　　] /ὁ λογιστὴς εἶ(πεν)·
　　　]. . . . . . .ιακαρ. . . .[　　　]. . .ςιν. /ὁ λογιστὴ[ς εἶ(πεν)·]
　　　　　　]. . . . . .[　　　　　　]. . . Πεκῦσις ἀνὴρ [
　　　　　　　　　　　　　]　　(vac.)　　　[
220　　　　　　　　　　　　]. . . . .[

　　　　　·　　　·　　　·　　　·

200 l. ὑποσημειωσαμένων　　　208 l. ἀσφάλειαν; ασφαλ`ε´ιαν?　　　210 High spot of ink before
ἀνεγνώσθη, perhaps accidental　　212 ἴδια　　　213 l. ἀσφάλειαν　　　219 Possibly a further
letter after ρ?

. . . .

πηρέτου καὶ Εὐλογίου π[α]ρ[έδρου
'Ισίου Παγγᾶ. ἡ μὲν εχ. . . . . [.] . . . . [
ὑπομ[[ο]]νημ[
ἔλεγχον παραϲτη . . . . [
225   μένων τοῦ οἰκ[*c.* 7   ] . . . [
φυλακίοιϲ κατακει . . . . [
. . ιουμεν ιϲ . . . [
[.] . . ντο οικο . . [

. . . .

222 παγ'γα   224 ελεγ'χον   226 l. (-)φυλακείοιϲ?

'Minutes for the month of Phamenoth of the year 19 and 9, before Dioscurides, *curator*, for filing.

'[Date, place.] In the presence of . . . leading citizen(s) and Tiro son of Heracleides and the majority of the *demotae*, through Sarapion son of Taus. . . and Parammon and Ammon and Ammonius and others. The *curator* said, "In the beginning you were given orders by Sabinianus who then adorned the throne of the praesidiate that either the landowners or the councillors should collect a sum of money from the *pagani*; you collected as you were instructed. But now I have received a letter from the Nobility of my lord Flavius Magnus, *vir perfectissimus*, prefect of Egypt, . . . in full to the last penny. Since, then, I summoned you (as) the original purchasers of the tunics named and sent by the said former *praeses* Sabinianus to the end that the *demotae* may get the money decreed for them by the Virtue of my aforesaid lord Flavius Magnus, *vir perfectissimus*, prefect of Egypt, I urge you to give them the money, and if the councillors or landowners are willing to buy the tunics which you said you had brought, in accordance with the instructions from superior authority, they may sell them for what price they wish." Leucadius answered, "My lord Sabinianus, *vir perfectissimus*, former *praeses*, ordered us to go to Tyre and carry out the compulsory purchase of the *paragaudae* and I sent the assistant in place of myself and he has effected the purchase at a price per tunic of 65,000 den. excluding expenses, and the tunics were brought and they are here, and if you want (me) to bring them to you and to distribute them to whom you wish, just say; all I want is a guarantee . . ." The *curator* said, "The *pagani* are not taking the tunics since they were not ordered to take them, but the money which they gave unwillingly. If, then, you have collected the tunics, you can pass them on to your fellow councillors who were ordered to buy them or to the landowners, and give the money to the *pagani*; do so." Leucadius, prytanis, said, "I have nothing to do with the *pagani*. The *paragaudae* were collected; take them, give me a guarantee and give them to whom you want." The *curator* said, ". . . to give (it) back to the last penny." Leucadius, prytanis, said, "You take the tunics and sell them or do what you like; just give me a guarantee. I have done my duty." The *curator* said, "How many tunics did you collect with the 7,000 talents from the *demotae*?" Leucadius, prytanis, said, "Altogether 150 tunics were collected, at 65,000 den. per tunic plus 5,000 den. for expenses. I give you the figures per unit as ordered by my lord Sabinianus, *vir perfectissimus*, former *praeses*." The *curator* said, ". . . or give the tunics to whom you want for what price you want; it is absolutely necessary, in accordance with the order of my lord Flavius Magnus, *vir perfectissimus*, prefect of Egypt, that the *demotae* get back their own money to the last penny."'

(39-77) 'Year 19 and 9, Phamenoth 7. In the consulship of Proculus and Paulinus. [Location, in the presence of . . .]phanes, assessor. Theon, advocate, said, "(My client is) Sarapion son of Aphynchius, against his wife Helen, who is present. My client used the petitionary procedure, pleading before the then office of *praeses*, to all appearances because he observed his wife was being defrauded, but in reality he regarded these objects which had been transferred by him to his wife as his own property and so with all the pressure he could muster he employed the same petition to obtain satisfaction." While he continued speaking, the *curator* said, "It was superfluous for him to petition the *praeses*. Since the law is clear that the local judges are to hear such(?) cases, I accord a hearing to the affair and will listen to the suit." Theon, advocate, said, "The wife has come forward, [contradicting?] what has been said and is being said by her husband. He, then, on getting hold of his own children's gold jewellery, deposited it with his own wife. As though for greater security the girl deposited these goods with my client's mother. She, acting well, when . . . making up a will wished all the objects to be restored to the girl." While he continued speaking, the *curator* said, "Does the will proclaim it to be a deposit, and that it must be restored to the girl, or not?" Theon, advocate, said, "It does so, and I will read it." The *curator* said, "Read it." It was read; after the reading, the *curator* said, "Who brought the will to the *curator's* office for opening?" Theon, advocate, said, "We did, and Demeas raised no objections there. But when it seemed that time was running on and that the woman who held the objects—Tapatrinis, who is present—was delaying, because of this we were forced to . . . the office of the *praeses* . . . let there be no . . . before judgement, but let the gold be given back to the girl in accordance with the wish of my client's mother." Demeas answered, "I gave it to her." Theon, advocate, said, "The girl has come forward, and so has she who has the gold. Nothing further remains than for Your Sagacity, annoyed that someone dares to act in defiance of an actual will, to declare that the woman holding (the objects) must return them to us; for Your Grace observes that the young woman has become (entitled to act?) by the *ius liberorum*." Ammonius, advocate, said, "Permit me to speak." Theon, advocate, said, "I object . . . " Ammonius, advocate, said, "I speak against the charge." Theon, advocate, said, "He is talking rubbish; let him say who gave him instructions." The *curator* said, "In what capacity do you speak in opposition?" Ammonius, advocate, said, "I speak in opposition as the father of the girl who is present, and because the instructions of Alexandra were carried out." The *curator* said, "How long ago did Alexandra die?" Demeas answered, "Three years ago." Ammonius, advocate, said, "Let the dispositions of the will be valid." While he continued speaking, the *curator* said, "Whether the objects are with the father or with the husband or with Tapatrine here present, it will be necessary in accordance with the will . . . If she wishes of her own volition to give them to her husband, she has the right, [since?] she has become mother of three(?) children to her husband, of the absolute enjoyment as her own property of the things bequeathed her by her deceased mother-in-law."'

(78-97) 'Year 19 and 9, Phamenoth 17. At the Capitolium, in the presence of Horion and Heras, assistants, and Eulogius, assessor. The *curator* said, "An order of my lord the prefect of Egypt, Flavius Magnus, *vir perfectissimus*, has been brought before my humble self by Aeithales from the territory of the Mastitae, concerning property belonging to the child Isis, who is in his guardianship, which is being detained by Philammon, here present, and his brothers, heirs of Boccas. So, keeping in my heart the fear of the Nobility of so great an official, I have communicated his orders to the parties in the case, and I have also brought them in so that we may know what mutual arrangements they have come to." Philammon answered, "We made an agreement, and I have a document about this." The *curator* said, "Let it be read." And it was read as follows. After the reading, Aeithales answered, "Out of this property he owed me fifty talents in money, which he wrote to me that he would repay within the appointed time, and I have the document attesting the debt." The *curator* said, "The order of my lord the prefect of Egypt, Flavius Magnus, *vir perfectissimus*, has been carried out; the document of discharge between you shows both sides to be in agreement. Wherefore you will depart, abiding by the conditions of the agreements made between you. As regards the document which Aeithales mentions concerning the debt of fifty talents, at the proper time he is to sue the debtor regarding the obligation contained therein."'

(98-131) 'Year 19 and 9, Phamenoth 17. At the accounts-office. In the presence of Horion and Heras, assistants, and Eulogius, assessor. Theon, advocate, said, "(My client is) Tachonsis daughter of Amois from the village of Ision Panga, against Syrus, a Libyan, who is present. Great is the aberration that has occurred. For being a Libyan immigrant . . . chancing on the absence of my client, he has occupied a piece of property belonging to her, and if (he is confirmed?) in control of it . . . from registrations of cession or from her father's will . . . requesting(?) that he desist from the forceful behaviour he uses against us. Because of this we petitioned the office of the *praeses* and we are present here to obtain satisfaction." The *curator* said, "What does Syrus say to this? On what grounds do you occupy the property?" Syrus answered, "In succession to her(?) father." The *curator* said, "Produce the evidence to justify your control.' Syrus answered, "Let her say from whom she claims (control)." Theon, advocate, said, "Tachonsis is the daughter of Amois. Amois . . . Syrus . . ." The *curator* said, "[? No one else] inherited along with the woman?" Tachonsis answered, "I used to have a brother, but he died." The *curator* said, "Did you alone inherit from your father?" She answered, "Yes." The *curator* said, "Whose was this property, your mother's or your father's?" Tachonsis answered, "My father had it from my grandfather, and I from my father." The *curator* said, "Your brother sold nothing while he was still alive?"

Tachonsis answered, "No." Theon, advocate, said, "Let him produce the proofs to justify his control or let him withdraw." Syrus answered, "The day after tomorrow I will produce them, for a courier came and brought them to me from Alexandria." The *curator* said, "You are Libyan by race?" He answered, "Yes." The *curator* said, "He admits himself that he is foreign to this community; and I recall how when the woman presented my humble self with the order of my lord Sabinianus, who then adorned the throne of the praesidiate . . . Since therefore [he declares(?)] that today the documents have been conveyed to him locally and that the day after tomorrow he will bring the proofs, he can control . . . in respect of the specified sections. If he does not procure (them), he is to have nothing to do with the property coming to the woman by inheritance . . . "'

(132-3) 'In the consulship of Proculus and Paulinus, *viri clarissimi*. In the consulship (*vac.*)'

(134-55) 'Year 19 and 9, Phamenoth 21. In the temple of Hadrian, in the presence of Berenicianus, aide, and Theodorus alias Horion and Ammonas and Ischyrion son of Anubion, the four of them signatories, and Diogenes, notary, and Horion, assistant. Diogenes, notary, said, "Tanechontis, falling ill, summoned me and requested a will to be written for her . . . Heraclas, keeper of the records . . . in the case of her death, with its presentation(?) for opening. Since therefore she has died, today the will is presented to Your Grace for opening." The *curator* said, "You, Heraclas, were entrusted with presenting the document for opening?" He answered, "Yes." The *curator* said to Diogenes, "Did you make out the document in accordance with the wishes of Tanechontis?" He answered, "Yes." The *curator* said, "In the presence of whom?" He answered, "The signatories." The *curator* said, "How many signatories are there?" Diogenes said, "Seven, and four are present." The *curator* said, "Let the four subscribe that they have recognized their own seals." When the signatories who were present had subscribed that they had recognized their own seals, the *curator* said, "Let the document be opened and read." And the document of Tanechontis, of local origin, being opened and read, dated to the current consulship, Phamenoth 20, after the reading the *curator* said, "The body of the deceased will be handed over for burial; the inscribed heirs will see to it that they provide copies of the will when they obtain the original . . . ".'

(156-80) 'Year 19 and 9, Phamenoth 22. At the Capitolium, in the presence of Horion, assistant, and Eulogius, assessor. Ammonius, advocate, said, "(My client is) Chaeremon alias Ischyrion, councillor of the city of . . . , against Thaesis daughter of Heraclas, from this city, who is present. There belongs to my client a house in the same city which Hermias, surveyor, son of Papirion . . . But he crossed over to the Oasis . . . putting it under seals . . . requesting possession of the property and that the seals should be removed. By Your Grace's forethought it has been commanded that this should happen, and since today Hermias is absent on the appointed day but he is very much a boy under his mother's control and she is present we request that your instruction be put into effect." The *curator* said, "What does Thaesis say? Where is your son Hermias?" She answered, "He went off to the Oasis. We renounced him; I have nothing to do with him, nor did his father . . . we repudiated him before the court of the *praeses* . . . " The *curator* said, "The laws order . . . Since therefore [Chaeremon has obtained a decision of?] the *praeses* concerning the possession of his own house, and . . . " Ammonius, advocate, said, "We request . . . " The *curator* said, "Tomorrow it shall be as you have requested."'

(181-213) 'Year 19 and 9, Phamenoth 19. At the gymnasium, in the presence of Capitolinus, local former magistrate, and Sarapion son of Hermias and Ision son of Heras and Amoitas son of Silvanus and Horion son of Horion, the four of them signatories, and Horion, assistant, and Eulogius, assessor. Poemenius, advocate, said, "The common . . . ordained for all . . . his own wish . . . and summoning the most-respected Capitolinus, councillor of this community, he provided him with his instructions, entrusting him in the case of his death with their presentation to Your Experience as is customary so that what was written therein might be opened and read. For this reason he has presented himself here in fulfilment of (Besarion's) wish and requests that the opening of the will should take place in accordance with the laws." The *curator* said, "What does Capitolinus, here present, say? Did the deceased deposit this document with you?" He answered, "Yes." [The *curator* said, "How many are the signatories?" He answered,] "They are seven, . . . " The *curator* said, "Who is the notary who drew up the will?" Poemenius, advocate, said, "I am." The *curator* said, "Let each of the signatories here present subscribe that he has recognized his own script and seal." When the signatories present had subscribed that they had recognized their own seals, the *curator* said, "Let the document be opened and read." After the reading of the document of . . . Besarion, veteran resident in this city, dated to the consulship of our masters Crispus and Constantinus the most noble Caesars for the 3rd time, [month and day], Poemenius, advocate, said, "Let there be read also the . . . and we beg to obtain the original, subject to our providing copies, for the security of the heirs." The *curator* said, "The body of the deceased will be handed over for burial. The document made by Besarion, veteran, has been read in the presence of my humble self, and the heirs may give . . . ".'

1 The writing is at the right-hand edge, upside-down in comparison with 2–4, and washed out except for the first letter. Was λογιϲτοῦ intended? The form of the initial (undeleted) letter resembles λ of λογιϲτοῦ in 4.

2 The line is in the same hand as 3–4 but written much smaller. μη(νόϲ) transcribed by analogy with 3. Thereafter only scanty ink traces, and the reduced scale makes estimating the number of letters difficult. It is not clear how far the writer went; the right half of the line is blank, and if this were an abandoned title he might have stopped at an otherwise irrational point. There is no obvious reason why the title should have been written twice otherwise.

3–4 Cf. **3759** 42. There is no day of the month in that instance. After φ in 3, the rest of Φαμϵ[ν]ωθ is very uncertain indeed.

4 The line begins below ἐπί in 3.

5 Traces of the first half of the line are extremely scanty, and indicated numbers of letters present or absent are little more than conjecture. We expect year-sign, year-numbers (19 and 9, cf. l. 39 etc.), month (Phamenoth, cf. 3), and a day-number (7 (cf. l. 39) or lower(?)), and location (locations elsewhere are ἐν τῷ Ἀδριανίῳ (134), πρὸϲ τῷ Καπιτωλίῳ (78, 156), λογιϲτηρίῳ (98), and γυμναϲίῳ (181)); but I cannot claim to recognize any of this here.

ἐπὶ παρόντων. This formula occurs several times in this text (78, 98, 134, 156, and 181); also in **3757** 3, **3759** 1, and **3767** 1. See 156–8 n. below.

The second half of the line will have contained names and possibly titles; damage is such that scarcely any letters can be certainly identified.

αρχο. Cf. XXII **2346** 23 ἀρχοντικῶν? Note δημοτῶν there which occurs in the next line here.

6 προπολ(ιτευομένων) (or -ου?). See A. K. Bowman, *The Town Councils of Roman Egypt*, esp. 155–8; a different view of πολιτευόμενοι is given by H. Geremek, *Anag.* 1 (1981) 231–47. See too LI **3627** 1 n.

δημοτῶν. The same group are elsewhere described as παγανοί (9, 11, etc.); compare especially 13 and 38 (δημότας) with 25 (παγανοί). The words here appear to be used interchangeably to describe those with no official positions, in effect the lower classes. The interchangeability excludes any sense of town-dwellers contrasted with country-dwellers (XXII **2346** 23 n.). For παγανοί see further *ZPE* 62 (1986) 66–7.

The feminine Ταυϲ-, if right, is unexpected.

8 Sabinianus was already known as *praeses Mercurianae* (for this, and not *Herculia*, as his area of authority see J. D. Thomas, *BASP* 21 (1984) 225–34), see J. Lallemand, *L'Administration civile* 256. To the references there given add XLV **3261**, which provides our latest date for him in office (AD 324). He is out of office by the date of the present hearing (late February–early March 325) and the text does not indicate the interval that has elapsed since he was in office.

κτήτορας. Lat. *possessores*. See A. Segré, *Traditio* 5 (1947) 113–14; A. C. Johnson and L. C. West, *Byzantine Egypt: Economic Studies* 13–16.

9 παγανούς. Cf. 6 n.; G. H. R. Horsley, *New Documents Illustrating Early Christianity* i no. 44.

ἀπῃτήϲατϵ [κ]α[θ]ώς. The reading is suspect. ϵ is the difficult letter: traces are attributed to it (as an extended centre bar) which if attributed to the word following would mean that the space and traces would be too extensive for καθώς.

10 ἀνδρείας. See **3757** 9 n.

11 A crease (where the roll was flattened) has caused severe damage to the first half of this line. Traces are visible almost all the way along but no letters are certain and what is transcribed is very conjectural. ἀποκαταϲταθῆναι may be a possibility.

μέχρι ἀϲϲαρίου ἑνός. Again in 30 and 38. Cf. **3756** 12 n.

12 ϲυνωνητάϲ. For ϲυνωνή (*coemptio*) see J.-M. Carrié, *Proc. XVI Congr. Papyrology* (1981) 432–3.

ϲτιχαρίων. For *vestis militaris* see Carrié, op. cit. 434–5; also XLVIII **3424** 2 n., 9 n. Carrié's interpretation of the system is in large part supported by **3758**. For prices see 21 n. below.

14 ἀρετῆς. Later the use of this honorific becomes more diffuse, but in the late third and fourth centuries its application is confined to the prefect, *praeses*, *rationalis* (IX **1204** 4; P. Harr. 160. 8 (see *ZPE* 37 (1980) 237)), and *dux* (VIII **1103** 4).

18 Another crease has damaged the middle of this line, cf. 11 n. Leucadius is a previously unrecorded

prytanis of Oxyrhynchus, cf. 28, 30, 33. He can scarcely be identical with the Leucadius active in P. Mert. 36, AD 360. Flavius Leucadius (almost certainly Dioscurides' successor) is attested as logistes from July/Aug. 325 (I 52; see Appendix I below), so that suggesting prytanis and logistes were the same man would require a change of prytanis during the year of office (324/5); there is no evidence of compatibility of tenure of the two offices. Leucadius' words are introduced differently from elsewhere in this text (28, 30, 33): damage is severe, but crossed rho of ἀπε[κ]ρ(ίνατο) is reasonably clear (the form of the abbreviation is standard, see R. A. Coles, *Reports of Proceedings* 45 n. 3, where however I inaccurately represented the form, and **3757** 13 n.).

20 παραγαύδια (cf. 29) are here obviously equated with cτιχάρια. The association of *paragaudae* with purple (R. Macmullen, *Aeg.* 38 (1958) 187; P. J. Sijpesteijn, *ZPE* 21 (1976) 177-8) fits well with their Tyrian provenance here (see 19). For *paragaudae* see also *Aeg.* 43 (1963) 4-5 (this text republished as P. Med. II 46). For the use of purple garments note M. Reinhold, *History of Purple as a Status Symbol in Antiquity* (Coll. Latomus 116).

21 Cf. 32-4. The 'expenses' are given in 34 as 5,000 den./tunic, and the arithmetic is correct as given there. That is to say, the *coemptores* collected 7,000 tal. = 10,500,000 den. (1 tal. = 1500 den.) and bought 150 sticharia, giving a unit price of 70,000 den. including expenses or 65,000 den. net of expenses. The price per sticharion works out as 43 tal. 500 den. excluding expenses, or 46 tal. 1,000 den. including them (33-4). This is for a Tyrian sticharion, see 19 with 20 n. above. The expenses total 500 talents. A breakdown is hardly possible, but presumably travel costs accounted for part of this. Consulting the table in Appendix III below will give some idea of the buying power of 500 talents at this time. We have evidence for Egyptian sticharion prices neatly bracketing this date (325), namely XLIV **3194** (4,000 dr. = 1,000 den. in 323) and PSI IV 309 re-edited by R. S. Bagnall, *Stud. Pap.* 21 (1982) 87-91 (1 tal. in 327). Both of these are 'official' prices, that is to say the amount paid or refunded by the government, and were further reduced by a 6⅛% deduction. (A different explanation is offered by J.-M. Carrié, op. cit. (12 n.), 435.) See also R. S. Bagnall, *Currency and Inflation in Fourth-century Egypt* (*BASP* suppl. 5) 69. **3776** 27 records a price for a pair of third-grade sticharia in 343 as 133 tal. 500 den. Comparison of the dalmatic prices there with the earlier ones in **3765** 12-13 (*c.*327) could suggest that the local price for a sticharion at the earlier date might have been of the order of 6-10 talents. If so, this would make clear the discrepancy between the real cost of the garments and the miserable recompense offered by the government. Cf. CPR VIII p. 82. The Tyrian figure of 43 tal. 500 den. may be sufficiently explained by the luxury nature of the goods, cf. 20 n.

24 Another crease has severely damaged this line, cf. 11 n. There are occasional traces in the indicated initial lacuna.

30 A crease has severely damaged the first half of this line, cf. 11 n.

32-4 See 21 n.

39 For the consuls cf. **3756** 26 n.

39-77 This case is a clear example of abridgement in drafting the proceedings: note, e.g., the introduction of names into the argument (e.g. Demeas, 56) without any explanation of who they are. Similarly unexplained is, e.g., ταῦτα in 44.

41 Theon, advocate, recurs in 99. Other 'statements of client' of this type are in 99-100, 158-9, 222(?); M. *Chr.* 97 i 3 and P. Bour. 20. 2; also **3759** 2-3 and M. *Chr.* 93. 2 and the texts traditionally described as *narratio* documents such as P. Col. VII 174, of which the most recent treatment is by N. Lewis, P. Rainer. Cent. pp. 121-6.

Here and later a rho with a horizontal cutting the descender represents ῥ(ήτωρ): this is a common convention in records of proceedings.

ἐπὶ παρούcῃ. Cf. 156-8 n. below.

42 ὁ βοηθούμενος. Cf. 51, 61, 159; P. Lips. 33 ii 19, P. Bour. 20. 5, 30, and M. *Chr.* 300. 2, 4, 6.

λόγῳ μὲν καὶ τῷ δοκεῖν. Cf. SB V 7696. 30.

43 τὴν ἡγεμονίαν τὴν τότε. See the introduction above, on ll. 5-38.

45 ⟦ολο⟧. The letters are small and close to the word before. The writer, before proceeding, deleted them and wrote the logistes' title more prominently. The reason for the rewriting at the end of the line (note that the readings are identical: this is not a correction) seems to be no more than clarity following on an accidental blot obscuring ωc of περιττῶc. -

46-7 χαμαιδικαcτάc. χαμαιδικαcτήc is usually rendered *iudex pedaneus* = *iudex delegatus*. In this case there clearly had been delegation, directly or indirectly (τὴν τότε, 43) from the *praes*, but the wording in 46-7 implies that a case of this nature should have gone straight to the χαμαιδικαcτήc; we may suppose that the equivalence arises precisely because the local or minor judiciary often were the delegated judges.

47 ἀκοῦϲαι τῶν. The reading is more assured than the dots indicate; the insertion of ⟨τοιούτων⟩ seems essential.

48 ἕϲτηκεν. Cf. P. Lips. 38. 3; P. Bour. 20. 25, and *ZPE* 34 (1979) 106 (l. 2).

49 The repeated then deleted speech-introduction suggests that an intervening utterance by another speaker has been omitted in this version of the proceedings.

ἐκγόνων. Cf. 65, 74–7 with nn.

56 For the *curator civitatis* as competent official in cases of *apertura testamenti* cf. 141–2 n. below.

58 Ταπατρίνιοϲ. Contrast 72 Ταπατρίνη. The introduction calls attention to a change of pen (or possibly hand) in this line: it comes between γ and κ of ἀνάγκην. Note the different style after this in the speech-introductions for the logistes.

60 Traces of a short interlineation above the beginning of the line.

61 The interlinear additions here and in 65, 75, and 77 are by the hand/pen responsible for ll. 39–58 of this section.

63 ἀγχίνοιαν. See H. Zilliacus, *Unters. zu den abstrakten Anredeformen* 49, 64, 105.

65 ἐμμέλια (= ἐμμέλεια). See Zilliacus, op. cit. (63 n.), 45, 47, 67, 106; CPR V 12. 5 n.

τέκνων δικαίῳ. For the *ius liberorum* cf. the references collected in P. Köln III 150. 3–4 n.; add P. Mich. XV 719. 5–6 n. with Appendix II, pp. 158–71. The grammar seems odd. The possessor of this right is usually described as χρηματίζουϲα τέκνων δικαίῳ. In some sense χρηματίζουϲα must be understood here. The relevance presumably is that acting without a guardian Helen can dispose of property left to her (52–4) without her husband's control, cf. 74–7. Ammonius, advocate, recurs in 157 and in **3764** 5, 16. The grounds for Theon's objection at the end of the line are not clear. Ammonius' status as an advocate seems to have been at issue in some way: the relationship between Theon and Ammonius is complex and not yet fully understood.

67 It was possibly intended to delete ληρεῖ together with οὐδέν at the end of 66.

71 There is an ink spot in the left margin level with this line; whether it is accidental, or was intended to be indicative, is not clear.

73 The initial traces are insufficient for a decision between βούλημα/βουλημάτιον.

74–5 A wider space between these lines, perhaps because of pre-existing surface damage.

74–7 For the *ius liberorum* cf. 65 n. above.

75 I have failed to read the mid-line supralineation. I do not think it can simply be γ ΄, i.e. (τριῶν) τέκνων. It would be possible to read γάρ, but grammar would then seem to require the deletion of τῷ ἀνδρί at the beginning of the line, which is not indicated in the manuscript.

78 πρὸϲ τῷ Καπιτωλίῳ. See **3757** 3 n. Note that in the hearing starting at l. 98 on the same day the location is different (the λογιϲτήριον).

81 There is an annotation in the left margin, of uncertain significance; it resembles a large mu with a vertical line (a rho?) through it. It is clearly not a κρίϲιϲ-indicator (cf. R. A. Coles, *Reports of Proceedings* 54 n. 3) at this point (contrast 92 and n.). Does it indicate in some way that the revised version of this section (= **3757**) is to be found on the other side? It is not simply a deleted start to Μάγνου, begun too far to the left.

τῇ ἐμῇ μετριότητι. For μετριότηϲ, Lat. *modicitas, mediocritas*, see H. Zilliacus, *Unters. zu den abstrakten Anredeformen* 79, 95, 108; *ZPE* 10 (1973) 137.

83 The interlinear corrections here and in 85 (twice) and 89 and 91 are in a smaller more slanting hand than the main hand of 79–97. The correction in 95 may also be the work of this corrector. See 94 n.

85 There are two levels of interlinear correction, apparently both by the same hand. ων of ἔχων was first deleted and οντεϲ inserted above; then εχ and οντεϲ were struck out and τοίνυν ἔχων written higher up still. For the damaged letters before τῆϲ, see **3757** 9 n.

92 For the ecthesis, locating the *curator*'s κρίϲιϲ, cf. R. A. Coles, *Reports of Proceedings* 54 n. 3. Contrast e.g. the format in 108, where the *curator*'s utterance begins the line but is not his κρίϲιϲ.

94 The corrections here and in 97 (see also the app. crit.) are in a different script (greyer and less crisp) from those listed in 83 n., and may be from a different hand.

98 πρὸϲ τῷ λ[ο]γιϲτ[ηρίῳ. Note that in the hearing that began at l. 78 on the same day the location is different (the Καπιτώλιον). For the λογιϲτήριον cf. L 3576 18–19 n.; for other locations for hearings before the logistes see **3757** 3 n.

100 Ἰϲίου Παγγᾶ. See A. Calderini, *Diz. geogr.* iii. 35; P. Pruneti, *I centri abitati dell'Ossirinchite* 71–2.

ἐπὶ παρόντι. Cf. 156–8 n. below.

101 πάροικοϲ. Cf. e.g. ξένοϲ (cf. 122 below) καὶ πάροικοϲ, L 3584 5. Note P. Harr. II 239. 1 n.

107 The hearing of the case was clearly delegated by the *praeses* to the *curator* as the local official, cf. 123-4.

112-13 μή τι[νεc cυνεκλη]ρ[ο]νόμηcαν. The restoration is conjectural but must represent the general sense.

118 αὐ (= οὐ). Cf. e.g. P. Sak. 32 (= P. Thead. 14). 31; P. Lips. 32 (= M. *Chr.* 93). 5; F. T. Gignac, *Grammar* i 217.

119-20 μετὰ τὴν αὔριον. Cf. 127. The next day (Phamenoth 18 = 14 March 325) was a Sunday, on which no court proceedings would be held (cf. **3759** introd. and 38 n.); for the system of reckoning see V. Grumel, *La Chronologie* p. 316.

120 οὐερεδάριοc. Lat. *veredarius*. The word is already attested several times elsewhere in papyri in the spelling βερεδάριοc/βεριδάριοc. See B. Meinersmann, *Lat. Wörter u. Namen* 10; S. Daris, *Il lessico latino nel greco d'Egitto* 33; and now especially F. Paschoud, *Bonner Hist.-Aug.-Colloquium 1979/1981* (Bonn 1983) 215-43, esp. 238-43.

120-1 οὐερεδάριοc γὰρ ἐλθὼν ἤγαγέν με (l. μοι) ἀπὸ Ἀλεξαγδρε[ί]αc. This presumably has nothing to do with the fact that Syrus was an immigrant to the Oxyrhynchite nome, cf. 121-2; rather, the original documents to support his occupancy of the property (γνωρίcματα, 110; ἀποδείξειc, 119, 128; βιβλία, 127) had been filed in one of the Alexandrian record-offices and copies were now being brought out to him.

121 For Libya see J. Mathwich, *ŽPE* 15 (1974) 74-5; A. Calderini, *Diz. geogr.* iii. 199-201.

122 ξένος εἶναι τῆς πολιτίας. Is this not just a reference to the Oxyrhynchite nome but charged with a wider implication, that since the Diocletianic reorganization (see the article by Mathwich cited above) Syrus belonged to a totally different province, viz. Libya Inferior? Such, however, is not the sense carried by τῆcδε τῆc πολιτίαc in 188.

123 τῇ ἐμῇ μετριότητι. Cf. 81 n.

124 τοῦ διακοcμήcαντοc τὸν θρόνον τῆc ἡγεμονίαc. Cf. 7-8, and **3756** 7 and n. For Sabinianus, *praeses Mercurianae* cf. 8 n. above.

127 μετὰ τὴν αὔριον. See 119-20 n.

131 There are a few scanty traces of ink on loose fibres besides the few traces indicated.

134 ἐν τῷ Ἀδριανίῳ. Cf. the note to P. Harr. 160. 2, re-ed. *ŽPE* 37 (1980) 237-8. Further examples are in **3767** 1 and **3764** 14, and cf. L **3576** 18-19 n. For other locations of hearings before the logistes see **3757** 3 n.

Βερεν[ι]κι[α]ν[ο]ῦ βρ[η]θ(οῦ). Is this man possibly to be identified with the strategus (by this time a locally recruited post of course) of two years later, no. 121 in J. E. G. Whitehorne's list, *ŽPE* 29 (1978) 184?

136 ταβελλίωνοc. See A. Berger, *Enc. Dict.* s.v. *tabellio*, with references.

139 εντο[. There is hardly room for anything further. Perhaps ἐντο|λάc or the like (cf. 188), but the beginning of 140 is too damaged to allow confirmation.

140 After ἀπέλθοι, ἐπενεγκεῖν (cf. 189) *vel sim.* is expected, but I cannot read the traces as ἐπ[.

141 ἐμμελείᾳ. See 65 n. above.

141-2 For the *curator civitatis* as competent official in cases of *apertura testamenti* cf. 56 above. This is yet another area in which the *curator* encroaches on functions which were formerly those of the strategus, cf. B. R. Rees, *JJP* 7-8 (1953-4) 86 (for the strategus, cf. e.g. P. Mert. II 75 introd.; R. Taubenschlag, *Law*² 203-4).

146 ἑπτά. For seven-witness peregrine wills see P. Col. VII 188. 26-31 n.; the evidence of that papyrus is usefully consolidated by the present text of just five years later.

τέccαρεc. Cf. e.g. BGU I 361 iii 2, 15. Four is of course the required *maior pars* of the full complement of seven, cf. H. Kreller, *Erbr. Unters.* 402-3.

146-7 Cf. 198-9 below. The first three words of 147 are very conjectural; τε of τέc[ca]ρ[ε]c is reasonably secure, and suggests the reading.

148 Seemingly not παρόντων or τεccάρων at the beginning.

148-9 ἐπεγνωκέναι ἑαυτῶν τὰc cφραγῖδαc. Cf. H. Kreller, op. cit. 402.

151 φ of Φαμενώθ corr. from π, the scribe having changed an unfinished ὑπατείαν Πρόκλου to τὴν αὐτὴν ὑπατείαν and then again to τὴν ἐνεcτῶcαν ὑπατείαν?

154 Cf. D. Just. 10. 2. 4. 3, *heredem enim exemplum debere dare, tabulas vero authenticas ipsum retinere*. The requirement that the original will and not a copy of it be deposited in the government records (M. Kaser, *Das röm. Privatrecht* i² 693; H. Kreller, op. cit. 405) is clearly not yet applicable here, and αὐθεντικόν is not to be understood in its sense of 'officially certified copy', for which see R. A. Coles, *Reports of Proceedings* 24, 54, with references.

156 πρὸc τῷ Καπιτωλίῳ. Cf. 78 above (= **3757** 3).

156-8 ἐπὶ παρόντων (156), ἐπὶ παρούcῃ (158). Formulae of this type were discussed in my *Reports of*

Proceedings, esp. p. 33, but these logistes-texts add two new elements. First, the widespread use of the ἐπὶ παρόντων type to cover court officials etc. and also witnesses in cases of *apertura testamenti* (cf. 134 ff. above); I only quoted one uncertain example of this formula (op. cit. 33 n. 1), in P. Phil. 3. 2. The second is the use of the dative ἐπὶ παρόντι type to denote the defendant, occurring here each time in a statement of his client's identity by the advocate for the plaintiff. None of the examples I cited op. cit. 33 n. 3 is exactly parallel for this usage.

For ἐπὶ παρόντων in these texts cf. **3757** 3; **3758** 5, 78, 98, 134, 181; **3759** 1; **3764** 14; **3767** 1.

For ἐπὶ παρόντι/παρούσῃ cf. **3758** 41 (the deduction regarding the significance of the formula has been particularly useful here in disentangling the persons in the case), and 100.

158 τῇ[c *c.* 7] πόλεως. There is no direct indication elsewhere as to which city this is; nevertheless, the contrast with 159 ἀπὸ τῆςδε τῆς πόλεως followed by 160 ἐπὶ τῆς αὐτῆς πόλεως strongly implies that Chaeremon alias Ischyrion came from elsewhere than Oxyrhynchus.

159 τῷ βοηθουμένῳ, 'my client'. Cf. 42 n.

160 Ἑρμείας γεωμέτρης. Cf. 166-7 παῖς ὑποχίριος. For minors holding office cf. N. Lewis, *BASP* 16 (1979) 117-19, with P. Leit. 8 and the list of examples ibid. p. 21; he concludes that 'under age' is likely to mean 'less than 25'. On γεωμέτραι see F. Oertel, *Die Liturgie* 181; J. Lallemand, *L'Admin. civile* 180; also H. Kupiszewski, *JJP* 6 (1952) 257-9.

Is performance of the office elsewhere than one's place of origin (manifestly Oxyrhynchus, in Hermias' case) the explanation for Hermias' departure for the Oasis?

164 τῆς cῆς ἐμμελείας. See 65 n.

165-7 These lines do not represent a request for a judgement against Hermias *in absentia*: Hermias is a minor but his mother is present and she can (but contrast 169) receive judgement on his behalf (cf. R. Taubenschlag, *Law²* 145, on a father's position in these circumstances). For the identification of Thaesis as the formal defendant in the hearing see 156-8 n. For *materna potestas* see Taubenschlag, op. cit. 149-57 with references on p. 149; J. Modrzejewski, *JJP* 9-10 (1955-6) 355-7. Thaesis should exercise *materna potestas* (see 169 for her claim to have abdicated it, which is a separate issue) because the father has died. Papirion (161) takes no active part in these proceedings (in so far as the text has been read, but τῆς μητρὸς παρούσης for example (166) excludes the possibility), and presumably he died subsequent to the action attested in ἀπεκηρύξα‵μεν′ in 169 (is the correction to the plural (cf. 170 too) of subtle significance?).

166 κυρίᾳ. Cf. **3759** 18 n., 37 n.

167 For ὑποχείριος cf. R. Taubenschlag, *Law²* 131⁴.

169 ἀπεκηρύξα‵μεν′. On ἀποκήρυξις see M. Wurm, *Apokeryxis, Abdicatio und Exheredatio* (Münch. Beitr. 60, Munich 1972); M. Kaser, *Das röm. Privatrecht* ii. 213; R. Taubenschlag, *Law²* 52, 137-8; S. Jameson, *Hist.* 24 (1975) 290. The present text notably attests the persistence of the practice despite the recent injunction of Diocletian, Cod. Just. 8. 46. 6 (AD 288).

οὐκ ἔχω πρᾶγμα πρὸς αὐτόν. Presumably *materna potestas* was equally annulled by ἀποκήρυξις, although the implication of the plural ἀπεκηρύξαμεν must be that the rejection took place in the father's lifetime and thus that it was *patria potestas* that had been annulled and the question of *materna potestas* does not arise. Nevertheless, *materna potestas* over Hermias, whether it truly existed or not, must constitute the grounds on which Thaesis has been brought to court as defendant.

176 ρc οcε. The division is justified by the finial to first sigma, space, and enlarged second omicron. Divide further ὁ cε-?

179 The residual traces assigned to this line pose a problem because they are on a glue-stained area which was once covered by a kollesis. Possibly a strip had lifted off before these proceedings were written and 179 was then written on the exposed surface. But the problem is complicated by the appearance of similar traces level with the line above (where there has been surface loss before]ν δημοcι‗ ‗ [) which interfere with the ductus of the definite surviving letters.

180 Contrast 165-7 n. In fact a judgement *in absentia* must be what we have here, if Thaesis' claim of ἀποκήρυξις (169) is accepted. However, although ἀποκήρυξις was widely practised it had nevertheless been expressly forbidden by Diocletian (Cod. Just. 8. 46. 6, AD 288) so that it is quite likely that the *curator's* court would not accept Thaesis' denial of responsibility for her son on such grounds. Could οἱ νόμοι κελεύ[ουcιν, 171-2, refer to legislation on this subject?

αὔριον = Phamenoth 23 = Friday, 19 March 325.

181 Φαμενὼθ ιθ (the reading is clear and κθ is not possible) breaks the chronological sequence of the hearings (see the introd. above).

γυμνασίῳ. For other locations for hearings before the logistes see **3757** 3 n.

184 Poemenius is ταβελλίων as well as ῥήτωρ, see 197; cf. 136-7 above. He recurs as ῥήτωρ in **3759** 2 (2 October 325).

186-7 τῆς ἑαυ[το]ῦ γνώμης. Identification of the deceased, namely the veteran Besarion (cf. 202, 211), must precede this somewhere, but I have failed to discern it in the traces.

187-8 αἰδεσιμώτατον. This is an early example of the use of this honorific epithet. See H. Zilliacus, *Unters. zu den abstrakten Anredeformen* 60, 83.

189 παρασχ[ό]μενος. An interlineation above the end of this word (cf. app. crit.)?

εἰ τοῦ βίου ἀπέλθοι. Cf. 140.

190 ἐντρεχία. Lat. *experientia*. See Zilliacus, op. cit. 62, 67, 88. γνωσθῆναι is understandable but one suspects an error of omission and that ἀναγνωσθῆναι was intended.

195 The reference is to the number of signatories, cf. 146. As in that case, there were seven signatories and four (cf. 183-4) are present for the opening of the will.

196 More traces of ink actually survive at the beginning than the transcription indicates, but they are on a twisted and distorted 'rope' of loose fibres.

202 The damaged traces before Βησαρίωνος are presumably from his first name (if there are not too many letters for just that), and the first letter may be φ or ι, but I have failed to read what is left as part of Φλαουίου. For the use of this *gentilicium* by soldiers and veterans see J. G. Keenan, *ZPE* 11 (1973) 33-63, esp. 49-50 (50 n. 48 cites some rare examples of military Aurelii in this period); ibid. 13 (1974) 283-304. Note that the *curator civitatis* in the present hearing (Dioscurides alias Julianus) was still Valerius in the following month (XLIII **3125**), although a senior official (a *magister privatae*) in that same document bears the *gentilicium* Flavius. Οὐαλερίου does not seem possible here. We do not know either the precise date at which the use of the *gentilicium* Flavius was instituted in place of Valerius (Keenan cites an example of Flavius dated 13 January 325, *ZPE* 11 (1973) 48), nor the mechanics of its allocation (on which see Keenan, *ZPE* 13 (1974) 297-301), and with allocations on an individual or category basis such discrepancies need not surprise us.

203-5 The year is the preceding year, 324. The use of this particular consular formula in Egypt is so far attested only for December, see R. S. Bagnall and K. A. Worp, *Chronological Systems of Byzantine Egypt* 109. Since the clerk may have applied the formula retrospectively, ignoring the actual form which was revealed when the will was opened, we cannot be certain that the will was drawn up in the last months of the year, after the defeat of Licinius.

206 Or ὑπο- at end?

207 Cf. SB I 4426. 8 ἀποδοῦναι τὸ χρεών = 'die', XXXIV **2713** 6-7 (see *BL* VI p. 111); a comparable expression seems likely here.

210 τῇ ἐμῇ μετριότητι. Cf. 81 n.

212 Or κατα.. at end? But the last two traces are difficult to read on this interpretation.

215 The number of letters indicated is only approximate, as elsewhere in this fragment (especially 216 and 220).

218-19 The traces shown as from the earlier parts of these lines are on a piece linked to the main fragment by a twisted mass of loose fibres, and their vertical position and thus line-assignment are not certain.

219 There is space for another line between this and 220, but no ink survives and we may have here a space between records of different hearings, as earlier in the roll.

221 Presumably we are at the commencement of a report here, cf. 79, 99, 157, 184. Restore ὑ]πηρέτου. It is uncertain whether 220 should form part of this report (cf. 219 n.). 221 is likely to have continued with the opening speech for the advocate for the prosecution, briefly identifying his client (cf. e.g. 99-100), here apparently without indicating the presence of the defendant; hence the punctuation adopted in 222.

221-8 The articulation is uncertain at many places in this fragment, and the choice in the transcript is frequently arbitrary.

222 Ἰσίου Παγγᾶ is presumably the domicile of one of the parties in the case, cf. 100. Cf. 221 n. After ἡ μέν, I can discern neither a personal name nor e.g. ἔχουσα.

226-8 There are wider spaces between 226, 227, and 228 than elsewhere on this fragment (221-8); the reason is not apparent.

3759. Proceedings before the Logistes

11 1B.145/G (a)   24.5 × 55 cm   2 October 325

This report of proceedings before the logistes is self-standing and complete except for intermittent damage down the right edge. It was written *transversa charta* (see **3758** introd.) on the back of a piece cut from a roll of declarations of prices made to the logistes by the various guilds; the declarations thus preserved are published above as **3747–53**. **3759** begins at the **3753** end. Written up the margin between **3747** and **3748** (thus across the fibres and at the end of the off-cut piece) is a single line which constitutes a label for the proceedings; this 'label' is transcribed below as l. 42.

The basic issue in the case appears to have been the ownership of some buildings or building-land, and other officials (the prefect, the strategus) had already been involved. The sequence of events may be deduced as follows: (*a*) proceedings (more than one hearing presumably) before the strategus (7, 18–20); the defendants did not appear and a decision (19) was given against them *in absentia*. (*b*) Instructions passed from the strategus through the *praepositus pagi* to the village officials (8), but without result (9). (*c*) A petition to the prefect (10, 21, 23, 29) enclosing the strategus' ὑπομνήματα (7). (*d*) The prefect's subscription to the petition (14) delegates the case to the *curator* (also 7, 11). (*e*) The prosecution therefore sends an ἐπίσταλμα, an officially recognized private *denuntiatio*, to the defendants (25–6), only apparently to a different set of defendants (24, 28). The present hearing (*f*) is consequent on the ἐπίσταλμα, but is complicated by the apparent perversity of the prosecution in bringing the action against different persons. The time before ((*a*) above) the defendants had failed to appear, and now again it seems that persons concerned were not present (39–40). If Ischyrion the defending advocate is acting on behalf of the newly prosecuted persons, then the original defendants not unreasonably still failed to appear. Much of the current hearing is taken up with Ischyrion's objections to the prosecution's change of course and, presumably, by implication to the consequent application of the original default procedure to his new clients who had (because not previously summoned) not so been at fault; it is not clear if they are present at the current hearing (cf. 39–40, and 37 n.), but that is a separate issue. At the end of the day the logistes postpones continuation of the proceedings, since the next day is Sunday, and puts off a decision yet again, to give all concerned one more chance to appear: but this time, all present or not, a decision is promised.

There are two points of prosopographical interest. The prefect Flavius Magnus is known from this text (which gives the latest date we have for him) and **3756–8** only; his tenure is discussed in **3756** 9 n. The date of the proceedings falls within the known tenure of the logistes Flavius Leucadius; his name does not appear within the proceedings themselves but he is named in the docket on the back (42). For the evidence for his tenure see Appendix I below.

Line 38 contains the earliest papyrological reference to Sunday as the Lord's Day;

cf. XLVIII **3407** introd. and 15–16 n. For the cessation of legal business on Sunday see Cod. Just. 3. 12. 2(3) (AD 321) cited in **3407** 15–16 n.: *omnes iudices . . . venerabili die solis quiescant.* See further 38 n. below. Contrast **3741**.

For kollesis-locations and kollema-sizes on this piece of papyrus cf. the introd. to **3747–53**.

(ἔτους) κϛ´ ´καὶ ιϛ´ ´καὶ βϛ´ ´, Φαῶφι ϛ´. ἐν τῷ Κορίῳ ἱερῷ. ἐπὶ παρό[ντων]
Διονυσοδώρου ὑπηρέτου καὶ Φανίου παρέδρου, Ποιμένιος ῥ(ήτωρ) ε[ἶ(πεν)·
Χαι-?]

ῥήμων ἀπὸ τῶν αὐτόθι ἐντυγχάνει. οὐ δικαστήριον ε . . . . θ . . . . [συγ-]
κροτεῖν ἦλθον, μὴ τοῦτο νομίςῃς, καὶ ἑξῆς λέγοντος Ἰςχυρίων ῥ(ήτωρ)
εἶ(πεν)· παρα-

5 γράφομαι· πρὸ[ς] τίνα λέγει εἰπάτω. Ποιμένιος ῥ(ήτωρ) εἶ(πεν)· ὁ κύριός
μου διαςημ(ότατος)

ἔπαρχος τῆς Αἰγύπτου Φλάουιος Μάγνος πρὸς τὰ αὐτοτελῶς γενόμενα
ὑπομνήματα παρὰ τῇ ςτρατηγίᾳ βοηθόν ςε δέδωκεν. καὶ γὰρ ἐπι-
ςτάλματα ἐγένετο παρὰ τοῦ πραι(ποςίτου) πρὸς τοὺς δημοςίους π[ερὶ τοῦ]
παραδοῦναι τὴν νομήν. ἧττον ἐφρόντιςαν πρὸς τοῦτο κ[αὶ ἀνη-]

10 νέγκαμεν ἐπὶ τὸν κύριόν μου ⟦.⟧ τὸν ἔπαρχον καὶ . . . [c. 4]
τερόν ςε βοηθὸν ἔςχαμεν καὶ ἀξιοῦμεν τὴν νομὴν . . [. . παραδο-]
θῆναι. |ὁ λογιςτὴς εἶ(πεν)· τί προςέταξ[ε]ν ὁ δεςπότης μου [διαςημότατος]
ἔπαρχος τῆς Αἰγύπτου Φλάουιος Μάγνος; ⟦Ποιμένιος ῥ(ήτωρ) εἶ(πεν)·
ἀνα-⟧

⟦γ.⟧ καὶ ἀνεγνώςθη οὕτως· ὁ λογιςτὴς τὰ κατὰ νόμους ὁριςθέντα

15 ἐπιτελῆ καταςτήςει, ὥςτε ςυνχώρηςον ἀναγνῶναι τὰ ὑπομνήματα ἀφ´ ὧν ἐντελέςτερον . . . [.] . εἰ ὅτι οὐδὲν ἕτερον ὑπ[ο-]
λείπεταί μοι ἢ εἰςαχθῆναι εἰς τὴν νομὴν τῶν οἰκοπέ[δων.]
κατὰ κυρίαν γὰρ ἀπελίφθης[α]ν οἱ ἀντίδικοι. οὐ παρεληλυ-
θότες εἰς τὸ δικαςτήριον κατὰ κυρίαν, ἀπόφαςιν ἐδέξαν[το]

20 καὶ ἔξωροι γεγόναςι κατὰ τοὺς νόμους. |ὁ λογιςτὴς εἶ(πεν)·
πρὸς τίνα λέγει εἰπάτω. Ποιμένιος ῥ(ήτωρ) εἶ(πεν)· κατὰ Ἀράχθου ἀνήνεγκε
καὶ Εὐδαίμονα καὶ Φίβιος καὶ τῶν ςὺν αὐτοῖς. Ἰςχυρίων ῥ(ήτωρ) εἶ(πεν)·
μαρτύρομαι ὅτι κατά τινων ἀνήνεγκεν ἐπὶ τὸν κύριόν μου τὸν

1 l. Κορείῳ   4 ει᾽) and so *passim*   5 διαςημϛ   8 Trace above second a of παρά perhaps
a more clearly written a   9 ητ᾽τον   18 l. ἀπελείφθηςαν; ουπαρ written over washed-out letters
22 l. Εὐδαίμονος; ςὺν

ἔπαρχον καὶ κατ' ἑτέρων εἰσάγει νῦν. τοῦτο μαρτύριον ἔσται μοι

25   τῆς παραγραφῆς. /ὁ λογιστὴς εἶ(πεν)· αὐτὸ τὸ ἐπίσταλμα
ὃ ἐπέστειλας τῷ ἀντιδικοῦντί coι ἀνάγνωθι. καὶ ἀνεγνώcθη·
μετὰ τὴν ἀνάγνωcιν Ἰcχυρίων ῥ(ήτωρ) εἶ(πεν)· παραγραφὴν ἐπηγ-
γιλάμην· περὶ ἑτέρων προcώπων τὴν δίκην νῦν εἰcάγει,
περί τινων ἀνενεγκὼν ἐπὶ τὸν κύριόν μου τὸν ἔπαρχον.

30   τὴν οὖν παραγραφὴν ἐπηγγιλάμην θαυμαcτὴν
οὖcαν καὶ ἐννομωτάτην· ὡc οὐδαμῶc δύναται
εἰcαγώγιμον ποιεῖν τὸ πρᾶγμα ὁ ἀντίδικοc. καὶ ἑξῆc
λέγοντοc Ποιμένιοc ῥ(ήτωρ) εἶ(πεν)· μαρτύρομαι τὴν φωνὴν
αὐτοῦ ὅτι μὴ δύναται εἰcαγώγιμον εἶναι τὴν δίκην

35   ὅπωc ἀξιῶ ἤδη εἰc νομὴν πέμπεcθαι τῶν οἰκοπέδων.
/ὁ λογ(ιcτὴc) εἶ(πεν)· ἐπειδὴ ἑcπέραc ἐγένετο πρόκριμα οὐδὲν
ἔcται τῆc κυρίαc μήπω ἐνcτάcηc. ἐπείπερ μέροc τι
τῆc ἐπιούcηc κυριακῆc ἱερᾶc ἐπέκυψεν, ὑπε[ρ-]
τεθήcεται μετὰ τὴν κυριακὴν ἡ δίκη μέχρι [οὗ ἀμ]φότερα

40   τὰ μέρη παρέcεται πρὸc δικαιολογίαν. ἐὰν ⟦γὰρ⟧ ʼδέʼ τιc ἀπολ[ει-]
φθῇ εἴ τι παρίcταται τῇ ἐμῇ μετριότητι ἀποκριθήcομ[αι.]

Back   ὑπομν(ήματα) μη(νὸc) Φαῶφι κϛʹʹ ιϛʹʹ βϛʹʹ ἐπὶ Λευκαδίου λογιcτοῦ.

24 l. καθ'   27-8, 30 l. ἐπηγγειλάμην   36 λογ'; l. ἑcπέρα   41 παρῖcταται   42 υπομν∫μη̄

'Year 20, 10, and 2, Phaophi 5. In the temple of Kore. In the presence of Dionysodorus, assistant, and Phanias, assessor, Poemenius, advocate, said, "[Chae?]remon of this locality petitions. I have not come [trying?] to contrive a hearing—do not think this", and while he continued speaking, Ischyrion, advocate, said, "I object. Let him say against whom he speaks." Poemenius, advocate, said, "My lord the prefect of Egypt Flavius Magnus, *vir perfectissimus*, in response to minutes made independently at the strategus' office, gave you as our helper. Communications had passed from the *praepositus* to the village officials concerning the transference of possession. They paid no attention to this, and we petitioned before my lord the prefect and we obtained you . . . as a helper and we request that possession . . . be transferred." The *curator* said, "What did my master the prefect of Egypt Flavius Magnus, *vir perfectissimus*, ordain?" And there was read as follows: " 'The *curator* is to put into effect what has been decided in accordance with the law'; therefore assent to the reading of the minutes, from which . . . more completely that nothing else remains for me except to be installed in possession of the sites, inasmuch as on the appointed day the defendants did not appear; not having come to the court on the appointed day, they were given a decision and have been decreed out of time in accordance with the laws." The *curator* said, "Let him say against whom he speaks." Poemenius, advocate, said, "He petitioned against Harachthes and Eudaemon and Phibis and those with them." Ischyrion, advocate, said, "I call you to witness that he petitioned against certain persons before my lord the prefect and it is against different persons that he now brings a case. This will be the evidence for my objection." The *curator* said, "Read out the actual communication which you sent to your adversary." And it was read; after the reading, Ischyrion, advocate, said, "I gave notice of my objection. After petitioning my lord the prefect regarding certain persons, he is now bringing a case in respect of different persons. So I gave notice of my objection which is admirable and absolutely within the law; thus in no way can my adversary make the case tenable." While he was continuing to speak, Poemenius, advocate, said, "I call his own words to witness, that the case is untenable; so that I now request to be assigned possession of the sites." The *curator* said, "Since the hour of *vespera* has passed, there shall be no prejudgement, the appointed day not yet having arrived. Since some part of the coming sacred Lord's Day has supervened, the case will be deferred till (the day?) after the Lord's Day, until both the parties shall be present for judgement. But if anyone is absent, I shall give such decision as occurs to my humble self."'

(Back) 'Minutes for the month of Phaophi, (year) 20, 10, and 2, before Leucadius, *curator*.'

1 ἐν τῷ Κορίῳ ἱερῷ. For the cult of Kore at Oxyrhynchus, and her temples, cf. XII **1449**, esp. 52 ἐν ἱερῷ τῆς Κόρης. For other locations for hearings before the logistes see **3757** 3 n.

2 Poemenius has appeared in **3758** 184; see n.

For the form of ῥ(ήτωρ) see **3758** 41 n.

2–3 Χαι-?]ρήμων ἀπὸ τῶν αὐτόθι ἐντυγχάνει. For such 'statements of client' at the start of a hearing cf. **3758** 41 n.

3–4 δικαστήριον . . . [cυγ]κροτεῖν. Cf. XLIII **3126** i 10–11 and n. The damaged passage in 3 here presumably contained a word meaning 'wishing', 'trying', or the like, but I have failed to read it.

5 πρὸ[c] τίνα λέγει εἰπάτω. Note that Poemenius' statement of client in 2–3 omits the ἐπὶ παρόντι-type phrase denoting the defendant (cf. **3758** 156–8 n.).

12 [διαcημότατοc]. The supplement is hardly in doubt. Scanty traces in fact survive of the opening letters but I cannot allocate them to particular letters.

13 ff. It is unclear why Poemenius' speech-introduction was deleted. He probably read the quotation that follows (cf. Ischyrion, in 25–7). If I understand the structure of 14–20 rightly, and am correct in supposing the quotation to end at 15, then the speech following has no speaker's introduction. This will be regardless of the identity of the quotation-reader, though ὥcτε (15) suggests that quotation-reader and speech-speaker must be the same.

15 For ὥcτε followed by the imperative cf. Mayser ii 1 p. 300 and ii 3 p. 97. At end, υπομ), i.e. ὑπομ( ), was first written.

17 End of οἰκοπέ[δων] is not clear and the lacuna is scarcely adequate for three letters. Was the word abbreviated in some way? For οἰκόπεδα see G. Husson, *Oikia* 209–11.

18 κατὰ κυρίαν. See A.-J. Boyé, *La Denuntiatio* 214 n. 32; R. Taubenschlag, *Opera Minora* ii 179 ff.; BGU XV 2467. 24b n.; and 37 n. below. For judgements *in absentia* see also T. C. Skeat and E. P. Wegener, *JEA* 21 (1935) 241–2.

21 Possibly ἀνήνεγκε[ν] at end. [Chae?]remon (2–3) is the subject.

25–6 Unexpectedly, the logistes' words only seem to make sense if addressed to Poemenius, in spite of Ischyrion's intervention in 22–5. The logistes will then be seeking to establish from Poemenius the precise identity of the persons against whom the prosecution's action is presently directed (thus this ἐπίcταλμα will be the *denuntiatio*), and this will explain Ischyrion's outburst in 27 ff. This copy of the proceedings does not quote this ἐπίcταλμα; is this important information omitted because this copy was made for the prosecution, for whom its inclusion would seem unfavourable?

36 ἑcπέραc (l. ἑcπέρα) ἐγένετο. For the technical use of ἑcπέρα to denote the hour before sunset cf. V. Grumel, *La Chronologie* 164.

37 τῆc κυρίαc. Contrast κατὰ κυρίαν, 18 and 19, the *dies legitimus* or *supremus* which has already passed. The defendants failed to appear then, and judgement was given against them. It seems to have been ineffectual and now the new hearing has its own *dies legitimus* or *supremus* and again the defendants (their identity is not clear, cf. 21–9) have apparently so far failed to turn up (cf. 39–40) although Ischyrion the advocate is present. Whether after this further delay effective justice was anywhere nearer attainment we are not told.

38 κυριακῆc. Cf. the introduction. This example of κυριακή, 'the Lord's Day', is at the same time the earliest from papyri and precisely dated; it also shows that the substantival usage was already current. On days of the week see XLIV **3174** 17 n. 3 October 325 was indeed a Sunday, as can be calculated by the tables in V. Grumel, *La Chronologie* 316. For Sunday see further W. Rordorf, *Der Sonntag* (*Abhandl. zur Theol. d. Alten u. Neuen Test.*, 43) (Zürich, 1962; Engl. transl. by A. A. K. Graham, London, 1968).

ἐπέκυψεν. Cf. Theophylactus Simocatta III 16. 2, ἐπεὶ χειμῶνος ὥρα παρέκυπτεν. The implication in the papyrus must be that the 24-hour day of the week was here considered as beginning at sunset with the 'first hour of the night'. In Oxyrhynchus at the date of **3759** this would have been approximately 5.40 p.m., see

F. K. Ginzel, *Handb. der math. u. techn. Chronologie* ii 165–7. The meaning of $\mu\acute{\epsilon}\rho o\varsigma\ \tau\iota\ldots\ \acute{\epsilon}\pi\acute{\epsilon}\kappa\upsilon\psi\epsilon\nu$ will presumably be that the court session has run on past that time. Cf. 36 n. on *vespera*.

42 For the docket cf. the title to **3758**, ll. 3–4. Note here that it comes at the foot-end of the proceedings; and that if it was to serve as a 'label' for the roll, as surely it was, then the curvature of the roll was reversed on rolling.

3760–3763. Declarations of Prices

4 1B.76/p　　　　　　　　　　33 × 24.5 cm　　　　　　　　　　326?

The front of this papyrus was used for a series of declarations of prices by guilds. In all parts of five declarations are preserved. I do not transcribe the first item: there are a few scattered traces from line-ends only, few of them identifiable as particular letters. The second declaration is that of the $\grave{\epsilon}\lambda\alpha\iota o\upsilon\rho\gamma o\acute{\iota}$, the third that of the $\grave{\alpha}\rho\tau\upsilon\mu\alpha\tau o\pi\hat{\omega}\lambda\alpha\iota$, and the fourth that of the $\kappa\acute{\alpha}\pi\eta\lambda o\iota$; of the last one little survives but the subscription, from which the guild cannot be identified. The three guilds identified here recur in the same order in **3738–40**; cf. also **3765** 1–4.

As usual, the text is not a $\tau\acute{o}\mu o\varsigma\ \varsigma\upsilon\gamma\kappa o\lambda\lambda\acute{\eta}\varsigma\iota\mu o\varsigma$. For the regular format in such declarations see **3731** introd. As far as can be ascertained the main bodies of the declarations are in the same hand (this is certainly true for **3760–1**; **3762** is too damaged for certainty, while almost nothing survives from the other two), as would in any case be expected. Names of declarants and the prices were presumably later insertions, although the only evidence for this is the slightly narrower space into which **3760** 6 has been squeezed. I suppose that the insertions were made in the logistes' bureau by the scribe who had drafted the declarations in advance. The subscriptions are all in different hands. There is one kollesis, after **3761**, clearly of the three-layer type (cf. P. Harr. II 212 introd. and LI **3624–6** introd.). The strip-construction (*pace* I. H. M. Hendriks, *ZPE* 37 (1980) 121 ff.: his views were restated in a modified form in *Atti del XVII Congresso int. di Papirologia* (Napoli, 1984), 31–7; see P. Harr. II 214 introd.) of the left-hand kollema is particularly clear, and the width of the strips fluctuates, from a substantial 3.5 cm (or possibly more) down to 2 cm.

For the date see **3760** introd.

On the back is an extensive official document of *c*.337 whose publication is reserved for a later volume.

3760. Declaration of Prices

For some general comments on this roll see the introduction just above to **3760–3**. The upper part of the roll is mostly missing, and it is here that it survives most fully. The date (see 1 n.) and the identity of the logistes are highly conjectural, but the proposed combination (1–2) seems the best since the prices of $\phi\acute{\alpha}\beta\alpha$ and $\kappa\acute{\upsilon}\mu\iota\nu o\nu$ (**3761** 13–14, at 6 and 8 tal./art.) are the same as in **3765** 1–2 of *c*. 327 and ought not to be too distant in date, while the prices declared by the $\kappa\acute{\alpha}\pi\eta\lambda o\iota$ (**3762** 15–16) are in one case slightly lower than is listed for the corresponding items in **3765** 3–4 so that the **3760–3** roll may be expected to be slightly earlier than **3765** (but cf. **3773** for seasonal variation in wine prices).

The guild here is that of the ἐλαιουργοί, who also appear in **3738**.

. . . . .

Κᾳί[ca]ρϙ[c τὸ α΄, (month) λ΄.]
Φ[λ](αουίῳ) Λεϙϰ[αδίῳ λογ](ιcτῇ) ['Ο]ξ[(υρυγχίτου)]
[π]αρὰ τ[ο]ῦ ϰ[οινο]ῦ τῶν
ἐλαιοϋργῶν τῆc λαμ(πρᾶc) 'Οξ(υρυγχιτῶν)
5   πόλεωc δι' ἐμοῦ Αὐρηλίου
. . . . τι . . ατοc.
προcφωνῶ τὴν ἑξῆc
ἐνγεγρ(αμμένην) τιμὴν ὧν χιρίζω
ὠνίων καὶ ὀμνύω τὸν
10   θεῖον ὅρκον μηδὲν διεψεῦcθαι. ἔcτι δέ·
λαχανοcπέρμου
(ἀρτάβηc) α τάλ(αντα) ιε.

_____

(m. 2)   Αὐρήλιοc . . . τι . . αc
15   ἐπιδέδωκα ὡc πρόϰ(ειται).
Αὐρ(ήλιοc) Διονύcιοc ἔγρ(αψα) ὑ(πὲρ)
αὐτοῦ γρ(άμματα) μὴ εἰδ(ότοc).

2 φ[λ]΄   4 λαμοξ΄   8 ενγεγρ∫   13 ⸗? ταλ΄   15 προ^ϰ   16 αυρ∫, εγρ∫υ)
17 γρ∫, ει^δ

(2 ff.) 'To Flavius Leucadius, *curator* of the Oxyrhynchite, from the guild of the oil-workers of the illustrious city of the Oxyrhynchites, through me Aurelius . . . son of . . . . I declare the price entered below for the goods which I handle, and I swear the divine oath that I have been deceitful in nothing. As follows:

'Vegetable seed   1 art.   tal. 15.'

(m. 2) 'I, Aurelius . . ., presented this as aforesaid. I, Aurelius Dionysius, wrote on his behalf as he is illiterate.'

1 The date is restored as the end of the consular formula for 326, for which see R. S. Bagnall and K. A. Worp, *The Chronological Systems of Byzantine Egypt* 109; but the restoration is very conjectural, see the introd. above.

2 Cf. 1 n. and the introd. above. For Flavius Leucadius, *curator*, see Appendix I below. He was certainly in office for much of 326 so that this text as it stands can add nothing to our knowledge of his term of office.

4–5 τῆc λαμ(πρᾶc) 'Οξ(υρυγχιτῶν) πόλεωc. Cf. **3748** 7 n.

6 This line is a subsequent insertion in a ready prepared text, but by the same hand; the space above and below it is less than elsewhere in the text.

12 λαχανοcπέρμου. For ἔλαιον (cf. 4 ἐλαιουργῶν) = vegetable oil see LI **3639** 10–11 n. and **3738** 5–6 n.

3761. DECLARATION OF PRICES

See the introduction above to **3760–3** for general comments on this roll. The guild here is identified as that of the ἀρτυματοπῶλαι by comparison with the sequence **3738–40** where the items declared by the ἀρτυματοπῶλαι (**3739**) are lost but total the same number as here and are likewise preceded by the declaration of the ἐλαιουργοί (**3738**) and followed by that of the κάπηλοι (**3740**). Note also **3765** 1–4, where the last two items declared here are likewise followed by the items declared by the κάπηλοι (**3740, 3762**).

>   •   •   •   •   •
>
>   [. . . .]. [
>   τιμὴν ὧν [
>   καὶ ὀμνυ[
>   κον μηδ[ὲν
> 5   ἔϲτ[ι δέ·
>   ϲηϲάμο[υ
>   μελανθίου [
>   κόρου ξηρ[οῦ
>   ὀριγάνου . . .[   ]. . . .[
> 10   ϲινάπεωϲ [(ἀρτάβηϲ) α?] τ[ά]λ(αντα)   η
>   μ. . . .[.]. (ἀρτάβηϲ?) α [τά]λ(αντα)   δ
>   κνήκου   (ἀρτάβηϲ?) α τ[ά]λ[(αντα)]   .
>   φάβατοϲ   (ἀρτάβηϲ) α τάλ(αντα)   ϛ
> 14   κυμίνου   (ἀρτάβηϲ) α τ[ά]λ(αντα)   η
>
> (m. 2)   Αὐρ(ήλιοϲ) Ἡρακλῆ[ϲ] ἐπ[ι]δέδωκα πρ(οϲφωνῶν)
>   ὡϲ πρόκ(ειται). Αὐρ(ήλιοϲ) Θέων ἔγρ(αψα) ὑ(πὲρ) αὐτοῦ
>   γρ(άμματα) μὴ εἰ[(δότοϲ)].

8 l. κορίου   13–14 ÷? See 11–14n.   ταλ'; so presumably in 10–12   15 αυρ∫, πρ∫
16 προ^κ αυρ∫, εγρ∫υ), γρ∫?

6 ϲηϲάμο[υ, 'sesame'. M. Schnebel, *Die Landwirtschaft* 197–200.

7 μελανθίου, 'black cummin'. Schnebel, op. cit. 205–6.

8 κόρου (l. κορίου) ξηρ[οῦ, 'dried coriander'. Cf. P. Teb. II 314. 17–18 κορέου ξηρο[ῦ], and Schnebel, op. cit. 207.

9 The traces exclude Ἡρακλεωτικ-, λευκ-, μελ-, cf. LSJ s.v. ὀρίγανον.

10 ϲινάπεωϲ, 'mustard'. The reading is uncertain, especially initial sigma. See Schnebel, op. cit. 205.

11–14 Note the app. crit. on the abbreviation for ἀρτάβηϲ in 13–14, which actually appears more as a straight horizontal without (apparently) benefit of a dot. That the items in 13–14 were measured by the artaba is shown by **3765** 1–2. The unit in 12 is not certainly the artaba, and 11 is even more uncertain. That one item declared by this guild was differently measured is shown by **3739** 18.

11 μήκωνος (cf. Schnebel, op. cit. 206) cannot be read.
12 κνήκου, 'safflower'. Schnebel, op. cit. 202; BGU XV 2484. 4 n.
13 φάβατος, 'beans': cf. §1. 9-10 of the Price Edict ed. Giacchero, with Lauffer's commentary, *Diokletians Preisedikt* p. 215.
14 κυμίνου, 'cummin'. Schnebel, op. cit. 205-6.
16 For Aurelius Theon see Appendix IV below.

3762. DECLARATION OF PRICES

See the introduction above to **3760-3** for general comments on this roll. The surface here has suffered severe abrasion, especially at the top. The guild here is that of the κάπηλοι, who recur—likewise preceded by the ἀρτυματοπῶλαι—in **3740**. Cf. also **3765** 3-4.

```
        .       .     .      .
    [        c. 16        ] . . . [
    [        c. 16        ] . . . . [
    [       c. 14       ] . . . . . [
    [      c. 11       ] . . . . . . . [
5   [παρὰ τοῦ κ]οινοῦ [τ]ῶν καπ[ήλων]
    [ . . ] . . . . . . . . . . . [
    [ . . . ] . . . . . . . . . . . [
    [ . . ] . μου καὶ . . . [
    προσφωνῶ τὴ[ν ἑξῆc]
10  ἐνγεγραμμένην τ[ιμὴν]
    ὧν [χιρί]ζω ὠνίω[ν καὶ] ὀ-
    μνύω τὸν θεῖ[ον ὅ]ρκον
    μηδὲν διεψεῦcθαι.
            ἔcτι δέ·
15  οἴν[ο]υ 'Οαcιτικοῦ  (ξέcτου) α (δηνάρια) υ
    κυ[ι]δίου Θηβαικοῦ  (ξέcτου) α (δηνάρια) τ[ο]ε
```

_____

(m. 2)   Αὐρ(ήλιος) Ἄμμων προcφ(ωνῶ) ὡς πρόκ(ειται).
    Αὐρ(ήλιος) Ὡρίων ἔγρ(αψα) ὑ(πὲρ) αὐτοῦ
    γρ(άμματα) μὴ εἰδ(ότος).

15, 16 ✗   17 προcφ ΄, προ^κ 18 εγρ∫υ)   19 γρ∫, ει^δ

(5 ff.) '. . . from the guild of the tavern-keepers . . . I declare the price entered below for the goods which I handle and I swear the divine oath that I have been deceitful in nothing. As follows:

'Oasite wine   1 sextarius   den. 400

'Theban (wine) of Cnidian type 1 sextarius   den. 375(?).'

(m. 2) 'I, Aurelius Ammon, declare as aforesaid. I, Aurelius Horion, wrote on his behalf as he is illiterate.'

1–4 Cf. **3760** 1–2 and the introd. there and 1 n. If the reconstruction of that text is correct, then since the declarations in the roll will follow the same initial format 1 here should be the top line, 1–3 preserve the consular date followed by month and day, and 4 the address to the logistes. But none of this can be confirmed from the exiguous remains.

5 καπ[ήλων]. See **3740** 7 n.

6–8 λων of καπήλων may have run on to 6. Comparing 17 and **3760**, these lines should run τῆς λαμ(πρᾶς) Ὀξ(υρυγχιτῶν) πόλεως δι' ἐμοῦ Αὐρηλίου Ἄμμωνος followed by a patronymic; other such documents may have μηνιάρχου besides or in place of the patronymic. However, I have failed to equate this with the damaged traces. Letters read in 8 are difficult.

15–16 Cf. **3740** 16–17 n.

18 For Horion cf. Appendix IV below.

3763. Declaration of Prices

See the introduction above to **3760–3** for general comments on this roll. Virtually nothing survives of this last declaration except part of the subscription, and that tells us nothing except that the guild was represented by a single declarant who was called Aurelius A- or Ha-. We print the text simply for completeness' sake and in case these scanty remains might somehow help in establishing the continued guild sequence. For a possible identity see 3 n.

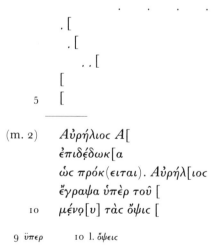

```
          . [
           . [
             . . [
          [
    5     [
          _____

 (m. 2)   Αὐρήλιος Α[
          ἐπιδέδωκ[α
          ὡς πρόκ(ειται). Αὐρήλ[ιος
          ἔγραψα ὑπὲρ τοῦ [
   10     μένο[υ] τὰς ὄψις [
```

8 προ^κ   9 ὕπερ   10 l. ὄψεις

3 Tentatively, the traces could be οἰ[, i.e. οἴ[νου Ὀξυρυγχιτικοῦ, from the guild that follows the κάπηλοι (**3762**) in the extracted sequence of items in **3765** (5–7 together, probably; the items declared by the κάπηλοι are in 3–4).

9–10 E.g. βεβλαμ]μένο[υ].

3764. PROCEEDINGS

70/16 bis (a)
+71/51 (b)   25.5 × 31.5 cm   c. 326

The back of the roll of price-declarations of which **3732–5** are preserved has been used to record proceedings; we have here 13 lines from the end of one case and 12 lines from the beginning of the next. Curiously, the logistes seems not to have been the presiding official (the declarations came into his bureau, admittedly fourteen years earlier); the second case here is held before a διαιτητής, a delegated arbitrator, who was an otherwise unrecorded member of the Oxyrhynchite council. The presiding official in the first case must be identified at 7, but I have failed so far to read the title, see n.

The first case (8) provides our second reference to Ti. Flavius Laetus, *praefectus Aegypti* (cf. LI **3620**), which gives us an approximate date for the hearings (they were both held on the same day, 14).

The details in each case are far from clear. The first appears to concern the disputed ownership of some property and the rents payable for its occupation, perhaps to a girl minor. The prefect had pronounced conditionally in favour of the minor, but the presiding official here defers a decision until he has more information at his disposal. The second case hinges on the non-appearance of one of the parties and the possibility of a judgment by default (cf. **3759**). The arbitrator seems ill-informed (23) of the details of his own position.

```
          .     .    .     .    .
. . . . . . . . . . . αι . . . . . . [        c. 30              ]
cτεγανόμια παρεσχηκότων τῇ παιδὶ ὁ μὲν Ἱέραξ διεβεβαιώcατο
[ἐ]πὶ χρόνον ᾠκηκέναι, cτεγανόμια δὲ παρεσχηκέναι
Θαήcει τινί· ὁ δὲ Θῶνιος ἐν τάξει κηδεμόνος φαίνεται ἑcτηκώς.
5  Ἀμμώνιος ῥ(ήτωρ) εἶ(πεν)· ἡμεῖc ἐπριάμεθα τὸ οἰκόπεδον· δειξάτω βία[ν.]
   ἀλλ᾽ οὐδὲν ἐδίχθη ⟦τῶν ἐπὶ τοῦ⟧ ‵ὧν ἐδίδαξαν τὸ μεγαλεῖον τοῦ ′ κυρίου μου
       .        ‵διαcημ(οτάτου) ′ ἐπάρχου ⟦πεπραγμένων⟧ ‵τῆc Αἰγύπτου ′.
   /. [. ] . . [.  εἶ](πεν)· ἐπειδὴ προcέταξεν ὁ κύριόc μου διαcημότατοc ἔπαρχοc
   τῆc Αἰγύπτου Φλάουιος Λαῖτος εἰ ε[ὑ]ρεθείη ἡ παῖc ἐκ cυμφών[ου]
   ἐκβληθεῖcα ⟦. .⟧ τῆc οἰκεία[c] ταύτην εἰcάξαι εἰc τὴν νομήν, ἐπεὶ τ . . . . .
10 τουτ[1-2] . [. ] . προχενομενο[. κ]αὶ ἕτερά τινα δίκαια περὶ δεcποτίαc
   ἀμφότερα μέρη κατέθετο, ἔτι τ[ῶ]ν χρόνων ἐνδιδόντων δύναcθ⟦αι⟧ε
   α . . . . τω[. ] ἀναδιδάξαι καὶ ὅρου τυχεῖν ⟦παρὰ τῆc ἡμετέραc⟧
   ⟦μετριότητοc⟧.
```

2 ἱέραξ?   6 ἀλλ᾽ added in margin; l. ἐδείχθη; διαcημʃ   9 l. οἰκίαc   10].[: a long descender (ι, ρ, φ, or ψ?)   13 Extent of deletion not quite certain

τῇ αὐτῇ ἡμέρᾳ, πρὸς τῷ Ἀδριανίῳ. ἐπὶ παρόντων Παύλου προσθυρέου,

15   ἐπὶ Ἀςκληπ[ιά]δρ[υ] Διονυσοδώρου β[ο]υλ(ευτοῦ) διαιτητοῦ.

Ἀμμώνιος ῥ(ήτωρ) εἶ(πεν)· Ὠριγένης πρὸς ἀντιδίκους Ἀρτεμιδώραν καὶ κληρο-

νόμους Ε.[3-4].ου. ὡς μὲν δι[αιτητὴς εἶ] ἡμῖν αἱρουμένοις καὶ τοῖς ἀντιδίκοις

τοῦτο οὐ μόνον διδάςκει ὁ παρὼ[ν] λόγος ἀλλὰ καὶ τὰ ἐπιστάλματα τοῦ ἀξιολο-

γωτάτου π[ρυ]τάνεως πε . . . [.] . . ἐπειδὴ δὲ ἀπ' ἐκείνης τῆς ἡμέρας

20   [κα]θ' ἣν ἐ[π]εςτάλης σήμερον χρόνοι πληροῦνται, διὰ τοῦτο πάρες[μεν] [ἀ]ξιοῦντες ἐπισημήνασθαι μὲν τὴν ἀπόλιψιν τὴν τῶν ἀντιδί[κων], συνχωρῆσαι δὲ ἡμῖν τὰ αἴτια τῆς ὑποθέσεως εἰπεῖν. /ὁ δι-

αιτητὴς εἶ(πεν)· δεῖξον πότε ἐπεστάλην διαιτητὴς γενέσθαι ὑμῶν.

[Ἀμμώνι]ος ῥ(ήτωρ) εἶ(πεν)· κατὰ τὴν κγ′ τοῦ Χοιὰκ μηνὸς ἐπεστάλης

25   [*c.* 20   ].[*c.* 10   ] . . . . [. .]η . . . ςε[*c.* 7   ]

14 l. Ἀδριανείῳ, παρόντος, προσθυραίου   15 β[ο]υλ   20-1 Ends of lines obscured by ink-blots
21 l. ἀπόλειψιν

'"... (of?) those who have paid rents to the girl, Hierax on the one hand confirmed that he had lived there for some time but paid the rents to one Thaesis; Thonius on the other hand is here present in court in his capacity as guardian." Ammonius, advocate, said, "We bought the property; let him prove violence. But none of the story they told the Highness of my lord the prefect of Egypt, *vir perfectissimus*, was proved." [The?] ... said, "Since my lord the prefect of Egypt, Flavius Laetus, *vir perfectissimus*, instructed that if the girl should be found to have been indisputably thrown out of the house she should be installed in possession, (and?) since ... and both sides have put forward further claims regarding ownership, you may, since the time still admits of it, ... inform (me?) and obtain a ruling."'

(14 ff.) 'On the same day, at the Hadrianeum. In the presence of Paul, doorkeeper; before Asclepiades son of Dionysodorus, councillor, arbitrator. Ammonius, advocate, said, "(My client is) Horigenes against his adversaries Artemidora and the heirs of ... That you are the arbitrator whom we and our adversaries chose not only the present discussion tells us but so also the instructions of the most respected prytanis ... Since from that day on which you were appointed today the time is up, for this reason we are present requesting that you take note of the default of our adversaries, and that you allow us to state the origins of the suit." The arbitrator said, "Show when I was appointed to be your arbitrator." Ammonius, advocate, said, "On the 23rd of the month of Choiak you were appointed ..."'

6 τὸ μεγαλεῖον. Cf. CPR V 12. 4 and n.

7 This must be the title or possibly the name of the presiding official at the beginning of the line, but I have failed to read it. At any rate the reading is not /ὁ λογιςτὴς εἶ(πεν).

8 Ti. Flavius Laetus was known as prefect of Egypt on 2 February 326 (LI **3620**). His predecessor Flavius Magnus was still in office on 2 October 325 (**3759**); his next known successor Septimius Zenius was in office in Oct./Nov. 327 (P. Harr. II 215 recto). See *BASP* 22 (1985) 25-7 for another prefect in this period.

9 τρίγνν would suit very well at the end but it leaves us without a connective.

14 Ἀδριανίῳ ... προσθυρέου (l. Ἀδριανείῳ, προσθυραίου). For the doorkeepers of the prison in the

Hadrianeum cf. L **3576** 18–19n. There are now several items of evidence to support προϲθυραῖοϲ; προϲθυρεύϲ may well not exist. For the ἐπὶ παρόντων formula cf. **3758** 156–8n. The formulaic plural is inappropriate here.

16–17 'Ωριγένηϲ κτλ. For 'statements of client' of this type cf. **3758** 41n.

18–19 ἀξιολογωτάτου. See H. Geremek, *JJP* 16–17 (1971) 162–4.

24 Choiak 23 = 19 December (the year can really only be 325 or 326, so that leap-year calculations are irrelevant). There are no grounds for linking the prefecture of Laetus (8) with this date.

3765. Summary of Prices Declared; and Declaration of Prices by the Guild of Goldsmiths

3 1B.77/B(7)a   76.5 × 8 cm   *c.* 327

This text is without parallel in this archive or elsewhere. Four fragments combine into a long strip from the top edge of a roll and preserve the tops of seven columns. The seventh column is the beginning of the declaration by the goldsmiths (cf. **3768**) to the logistes Flavius Thannyras (see 49n. and Appendix I below) previously known only from I **83** and **83a** (16 January 327). The six preceding columns have extracted the items and prices declared in such declarations, arranged in no immediately discernible order and with no divisions between the guilds. Prices are in the same hand as the items; there is some evidence of in-filling (blacker ink in cols. ii, iii, vi) but this is not consistent. Apart from the loss of an unknown number of columns at the beginning with yet more extracted items and prices, I believe that we have the beginning of a roll of declarations; that the declaration of the goldsmiths came first in the series, and that it was prefaced either by a summary of the items and prices declared the previous month, or (if prices were inserted) by the items and current prices extracted from the declarations that immediately followed.

The summarized items and prices can be compared in some six places with items and prices in our complete declarations. The two clearest and best-preserved passages are both echoed in declarations of a couple of years or so later: with 18–23 cf. P. Harr. I 73 ii (re-ed. *ZPE* 37 (1980) 231) and with 32–40 cf. XXXI **2570** iii republished below as **3766** v. The comparison enables us further to revise the text of P. Harr. 73 (see below, 21 n.). The later prices generally show an increase, varying up to 300% (18, cf. 23), but in one instance (33) there is no change and in another (35) the price two years later was lower! Also with 1–2 cf. **3761** 13–14; with 3–4 cf. **3740** 16–17 and **3762** 15–16; with 9–11 perhaps cf. **3753** 17–19 (and therefore possibly with 8 cf. **3752** 19); with 12–15 cf. **3776** 15–19 and LI **3626** 16–20.

I have suggested in *ZPE* 39 (1980) 115 that, whatever the original basis for the order of the guilds, the declarations would be drawn up by copying the previous month's roll. They should thus preserve a consistent order, and it would be reasonable to suppose that **3765**'s extracts follow this same order. That this is to a certain extent so is shown by 1–4, which follow the order of **3739–40** and **3761–2**, and 8–11, which may tally with **3752–3**. This information in turn may justify the use of **3765** as a vital factor in creating the framework for the sequence of guilds proposed in Appendix II below. (The item in 16, priced at 80 tal., should on this basis be the same item that recurs in P. Harr. 73. 20 as re-edited in *ZPE* 37 (1980) 231, apparently only 1,000 den. a couple of years or so later. Although some prices might drop (cf. 35), this is inconceivable; the answer might be that a figure in talents preceded the denarii in P. Harr. 73. 20. P. Harr. 73 i may on the other hand be a different guild, declaring at least two (ll. 20–1) and possibly more different items; but in **3765**, 16–17 (plus more preceding, lost?) surely belong together, and inasmuch as they are dyestuffs they naturally adjoin 18–23, declared by the βαφεῖς; see P. Harr. 73 as re-edited.)

Written along the fibres; the text is not a τόμος cυγκολλήcιμος. Visible kollema-widths are 22 cm, 20 cm, and 18.5 cm. There is no kollesis between cols. vi and vii. The back is blank.

col. i

φάβατος	(ἀρτάβης) α	τάλ(αντα) ϛ
κυ[μί]νου	(ἀρτάβης) α	τάλ(αντα) η
οἴνου Ὀαϲιτικοῦ	ξ(έcτου) α	(δηνάρια) φ
κνιδίου Θηβαϊκ[ο]ῦ	ξ(έcτου) α	(δηνάρια) τοϛ
5 οἴνου Ὀξυρυγχ[ιτικοῦ]	ξ(έcτου) α	(δηνάρια) τοϛ
ὄξους Ὀξυρυγχ[ιτικο]ῦ	ξ(έcτου) α	(δηνάρια) τ
[. .] . [. . Ὀ]ξυρυ[γχιτικ-?		]

. . . . .

col. ii

ὑποδεεϲτέρων χωρικῶν λί(τρας) α		(δηνάρια) φ
cτιππίου τὸ δεϲμίδιον α ′ ἄγον ὁλκ(ῆς) μ(νᾶς) ε		
10 τοῦ μὲν ἐξόχο[υ]		τάλ(αντα) β (δηνάρια) ψν
τοῦ δὲ κοινοῦ		τάλ(αντα) β
ὀθόνης παντοίας δελματικ(ῶν) ταρcι-		
κῶν γυναικ(είων) α εἰδέας ζ(εύγους) α		τάλ(αντα) μ
β εἰδέας	[ζ(εύγουc) α]	τά[λ(αντα)] λ (δηνάρια?) . . .
15 [γ εἰ]δέας [		]

. . . . .

1 ⲧ, ταλ′   3 ✕   6 ✕?   8 ⳑ   9 ολᴷ μʃ   12 δελματιᴷ   13 γυναιᴷ

col. iii

Νικαϊνῆ[c]	λί(τρας) α	τάλ(αντα) π
ῥιζείν[η]c	λί(τρας) α	τάλ(αντα) γ
πορφύρα[c ἐ]ντοπ(ίου)	λί(τρας) α	τάλ(αντα) β
κοκκίνου α	λί(τρας) α	τάλ(αντα) η
20 β κοκκίνου	λί(τρας) α	τάλ(αντα) β

ϲανδυκίνου καὶ χλωροῦ καὶ
   καλλαΐνων καὶ τῶ[ν .] . . [.] . . ` . ´ λί(τρας) α τάλ(αντον) α (δηνάρια) . [
[ῥ]οδίνου   λί(τρας) α   τάλ(αντον) α [   ]

. . . . .

col. iv

θηλιῶν ὁμοίως (πρωτο)βόλου		τάλ[(αντα)] ϲ
25 (δευτερο)βόλου		τάλ(αντα) ρν
τελείας		τάλ(αντα) ρ
ταύρου τελείου		τάλ(αντα) ϲλ
ὑποδεεϲτέρου		τάλ(αντα) ϲ
κρέως μοϲχ[ε]ί[ο]υ	λί(τρας) α	(δηνάρια?) . [.] .
30 βοὸς τελείας		τάλ(αντα) ρ
[.] . . [. .] . . . . . [ ]		τά[λ(αντ-)]

. . . . .

col. v

ϲτύρακος ἐλαφροῦ	λί(τρας) α	τάλ(αντα) δ
κόϲτου	[λ]ί(τρας) [α	τά]λ(αντα) ϛ
μαϲτίκης	λί(τρας) α	[τάλ(αντα)] δ
35 ἀμμώμου	λ[ί(τρας)] α	[τάλ(αντα)] η
βδέλλη[ϲ]	λί(τρας) α	τ[άλ(αντα)] ε
καϲίας	λί(τρας) α	τάλ(αντα) ϛ
καϲάμο[υ]	λί(τρας) α	τάλ(αντον) α (δηνάρια) φ
ψιμιτ[ίου]	λί(τρας) α	[ ] .
40 . . . . [		]

. . . . .

<hr>

16 νικαϊνης   17 l. ῥιζίνης   18 εντοπ´   24 l. θηλειῶν; αβολου   25 β βολου
29 Beginning of κρέως corr.?   ✕?   30 l. βοός   31 Only occasional ink spots survive of the
item in this line   32 An unexplained mark in the upper margin above the beginning of this line
34 l. μαϲτίχης   35 l. ἀμώμου   39 l. ψιμνθίου

col. vi

ὑποδεεστέρας	τάλ(αντα) κ
βοΐνης τελείας	τάλ(αντα) κ
ὑποδεεστέρας	[τά]λ(αντα) ιε
αἰγίου τελείου	τ̣ά̣λ(αντα) δ
45 ὑπ[οδε]εστέρας	τάλ(αντα) β
προβατίου τελείου	τάλ(αντα) β
ὑπο[δεεστ]έ[ρου	τά]λ(αντον) α̣
...[c. 9].[	].[ ]

. . . . .

col. vii

(m. 2)	Φλαουίῳ Θαν[ν]υρᾷ
50	λογιστῇ Ὀξυρυγχίτου
	παρὰ τοῦ κοινοῦ τῶν
	χρυσοχόων τῆς λαμ(πρᾶς)
	καὶ λαμ[(προτάτης) Ὀ]ξ(υρυγχιτῶν) πόλεως
	δι᾽ ἡμ[ῶ]ν̣ τῶν μηνι-
55	αρχ[ῶν Α]ὐρηλίων
(m. 3)	Ἀμμωνί[ο]υ̣ καὶ τοῦ ἀδελφοῦ
	.[c. 15]...

. . . . .

44 l. αἰγείου   45 l. ὑποδεεστέρου   46 l. προβατείου   52 λαμϲ   53 [ο]ξ´

(1–7)	'Beans	1 art.	tal. 6
	'Cummin	1 art.	tal. 8
	'Oasite wine	1 sextarius	den. 500
	'Theban (wine)		
	of Cnidian type	1 sextarius	den. 375
	'Oxyrhynchite wine	1 sextarius	den. 375
	'Oxyrhynchite cheap		
	wine	1 sextarius	den. 300
	'Oxyrhynchite(?) [ ]	[	]

(8–15)	'Inferior, local	1 lb.	den. 500
	'Tow, per single bundle having a weight of 5 minas,		
	superior quality		tal. 2 den. 750
	standard quality		tal. 2
	'Linen of all kinds: ladies' Tarsian sleeved tunics,		
	1st quality	1 pr.	tal. 40
	2nd quality	[1 pr.]	tal. 30(?) den.? ...
	3rd quality	[	]

(16–23)	'Nicaean (purple)	1 lb.	tal. 80
	'Root (purple)	1 lb.	tal. 3
	'Local purple	1 lb.	tal. 2
	'Scarlet, 1st grade	1 lb.	tal. 8
	'2nd grade scarlet	1 lb.	tal. 2
	'Bright red, and yellow orpiment(?), and		
	blue-green and . . .	1 lb.	tal. 1 den. . . .
	'Pink	1 lb.	tal. 1 [ ]

(24–31)	'Females likewise: at 1st tooth-change		tal. 200
	at 2nd tooth-change		tal. 150
	full-grown		tal. 100
	'Bull, full-grown		tal. 230
	inferior		tal. 200
	'Veal	1 lb.	den.? . . .
	'Cow, full-grown		tal. 100
	inferior(?)		tal. [ ]

(32–40)	'Storax, dwarf	1 lb.	tal. 4
	'Costmary	1 lb.	tal. 6
	'Mastic	1 lb.	tal. 4
	'Amomum	1 lb.	tal. 8
	'Bdellium	1 lb.	tal. 5
	'Cassia	1 lb.	tal. 6
	'Cassamum	1 lb.	tal. 1 den. 500(?)
	'White lead	1 lb.	[ ]
	'. . . .	[	]

(41–8)	'inferior	tal. 20
	'Oxhide, from a full-grown animal	tal. 20
	inferior	tal. 15
	'Goatskin, from a full-grown animal	tal. 4
	inferior	tal. 2
	'Sheepskin, from a full-grown animal	tal. 2
	inferior	tal. 1
	'. . . [	]

(49 ff.) (m. 2) 'To Flavius Thannyras, *curator* of the Oxyrhynchite, from the guild of the goldsmiths of the illustrious and most illustrious city of the Oxyrhynchites, through us the monthly presidents Aurelii' (m. 3) 'Ammonius and his brother . . . '

1–2 Cf. **3761** 13–14.

3 ξ(ἑϲτου). For the form of the abbreviation see **3740** 16–17 n.

3–4 Cf. **3740** 16–17 n.

5 On Oxyrhynchite wine note **3740** 7 n.

8 Perhaps linen, cf. **3752** 19 and the introd. above, and n. 16 on Appendix III below.

9–11 These items will perhaps derive from a declaration by the ϲτιπποχειριϲταί, despite the variant wording in **3753**, our sole declaration by them. The third grade (ὑποδεεϲτέρων χωρικῶν there) is absent here, by accident or design. For conversion from minas to pounds see D. W. Rathbone, *ZPE* 53 (1983) 267; 5 minas = 5.20833 lb.

12–15 Cf. **3776** 15–19, and also LI **3626** 16–20.

13 ζ(εὔγουϲ). Cf. **3776** 17 n. The abbreviation is a zeta with an oblique stroke rising to the right at a shallow angle to cut the lower horizontal.

14 The reading of the price is very uncertain.

16–17 On these two items cf. the introd. above. The two adjectives, without further specification, will surely derive from the declaration of one guild. The price-difference between the two items is notable. For dyestuffs in general see H. Dürbeck, *Zur Charakteristik der griechischen Farbenbezeichnungen* (Bonn, 1977).

Νικαϊνῆ[c]. I presume this is the same as πορφύρας Νεικαηνῆς κοκκηρᾶς of the Price Edict, §24. 8 ed. Giacchero. For the spelling cf. Νεικαϊνῆς of the Megara IV copy, reported in Lauffer's apparatus. The high price compared with the dyestuffs following is appropriate for a genuine import. Lauffer's edition gives a bibliography for the type, p. 271; Νικαεινῆς πορφύρας also in P. Strasb. 131. 7.

For ῥιζείνης cf. P. Holm. 26. 28 (now re-ed. R. Halleux, *Les Alchim. grecs* i (1981)) and P. Strasb. 131. 6, 8. I. Andorlini, in M. Manfredi *et al.*, *Trenta testi greci (editi in occ. del XVII Congr. int. di Pap.)* (Florence, 1983) 18. 24 n., supposes equivalence with πορφύρα ἐντόπιος in P. Harr. I 73. 40 (re-ed. R. A. Coles, *ZPE* 37 (1980) 231), but the lower price for the latter in the next line here (18) implies a distinction between the two grades. For purple see also G. H. R. Horsley, *New Documents Illustrating Early Christianity* iii (1983) 53–4.

18–23 Cf. the declaration of the βαφεῖς, P. Harr. 73 re-ed. R. A. Coles, op. cit. The numismatic information in R. S. Bagnall, *Currency and Inflation in Fourth-century Egypt* (*BASP* suppl. 5 (1985)) 37 could suggest that P. Harr. 73 will date not earlier than 330; on the other hand, the modest increase in the price of first-grade κόκκινος (cf. the table in Appendix III below) does not well accord with this.

18 πορφύρα[c]. Cf. M. Manfredi *et al.*, op. cit. 18. 24 n.

19–20 κοκκίνου. Cf. M. Manfredi *et al.*, op. cit. 18. 26 n.; P. Laur. III 82. 2 n.

20 β κοκκίνου. This confirms the reading of the less legible parallel passage in P. Harr. 73. 42 (as re-ed. loc. cit.).

21 cανδυκίνου will presumably be the word I could not read at the beginning of P. Harr. 73. 43 (as re-ed. loc. cit.). Cf. P. Laur. III 82. 4 n.; M. Manfredi *et al.*, op. cit. 19. 7 n.

χλωροῦ. Cf. M. Manfredi *et al.*, op. cit. 18. 25 n. An identification with trisulphide of arsenic (*ZPE* 37 (1980) 234) may not be correct: Miss Gillian Eastwood informs me that textile dyes should be organic. (ἀρcενικόν nevertheless features in two dye recipes, Halleux, op. cit. 150 with p. 204 n. Thphr. *Lap.* 51 refers to painters' pigments, not dyestuffs (rejecting with Eichholz the reading βαφεῖς). The edition by Caley and Richards, *Theophrastus on Stones* pp. 171–2, has a useful note on ἀρcενικόν.)

22 καλλαῖνων. Note P. J. Sijpesteijn, *ZPE* 30 (1978) 233–4; M. Manfredi *et al.*, op. cit. 18. 21 n. I cannot make out the last word of the substances listed in 21–2. cυγχρόων (cf. P. Harr. 73. 44 as re-ed. loc. cit.) must be a likely candidate, but I cannot claim to see it.

24–30 For a revised version of the Price Edict's §30 (ed. Giacchero) see M. H. Crawford and J. M. Reynolds, *ZPE* 34 (1979) 177–8 with commentary on pp. 198–9.

24–6 For the meaning of the terms (πρωτο)βόλου and (δευτερο)βόλου see CPR VI p. 20. Comparison with the Price Edict (§30, as revised, see 24–30 n. above) suggests that the animals listed here may be female donkeys. Both in the Edict and here the price is approximately on a par with that for bulls (230 tal. here, 27). The value of a female donkey reduces with age, presumably because of the reduced breeding potential. However, the fourth-century donkey prices listed by R. S. Bagnall, op. cit. (18–23 n. above) 67–8 have reached nowhere near **3765**'s prices (c. 327) by 331, the latest example he lists (40 tal.), and it may be that horses are meant here, cf. his list of prices for them on p. 68.

29 For fourth-century meat prices see Bagnall, op. cit. 67.

31 One might guess ὑποδεεcτέρας came in this line, but the traces are too scanty for any indication.

32–40 For the commentary on these items declared by the μυροπῶλαι see **3766**.

35 Not clear if αμμ- or αμ- was intended.

37 Initial κ oddly written; perhaps there has been a correction.

38 The denarius-figure is uncertain, but ψ is the only alternative to φ; if ψ, a trace to the right may be from a second letter, probably ν. φ (= $\frac{1}{3}$ tal.) and ψν (= $\frac{1}{2}$ tal.) are likely quantities.

40 Presumably cανδυκίου, cf. **3766** 96, but I cannot claim to read it in the scattered and broken traces.

41–7 These entries must refer to hides. For the ox-hides the noun implied is βύρcης, cf. §8. 6a, 9 in the Price Edict (ed. Giacchero); for the other hides the noun is δέρματος. The feminine ending in 45 must be an error.

49 The *curator*'s name: the sole alleged evidence for the spelling Thennyras is I **83** with its duplicate **83a**. The original of **83** is missing and I have no photograph; the name is awkwardly written in **83a** but alpha seems preferable to epsilon.

52 We may conclude from **3773** (see the introd. to that text) that the goldsmiths declared the price of the gold solidus (cf. **3768** introd.).

3766. Declarations of Prices

4 1B.76/3(c)   41 × 27 cm   27 October 329

Under this number we republish **XXXI 2570** ii–iii (here cols. iv–v) together with a new joining fragment which completes **2570** i (here col. iii) and adds a further column before that (col. ii). There are extremely scanty traces of a yet further preceding column which we do not transcribe. The guilds now represented are the fish-merchants (ἰχθυοπῶλαι, col. ii), the fullers (κναφεῖϲ, col. iii), the potters of earthenware pottery (κεραμεῖϲ κεραμικοῦ κεράμου, col. iv) and the perfume-sellers (μυροπῶλαι, col. v). Suggested readings for **2570** in *BL* VI (p. 110) are all mistaken.

The identification of the fish-merchants in col. ii supports the identification of this guild in PSI III 202 col. ii, proposed in *ZPE* 37 (1980) 230, since in both declarations what is declared is the price of ἰχθύων παντοίων. Not enough survives to identify the guild of our col. i, unfortunately; the knowledge would have helped—one way or the other—with the problem of the order of the guilds, since in PSI 202 the χοιρομάγειροι precede the ἰχθυοπῶλαι. The next two guilds are still sole representatives, but documentation on the μυροπῶλαι is accumulating: cf. **3731**, **3733**, and **3765**. The surviving guilds in **3766** are arranged roughly alphabetically, but this may not be deliberate.

As regards col. iv, for pottery manufacture in Egypt see now H. M. Cockle, *JRS* 71 (1981) 87–97 with L **3595–7**.

The logistes to whom the declarations are addressed, Flavius Julianus, is known from several texts (see Appendix I below); this one is still the earliest evidence for his tenure. See **3755** 27–8 n. regarding his family and probable earlier career.

Kolleseis occur between cols. i and ii and between cols. iv and v. This is fortuitous; the text is clearly not a τόμοϲ ϲυγκολλήϲιμοϲ. The kollema bearing ii–iv is approximately 20 cm wide (the visible width of the sheet).

Distinction of hands poses a problem, as often in these declarations. For the expected format in texts of this type see **3731** introd. As far as the preliminary drafting goes, there are frequent changes of style and one gets the impression that, at the minimum, the upper parts of the texts are due to one hand and the lower parts (generally, προϲφων- onwards) to another. As for the insertions, the prices in cols. ii and iv are added in a different hand. In cols. iii and v they are in the same hand as the draft; the single example in iii shows no sign of being a later insertion, but several of the prices in v are clearly so. As for the subscriptions, a hypographeus was employed in cols. iii–iv, Aurelius Horion. If he were responsible for the name-insertions (probable in col. ii, possible in col. v), he will have been a scribe in the logistes' bureau. See Appendix IV below. Insertion of the price in col. ii may be by his hand. The subscription in col. v could be an autograph; that in col. ii is too badly damaged to allow certainty, but may also be an autograph.

I have numbered the lines of the five columns continuously throughout. I do not repeat the inconvenient line-numbering of the *ed. pr.*

On the other side, along the fibres, is **3767**. The new piece supplies the beginning of the report of proceedings, **XXXI 2562**, and the whole is now re-edited as **3767**. The minimum interval before reuse of the declarations to take the obsolete proceedings on the back would be a month, the maximum interval thirteen months: see **3767** introd.

col. ii

. . . .

```
         [      c. 11      ].[   c. 7   ]
         [      c. 14      ].[  c. 4   ]
         [      c. 12      ]....[ c. 3 ]
         [      c. 15      ].[.].[.]
 5      ....[    c. 8    τῶ]ν ἰχθυ-
        ρπωλ[ῶ]ν τ[ῆ]ς [λα]μ[(πρᾶc) κ]αὶ λαμ(προτάτηc) Ὀ[ξ](υρυγχιτῶν)
        [......]..[...] Αὐρ(ηλίου)
(m. 2)  [....].[....] Παμούνιος
(m. 1?) προ[c]φ[ω]νῷ ἰδίῳ τι-
 10     [μή]ματι τὴν ἑξῆc
        [ἐγ]γεγραμμένην τι-
        [μ]ὴν ἐ[πὶ] τοῦδε τοῦ
        μ[ηνὸc] ὧν χιρίζω ὠνί-
        ων καὶ [ὀ]μ[ν]ύῳ τ[ὸ]ν
 15     θεῖον ὅρ[κο]ν μηδὲν δι-
        εψεῦcθ[αι. ἔc]τι δέ·
        ἰ[χ]θύων παντοίων
              λί(τραc) α [(δηνάρια)] (m. 2) φ.
```

```
(m. 3)        Αὐρ(ήλιος) ...... ειαρχης
 20     [...].[..].[...]...ε..
        ..β[....] ἐπιδέ[δ]ω-
        κα π[ροc]φ(ωνῶν) ὡ[c] πρόκ(ειται).
```

col. iii

```
(m. 1)  [ὑπατ]είαc τῶν
        [δεcποτ]ῶν ἡμῶν
 25     [Κωνcταν]τίνου Αὐγούc[του]
```

5 ἰχθυ	6 λαμ̣	7 αυρ″: rewritten?	9 ἰδιω	13 l. χειρίζω	17 ἰ[χ]θυων
18 λ	19 αυρ′?	22 προ^κ?			

[τὸ η ΄ καὶ] Κωνσταντίνο[υ]

[τοῦ ἐπιφ]ανεστάτου Καίϲαροϲ

[τὸ δ΄,] Φαῶφι λ⁻.

[Φλαου]ίῳ Ἰουλιανῷ λογ(ιϲτῇ) Ὀξ(υρυγχίτου)

30 [παρ]ὰ τοῦ κο[ι]νοῦ τῶν κναφέ-

[ω]ν τῆϲ λαμ(πρᾶϲ) κᾳὶ λαμ(προτάτηϲ) Ὀξ(υρυγχιτῶν) πόλεῳϲ

[δι᾽ ἡμ]ῷν μηνιαρχῶν Αὐρ(ηλίων)

(m. 1, added?) Γερμα[νοῦ] Πλουτίωνοϲ καὶ Ϲαρα-

πίωνοϲ Διοϲκόρου καὶ Θε[ογν]ώϲ-

35 του Νείλου καὶ Θῶνι̣[οϲ ?Φι]λο-

ξένου. (m. 1?) προϲφωνοῦ[μ]ε̣ν

ἰδίῳ τιμήμ[α]τι τὴν ἑξῆϲ

ἐνγεγραμμένην τιμὴν

ἐ̣π̣ὶ τοῦδε τοῦ μη[νὸϲ ὦν]

40 χιρ̣ί̣[ζο]μεν ὠν[ίων] καὶ

ὀμν[ύο]μ̣[εν τὸν θεῖο]ν

ὄρκον μηδ[ὲν διε]ψεῦϲθαι.

[ἔϲτι δ]έ̣·

44 νίτρου Ἀραβικοῦ κε̣ν̣(τηναρίου) α (δηνάρια) (m. 1, added?) φ.

_____

(m. 2) Αὐρ(ήλιοι) Γερμανὸϲ καὶ Ϲαραπίω[ν] καὶ

Θεόγνωϲτοϲ καὶ Θῶνιϲ ἐπιδε-

δώκαμεν προϲφ(ωνοῦντεϲ) ὡϲ πρόκ(ειται). Αὐρ(ήλιοϲ) Ὠρίω[ν]

ἔγρ(αψα) ὑ(πὲρ) αὐτ(ῶν) γρ(άμματα) μὴ εἰ̣δ̣(ότων).

col. iv

(m. 1) ὑ̣π̣α̣τ̣ε̣ίᾳϲ τῷν̣

50 δ̣εϲποτῶν ἡ[μῶν]

Κωνϲταντίνου

Αὐγούϲτου τὸ η΄κᾳὶ

Κωνϲταντίνου τοῦ̣

ἐπιφανεϲτάτου Καίϲ[α]ρ̣οϲ

29 [φλαου]ιωϊουλιανωλογʃ(?)οξ΄   31 λαμʃοξ΄   32 Ductus of Αὐρ(ηλίων) not clear: some interference with the line above   37 ϊδιω   38 l. ἐγγεγραμμένην   40 χ re-written; l. χειρίζομεν   43 Trace is a horizontal finishing-stroke   44 κενʃ, ✳   45 αυρ΄   47 προϲφ΄, προᵏαυρ΄   48 εγρʃυ)αυτºγρʃ, ει̣ᵈ?

55 τὸ δ΄, Φαῶφι λ‾.

  Φλαουίῳ Ἰουλιαν̣ῷ

   λογιστῇ Ὀξυρ[υγ]χίτου

  παρὰ τοῦ κοινοῦ τῶν

  κεραμέων κεραμικοῦ

60 [κ]εράμου τ̣ῆς λ[α]μ(πρᾶς) καὶ λαμ(προτάτης) Ὀξ(υρυγχιτῶν)

  [πό]λ̣εως δι᾽ ἐμοῦ Α[ὐρ](ηλίου)

(m. 1, added?) Δημητρί̣ο̣υ [Μ]έ̣λ̣α̣[νο]ς.

 (m. 1?) προσφωνῶ ἰδ[ίῳ] τ̣ι-

   μήματι τὴν ἑξῇ[ς ἐ]ν-

65 γεγραμμέν̣ην [τιμὴν]

  ἐπὶ τοῦδε τοῦ [μηνὸ]ς

  ὧν χιρίζω ὠ̣[νίων]

  καὶ ὀμν̣ύω τὸν θεῖ[ον]

  ὅρκον μηδὲν δι̣ε-

70 ψεῦσθαι. ἔστι δέ·

  πίσσης ξηρᾶς ζ̣ι̣ρ̣ι-

  τικῆς κεν(τηναρίου) α τάλ(αντα) (m. ?, added) γ

(m. 1?) Τρῳαδ[η]ς̣ίας κε[ν](τηναρίου) [α   ]

  ———

(m. 2) Αὐρ(ήλιος) Δημήτριος ἐπιδέ[δω-]

75 κα προσφ(ωνῶν) ὡς πρόκ(ειται). Α(ὐρήλιος) Ὠρί[ων]

  ἔγρ(αψα) ὑ(πὲρ) αὐτο[ῦ] γρ(άμματα) μὴ ε̣ἰδότος.

     col. v

(m. 1) ὑπατείας τ̣ῶν δε̣ςποτῶν ἡμῶν Κ̣ω[νςταντίνου Αὐγούςτου τὸ η ΄ καὶ]

  Κωνσταντίνου τοῦ ἐπιφανεστάτου Κ[αίσαρος τὸ δ΄, Φαῶφι λ‾.]

  Φλαουίῳ Ἰουλιανῷ   λ[ογιστῇ Ὀξυρυγχίτου]

80 παρὰ τοῦ̣ κ̣οινοῦ τῶν μυροπωλῶν [τῆς λαμ(πρᾶς) καὶ λαμ(προτάτης)

  Ὀξ(υρυγχιτῶν) πόλεως δι᾽ ἐμοῦ Αὐρ(ηλίου)]

(m. 2?) Θωνίου Θέωνος. (m. 1?) προσφωνῶ ἰδίῳ τ̣ι[μήματι τὴν ἑξῆς ἐγγεγραμ-

        μένην]

56 φλαουιῳϊουλιαν̣ω   60 λαμ/οξ΄   61 α[υρ]΄   63 ϊδ[ιω]   64 l. ἐγ-   67 l.
χειρίζω 72 κεν/, ταλ΄   73 κεν/   74 αυρ΄   75 προσφ΄, προ\^κ α‾   76 εγρ/υ), γρ/
79 φλαουιῳϊουλιανω   81 ϊδιω?

τιμὴν ἐπὶ τοῦδε τοῦ μηνὸς ὧν χ[ειρίζω ὠνίων, καὶ ὀμνύω τὸν θεῖον]
ὅρκον μηδὲν διεψεῦςθαι.   [ἔςτι δέ·]

84	πιπέρεως	λί(τρας) α	τάλ(αντα)	(m. 1, added)	ιβ
(m. 1?)	λιβάνου	λί(τρας) α	τάλ(αντα)	(m. 1, added)	β
(m. 1?)	μαλαβάθρου	λί(τρας) α	τάλ(αντα)	(m. 1, added)	ν
(m. 1?)	cτύρακος ὑψηλοῦ	λί(τρας) α	τάλ(αντα)	(m. 1, added)	κ
(m. 1?)	cτύρακος ἐλαφροῦ	λί(τρας) α	τάλ(αντα)	(m. 1, added)	ι
(m. 1?)	κόcτου	λί(τρας) α	τάλ(αντα)	(m. 1, added)	ϛ
(m. 1?)	μαcτίκης	λί(τρας) α	τάλ(αντα)	(m. 1, added)	ι
(m. 1?)	ἀμώμου	λί(τρας) α	τάλ(αντα)	(m. 1, added)	ϛ
(m. 1?)	βδέλλης	λί(τρας) α	τάλ(αντα)	(m. 1, added)	ζ
(m. 1?)	καcίας	λί(τρας) α	τάλ(αντα)	(m. 1, added)	.
(m. 1?)	καcάμου	λί(τρας) α	τάλ(αντα)	(m. 1, added)	β
(m. 1?)	ψιμιτίου	λί(τρας) α	τάλ(αντον)	(m. 1, added)	α (δηνάρια) Ά
(m. 1?)	[c]ανδυκίου	λί(τρας) α	τάλ(αντα)	(m. 1, added)	δ
(m. 1?)	ζμύρνης	λί(τρας) α	τάλ(αντα) [		]

(98–112 to right of 84–97)

98	[		]
	[.] . [		]
100	μοχλω . . [		]
	[ζ]ινκιπέρεως [		]
	πατήμ[ατος		]
	ἀcφαλαν[θ]ίου	λί(τρας) α	τ[άλ(αντα)]
	ἀρναβωρατίων	λ[ί(τρας) α	]
105	cαcέλεως	λί(τρας) α	(δηνάρια) (m. 1, added) Ά
(m. 1?)	cφαγνίου	λί(τρας) α	(δηνάρια) (m. 1, added) Ά
(m. 1?)	εἰρωνων	λί(τρας) α	(δηνάρια) (m. 1, added) Ά
(m. 1?)	ἐλενιδίων	λί(τρας) α	(δηνάρια) (m. 1, added) Ά
(m. 1?)	ἀλκεωτίδων	λί(τρας) α	(δηνάρια) (m. 1, added) Ά
(m. 1?)	ὀνυχίων	λ[ί(τρας)] α [	]
111	ξυλομα[cτίχης		]
	αλ[ιμαcτου?		]

(113 below 97)

(m. 4)   Αὐρ(ήλιος) Θω . . . . [.] . . . . . . [

84 λ, ταλ   85 ταλ´ and so elsewhere; the diagonal may be omitted, as in 84   αλ re-inked in 85
90 l. μαcτίχης   95 l. ψιμυθίου, ✶   101 l. ζιγγιβέρεως   103 l. ἀcπαλάθου?   113 αυρ´

Col. ii

'. . . the fish-merchants of the illustrious and most illustrious city of the Oxyrhynchites, . . . Aurelius' (m. 2) '. . . son of Pamunis.' (m. 1?) 'At my own risk I declare the price entered below for the present month for the goods which I handle, and I swear the divine oath that I have been deceitful in nothing. As follows:

'All sorts of fish   1 lb.   den.' (m. 2) '500.'

(m. 3) 'I, Aurelius . . ., presented this, making my declaration as aforesaid.'

Col. iii

(m. 1) 'In the consulship of our masters Constantinus Augustus for the 8th time and Constantinus the most noble Caesar for the 4th time, Phaophi 30. To Flavius Julianus, *curator* of the Oxyrhynchite, from the guild of the fullers of the illustrious and most illustrious city of the Oxyrhynchites, through us monthly presidents Aurelii' (m. 1, added?) 'Germanus son of Plution and Sarapion son of Dioscorus and Theognostus son of Nilus and Thonis son of Philoxenus.' (m. 1?) 'At our own risk we declare the price entered below for the present month for the goods which we handle, and we swear the divine oath that we have been deceitful in nothing. As follows:

'Arabian soda   100 lb.   den.' (m. 1, added?) '500.'

(m. 2) 'We, Aurelii Germanus and Sarapion and Theognostus and Thonis, presented this, making our declaration as aforesaid. I, Aurelius Horion, wrote on their behalf as they are illiterate.'

Col. iv

(m. 1) 'In the consulship of our masters Constantinus Augustus for the 8th time and Constantinus the most noble Caesar for the 4th time, Phaophi 30. To Flavius Julianus, *curator* of the Oxyrhynchite, from the guild of the potters of earthenware pottery of the illustrious and most illustrious city of the Oxyrhynchites, through me Aurelius' (m. 1, added?) 'Demetrius son of (?)Melas.' (m. 1?) 'At my own risk I declare the price entered below for the present month for the goods which I handle, and I swear the divine oath that I have been deceitful in nothing. As follows:

'Dry pitch, Siritic   100 lbs.   tal.' (m. ?, added) '3'.

(m. 1?) 'Troadensian   100 lbs.   [   ]

(m. 2) 'I, Aurelius Demetrius, presented this, making my declaration as aforesaid. I, Aurelius Horion, wrote on his behalf as he is illiterate.'

Col. v

(m. 1) 'In the consulship of our masters Constantinus Augustus for the 8th time and Constantinus the most noble Caesar for the 4th time, Phaophi 30. To Flavius Julianus, *curator* of the Oxyrhynchite, from the guild of the perfume-sellers of the illustrious and most illustrious city of the Oxyrhynchites, through me Aurelius' (m. 2?) 'Thonius son of Theon.' (m. 1?) 'At my own risk I declare the price entered below for the present month for the goods which I handle, and I swear the divine oath that I have been deceitful in nothing. As follows:

'Pepper	1 lb.	tal.' (m. 1, added) '12'.
(m. 1?) 'Incense	1 lb.	tal.' (m. 1, added) '2'.
(m. 1?) 'Malabathrum	1 lb.	tal.' (m. 1, added) '50'.
(m. 1?) 'Storax, tall	1 lb.	tal.' (m. 1, added) '20'.
(m. 1?) 'Storax, dwarf	1 lb.	tal.' (m. 1, added) '10'.
(m. 1?) 'Costmary	1 lb.	tal.' (m. 1, added) '6'.
(m. 1?) 'Mastic	1 lb.	tal.' (m. 1, added) '10'.
(m. 1?) 'Amomum	1 lb.	tal.' (m. 1, added) '6'.
(m. 1?) 'Bdellium	1 lb.	tal.' (m. 1, added) '7'.
(m. 1?) 'Cassia	1 lb.	tal.' (m. 1, added) '.'.
(m. 1?) 'Cassamum	1 lb.	tal.' (m. 1, added) '2'.
(m. 1?) 'White lead	1 lb.	tal.' (m. 1, added) '1, den. 1,000'.
(m. 1?) 'Sandyx	1 lb.	tal.' (m. 1, added) '4'.
(m. 1?) 'Myrrh	1 lb.	tal. [ ]

(l. 100) '. . .   [   ]

'Ginger   [   ]

'Pounded spice(?)   [   ]

'Camel's thorn(?)	1 lb.	tal. [	]
'Zedoary	1 lb.	[	]
'Hartwort	1 lb.	den.' (m. 1, added) '1,000'.	
(m. 1?) 'Sphagnium	1 lb.	den.' (m. 1, added) '1,000'.	
(m. 1?) '. . .	1 lb.	den.' (m. 1, added) '1,000'.	
(m. 1?) 'Elecampane	1 lb.	den.' (m. 1, added) '1,000'.	
(m. 1?) '. . .	1 lb.	den.' (m. 1, added) '1,000'.	
(m. 1?) '. . .	1 lb.	[	]
'Mastic wood	[		]
'. . .	[		]
(m. 4) 'I, Aurelius Thonius, . . . '			

19–22 The subscription is puzzling, although I can make very little of much of it and what is transcribed is very hazardous. The surface is almost entirely abraded. If 21–2 are correct the subscription is autograph. What occupied all the preceding space, since there was but one declarant (cf. 8 with the singular verbs in 9, 13, and 14 as well as 21–2), is far from clear. -ειαρχης (19) hardly suggests a personal name; did the declarant somehow describe himself as μηνειάρχης (a very short name could precede: but what of 20–1?), abnormally? The space allocated to the name will of course have to fit with 8 as well.

22 Reading very uncertain. No trace of ink below this line; unless another line has been totally lost, προςφωνῶν must have been abbreviated although no mark of abbreviation survives.

25 The consular formula as lemmatized in R. S. Bagnall and K. A. Worp, *The Chronological Systems of Byzantine Egypt* 109 has Cεβαςτοῦ, not Aὐγούςτου. For the latter as the normal Oxyrhynchite form see LI **3620** 2 n.

44 νίτρου Ἀραβικοῦ. For νίτρον see A. Lucas, *Anc. Egyptian Materials and Industries*, 4th edn. rev. J. R. Harris (1962) 263–7; also M. Manfredi *et al.*, *Trenta testi greci (editi in occ. del XVII Congr. int. di Pap.)* (Florence, 1983) 22. 17 n., and M. Amelotti and L. Migliardi Zingale, *Scritti in onore di Orsolina Montevecchi* p. 5 with n. 7, from which it appears that the Arabian variety is new. The *aphronitri* of the Price Edict (two grades, §33. 38–9 as revised by M. H. Crawford and J. M. Reynolds, *ZPE* 34 (1979) 180 with commentary p. 203; the price of the better grade restored as 100 den./lb.) is so differently priced that it must be a different substance, unless the Edict's price is wrongly given.

62 The reading of the patronymic is very conjectural.

71–3 Cιριτικῆc and Tρωαδηcίαc first read by H. M. Cockle, *JRS* 71 (1981) 95. See further the note on L **3596** 19.

79 Probably a space between λ[ογιcτῇ and 'Oξυρυγχίτου.

84 ff. It is by no means apparent that all the prices have been added, but some are clearly so (e.g. 84); on this basis the deduction is made for the rest. On the import of aromatics see *BASP* 21 (1984), 39–47.

84 πιπέρεωc. See V. Gazza, *Aeg.* 36 (1956) 92; M. Manfredi *et al.*, op. cit., 19. 8 n.; M. H. Crawford and J. M. Reynolds, *ZPE* 34 (1979) 207; H. Harrauer and P. J. Sijpesteijn, *Medizinische Rezepte* (Vienna, 1981) p. 8.

85 λιβάνου. See Gazza, op. cit. 87–8; Harrauer–Sijpesteijn, op. cit. p. 10; S. Lauffer, *Diokletians Preisedikt* 285; P. Coll. Youtie II 87. 6 n. and L. C. Youtie, *ZPE* 27 (1977) 145.

86 μαλαβάθρου. A. Lucas, op. cit. 308; *Dai papiri della Società italiana (Omaggio all' XI Congr. int. di Pap.)* (Florence, 1965), no. 12. 11 n.; Lauffer, op. cit. 287; Crawford–Reynolds, op. cit. 204 (on §34. 2–3 of the Aezani copy of the Price Edict). At 60 den./lb. for the cheaper grade (§34. 3) this cannot be equivalent to the item in our declarations, which is consistently the guild's top-priced item.

87–8 cτύρακοc. See XXXI **2570**, n. ad loc.; *Dai papiri* (cited above), no. 12. 10 n.; Lauffer, op. cit. 285; P. Vindob. Worp p. 156 (this text, no. 20, is re-ed. Harrauer–Sijpesteijn op. cit., text no. 1); Gazza, op. cit. 98; P. Coll. Youtie II 86. 4 n.

89 κόcτου. See Gazza, op. cit. 85; P. Coll. Youtie II 86. 3 n.; Crawford–Reynolds, op. cit. 204; Harrauer–Sijpesteijn, op. cit. p. 26; P. Haun. II 20. 11 n.; CPR IX 78. 3 n.

90 μαcτίκηc (l. μαcτίχηc). See P. Coll. Youtie II 86. 5 n.; P. Haun. II 20. 7 n.; *Dai papiri*, no. 12. 9 n.; Crawford–Reynolds, op. cit. 205; Lauffer, op. cit. 285; L. C. Youtie, *ZPE* 27 (1977) 145; Harrauer–Sijpesteijn, op. cit. p. 9.

91 ἀμώμου. P. Coll. Youtie II 86. 2 n.; *Dai papiri*, no. 12. 19 n.; Lauffer, op. cit. 286.

92 βδέλλης. Lauffer, op. cit. 284; J. Hengstl, *ZPE* 30 (1978) 245–6.

93 καcίαc. Lauffer, op. cit. 284; Crawford–Reynolds, op. cit. 204–5; Ann Hanson, *TAPA* 103 (1972) 164.

94 κασάμου. κα[λ]άμου *ed. pr.*, but traces of all the letters are present. The first published suspicion of this reading was due to D. Hagedorn as reported by A. Bülow-Jacobsen, P. Haun. II 20. 6 n., and is confirmed by the passages in **3731**, **3733**, and **3765**.

95 ψιμιτίου. See Gazza, op. cit. 105; Lauffer, op. cit. 288; Harrauer-Sijpesteijn, op. cit. p. 6.

96 [c]ανδυκίου. See Crawford-Reynolds, op. cit. 209, and cf. **3765** 21 n.

97 ζμύρνης. Gazza, op. cit. 97-8; *Dai papiri*, no. 12. 13 n.; Lauffer, op. cit. 288; Harrauer-Sijpesteijn, op. cit. p. 5; Hanson, op. cit. 164; Crawford-Reynolds, op. cit. 206.

100 Note Crawford-Reynolds, op. cit. 206 (§34. 25 n.).

101 [ζ]ιγκιπέρεως. Gazza, op. cit. 82; Lauffer, op. cit. 287; Harrauer-Sijpesteijn, op. cit. p. 8.

102 πατήμ[ατος. See XXXI **2570**, n. ad loc.

103 ἀсφαλαν[θ]ίου. There is some uncertainty as to whether this should be equated with ἀσπάλαθος or with ἄσφαλτος. See Crawford-Reynolds, op. cit. 207. If it is at all correct to equate our item here with §34. 70 of the Edict (as revised by Crawford-Reynolds: *aspalathi* in the Latin, ἀσπάλτου in the Greek), the form of the word here and in **3733** suggests the equation with ἀσπάλαθος is more likely. For ἄσφαλτος see Lauffer, op. cit. 289; Gazza, op. cit. 101; *Dai papiri*, no. 12. 16 n.; M. Manfredi *et al.*, op. cit. (see 44 n.), 19. 5 n.

104 ἀρναβωρατίων. The reading at the end is uncertain: ἀρναβωρατικόν could also be read, but a genitive is expected. See XXXI **2570** n. ad loc.; also Lauffer, op. cit. 288, but for the revised text of the Edict at this point (§34. 64-5) see Crawford-Reynolds, op. cit. 183.

105 cαсέλεως. cαγέλεως or cατέλεως *ed. pr*, 'unknown'. The new reading (confirmed by **3733** 23) allows comparison with cέсελις, Gazza, op. cit. 96; see also P. Haun. II 20. 12 n.

106 сφαγνίου. The word is still not evidenced from elsewhere. Note that LSJ s.v. сφάγνος gives an equation with ἀσπάλαθος, cf. 103 n. above.

107 εἰρωνων. 'Unknown', *ed. pr.* Note Crawford-Reynolds, op. cit. 209, suggesting a possible equation with the Edict's *ireos* (§34. 82); the Greek version is lost at this point. For this substance see Gazza, op. cit. 82; Harrauer-Sijpesteijn, op. cit. p. 14. Possibly cf. ἐλαίου εἰρίνου, §34. 46 in the Price Edict ed. Giacchero, with Lauffer, op. cit. 287?

108 ἐλενιδίων. See Crawford-Reynolds, op. cit. 210.

109 ἀλκεωτίδων. ἀλκεωτίδος *ed. pr.*, 'unknown; a herb, "elk's ear"?'

110 ὀνυχίων. Cf. *ed. pr.*, n. ad loc., also VIII **1142** 4 n.

111 ξυλομα[cτίχης. Cf. **3733** 29 ξυλομαcτίκη[c]. Cf. Crawford-Reynolds, op. cit. 209 (= §34. 79 in their revised version of this part of the Price Edict; the entry is absent in Lauffer's edition).

112 αλ[ιμαстου? This line omitted altogether in the *ed. pr.* Cf. **3733** 30 αλιμαстου. ἀλαcάνθου (cf. §34. 97 in the Price Edict with Crawford-Reynolds, op. cit. 210) cannot be read there.

113 The line must surely read Αὐρ(ήλιος) Θώνιος ἐπιδέδωκα προσφ(ωνῶν) ὡς πρόκ(ειται), cf. 46-7 and 74-5, but I cannot claim to link the traces to this reading beyond Θω-. The subscription of a ὑπογραφεύς could have followed; there could just be room in the rest of this one (wide) line.

3767. PROCEEDINGS BEFORE THE LOGISTES

4 1B.76/3(c)   27 × 41 cm   30 December 329 or 330

Under this number we republish **XXXI 2562** together with an additional dozen lines which adjoin at the top and stretch back to the beginning of the report; **2562** had the end, so that now we have the full extent (although lacunose) of the proceedings. The line-numbering of the *ed. pr.* is added in brackets. On the first-written side is **3766**, which republishes and extends **XXXI 2570**.

The new piece makes it clear that the presiding official is not the logothetes but the logistes (as was to be expected, since the documents on the other side came into his bureau). The logistes is not named but must have been Flavius Julianus.

The date is Tybi 4 of a year which must fall in the prefecture of Flavius Magnilianus (his predecessor Septimius Zenius in office 19 August 328, XLIII **3126**; Magnilianus in office 12 January 330, XLVII **3350**), but later than the declarations to the logistes written first on the other side (**3766**, 27 October 329). At the other end both papyrus and prefect are limited by the prefecture of Florentius, only attested so far in hagiographical sources for some time in 331: see J. Lallemand, *L'Admin. civile* 241. Possible dates are thus 30 December 329 or 30 December 330. The first of these was a Tuesday, the second a Wednesday (V. Grumel, *La Chronologie* p. 316); i.e. one cannot exclude one of the choices on the basis of its being a Sunday, cf. **3759**. The papyrus roll with the declarations preserved in part as **3766** (27 October 329) would not have been considered scrap paper at least until it was superseded by the next month's declarations (which would be dated 26 November), so that the minimum interval before partial reuse as **3767** would be a month.

Written along the fibres in *transversa charta* form. For the kolleseis, see **3766** introd.

[Year,   ] *Τῦβι δϛ΄, ἐν τῷ Ἀδριανίῳ. ἐπὶ παρόντων* ⟦. . . . .⟧
[*Cερήνου καὶ Πετρ*]*ωνίου καὶ Χωοῦ καὶ Ὠρίωνος ἀπὸ εἰρηναρχῶν τῶν*
                                       πάντων
[*c.* 15   ]. . . *καὶ Τιθοῦς καὶ Cαραπᾶ ὑπηρετῶν καὶ Εὐαγγέλου*
                                      παρέδρου,
[*Δίδυμος εἶ*(*πεν*)· . .].[.]. . . .`.´ *ἀνήνεγκα ἐπὶ τὸν κύριόν ·μου τὸν*
                           διαc(*ημότατον*) *ἔπαρχον τῆς*
5   [*Αἰγύπτου*] *Φ*[*λ*]*άουϊον Μαγνιλιανὸν περὶ ἡμετέρων πραγμάτων καὶ ἔϛωϛέ*
     [*μοι τὰ δίκαια;*] *ἀπέλαβον οὖν τὰ ἡμέτερα.* /*ὁ λογιστὴς εἶ*(*πεν*)· *ἀν*[*άγνω*]*θι τί*
     [*προσέταξεν ὁ κύ*]*ριός μου ὁ διαc*(*ημότατος*) *ἔπαρχος τῆς Αἰγύπτου*
                             Φλάου[*ϊος Μαγνιλιανός.*]
     κ[*αὶ ἀνεγν*]*ώϲθη οὕτωϲ· Φλά*[*ουϊο*]*ϲ Μαγνιλιανὸς λογιστῇ Ὀξυρ*[*υγχίτου*]
     χαίρειν. ἀφαίρεσιν ὑπομεμε[*νηκ*]*έναι διαφ*⟦*αι*⟧`*ε*´*ρόντων* [*ἑαυτῷ;*]
10 *εἰδῶν ὑπό τινων Δίδυμος λίβ*[*ε*]*λλον ἐπιδοὺς τῇ ἐμῇ* [*c.* 7]
     οὗ τὸ ἀντίγραφον τούτοις μου τοῖς γ[*ράμμασιν*] *ὑποταγῆναι προ*[*σέταξα*]
     [. . .].*ι νῦν ηξ*. . .[.].[. . .].*οϲτ*.[. .].[. . .]. .[.]. .*cιν του.ου* [5–10]
     [2–3].*cιν φρόν*[*τ*]*ι*[*c*]*ον* . . . . . .[. . .]*ω παρασχεῖν εἰ τὰς ἀποδείξιϲ τῆϲ*
     γεγενημένης ὑπο. . . .*ν πρὸ δίκης ἀφαιρέσεως παράσχοι. ἔρρωσο.*
15 *μετὰ* [*τὴ*]*ν ἀνάγνωσιν* /*ὁ λογιστὴς εἶ*(*πεν*)· *τί λέγουσι οἱ παρόντες ἄγροικοι*
(5) *Cερῆνος καὶ Πετρ*⟦*ος*⟧*ώνιος καὶ Χωοῦς καὶ Ὠρίων; ἐπηκούσατε*

1 l. *Ἀδριανείῳ*   3 *ὑπηρετων*   4 *διαc∫*; so in 7, 17, 24   6 *ει*⟩ and so *passim*   9 First *ν* of *διαφερόντων* rewritten   13 l. *ἀποδείξεις*

[τῆ]ς προστάξε[ω]ς τοῦ κυρίου μ[ου διας](ημοτάτου) ἐπάρχο[υ τῆ]ς
         Αἰγύπτου Φλαουΐου Μαγνιλιανοῦ
[καὶ] τῶν ὑπὸ Διδύμου κατατεθέντων ἐπὶ τῶν ὑπομνημάτων
ὡς εἴη πληρωθεὶς τῶν εἰδῶν αὐτοῦ· κατάθεςθ⟦αι⟧ `ε´ τοίνυν καὶ ὑμῖς
20   τί ἐπράξατε ἐπὶ τούτοις· ἢ πέρα ἀπήτησεν ὑμᾶς ὁ Δίδυμος;
(10)   οἱ προειρημένοι ἀπεκρ(ίναντο)· εἴ τι ἐκρί[θ]ημεν ἐν τῷ κυριακῷ, δεδώκαμεν·
       καὶ ἐπίσθημεν πρὸς ἑαυτούς. /ὁ λο[γι]ς[τὴ]ς [εἶ](πεν)· καὶ ἡ προφορὰ
                                                                      Διδύμου
       καὶ ἡ τῶν ἀγροίκων ἐμφέρεται τοῖς ὑπ[ο]μνήμασιν· τῆς γὰρ προστ[ά]ξ[εως]
       τοῦ κυρίου μου διας(ημοτάτου) ἐπάρχου προςταττούςης τὰ ταῖς ἀληθείαις
                                                                      χρεω[ςτού-]
25   μενα ἀποκατασταθῆναι, τοῦτο γεγένηται κατὰ τὰ προςφωνηθ[έντα,]
(15)   ὡς εἶπο⟦μ⟧ν, ⟦ἐπι . . ⟧ ὑ[πὸ ἀμ]φοτέρων τῶν μερῶν ἐπὶ ὑπομ[νημά-]
       των.

19 ὑμις; l. ὑμεῖς   20 ὑμας   22 l. ἐπείςθημεν   23 Third ε of ἐμφέρεται corr. from α

'[Year,] Tybi 4, in the Hadrianeum. In the presence of Serenus and Petronius and Chöous and Horion, ex-eirenarchs, all . . . and Tithoes and Sarapas, assistants, and Euangelus, assessor, Didymus said, "I sent up (a petition?) to my lord the prefect of Egypt, Flavius Magnilianus, *vir perfectissimus*, about our affairs and he (confirmed my rights?). So I recovered my property." The *curator* said, "Read what my lord the prefect of Egypt, Flavius Magnilianus, *vir perfectissimus*, instructed." And there was read as follows: "Flavius Magnilianus to the *curator* of the Oxyrhynchite, greetings. Didymus, having presented a petition to my . . . that he had suffered the theft by certain persons of goods belonging to himself, the copy of which I have ordered to be subjoined to this my letter, . . . see to it . . . provide . . . if he should provide the proofs of the theft that occurred . . . before the court case. Farewell." After the reading the *curator* said, "What do the peasants who are present say, Serenus and Petronius and Chöous and Horion? You have listened to the ordinance of my lord prefect of Egypt, Flavius Magnilianus, *vir perfectissimus*, and the depositions of Didymus on the record, that he has received his goods in full. Depose yourselves therefore what you did in this connection; or did Didymus demand too much from you?" The aforesaid persons answered, "Whatever we were assessed in the government account, we paid; and we came to an agreement among ourselves." The *curator* said, "The depositions both of Didymus and the peasants are entered in the minutes; for the ordinance of my lord prefect, *vir perfectissimus*, has ordained that what was genuinely owed should be paid back, and this has happened according to the declarations, as I said, by both sides on the record."'

1 The regnal-year notation presumably came in the lacuna. The possibilities are 24, 14, 6 and 25, 15, 7 (see the introduction above).

ἐν τῷ Ἀδριανίῳ. Cf. **3758** 134 n.

Possibly Ὡρίωνος under the deletion.

1–2 Serenus *et al.* are in effect one of the parties in the case (cf. 15–16), not assistants to the court as the persons named in 3 will be. This, then, runs counter to the rules of format proposed by me in *Reports of Proceedings* (= Pap. Brux. 4), esp. p. 33. See further **3758** 156–8 n.

3 Tithoes and Sarapas recur in P. Harr. I 160. 3, as re-ed. *ZPE* 37 (1980) 237, dated 'after *c.* AD 329–331'.

4 For the restoration of Δίδυμος εἶ(πεν) cf. 10. It was perhaps followed by a note of the month and the day, or more likely by an object (λίβελλον (cf. 10) vel sim.) for ἀνήνεγκα following.

7 Μαγνιλιανός at end must have been somewhat cramped.

9 ἀφαίρεςιν. See LI **3611** 7–10 n.

19 εἴη πληρωθείς. For the construction see F. T. Gignac, *Grammar* ii 305–7.

20 ἢ πέρα. ὑπὲρ ἅ cannot be read, although ηπερ might possibly be a phonetic variant of ὑπέρ.

21 For the abbreviation of ἀπεκρ(ίναντο) cf. **3757** 13 n.

22 For ἑαυτούς as first person reflexive see Gignac, *Grammar* ii 167.

3768. DECLARATIONS OF PRICES

A 6.B5/2(J) (5 iii 74)   15 × 9.5 cm   *c.* 332–6?

    This sequence of three price-declarations to the logistes contains those of the goldsmiths (cf. **3765**) and the silversmiths (cf. LI **3624**), and is likely therefore to have been the beginning of a roll of such declarations, cf. **3765** introd. If it was once preceded by columns of summarized prices, as in **3765**, no trace now remains. The blank spaces left in these declarations, see **3731** introd., were never filled in; cf. I **85** v–vi, re-ed. *ZPE* 39 (1980) 119–20, and LI **3626**. Was this roll never used?

    The sequence of guilds yielded by **3765** combined with this papyrus indicates that LI **3624–6** may also come from near the beginning of their roll; see Appendix II below.

    The declarations here break off before reaching the statement of the objects declared, as does the goldsmiths' declaration in **3765**. We may conclude from **3773** (see the introd. to that text) that the object of the goldsmiths' declaration was the gold solidus.

    The logistes, Flavius Asclepiades, is new. The papyrus preserves no date, and Asclepiades' position in the list of logistae is uncertain. The use of the *gentilicium* Flavius assures a placing *c.* 325 or later (J. G. Keenan, *ZPE* 11 (1973) 46, 49) but there is no adequate gap in fact until between Flavius Hermias and Flavius Paeanius alias Macrobius, *c.* 332–6. As well as being the earliest substantial gap in the period after *c.* 325, this is one of the longer gaps within the palaeographical date-range. But this must remain conjectural and I cannot exclude a placing somewhat later in the fourth century.

    All the writing on the papyrus is in one hand. There is one kollesis, at the right edge of col. ii. The back is blank.

col. i

Φλ(αουΐῳ) Ἀσκληπιάδη

λογιστῇ Ὀξυρυγχίτου

[παρὰ το]ῦ κ[ο]ι̣[νοῦ τῶν]

χρυσοχό[ω]ν̣ τῆ[ς αὐ-]

5   τῆς πόλεως

[   ] (vac.)

προσφ[ω]νοῦμεν

1 φλ′   5 Final c extended as filler-stroke

ἰδίῳ τιμήματι τὴ[ν]
ἑ[ξ]ῆϲ ἐνγεγρ[αμμέ-]

· · · · ·

col. ii

10 Φλ(αουΐῳ) Ἀϲκληπιάδῃ
λογιϲτῇ Ὀξυρυγχίτου
[παρ]ὰ τοῦ κοιν[ο]ῦ τῶν
ἀρ[γ]υροκ[όπων τ]ῆϲ αὐ-
τῆϲ πόλε[ω]ϲ
15 [   ]   (vac.)
προϲφωνοῦμεν
ἰδίῳ τιμήματι τὴν
ἑ[ξ]ῆϲ ἐνγεγραμμέ-
[ν]ην τιμὴν ὧν χι-
20 [ρίζ]ο[μ]εν ὤν[ί]ω[ν] κ[αὶ

· · · · ·

col. iii

[Φ]λ(αουΐῳ) Ἀϲκλ[ηπιάδῃ]
λογιϲτῇ [Ὀξυρυγχίτου]
[π]αρὰ τοῦ κο[ινοῦ τῶν]
[. . . . . .] . . [0-3 τῆϲ αὐτῆϲ]
25 πόλ[εω]ϲ   [   ]
(vac.)   [   ]
προϲφων[οῦ]μ[εν]
ἰδίῳ τιμήματ[ι τὴν]
ἑξῆϲ ἐνγεγρα[μμέ-]
30 νην τιμ[ὴν ὧν χει-]
ρίζομεν ὠ[νίων
[. . .] . . [

· · · · ·

9, 18, 29 l. ἐγγεγραμμένην   10 φλ´   14 Filler-stroke at end (cf. 5)   19-20 l. χειρίζομεν
21 [φ]λ´   25 πόλ[εω]ϲ: trace at end is of filler-stroke (cf. 5, 14 with app. crit.) rather than actual ϲ

'To Flavius Asclepiades, *curator* of the Oxyrhynchite, from the guild of the goldsmiths of the same city [*vac.*]. At our own risk we declare the (price) entered below . . .'

Col. ii

'To Flavius Asclepiades, *curator* of the Oxyrhynchite, from the guild of the silversmiths of the same city [*vac.*]. At our own risk we declare the price entered below for the goods which we handle and . . .'

Col. iii

'To Flavius Asclepiades, *curator* of the Oxyrhynchite, from the guild of the . . . of the same city [*vac.*]. At our own risk we declare the price entered below for the goods which we handle . . .'

5–7 Note the consistent plural drafting (cf. 16, 27) and the comparatively narrow space for the names (esp. in 26) if there were to be more than one declarant. Cf. I **85** i–iv (re-ed. *ZPE* 39 (1980) 116–19).

24 Traces are completely indeterminate: there is no chance of identifying the guild here (ἀρτοκόποι, cf. LI **3625**?) on their basis. Estimate of letters lost at the end (besides the necessary τῆς αὐτῆς) is variable, from none (cf. 21, 23) to three (cf. 22), since the break is approximately vertical.

3769. PETITION TO A SYNDIC

22 3B.16/K(1–2)a   12.5 × 12 cm   February/March 334

The details of this damaged petition are scarcely discernible. Nevertheless it is of interest for its addressee, Flavius Julianus, syndic, who appears again—but as Aurelius—in **3770**: see the introd. to that text. There are various possible explanations of the change of *gentilicium* from Aurelius to Flavius, but since **3769** (where he is Flavius) must antedate **3770** (where he is Aurelius), or at the very least date from the same day (**3769** was written in Phamenoth, **3770** on Phamenoth 30), this must strengthen the case for supposing that Aurelius as Julianus' *gentilicium* in **3770** is only a slip. A minor consequence is that **3770** is less likely to have been drafted at the syndic's bureau, where obviously the scribes would have known his correct current style.

The papyrus formed part of a τόμος cυγκολλήcιμος and there are scanty remains of the ends of some lines from the preceding entry, which we do not transcribe.

The back is blank.

> ὑπατείας Φλαουΐου ᾿Οπτάτου πατρι[κί]ου [καὶ ᾿Ανικίου]
> Παυλείνου τῶν λαμπροτάτων, Φαμεν[ὼθ   ]
> Φλαουΐῳ ᾿Ιουλιανῷ cυνδίκῳ νομοῦ ᾿Οξ[υρυγχίτου]
> παρὰ Αὐρηλίας Διεῦτος Ἀ̈ῢcιος ἀπὸ κώμης [*c.* 8   ]
> 5 ἐποφθαλμιῶν ἡμετέρων γῃδίω[ν . .]. . [*c.* 9   ]
> ἀπὸ τῆ[c] αὐτῆς κώμης πεντ. . .[*c.* 9   ?ριψοκίν-]
> δυνον ἑαυτὸν προτεῖναι προc. [
> . [.]. [.]ην ὁ προκίμενος Διον. . [

1 φλαουϊου   3 φλαουϊωϊουλιανω; superfluous ink after cυνδίκῳ perhaps just an accidental blot
4 c of Διεῦτος corr.; αϋcιος: υ partly obscured by ink, perhaps only a blot   8 l. προκείμενος

[κεφα]λαιωτῇ ϵἰρηναρχῶν [

10 [ἐπα]ρχικὸν δικαστήριον . [

[*c.* 5] . . αυτον δ[.] . ν . κα[

[ ] . . [. .] . . . ου ν . [.] . [

[ ] . . [.] . [

. . . . .

1 For the consuls cf. **3770** 18 and n.

5 For ἐποφθαλμιάω with the genitive cf. P. Sak. 43. 19, but here a dative could have followed, e.g. μέρει.

9 For irenarchs see P. Turner 41. 20–1 n., 42 introd. and N. Lewis, *The Compulsory Services of Roman Egypt* (= *Pap. Flor.* XI) 23–4. The irenarchs here will be village officials; for their κεφαλαιωτής cf. XIX **2233** 3–4 (with XXXI **2568** 1–3 n.) and L **3576** 21.

10 It is tempting to conjecture that the petitioner is requesting that the culprit be brought before the prefect's court under guard by the headman of the irenarchs.

3770. PETITION TO A SYNDIC

71/21(a)   20 × 23.5 cm   26 March 334

Aurelia Ptolema petitions Aurelius Julianus, syndic of Oxyrhynchus, because of the behaviour of her son-in-law.

The document is of particular interest for the style and title of the addressee. **3769** attests him as syndic in the same year and month (therefore the same day or earlier) but with the *gentilicium* Flavius. He is to be identified with the Flavius Julianus who was *curator civitatis* shortly before (see Appendix I below) and acting syndic shortly after the date of the present text (VI **901** and **3771**). For the significance of the *gentilicium*-change and for the office of syndic (and its relationship to the ἔκδικος) see **3771** 3 n. and **3769** introd.

There is one kollesis, of the usual three layers, about one quarter of the way across (the edge of the upper sheet bisecting ἀν/δρί, 4). The damage is such as to permit examination of the uppermost layer from behind.

The back is blank, as far as can be seen; it has been extensively covered with repair strips in antiquity.

Αὐρη[λίῳ] Ἰουλιανῷ cυνδίκῳ τῆc Ὀ[ξ]υρυγχ[ιτ]ῶν π[όλεωc]

(vac.)

παρὰ Αὐρηλί[α]c Πτολέμαc Διονυcίου ἀπὸ [τῆc] αὐτῆc π[όλεωc. τὴν]

ἡμετέρ[αν θ]υγατέραν Ἄριλλαν Διογένου[c . .] . . [.] . μη[*c.* 7   ]

ἐκδέδωκα ἀνδρὶ Θέωνί τινι πρὸc γά[μο]ν [.] . . [. . . .] . . . [*c.* 5   ]

3 l. θυγατέρα; Δ of Διογένου[c corr.

5   τουτ. [c. 5]. ρων ἐξ ἧς καὶ υἱὸν ἔϲχεν ἄρρ[ε]ϙα ὃν ἐγ[α]λα-
  κτοτρόφηϲεν ἐπὶ ἕνα ἥμιϲυ ἐνιαυτὸν [κ]αὶ οὔτε τῷ παιδὶ
  τὰς τροφὰς οὔτε τῇ γυναικὶ ἑαυτοῦ ἐ[π]εϙϙύρηϲεν ἀλλ' ἤδη
  καὶ ἐν ἀ[λλο]δαπῇ γενόμενος πολλῷ χρόνῳ τὰ μὲν ϲτρώματα αὐτοῦ
  λαβὼν α . . . . [.]ϲεν καὶ ἐν χηρείᾳ τὴν ἐμὴν θυγ[ατ]έρα καταλείψας

10   πιρᾶται καὶ τὰ ἕδνα ἅπερ τότε παρέϲχεν ἀπα[ιτ]εῖν με τῆς ἐμῆς
  ἀϲθενίας καταφρονήϲαϲ· ὅθεν οὐ φέρουϲα τὴν τοῦ ἀνδρὸς
  ἀϲυνειδηϲίαν ἐπιδίδωμι τὰ βιβλία ἀξιοῦ[ϲα] ϙἰ τῇ αὐτῇ [αὐθ]ᾳ-
  δίᾳ ἐπιμένοιϙν καὶ τοὺς νόμους παρεκτ. [3–4].τουϲ[c. 4]
  [.]. . ν δικαι[. .] γάμων ὡρισμένους ᾳ . . . [3–4]. ᾳ. [c. 6]

15   [. .].[.].. [. .]. τροφὰς τοῦ τε υἱοῦ αὐτοῦ καὶ τῆς γαμετ[ῆς] ὑπο
  [. . .].. [.]. . . [.]. μηδ[ὲ] βουλόμενον διδόναι μηδὲ βιοτιν αὐτό(ν)
  [. . .]. . . . [. . ἀλ]λοτριοῦϲθαι αὐτὴν τ[ο]ῦ ἀνδρός.
  [ὑ]πατείᾳ[ϲ] Φλ(αουίου) Ὀπτάτου πατρικίου καὶ Ἀνικίου Παυλίνου

19   τῶν λ[αμπροτάτ]ων, Φαμενὼθ λ΄.

      (vac.)

(m. 2)   [Αὐρ]ηλία Πτολέμα ἐπιδέδωκα.

5]αρων or]θρων   10 l. πειρᾶται   11 l. ἀϲθενείας   13 l. ἐπιμένοι   16 l. βιότιον?   αυτο̄
17 Long filler-stroke at end of line

  'To Aurelius Julianus, syndic of the city of the Oxyrhynchites, from Aurelia Ptolema, daughter of
Dionysius, from the same city. I gave our daughter Arilla (her father being Diogenes) . . . to a man, one Theon,
in marriage . . . He had a male child by her. She nursed the child for a year and a half. He provided no
maintenance for the child or for his wife, but having already been elsewhere for a long time, taking his bedding
he . . . , and leaving my daughter as a widow he tries even to demand back from me the bride-price he provided
at that time, scorning my powerlessness. Wherefore, since I cannot endure the man's lack of conscience, I
present this petition, requesting that if he persists in this same wilful behaviour and . . .

  'In the consulship of Flavius Optatus, patrician, and Anicius Paulinus, *viri clarissimi*, Phamenoth 30.'

  (m. 2) 'I, Aurelia Ptolema, presented this.'

  5 υἱὸν . . . ἄρρ[ε]ϙα. For υἱός used as a feminine cf. L. C. Youtie, *ZPE* 33 (1979) 210 and R. Hodot, ibid. 37
(1980) 105 n. 5.

  9 Not ἀπεδήμηϲεν: the fourth letter is not δ, nor are the remains wide enough.

  12 ἀϲυνειδηϲία. See John Chrysostom, *Homil. in Act. Ap.* 31. 4 (*PG.* 60. 234) ἀϲυνειδηϲίας ἀπίϲτου δόξαν
λαβών (cited, as Dr Holford-Strevens points out, in the Dimitrakos lexicon s.v.). Cf. the opposite εὐϲυνειδηϲία,
PSI V 452. 26, where it is used as an honorific (which is absent from the discussion of H. Zilliacus, *Unters. zu
den abstr. Anredeformen*).

  15 ὑπό? Or ἀπό?

  18 For these consuls and for Optatus' title of *patricius* note T. D. Barnes, *The New Empire of Diocletian and
Constantine* 107–8.

3771. Petition to an Acting Syndic

71/61(a)　　　　　　　　　12.5 × 16.5 cm　　　　　　　　　1 May 336

This is a duplicate of VI **901**. The new text confirms the addressee, Flavius Julianus, as acting *cύνδικος* instead of acting *ἔκδικος* (see B. R. Rees, *JJP* 6 (1952) 83 n. 66, and 3 n. below) and the two papyri combine to allow us to know more of the drama of the petitioner's story and to appreciate the real plight of her poor pigs.

The two texts are in the same hand, and the pattern of damage is similar which suggests that they may have been rolled up together when they were thrown away. **901** probably came from Grenfell and Hunt's first season (cf. VI preface); the inventory-number of **3771** indicates nothing about the time of its discovery. At any rate the first editors were clearly unaware of this text when they published **901**. The writer's spelling is much improved in **3771** (5 *ἑςπεριναῖς ὥραις*, 6 *χοῖροι*, etc.) except for the curious error in 1, see n., but the grammar remains incorrigible. **3771** possibly joins to the right of **901**. The back of **3771** is blank; contrast **901** introd.

The surface of **3771** is badly damaged but there appears to be a kollesis reaching about 2.5 cm from the left edge.

ὑπατείας Οὐιρίου Νεπωτιανοῦ καὶ Τεττ[ί]ου Cεκούνδου
τῶν λαμπροτάτων {λαμπροτάτων}, [Πα]χὼν ϛ⁻.
Φλαουΐῳ Ἰουλιανῷ διοικοῦντι cυνδικί[αν] Ὀξυρυγχίτου
παρὰ Αὐρηλίας Ἀλλοῦτος Θωνίου ἀπὸ κώμης Τααʽμʹ-
5　πεμοῦ εʹ πάγου. ἑςπεριναῖς ὥραις τῇ χ[θ]ὲς ἡ[μέρ]ᾳ
ἡμέτεροι χοῖροι δύο τὴν [ὁ]ρμὴν ποιού[μ]ενοι ἐπὶ ἡμέ-
τερον ἔδαφος γενόμενοι ⟨ἐν⟩ ὑδραγωγίῳ μ[η]χανῆς
τῶν ἡμετέρων π[ε]δῶν καὶ Παβάν[ου] τινὸς ἀπὸ τῆ[ς]
αὐτῆς κώ[μ]ης, ὁ προειρημένος Παβᾶνος π[αρατυ-]
10　χὼν ἔχων μετὰ χῖρας ξοΐδιον ἀνελεῖν τοὺς χοί-
ρους βουλόμ[ενος] καὶ τοῦτον ἐπιςχοῦςα ὡς μη-
δαμῶς ἀδ[ικ]η[θεὶς] ὑπὸ τῶν χοίρων καὶ ἀπο-
[ςχό]μενος [τῆς πρὸς] τοὺς [χοί]ρους ἐπελεύςεως
ἐ[μοὶ ἐπελήλυθε]ν βου[λόμ]ενός με καταποντίςαι
15　ἐν ὑδρα[γωγίῳ ὡς εἰ] μὴ ἔκ τινος προνοίας τὴν
[c. 3]ν τῶν ἐπαντλούντων βοῶν . . . . . [c. 3]
[c. 4]·[·]·· . . . . . [μη]ν ὑπ' αὐτοῦ ἐν [ὑδραγω]χί[ῳ]

1 οὐΐριου, τετʼτιου; l. Φακούνδου　　3 φλαουϊωϊουλιανω　　10 l. χεῖρας; ξοΐδιον　　12 l. ἀδικηθέντα
17 ὑπ

[　　　*c.* 12　　　]..[*c.* 5].[　　*c.* 11　　]
[　　　*c.* 12　　　]τι.[*c.* 3].[.].[　　*c.* 10　]
20 [　　　*c.* 13　　　]..[　　　*c.* 16　　　]

. . . . . .

'In the consulship of Virius Nepotianus and Tettius Secundus (*sic*), *viri clarissimi*, Pachon 6.

'To Flavius Julianus, acting syndic of the Oxyrhynchite, from Aurelia Allous daughter of Thonius from the village of Taampemou in the 5th pagus. In the evening hours yesterday our two pigs broke out on to our plot and got into the conduit of the waterwheel for our lands and those of one Pabanus from the same village. The said Pabanus happened by, having a chisel in his hands, and wanted to kill the pigs. I held him back, for the pigs had done him no wrong. He desisted from his onslaught on the pigs and came at me, wanting to push me under in the conduit, so that had I not by some providence . . . the . . . of the oxen working the irrigation, [I would have been?] . . . by him in the conduit . . . '

1 Ϲεκούνδου. The reading is quite clear, but there is no justification for the name. For the consuls see R. S. Bagnall and K. A. Worp, *The Chronological Systems of Byzantine Egypt* 110. The writer's error is the more extraordinary given the generally improved spelling here compared with the performance in **901**.

2 The slight indentation in this line does not occur in **901**.

3 Flavius Julianus is the former logistes or *curator civitatis*, attested in that office from 329 to 331. For his career see Appendix I below. I deal here with problems relating to the office of ϲύνδικοϲ in general and to his tenure of it in particular.

3769 of Feb./Mar. 334 attested him as syndic, not as acting syndic, with the *gentilicium* Flavius (he had already been Flavius as *curator*). **3770** again attested him as syndic in the same year, on 26 March, but with the *gentilicium* Aurelius. Now the present text and its duplicate VI **901** (see B. R. Rees, *JJP* 6 (1952) 83 n. 66: from a photograph I believe ϲγνδικίαν is justifiable) attest him a couple of years later (1 May 336) as acting syndic and Flavius again.

The standard reference for the ἔκδικοϲ/ϲύνδικοϲ/*defensor* in Egypt is still B. R. Rees, *JJP* 6 (1952) 73-102. Several new examples can be added to his list on pp. 101-2, and there have been several more recent discussions, none of them reaching significant conclusions radically different from those Rees could reach. These discussions are: A. K. Bowman, *Akten des XIII. intern. Papyrologenkongresses* (1971; publ. Munich 1974) 44; J. Lallemand, *L'Admin. civile* 114-18; A. K. Bowman, *Town Councils* 46-52, 124; J. G. Keenan, *ZPE* 11 (1973) 49, 60, ibid. 13 (1974) 291.

References from mid-fourth-century Egypt with named ἔκδικοι and ϲύνδικοι are as follows:

P. Strasb. 296	326	Aur. Ammonius alias Canobus, Aur. Nilammon alias Hierax, both ϲύνδικοι, ex-magistrates, and councillors	Hermop.
XLIV **3195**	331	Claudius Hermias, ἔκδικοϲ	Oxy.
P. Köln Panop. 30	331	Fl. Paniscus, ἔκδικοϲ	Panop.
PSI VII 767	331/2	Aur. Achillion, ἔκδικοϲ, διάδοχοϲ to *curator*	Oxy.
XII **1426**	332	,,　　,,　　,,	Oxy.
XLIII **3127**	332	,,　　,,　　,,	Oxy.
P. Cairo Preis. 7	iv	Sallustius Olympiodorus, ἔκδικοϲ	Hermop.
3769	334	Fl. Julianus, ϲύνδικοϲ	Oxy.
3770	334	Aur. Julianus, ϲύνδικοϲ	Oxy.
3771, VI **901**	336	Fl. Julianus, acting ϲύνδικοϲ	Oxy.
SB III 6294	336	Fl. Hermias, ϲύνδικοϲ	Oxy.
CPR V 9	339	Aur. Eulogius alias Euphronius, ἔκδικοϲ	Hermop.
P. Col. VII 175	340	[Fl.?] Didymion(?), ϲύνδικοϲ (see *ZPE* 45 (1982) 234)	Arsinoite

From the welter of conflicting and confusing information some facts may now be claimed to emerge. The ἔκδικος in the early fourth century was junior to the *curator* (witness the order in **3195** and elsewhere, and the position of the ἔκδικος as διάδοχος to the *curator*, PSI VII 767), the cύνδικος from the 330s apparently senior to him (two ex-*curatores* become cύνδικοι; contrast Lallemand, op. cit. 118). Nomenclature adds further proof in both directions: ἔκδικοι in this period can be Aurelii, if they do not carry another *nomen* like Claudius Hermias and Sallustius Olympiodorus. On the other hand cύνδικοι and acting cύνδικοι are Flavii after 325, except for the single anomalous case of Aur. Julianus (**3770**) who is Flavius in the same year (**3769**), and the pair who are Aurelii in 326 (P. Strasb. 296), a puzzle which I except from the discussion which follows and defer to the end of this note.

If a condition of the grant of the Flaviate was not only that the post should be of a certain status but that it should be a government post (army or civil service) as opposed to a municipal service post, then either the ekdikia rated too low, or it was not a government post, or both (in the first half of the fourth century, that is). The post of *curator* was a government one and its holders from 325 are Flavii (earlier they were Valerii). Early on the *gentilicium* probably lapsed on ending tenure of the post (XLV **3256** 1 n.); later the title was retained in an 'emeritus' capacity (I **66**). If in the 330s, the period relevant to the present text, the *gentilicium* would normally lapse, then it is most likely that the syndic was a government official. If the *gentilicium* was retained, then the post of syndic may still be a government one carrying the Flaviate; or it may be a senior municipal appointment filled by local 'elder statesmen' who would have the Flaviate if they had (as had both Julianus and Hermias) been in government service at the appropriate level, on a par with the office of *riparius* (P. Harr. II 218. 2 n.). Whatever the explanation, the attribution of the *gentilicium* Aurelius to Julianus in **3770** seems likely to be purely an error.

The odd man out is Fl. Paniscus, ἔκδικος (P. Köln Panop. 30). He may, of course, have the Flaviate by virtue of previous service in the army or in another capacity (for a possible early Flavius-veteran cf. **3758** 202 n.).

The other difficulty is posed by P. Strasb. 296, where two syndics occur in November 326, both of them Aurelii; they are also described as ex-magistrates and councillors (of Hermopolis). This is substantially later than the start of the allocation of the Flaviate. Admittedly we do not know the mechanism of the allocation (cf. **3758** 202 n.), and the evidence shows (e.g. XLIII **3125**) that some ranks received it before others. Nevertheless, since they are paired and bear municipal titles, these syndics of the Strasbourg text seem more akin to their namesakes from the beginning of the century (e.g. XXXIII **2665** and **2673**, M. *Chr.* 196) than to the Flaviate ex-*curator* syndics, seemingly without colleagues, of the 330s, and to suppose that the Strasbourg text is just too early for the Flaviate to have reached the syndics does not obviate the difficulties. Was there a change in the status and the number of holders of the cυνδικία between 326 and (at the latest) 334, so that the allocation of the Flaviate comes later than expected and P. Strasb. 296 may legitimately be segregated from the syndics of the 330s and 340s? (Cf. A. K. Bowman, *Akten XIII Papyrologenkongr.* 44.) Otherwise we must suppose that, like the *riparii*, the syndics are not Flavii in virtue of their office and that the holders of the office who are Flavii either carry the *gentilicium* by right of a previous office or have some unmentioned concurrent entitlement.

4–5 For Τααμπεμοῦ see P. Pruneti, *I centri abitati dell'Ossirinchite* (= Pap. Flor. IX) 188–9. Its location in the 5th pagus was already known (only from **901**).

5 ἑcπεριναῖc ὥραιc. Cf. LI **3620** 9–10.

7 The presence of oxen (ἐπαγτλούντων βοῶν, 16) indicates that the μηχανή here will be of the *sāqia*-type; the ὑδραγώγιον will be the exit-channel. Cf. L. Ménassa and P. Laferrière, *La Sāqia: technique et vocabulaire de la roue à eau égyptienne* (Cairo, IFAO), where note the diagram facing p. 26. On the *sāqia* see also J. P. Olesen, *Greek and Roman Mechanical Water-lifting Devices* (= *Phoenix* suppl. 16, 1984) 370–85; T. Schiøler, *Roman and Islamic Water-lifting Wheels* (Odense, 1973).

8 π[ε]δῶν. **901** 8 has πέδων. *Pace* Grenfell and Hunt, this is far more likely to be for πεδίων than παιδῶν: for loss of iota in these circumstances and for the accent-shift cf. F. T. Gignac, *Grammar* i 302–3.

10 ξοΐδιον. **901** read ξοίλιον, corrected in the app. crit. to ξύλιον, but from a photograph it is reasonably clear that the reading should be ξοΐδιον as here. Delete ξύλιον from LSJ.

12 ἀδ[ικ]η[θείc]. Cf. **901** 11 ἀδικηθεί[c] where ι is clear and ἀδικηθέγ[τα] cannot be read.

14 με. The damaged fibres at **901** 14 must be adjusted to allow μοι or μαι (in place of οι) at this point.

15 προνοίαc. The reference for ἀπόνοια from **901** 15 should be deleted from the lexica.

17]ημην **901**, but I cannot recognize the last trace here before [μη]ν as η. From this point **901** preserves rather more text than **3771**, whose remains are too scanty to permit placing what **901** supplies. **901** was read ὑπ᾽ αὐτοῦ [23 letters]κόψας ὡς ἐκ τῶν [18 letters]. . . . . ͅοͅις τινὰς παράγετε [26 letters] θρασύτητι [29 letters]ουͅςᾳ. [(breaks off).

3772. DECLARATION OF PRICES

71/21 bis (a)   6.5 × 10.5 cm   c. 338

This fragment from the top of a declaration of prices by the κοινὸν τῶν ἐκδοχέων is more of I **85**, republished by R. A. Coles in *ZPE* 39 (1980) 115–23. To be precise, it is more of the separate roll on which stand cols. v–vi of **85**. As in them, the spaces left blank were never filled in; the hand is identical; and the new piece shares all the peculiarities distinguishing this series from **85** i–iv which are set out in *ZPE* 39 (1980) 116 except possibly one (see 1 n. below). I believe that it may once have directly preceded **85** v, thus further separating the two parts of **85**, but I have not been able to confirm this by physically putting the papyri together.

For the *curator* addressed, Flavius Eusebius, see Appendix I below. **85** i–iv are precisely dated (26 November 338) but I prefer to assign a less specific date to this new piece since along with **85** v–vi it carries no indication of its date beyond having the same addressee as i–iv (see *ZPE* 39 (1980) 116).

Traces survive from the preceding column (-]ω from its first line and -]ν from its second) at the upper left edge here, slightly higher than ll. 1 and 2 respectively. The back is blank.

    Φλαουΐῳ Εὐσεβίῳ
    λογιστῇ Ὀξυρυγχίτου
    παρὰ τοῦ κοινοῦ τῶν
    ἐκδοχέων τῆς αὐ-
 5 τῆς πόλεως δι᾽ ἐμοῦ
    Αὐρηλίου (vac.)
    (vac.) προσφωνῶ
    ἰδίῳ τιμήματι τὴν
    ἑξῆς ἐνγεγραμμέ-
 10 νην τιμὴν ὧν χι-
    ρίζω ὠνίων ἐπὶ τοῦ-
    δε τοῦ μη[νὸ]ς καὶ
    ὀμνύω τὸ[ν θεῖο]ν
    [c. 5].[c. 6]

    . . . .

1 φλαουΐῳ? See n. 8 ἰδιω 9–10 l. ἐγγεγραμμένην 10–11 l. χειρίζω

'To Flavius Eusebius, *curator* of the Oxyrhynchite, from the guild of the middlemen(?) of the same city, through me Aurelius (*vac.*). I declare at my own risk the price entered below for the goods which I handle for this month, and I swear the divine . . . '

1 A spot of ink above υι of *Φλαουίῳ* may possibly be remains of a diaeresis over the iota; this would be contrary to the pattern of I **85** v–vi, see *ZPE* 39 (1980) 116.

4 *ἐκδοχέων*. Variously translated 'forwarding agents' (LSJ), 'middlemen' (XIV **1669** 2 n.), 'Spediteure' (M. San Nicolò, *Äg. Vereinswesen* (2nd edn., Munich 1972) i 129). The word receives no entry in *CGL*. Such broad terms leave one puzzled as to what item or items the *ἐκδοχεῖς* would have declared. They are frequently recorded as handling grain, but this was not their sole business; in XIV **1673** they are handling wine. Note also P. M. Fraser, *Ptolemaic Alexandria* i 186–7, ii 319–20, cited in the note to XLIX **3507** 25, where *ἐκδοχεῖς* also occur in a context which may concern wine.

3773. COMMODITY PRICES

3 1B.81/D(2)   21.5 × 22 cm   *c.* 340

A substantial sheet of papyrus records the fluctuations in the price of gold, silver, and five basic commodities in the Oxyrhynchite nome (presumably) over a period of more than a year. The front carries the month-by-month prices from Thoth to the end of the year, but must have run back into the preceding year or years, see 1–3 n. The back begins in Thoth of what is probably the following year, but breaks off after three months. A close parallel is provided by LI **3628–33**, but **3773** differs in recording the price-fluctuations month by month in one nome, whereas **3628–33** record the variations averaged over 4-month periods in a series of nomes. It would have been easy to put together information of this kind from a collection of documents such as **3773**; **3773** for its part can really only have been assembled from a collection of guild price-declarations of the type featured plentifully in the present volume. Indeed the order of the commodities reflects to a certain extent the sequence of guilds proposed in Appendix II below. There are two immediate consequences from this conclusion: first, that the prices listed in **3773** are genuine open-market prices, not for example the level of refunds offered by the government in cases of compulsory purchase; second, that the guild of goldsmiths—no declaration of theirs survives intact—declared the price of the gold solidus in terms of talents and denarii. For possible evidence for the goldsmiths' use of gold coins as a source of raw material for the articles they fashioned, cf. P. Rainer Cent. 161. 22–3, though that passage may be otherwise explained.

The papyrus is not dated, apart from the month notations, but for a guide to its probable placing see R. S. Bagnall, *Currency and Inflation in Fourth-century Egypt* (*BASP* suppl. 5 (1985)) 38. On economic grounds a likely date may be in the late 330s or early 340s. Comparing also the list of prices assembled by R. S. Bagnall and P. J. Sijpesteijn, *ZPE* 24 (1977) 117–18, while remembering their caveat on p. 115, **3773** should post-date the prices for wheat and barley in 338 (24 tal. and $13\frac{1}{3}$ tal., I **85**). For the price of the gold solidus see Bagnall, *Currency* 61–2; also **3628** 8 n. with references, and R. S. Bagnall and K. A. Worp, *ZPE* 46 (1982) 246–7. **3773**'s gold prices (190–$243\frac{1}{3}$ tal., see below,

= 13680–17520 tal./lb.) fit neatly at the proposed date into the price structure outlined by Bagnall, *Currency* 61. See also J.-M. Carrié, *Aeg.* 64 (1984) 219–20. There is little other documentation for the solidus close to the price range attested by **3773**, but **3773** ought to post-date the price of 183⅓ tal. evidenced from SPP XX 81. 22 (re-ed. *ZPE* 22 (1976) 101–5 = SB XIV 11593; undated but assigned to the end of Constantine's reign (A. H. M. Jones, *LRE* i 440) or to the early 340s by Bagnall–Sijpesteijn, *ZPE* 24 (1977) 123–4; 338–41, Bagnall, *Currency* 39); the same document gives a wheat price of 26 tal. P. Lond. II 427 (p. 311 = P. Abinn. 68) may be nearly contemporary with **3773**, the price of wheat being 50 tal./art.; P. Abinn. 43 has a barley price of 30 tal./art., higher than **3773**. Both these texts are discussed briefly by Bagnall, *Currency* 41. His lists on p. 64 give their date as 'ca 348–351' against *c.* 342–51 on pp. 41, 67, and 70.

The ratio of gold to silver is probably meant to be consistently—if not always calculated absolutely accurately, see 53 n.—1:14.4, or in other words 1 lb. silver costs 5 solidi. For this rate—not otherwise certainly documented before 397—see **3628** 9 n. (For P. Oslo III 162 and the meaning of μονάς see XLVIII **3402** 4–5 n. and LI **3636** 18 n.) The price of gold climbs through the period of the text, from a conjectured 206⅔ tal. (and perhaps 190 tal.) per solidus to 243⅓ tal., then drops to 240 tal. The price of silver follows suit, though the increases only take effect after a few months' delay; when the papyrus breaks off, the silver price has not yet settled to match the drop in the price of gold. For silver prices see LI **3624** 17 n. and Bagnall, *Currency* 28 and 62 (on p. 62 the figure for **3624** should read '45,333 T. 2000 dr.'). The other commodities show less a steady increase than an inconsistent irregular fluctuation. The changes up and down, from one month to the next, reach a magnitude of one-third and show only too clearly how unsafe a guide to inflation-rates isolated prices can be; while longer-term changes (but still within a year) reach no less than 77% (vegetable seed, from 45 up to 80 tal./artaba).

It will be useful to supplement the text and translation with the commodities and prices tabulated, see Table 1. Prices are in talents.

The price-fluctuations for the five commodities other than gold and silver are perhaps in part to be explained as seasonal variation. Perhaps wheat, barley, and wine will fit the anticipated pattern of the highest prices coming just before the harvest, but lentils hardly will. There is no obvious explanation for the drop in barley, lentil, and vegetable-seed prices in Mecheir. The price-difference for lentils between one Thoth and (I presume) the next is striking. The figures for vegetable-seed suggest an autumn crop. The comparative values of barley, lentils, and wheat accord neither with the values given in **3628–33** (tabulated p. 73) nor with the statement in XLVII **3345** 46–7 n. (AD 209) that lentils were generally equated or nearly equated with wheat. Note also LI **3625** 16 n. Known fourth-century prices for these commodities are listed by Bagnall, *Currency* 64–6.

The effects of inflation are reduced (but not entirely removed), for those in a position to profit, by the increase in the price of the solidus: e.g. the increase in the price

TABLE I. *Variations in commodity prices over fifteen months*

	Θώθ	Φα.	Ἀθ.	Χοι.	Τῦ.	Με.	Φαμ.	Φαρ.	Παχ.	Παῦ.	Ἐπ.	Μεc.	Θώθ	Φα.	Ἀθ.
νομcματίου (each)	190? See 8 n.	$206\frac{2}{3}$?	$233\frac{1}{3}$	$233\frac{1}{3}$?	$233\frac{1}{3}$	$233\frac{1}{3}$	$233\frac{1}{3}$	$233\frac{1}{3}$	$243\frac{1}{3}$	$243\frac{1}{3}$	$243\frac{1}{3}$	$243\frac{1}{3}$	$243\frac{1}{3}$	240	240
ἀcήμου 1 lb.		950?	$1{,}033\frac{1}{3}$	$1{,}033\frac{1}{3}$?	$1{,}033\frac{1}{3}$	$1{,}166\frac{2}{3}$	$1{,}166\frac{2}{3}$		$1{,}866\frac{2}{3}$	$1{,}866\frac{2}{3}$	$1{,}866\frac{2}{3}$	$1{,}866\frac{2}{3}$	$1{,}213\frac{1}{3}$	$1{,}213\frac{1}{3}$	$1{,}213\frac{1}{3}$
cίτου 1 art.		45?	45		45	$46\frac{2}{3}$	50		50	45	45	45	40	40	40?
κριθῆc 1 art.	20		20? or 25		25	20	25		15	15	20	20?	20	22	
φακοῦ 1 art.	20		22		25	22	25		20+	30	30?	30	35	30	
λαχανοcπέρμου 1 art.		50	50		50	45	50			75	75		80	75	
οἴνου 1 sext.		1	1		1	1	$1\frac{1}{3}$	$1\frac{1}{3}$	$1\frac{1}{3}$	$1\frac{1}{3}$	$1\frac{2}{3}$		1	1	

of lentils is approximately 50% from one year-beginning to the next, but in terms of the buying-power of the solidus the increase reduces to approximately 25%.

There are two kolleseis, at the extreme right edges of cols. i and iii. The visible sheet distance between them is approx. 15 cm. Col. iv on the back is written larger and more coarsely (only partially because of the coarser papyrus texture) than the front, but the hand is the same.

On the back, and visible either side of the column transcribed here, are the faded remains of two columns; after a general heading, sub-headings α΄ πάγου, β΄ πάγου, γ΄ πάγου, and δ΄ πάγου are visible. The order of writing of the two texts is not certain, and it is not clear if there has been any deliberate attempt to efface this other text. Blank areas below α΄ πάγου and β΄ πάγου may be due to absence of entries for these districts. The hand of this other text may be the same as that of **3773**.

col. i

	[			]
	[κριθῶν	] ạ	τάλ(αντα)	κ
	[φακοῦ	] α	τ̣άλ(αντα)	κ
	[			]
5	[			]
	[Φαῶφι]			
	[νομισματίου			].
	[ἀσήμου		]..[..]	ν̣
	[σίτου		]	με
10	[κριθῶν			]
	φ[ακοῦ			]
	λαχανο[σπέρ(μου)			].
	οἴνου	ξ(έστου) ạ	τ̣ά[λ(αντον)] α	
	Ἀθὺρ νομισματίου		τάλ(αντα) ϲ[λγ (δηνάρια)] φ	
15	ἀσήμου	λί(τρας) α	τάλ(αντα) Ἀλγ (δηνάρια) φ	
	σίτου	ἀ(ρτάβης) α	τάλ(αντα)	με
	κριθῶν	ἀ(ρτάβης) α	τάλ(αντα)	κ
	φακοῦ	ἀ(ρτάβης) α	τάλ(αντα)	κβ
	λαχανοσπέρ(μου)	ἀ̣(ρτάβης) α	τάλ(αντα)	ν
20	οἴνο[υ]	ξ̣(έστου) α	τάλ(αντον) α	

3 ταλˈ, and so below; the dot has been lost in 2   15 λ, ✳   16 α⸗

Χοιάκ

[νομ]ι[cμα]τί[ου   ].. φ

[ἀcήμου   ]..[..]. (δηνάρια) φ

.   .   .   .   .

col. ii

Τῦβι

25	ν[ομιc]μ[ατ]ίου		τάλ(αντα)	cλγ (δηνάρια) φ
ἀ[cή]μου	λί(τρας) α	τάλ(αντα)	Ἀλγ (δηνάρια) φ
cίτου	ἀ(ρτάβης) α	τάλ(αντα)	με
κριθῶν	ἀ(ρτάβης) α	τάλ(αντα)	κε
φακοῦ	ἀ(ρτάβης) α	τάλ(αντα)	κε
30	λαχανοcπέρ(μου)	ἀ(ρτάβης) α	τάλ(αντα)	ν
οἴνου	ἀ(ρτάβης) α	τάλ(αντον)	α

Μεχείρ

νομιcματίου		τάλ(αντα)	cλγ (δηνάρια) φ
ἀcήμου	λί(τρας) α	τάλ(αντα)	Ἀρξϛ (δηνάρια) Ἀ
35	cίτου	ἀ(ρτάβης) α	τάλ(αντα)	μϛ (δηνάρια) Ἀ
κριθῶν	ἀ(ρτάβης) α	τάλ(αντα)	κ
φακοῦ	ἀ(ρτάβης) α	τάλ(αντα)	κβ
λαχανοcπέρ(μου)	ἀ(ρτάβης) α	τάλ(αντα)	με
οἴνου	ξ(έcτου) α	τάλ(αντον)	α

40 Φαμενώθ

νομι[c]ματίου		τάλ(αντα)	cλγ (δηνάρια) φ
ἀcήμου	λί(τρας) α	τάλ(αντα)	Ἀρξϛ (δηνάρια) Ἀ
cίτου	ἀ(ρτάβης) α	τάλ(αντα)	ν
κριθῶν	ἀ(ρτάβης) α	τάλ(αντα)	κε
45	φακοῦ	ἀ(ρτάβης) α	τάλ(αντα)	κε
λαχανοcπέρ(μου)	ἀ(ρτάβης) α	τάλ(αντα)	ν
οἴνου	ξ(έcτου) α	τάλ(αντον)	α (δηνάρια) φ

Φ[αρ]μοῦθι

[νο]μιϲματίου		τάλ(αντα)	cλγ (δηνάρια) φ
50 | [| |].. . [   ]

.   .   .   .   .

31 ἀ(ρτάβης): l. ξ(έcτου)

col. iii

	οἴνου	ξ(έϲτου) α	ϝάλ(αντον) α	(δηνάρια) φ
	Παχὼν νομιϲματίο̣υ̣		[τά]λ(αντα) ϲμγ	(δηνάρια) φ
	ἀϲήμου	λί(τραϲ) α	τάλ(αντα) Ἄρπϛ	(δηνάρια) Ἀ
	ϲίτου	ἀ(ρτάβηϲ) α	τάλ(αντα) ν	
55	κριθῶν	ἀ(ρτάβηϲ) α	τάλ(αντα) ιε	
	φακοῦ	ἀ[(ρτάβηϲ) α]	τάλ(αντα) κ.	
	λαχανοϲπ[έ]ρ(μου)	ἀ(ρτάβηϲ) α	τάλ(αντα) [ ]	
	οἴνου	ξ(έϲτου) α	τάλ(αντον) [α]	(δηνάρια) φ
	Παῦνι νομιϲματίου		τάλ(αντα) ϲμγ	(δηνάρια) φ
60	ἀϲήμου	λί(τραϲ) α	τάλ(αντα) Ἄρπϛ	(δηνάρια) Ἀ
	ϲίτου	ἀ(ρτάβηϲ) α	τάλ(αντα) με	
	κριθῶν	ἀ(ρτάβηϲ) α	τάλ(αντα) ιε	
	φακοῦ	ἀ(ρτάβηϲ) α	τάλ(αντα) λ	
	λαχανοϲ(πέρμου?)	ἀ(ρτάβηϲ) α	τάλ(αντα) οε	
65	οἴνου	ξ(έϲτου) α	τάλ(αντον) α	(δηνάρια) φ
	Ἐπεὶφ νομιϲμ(ατίου)		τάλ(αντα) ϲμγ	(δηνάρια) φ
	ἀϲήμου	λί(τραϲ) α	τάλ(αντα) Ἄρπϛ	(δηνάρια) Ἀ
	ϲίτου	ἀ(ρτάβηϲ) α	τάλ(αντα) με	
	κριθῶν	ἀ(ρτάβηϲ) α	τάλ(αντα) κ	
70	φακοῦ	ἀ(ρτάβηϲ) α	[τάλ(αντα)] λ	
	λαχάνου	ἀ(ρτάβηϲ) α	τάλ(αντα) οε	
	οἴνου	ξ(έϲτου) α	τάλ(αντον) α	(δηνάρια) Ἀ
	Με̣ϲ̣ο̣ρὴ νομιϲμ(ατίου)		τάλ(αντα) ϛ[μγ]	(δηνάρια) φ
	ἀ̣ϲ̣ή̣μ̣ο̣υ̣		τάλ(αντα) Ἄρπϛ	(δηνάρια) Ἀ
75	ϲ̣ί̣τ̣ο̣υ̣		τάλ(αντα) με	
	κρ̣ι̣θ(ῶν)		τάλ(αντα) κ	
	φ[α]κ[ο]ῦ̣		[τά]λ(αντα) λ	
	[		]. [ ]	

.   .   .   .   .

64 λαχανοϲ pap.; l. λαχάνου (cf. 71)?   66 νομιϲμϛ   76 κριθ⁻?

(Back)   col. iv

    Θώθ

80   νομισματίου   τάλ(αντα) ϲμγ (δηνάρια) φ

       ἀϲήμου   λί(τρας) α   τάλ(αντα) Ἀϲιγ (δηνάρια) φ

       ϲίτου   ἀ(ρτάβης) α   (τάλαντα) μ

       κριθῶν   κ

       φακοῦ   λε

85   λαχ(ανοσπέρμου)   π

       οἴνου   α

    Φαῶφι

       νομισματίου   ϲμ

       ἀϲήμου   Ἀϲιγ (δηνάρια) φ

90   ϲίτου   μ

       κριθ(ῶν)   κβ

       φακοῦ   λ

       λαχαν(οσπέρμου)   οε

       οἴνου   α

95   Ἀθύρ

       νομισματίου   ϲμ

       ἀϲήμου   Ἀϲιγ (δηνάρια) φ

       [ϲ]ίτου   ἀ(ρτάβης) α   . .

          .   .   .   .   .

85 λαχ´ A large blot of ink after π, probably accidental   91 κριθ´   93 λαχαν´, altered from λαχανοϲ or λαχάνου   94 A dot below α, perhaps only a blot   98 See n.

(14–20)	'Hathyr. 1 solidus		233 tal.	500 den.
	Uncoined silver	1 lb.	1,033 tal.	500 den.
	Wheat	1 art.	45 tal.	
	Barley	1 art.	20 tal.	
	Lentils	1 art.	22 tal.	
	Vegetable seed	1 art.	50 tal.	
	Wine	1 sext.	1 tal.'	
(24–49)	'Tybi.			
	1 solidus		233 tal.	500 den.
	Uncoined silver	1 lb.	1,033 tal.	500 den.
	Wheat	1 art.	45 tal.	
	Barley	1 art.	25 tal.	
	Lentils	1 art.	25 tal.	
	Vegetable seed	1 art.	50 tal.	
	Wine	1 art.(!)	1 tal.	

Mecheir.
1 solidus		233 tal.	500 den.
Uncoined silver	1 lb.	1,166 tal.	1,000 den.
Wheat	1 art.	46 tal.	1,000 den.
Barley	1 art.	20 tal.	
Lentils	1 art.	22 tal.	
Vegetable seed	1 art.	45 tal.	
Wine	1 sext.	1 tal.	

Phamenoth.
1 solidus		233 tal.	500 den.
Uncoined silver	1 lb.	1,166 tal.	1,000 den.
Wheat	1 art.	50 tal.	
Barley	1 art.	25 tal.	
Lentils	1 art.	25 tal.	
Vegetable seed	1 art.	50 tal.	
Wine	1 sext.	1 tal.	500 den.

Pharmouthi.
1 solidus		233 tal.	500 den.'

(51-77)
'Wine	1 sext.	1 tal.	500 den.
Pachon. 1 solidus		243 tal.	500 den.
Uncoined silver	1 lb.	1,186 tal.	1,000 den.
Wheat	1 art.	50 tal.	
Barley	1 art.	15 tal.	
Lentils	1 art.	20 + tal.	
Vegetable seed	1 art.	[ ] tal.	
Wine	1 sext.	1 tal.	500 den.
Payni. 1 solidus		243 tal.	500 den.
Uncoined silver	1 lb.	1,186 tal.	1,000 den.
Wheat	1 art.	45 tal.	
Barley	1 art.	15 tal.	
Lentils	1 art.	30 tal.	
Vegetable seed	1 art.	75 tal.	
Wine	1 sext.	1 tal.	500 den.
Epeiph. 1 solidus		243 tal.	500 den.
Uncoined silver	1 lb.	1,186 tal.	1,000 den.
Wheat	1 art.	45 tal.	
Barley	1 art.	20 tal.	
Lentils	1 art.	30(?) tal.	
Vegetable seed	1 art.	75 tal.	
Wine	1 sext.	1 tal.	1,000 den.
Mesore. 1 solidus		243 tal.	500 den.
Uncoined silver		1,186 tal.	1,000 den.
Wheat		45 tal.	
Barley		20 tal.	
Lentils		30 tal.'	

(79-98)
'Thoth.			
1 solidus		243 tal.	500 den.
Uncoined silver	1 lb.	1,213 tal.	500 den.
Wheat	1 art.	40 tal.	
Barley		20	
Lentils		35	
Vegetable seed		80	
Wine		1	

Phaophi.			
1 solidus		240	
Uncoined silver		1,213	500 den.
Wheat		40	
Barley		22	
Lentils		30	
Vegetable seed		75	
Wine		1	
Hathyr.			
1 solidus		240	
Uncoined silver		1,213	500 den.
Wheat	1 art.	..'	

1–3 The prices in 2–3 must surely be for barley and lentils, comparing the prices in the table in the introduction above. Line 1 of the transcript, which though altogether lost would have been level with the top of the following column, would then contain wheat, and the Thoth prices for gold and silver must have come at the foot of the preceding column, so that the papyrus must have recorded prices back into the previous year.

7 The trace is not ϕ, i.e. 500 den. It could be from $\bar{A}$, 1,000 den., indicating a gold price of 206⅔ tal., correct in relation to the silver price (which was slow to adjust) the following month (1,033⅓ tal.).

8 If $\nu = 50$ is correct, the next price-step down for silver would be 950 tal./lb., indicating a gold price of 190 tal./solidus in Thoth or earlier (earlier is more likely, comparing the time-lag in other instances—see the tabulation in the introd.).

14 The price is restored by analogy with the prices from Tybi to Pharmouthi (col. ii). The price in Phaophi was probably less, cf. 7 n.

17 It is possible that *κε* was intended.

19 *λαχανοςπέρ(μου)*. The descender of rho is cut by an oblique stroke rising to the right at a shallow angle; so also in 30, 38, 46, 57.

22 The price may be 233⅓ tal. as in the following months.

23 The price may be 1,033⅓ tal. as in the preceding month and the following month, but I cannot confirm this from the scanty traces.

39 For the form of *ξ(ἕςτου)* see **3740** 16–17 n.

45 The papyrus is badly warped in the second part of the line but the reading is not in doubt.

50 Probably]*Ἀ̣ρ̣ξ̣*[, from the price for *ἄςημον*.

51 Two strokes in the margin above this line probably not significant.

53 This price corresponds to a price for the solidus of 237⅓ tal., which does not actually occur. Are we to suppose an error, in place of a continued 1,166⅔ tal. (34, 42, ?50), or were such variations in the proportion (cf. the introd.) admissible? Note that the rate of 1,186⅔ tal. for silver is sustained till the end of the year (60, 67, 74). When the silver rate eventually rises to match (apparently) the new solidus rate from Pachon, it is given (81, 89, 97) as 1,213⅓ tal. (corresponding to a solidus price of 242⅔ tal.) instead of the expected 1,216⅔ tal. which would accord strictly with the ratio of 1:14.4.

58 The missing numeral will hardly be other than *α*, cf. the tabulated prices in the introd. above.

73 Talents-figure read by analogy with 52, 59, 66, and 80.

98 *ἀ(ρτάβης) α* is a rationalization of the papyrus text which has a single alpha struck through, thus *α̸*. The talent-indication is omitted; the price is indicated as two units, but *μ* (the price in the two preceding months) is a possible alternative.

3774. Declaration to the Logistes

3 1B.81/B(1)a 8 × 11 cm 341

This document is primarily of interest for establishing the correct position of Flavius Eulogius in the logistae list, viz. between Flavius Eusebius (known 338) and Flavius Dionysarius (known from March 324): see Appendix I below.

The text is a nomination to a liturgy or liturgies whose identity is lost. For a list of such texts from the fourth century see CPR VII pp. 74–5. Add LI **3621** and **3623**; PSI XVII Congr. (= M. Manfredi *et al.*, *Trenta testi greci*, Florence 1983) no. 28; P. Harr. II 213.

There are traces of a four-layer kollesis in the left margin; the papyrus will once have formed part of a τόμος ϲυγκολλήϲιμοϲ.

The back is blank.

ὑπατείαϲ Ἀντωνίου Μαρκ[ελλίνου]
καὶ Πετρωνίου Προβίνου [τῶν λαμ(προτάτων).]
Φλαουΐῳ Εὐλογίῳ λογιϲτῇ [’Ὀξυρυγχίτου]
παρὰ τῶν ἀπὸ κώμηϲ Ϲεφὼ [ζ΄ πάγου?]
5   δι’ ἡμῶν [τ]ῶν δημοϲίων Α[ὐρηλίων]
Ψεναμούνιοϲ Ψόϊτοϲ μίζ[ονοϲ τῆϲ]
κώμηϲ καὶ Ἀχιλλέουϲ . . [. . . . .]
τεϲϲαλαρίου καὶ Εὐδαίμον[οϲ Ἱέρα-?]
κοϲ καὶ ⟨’Ι⟩ουϲτίνου Πτολε[μαίου]
10   κωμαρχῶν. ἀκουλούθ[ωϲ τοῖϲ]
προϲταχθεῖϲιν ὑπὸ τοῦ [δια-]
ϲημοτάτου ἡγημόνοϲ [τῆϲ Αὐγου-]
ϲταμνικῆϲ Φλαουΐου ’Ιο[υλίου]
Αὐϲονίου δίδομεν κ[ινδύνῳ]
15   ἡμῶν καὶ πάν[των τῶν ἀπὸ]
τῆϲ α[ὐ]τῆϲ ⟨κώ⟩μη[ϲ   c. 8   ]
[c. 7   ] . [

.   .   .   .   .

3 [’Ὀξυρυγχίτου]: the word was perhaps abbreviated   6 l. μείζονοϲ   7 καί corr. from διά?
8 l. τεϲϲεραρίου   10 l. ἀκολούθωϲ   12 l. ἡγεμόνοϲ

'In the consulship of Antonius Marcellinus and Petronius Probinus, [*viri clarissimi*(?).]

'To Flavius Eulogius, *curator* of the Oxyrhynchite, from the inhabitants of the village of Sepho in the 7th pagus, through us the public officials Aurelii Psenamounis son of Psois, headman of the village, and Achilles son of . . . , *tesserarius*, and Eudaemon son of Hierax(?) and Justinus son of Ptolemaeus, comarchs. In accordance with the instructions of the *praeses* of Augustamnica, Flavius Julius Ausonius, *vir perfectissimus*, we present at our own risk and that of all the inhabitants of the said village . . . '

4 For Ϲεφώ see P. Pruneti, *I centri abitati dell' Ossirinchite* 176–7.

8 τεϲϲαλαρίου. Cf. LI **3621** 5–6 n. **3774** is now the latest evidence for the office.

11–14 For Fl. Julius Ausonius see L **3576–9,** esp. **3576** 10–12 n. with references, and **3775**. Published texts show him as in office between at least 13 November 341 and 1 July 342. Information about him is insufficient to restrict the placing of **3774** within 341.

14–16 Restorations are conjectural, especially the imposed correction in 16.

3775. Petition to the Logistes

71/40(b)   18.4 × 10.5 cm   1 July 342

This darkened and fragile papyrus preserves the beginning of a report of proceedings before Flavius Julius Ausonius, *praeses Augustamnicae*, preceded in a separate column by a petition or application to Flavius Eutrygius, *curator* of the Oxyrhynchite, referring to the appended proceedings. The second column was very wide, given the need to put the consular formula of 1–3 into one line there, see 15 n.

The text is of interest as providing the earliest attestation of Flavius Eutrygius as logistes; see Appendix I below. It also supplies our latest date for Flavius Julius Ausonius as *praeses* (previously 5 May 342 from P. Harr. 65); see 3774 11–14 n.

The back is blank.

col. i

[ὑπατεία]ς τῶν δεσποτῶν ἡμῶν
[Κωνστα]ντίου τὸ γʹʹ καὶ Κώνσταντος
[τὸ β]ʹʹ Αὐγούστων, Ἐπεὶφ ζ.

     Φλαουΐ[ῳ Εὐ]τρυγίῳ λογιστῇ Ὀξ(υρυγχίτου)
5   παρὰ Α[ὐρηλί]ου Ἐξᾶ Στεφάνου ἀπὸ τῆς
     αὐτῆς π[όλε]ως. τῶν πραχθέντων
     ὑπομν[η]μάτων παρὰ τῇ ἀρετῇ τοῦ
     κυρίου [μου] διασημοτάτου ἡγεμόνος
     τῆς Ἀγουσ[τ]αμνικῆς Φλαουΐ[ο]υ
10   Ἰουλίου Α[ὐσο]νίου περὶ τοῦ παραδο-
     θῆναί μοι [τ]οῦ ἡμετέρου οἰκοπέδου
     τὴν νομὴ[ν] διὰ τῆς σῆς εὐτονίας
     εἴσον [τῷ βιβ]λιδί[ῳ] ὑποτάξας
     [. .]. [

       ·   ·   ·   ·   ·

col. ii

15   ὑπατείας τῶν δεσποτῶν ἡμ[ων

     εἰσαχθέντος Ἐξᾶ ἀπὸ τῆς [
     κληρονόμους Ἡρακλείδου [

4 οξʹ   7 ὑπομν[η]μᾱτων   9 l. Αὐγουςταμνικῆς; φλαουϊ[ο]υ   13 l. ἴςον   15 ὑπατειας?
16 An attempt made to wash out ξα of Ἐξᾶ?

ὑπήκου[c]ϵν, Ἄριος ῥ(ήτωρ) ϵἶ(πϵν)· ϵν[

ποι...αλ[..] τῶν νόμων δι[

20   λϵυτϵον ἐκῖνοι ἐλθόντϵς ϵ[

οἰκοῦϲιν ἐπϵὶ τῷ απαν[

ὑπὸ τῆϲ μϵγαλορρίαϲ τ.[

ἃ οὐδὲν [.].[...].πα[

τὰ πϵπρ[αγμένα?

25   ἡμϵρῶν.[

ἡγϵμον[-

[..]...[

·   ·   ·   ·   ·

18 ϵι)   20 l. ἐκϵῖνοι

(1–12) 'In the consulship of our masters Constantius for the 3rd time and Constans for the 2nd time, Augusti, Epeiph 7.

'To Flavius Eutrygius, *curator* of the Oxyrhynchite, from Aurelius Hexas son of Stephanus, from the same city. Subjoining to the petition a copy of the minutes transacted before the Virtue of my lord *praeses* of Augustamnica, Flavius Julius Ausonius, *vir perfectissimus*, concerning the restoration to me of the possession of our property through Your Vigour . . .'

7 ἀρϵτῇ. See **3758** 14 n.

12 ϵὐτονίαc. For the honorific use of this word cf. BGU III 786 ii 1 and P. Brem. 9. 18 (both ii AD).

14 [ἀξ]ι[ῶ]?

15 The proceedings in the following lines are before the *praeses* Fl. Julius Ausonius, see 6–10. Given his known tenure, the nearest preceding imperial consulate, and the date of the creation of Augustamnica, the consulship here has to be that of 342 as in 1–3.

15–16 Marks of ink before the beginnings of these lines perhaps accidental.

18 ὑπήκου[c]ϵν. Probably a variation of the κληθέντοc καὶ (μὴ) ὑπακούcαντοc formula, for which see R. A. Coles, *Reports of Proceedings* 31 n. 4.

For the form of ῥ(ήτωρ) see **3758** 41 n.

20 λϵυτϵον. ρυτϵον could also be read. There are unexplained traces both below (first ϵ) and above (ϵο) the word. If λϵυτϵον is correct, [βου]λϵυτέον? τὸ τϵ]λϵυτϵον (= τϵλϵυταῖον)?

22 μϵγαλορρίαc. Lat. *magnanimitas*. See H. Zilliacus, *Unters. zu den abstrakten Anredeformen* 72, 89, 106. More recently published examples are SB VI 9396. 1 and 9597. 3, PSI XIII 1342. 12 and XIV 1425. 2.

23 The beginning of the line could be otherwise articulated.

3776. DECLARATIONS OF PRICES

22 3B.14/C(2–3)b   14 × 26.8 cm   24 July 343

This papyrus preserves the declaration by the guild of ὀθονιοπῶλαι more or less intact, despite its tattered appearance, plus ends of lines and beginnings of lines of the preceding and following declarations respectively. The papyrus is not a τόμοc cυγκολλήcιμοc although there is a kollesis between cols. i and ii (note that a line-end from col. i overruns it). The same hand wrote the main body of all three declarations.

Curiously the declaration of the ὀθονιοπῶλαι in the centre column here is almost identical, word for word, with the later one of the ταρϲικάριοι in LI **3626** (25 January 359), although in the latter the prices were never filled in. The parallelism is so close that the commentary on **3626** will in large part serve for the present text too. The explanation why two different guilds should make an identical declaration (or conversely what the difference is between the ὀθονιοπῶλαι and the ταρϲικάριοι) is still to be found. The third column here is clearly from the declaration of another but closely related guild of textile-merchants who handle — *inter alia* — goods described as Laodicean, cf. **3626** 4 n.

The papyrus provides the latest attestation for the logistes Flavius Eutrygius, for whom see Appendix I below.

Only line-ends remain from the preceding declaration, which we do not transcribe. No indication survives of the guild or of the items declared. The subscription is autograph, by [Αὐρ]ήλιος Παθερμού[θιος?]. **3765** 9 ff. could lead us to expect the guild of ϲτιππoχειριϲταί to precede, but the space may not suit; also, for what it is worth, the declaration from them in **3753** (AD 319) has four declarants against one in the present instance.

Distinction of hands, as often in these series of declarations, is not always easy. Here at least all three subscriptions are autograph. The statement of the identity of the declarant is handled casually, in the one place where it survives (6), both in the early stopping of the first hand (at πόλεωϲ) and in the minimum possible insertion of just the one name. The series is probably consistently plural-drafted (χιρί]ζομεν survives among the tattered traces of col. i), single declarants in cols. i–ii notwithstanding. Early stop and plural drafting are features shared by I **85** i–iv (re-ed. R. A. Coles, *ZPE* 39 (1980) 115–23; cf. ibid. 115–16 for an analysis of the often more rigorously circumscribed bureaucratic forms of these documents). I have compared a photograph of **85** (dated 338, five years earlier) with **3776**; the main hands are similar in style, but not sufficiently similar (or dissimilar) to allow a decision that they are (or are not) the same.

The back is blank.

col. ii

 Φλαουΐῳ Εὐτρ[υγίῳ]
 λογιϲτῇ Ὀξυρυ[γχίτου]
 παρὰ τοῦ κοινο͜[ῦ τῶν]
 ὀθονιοπωλῶν τ[ῆϲ]
5 αὐτῆϲ πόλεωϲ (added, m. 1?)
 δι(ὰ) Ἀττίωνοϲ.
(m. 1) προϲφωνοῦμεν ἰδίῳ

5 Final ϲ extended to form filling-stroke 6 δι ᾽ατ᾽τιωνοϲ

τιμήματι τὴν ἑξῆς ἐγ-
γεγραμμένην τιμὴν
10 ὧν χιρίζομεν ὠνίων
εἶναι ἐπὶ τοῦδε τοῦ μηνὸς
καὶ ὀμνύομεν τὸν θεῖον
ὅρκον μηδὲν διεψεῦσθαι.
ἔστι δέ·

15 [ὀ]θό[νης π]αντοίας δαλματικ(ῶν)
[γυναικ(είων) τ]αρcικ(ῶν) μεγάλ(ου) μέτρ(ου)
     α [εἰδέα]c   ζ(εύγους) α   τάλ(αντα) (added, m. 1?) υ
(m. 1) β ε̣ἰ[δέ]αc   ζ(εύγους) α   τάλ(αντα) (added, m. 1?) cξϛ (δηνάρια) Ⱥ
(m. 1) γ [ε]ἰ̣δ̣έ̣α̣c   ζ(εύγους) α   τάλ(αντα) (added, m. 1?) c
(m. 1) ἀ̣ν̣α̣β[ολα]δ̣ί̣ων ὁμοίωc·
21   α ε̣ἰ̣δ̣έ̣α̣c   ζ(εύγους) α   τάλ(αντα) (added, m. 1?) c. [
(m. 1) β ε̣ἰ̣δ̣έ̣αc   ζ(εύγους) α   τάλ(αντα) (added, m. 1?) ϛ[
(m. 1) γ ε̣ἰ̣δ̣έαc   ζ(εύγους) α   τάλ(αντα) (added, m. 1?) ρ̣. . [
(m. 1) c[τ]ιχαρίων ὁ̣[μ]οίωc·
25   α′ εἰδέαc [
        β′ εἰδέαc   ζ(εύγους) α̣   τ̣άλ(αντα) (added, m. 1?) . . [
(m. 1) γ εἰδέαc   ζ(εύγους) α   τάλ(αντα) (added, m. 1?) ρλγ (δηνάρια) φ
(m. 1) φακιαλίων ὁμοίωc·
29   α εἰδεαc   ζ(εύγους) α   τάλ(αντα) (added, m. 1?) ρξ
(m. 1) β εἰδέαc   ζ(εύγους) α   τάλ(αντα) (added, m. 1?) ρκ
(m. 1) γ ε̣ἰ̣δέαc   ζ(εύγους) α   τάλ(αντα) (added, m. 1?) ρ
(m. 1) [ὑπατεία]c Φουρίου Πλακίδου καὶ Φλαουΐου
     ['Ρωμώλο]υ τῶν λαμ(προτάτων), 'Επεὶφ λ΄.

(m. 2)   [Αὐρ]ήλιος Ἀττίων προс-
35   [φ]ωνῶ ὡς πρόκιτε.

8-9 l. ἐγγεγραμμένην   10 l. χειρίζομεν   15 δαλματι^κ   16 ταρcι^κμεγαλ·   17 ff. ταλ·
33 λαμϩ   34 ατ'τιων   35 l. πρόκειται

col. iii

.   .   .   .   .

(m. 1)   εἶναι ἐπὶ τοῦδ[ε τοῦ μηνὸς]

καὶ ὀμ[νύομεν τὸν θεῖον ὅρκον]

μη[δ]ὲν ϙ[ιεψεῦϲθαι.]

[ἔϲτι δέ·]

40   ὡρ[α]ρ[ίων

Λαδικη[νῶν

[

ὑπϙδεεϲ[τερ-

δαλματικ( ) . [

45   μετρ( ) [

ὑπϙδε[εϲτερ-

ϲτιχαρί[ων

[. . . .] . . [

[. . . .] . . [

50   [

[

[

Ἐπεὶφ λ. [

_____

(m. 3)   Αὐρή[λιο-

55   προϲ[φων-

44 δαλματιᵏ

Col. ii

'To Flavius Eutrygius, *curator* of the Oxyrhynchite, from the guild of the linen-merchants of the same city' (added, m. 1?) 'through Attion.' (m. 1) 'At our own risk we declare the price entered below for the goods which we handle to be (the price) during this month, and we swear the divine oath that we have been deceitful in nothing. As follows:

'Linen of all kinds:

'Ladies' Tarsian sleeved tunics, large size:

'1st quality	1 pr.	tal.' (added, m. 1?) '400.'		
(m. 1) '2nd quality	1 pr.	tal.' (added, m. 1?) '266, den. 1,000.'		
(m. 1) '3rd quality	1 pr.	tal.' (added, m. 1?) '200.'		

(m. 1) 'Shawls likewise:

'1st quality	1 pr.	tal.' (added, m. 1?) '2 . . .'		
(m. 1) '2nd quality	1 pr.	tal.' (added, m. 1?).'200(?).'		
(m. 1) '3rd quality	1 pr.	tal.' (added, m. 1?) '1 . . .'		

(m. 1) 'Tunics likewise:
'1st quality   [
'2nd quality   1 pr.   tal.' (added, m. 1?) '. . .'
  (m. 1) '3rd quality 1 pr.   tal.' (added, m. 1?) '133, den. 500.'
  (m. 1) 'Facecloths likewise:
'1st quality   1 pr.   tal.' (added, m. 1?) '160.'
  (m. 1) '2nd quality 1 pr.   tal.' (added, m. 1?) '120.'
  (m. 1) '3rd quality 1 pr.   tal.' (added, m. 1?) '100.'
(m. 1) 'In the consulship of Furius Placidus and Flavius Romulus, *viri clarissimi*, Epeiph 30.'
(m. 2) 'I, Aurelius Attion, declare as aforesaid.'

6 Ἀττίωνος. Note **3746** introd. ad fin.

11 εἶναι and ἐπὶ τοῦδε τοῦ μηνός are among the variations found in the formula of these declarations; often both omitted, both occur in LI **3624–6** and in I **85** i–iv (*ZPE* 39 (1980) 116–19), while ἐπὶ τοῦδε τοῦ μηνός also occurs without εἶναι, in the same position (**85** vi) or preceding ὧν χειρίζω/-ομεν ὠνίων (**3766**).

15–19 These entries reappear in the earlier summary **3765** 12–15, of *c*. 327: the price of the first quality has increased tenfold between then and 343. See Appendix III below.

16 μέτρ(ου). The descender of rho is cut by an oblique stroke rising to the right at a shallow angle; so also in 45.

17 ζ(εύγους). The abbreviation is a very rapid cursive zeta with a horizontal cutting it in the middle. Cf. **3765** 13. The prices of the items in LI **3626** are calculated by the τετράλαccον. For the possibility of ζ(εύγους) being the correct expansion of the abbreviation cf. the comments on δίλαccον, **3626** 16–17 n. The equation complicates rather than eases the explanation of the -λαccον compounds. For pairs note also P. Mich. VIII 468. 10–11, perhaps contrasting 14–15 there.

18 Note that 66 tal. 1,000 den. = ⅔ of 100 tal. Cf. 27 and n.

20 Less likely is ἀραβ[ολ]αίων. Note LI **3626** 21 n.

21–3 The damaged prices must fall within a certain pattern. The second quality (22) may be just 200, although it could be more. The first quality is obviously over 200, and the one-third/two-thirds pattern is likely (cf. the amounts in 18 and 27). Likewise with the third quality, which is over 100 (but less than 200).

24 cτιχ( ) in LI **3626** 24 may presumably now be expanded to cτιχ(αρίων), cf. the note ad loc.

25 Scanty traces in fact survive of ζ(εύγους) a τάλ(αντα) but on scraps of loose fibre. No traces of the price survive.

27 a τάλ(αντα) must represent the writer's intention, but the strokes are reduced to no more than αλ. Note that 33 tal. 500 den. = ⅓ of 100 tal. Cf. 18 and n.

32 The consulship begins in ecthesis in the blank space left below the shorter preceding column.

37 ὀμ[νύομεν. The series is probably consistently plural-drafted, even though the declarant is single (as in cols. i–ii): cf. the introd. above.

40 For ὠράριον = Lat. *orarium*, 'napkin, handkerchief' LS (not in the *OLD*), see the *Edictum de Pretiis* ed. M. Giacchero, §26. 162–82, with the commentary of S. Lauffer, *Diokletians Preisedikt* 275. The edict lists ὠραρίων Λαδικηνῶν among other varieties.

41 Λαδικη[νῶν. Possibly abbreviated Λαδικ⸍?

43 For ὑποδεέcτεροc in these declarations cf. **3752** 19, **3753** 20, **3765** 8, 41, 43, 45, 47. καταδεέcτεροc is the adjective regularly used in the *Edictum de Pretiis*.

53 λ. Probably λ′ as in 33, but all except the left foot of λ is broken away.

APPENDIX I

THE *CURATORES CIVITATIS* OF OXYRHYNCHUS, 303-346

A by-product of the texts in this volume has been a substantial increase in our prosopographical data relating to the logistes or *curator civitatis*. I do not attempt any synthesis of his responsibilities etc.; for that the standard reference remains B. R. Rees, *JJP* 7-8 (1953-4) 83-105. On pp. 104-5 Rees provides a list of the then known holders of the office, which has been superseded by the list of K. A. Worp, *BASP* 13 (1976) 38-40; Worp's list in turn is rendered obsolete—for Oxyrhynchus up to 346—by the new list presented below. To the above bibliography add J. Lallemand, *L'Admin. civile* 107-14. J. G. Keenan discusses the status (Valerius or Flavius, as against Aurelius) of the *curator* in *ZPE* 11 (1973) 44-6, 49 and 13 (1974) 290-1, 294, 297, 302; add XLV **3256** 1 n., XLVI **3306** 1 n., **3308-11**. The length of tenure of the office is discussed by Rees, op. cit. 95-6 and Lallemand, op. cit. 113. Our new documentation greatly extends the data available as a basis for judgement; the shortest maximum-possible term that can be deduced from the list below is around one year, while the longest attested term is around five years (unless new evidence breaks the continuity of tenure) and the longest possible term around six years.

Aurelius Seuthes alias Horion
    Earlier career:
        297/8(?)   Gymnasiarch. XLV **3246** 6
                      For P. Oslo III 135 and some other contemporary mentions of a Seuthes simply,
                      see the introd. to P. Harr. II 230-4.
    Earliest attestation as logistes:
        303   **3727**
    Interim and undated attestations:
        305   VI **895**
        Feb./Mar. 306   **3728**
        29 May 306   VIII **1104**
                      XVII **2106**, XVIII **2187**, XXXIII **2673** carry references to an unnamed logistes
                      within this period; presumably he will be Seuthes alias Horion.
    Latest attestation as logistes:
        4 May 307   **3729**
    Out of office by:
        29-30 Sept. 308 P. Lond. inv. 2226 (J. Lallemand, *L'Admin. civile* 265).
    Out-of-office references:
        s.d. but
        assigned *c.* 308/9 XXXIII **2666**
        22 June 309   XXXIII **2667**. Line 18 implies that Seuthes was the direct predecessor of Heron.

Valerius Heron alias Sarapion
    Commenced office after:
        4 May 307   **3729**
    Earliest attestation as logistes:
        29-30 Sept. 308 P. Lond. inv. 2226 (J. Lallemand, *L'Admin. civile* 265).

Interim and undated attestations:
 28 June,
  year uncertain XLIV **3193**. See the discussion by J. R. Rea, LI **3618** 1–4 n.
 s.d. but
  assigned *c.* 308/9 XXXIII **2666**
 22 June 309 XXXIII **2667**
 c. 310–11 **3731**
 s.d. **3730**
 25 May 312 **3732–5**
 312 (27 Sept.?) **3736**
Latest attestation as logistes:
 27 Sept. 312 **3737, 3739, 3740**
Out of office by:
 16 Mar. 313 XLVI **3305**
Out-of-office references:
 317/18 XLV **3256** (Aurelius Heron alias Sarapion)

Valerius Ammonianus alias Gerontius (first period of office)
 Commenced office after:
  27 Sept. 312 **3737, 3739, 3740**
 Earliest attestation as logistes I:
  16 Mar. 313 XLVI **3305**
 Interim and undated attestations:
  s.d.
  (assigned *c.* 314) XLVI **3306** (Aurelius Ammonianus alias Gerontius)
  July–Sept. 313 **3741** introd.
  21 Feb. 316 VI **983** (= SB III 6003)
  25 Feb. 316 I **53**
  316 VI **896** (col. ii: 1 Apr. 316)
  1 Nov. 316 I **84** (= W. *Chr.* 197)
  26 Nov. 317 **3742**
 Latest attestation as logistes I:
  15 Jan. 318 XXXIII **2675**
 Out of office by:
  318 (month not
  determined) **3743, 3744, 3745**

Valerius Dioscurides alias Julianus (first period of office)
 Earlier career:
  It is not certain how many persons are involved in the following references, and which of them is to be identified with the later logistes. For a discussion see esp. J. G. Keenan, *ZPE* 11 (1973) 45–6 and 13 (1974) 297.
  Sept.? 271 XII **1413**. Julianus alias Dioscurides, exegetes. (For date see A. K. Bowman, *Town Councils of Roman Egypt* 151–3.)
  293 P. Vindob. Salomons 7. Aur. Julianus alias Dioscurides, ex-hypomnematographus and bouleutes of Alexandria, ex-prytanis and bouleutes of Oxyrhynchus.
  296 SB VI 9502. Aur. (rather than Val.: J. G. Keenan, *ZPE* 11 (1973) 45) Julianus alias Dioscurides, ex-hypomnematographus, ex-prytanis and gymnasiarch and bouleutes of Oxyrhynchus, protostates.
  17 July 299 P. Laur. III 67 (see IV p. 14). [Julianus] alias Dioscurides, hypomnematographus, bouleutes of Oxyrhynchus.
  304 XVIII **2187**. Dioscurides, ex-magistrate.
  iii–iv XIV **1747** 64. Dioscurides son of Julianus, γεουχῶν.

310 or 311?   P. Mert. II 90 (for date see XXXIII **2668** introd., with XLIII **3120** 8–9 n. and P. Coll. Youtie II 79). Aur. Dioscurides [al. Julianus], strategus. PSI VIII 886. 8 may provide a reference to his tenure, in 310/11. P. Köln IV 199. 13 (s.d.) may also refer to him.

22 Aug. 311   XXXIII **2668** (= SB VIII 9875 re-ed.). Aur. Dioscurides alias Julianus, strategus of the Oxyrhynchite.

Oct./Nov. 315   XXXI **2585**. Aur. Dioscurides alias Julianus, (ex-?)gymnasiarch, ex-prytanis and bouleutes of Oxyrhynchus. (On the titles, note A. K. Bowman, op. cit. 137 n. 27, and N. Lewis, *BASP* 7 (1970) 109–10. I have re-examined the original in an attempt to read γυμναϲιαρχήϲαν|τι in 3–4. Up to χ, traces are present of all the letters and none is really in doubt despite the damage; but I cannot elicit ηϲαν from what is left at the end of the line.)

Set out thus, the evidence supports the tentative suggestion of J. G. Keenan, *ZPE* 11 (1973) 45, that we are dealing with two members of the same family, probably father and son; the father being Julianus alias Dioscurides and the son the subsequent logistes Dioscurides alias Julianus. The attested offices would accord with the two distinct careers implied by this hypothesis. That the hypothesis is correct may reasonably be taken as proven by P. Harr. II 212, addressed to the logistes Dioscurides son of Julianus. The family was clearly of standing in both Alexandria and Oxyrhynchus. The references to the son as strategus of the Oxyrhynchite are not at variance with this theory, since by this date the strategus was of course no longer from a nome different from where he held office (XLIII **3123** 3 n.). For a third generation of this family cf. **3755** 27–8 n. and the entry below for Flavius Julianus.

Commenced office after:
15 Jan. 318   XXXIII **2675**
Only attestations as logistes I:
318 (month
not determined)   **3743, 3744, 3745**
Out of office by:
23–5(?)
Mar. 319   **3746**

Valerius Ammonianus alias Gerontius (second period of office)
Commenced office after:
318 (month
not determined)   **3743, 3744, 3745**
Earliest attestation as logistes II:
23–5(?)
Mar. 319   **3746** (logistes)
Interim and undated attestations:
26 Mar. 319   **3748–53** (acting logistes)
320 (month and
day lost)   **3754** (acting logistes)
Latest attestation as logistes II:
Jan./Feb. 320   PSI V 454, where J. R. Rea has re-read line 6 to give Γεροντίῳ [δι]οικοῦντ[ι λο]γιϲτίạ[ν Ὀξ(υρυγχίτου), i.e. acting logistes: this correction has not previously been published.
Out of office by:
27 Sept. 320   **3755**
Out-of-office references:
7 Nov. 331   PSI VII 767.28? [κληρο(νόμοι) Ἀμμω]νιανοῦ ἀπὸ λογιϲτῶν? (K. A. Worp by letter); cf. p. 226.
18 Sept. 334   PSI V 469, κληρονόμοιϲ Ἀμμωνιανοῦ ἀπὸ λογιϲτῶν (cf. K. A. Worp, *BASP* 13 (1976) 39).

Valerius Dioscurides alias Julianus (second period of office)
Commenced office after:
Jan./Feb. 320   PSI V 454 (see above)

Earliest attestation as logistes II:

27 Sept. 320   **3755**

Interim and undated attestations:

30 July 321   VI **900** (see XLVI **3305** 3 n.)

322 or 323   P. Harr. II 212. Dioscurides son of Julianus.

18 Jan. 323   I **42**. Dioscurides only. There is no need to consider whether Dioscurides may be a different logistes from Dioscurides alias Julianus; the Julianus was presumably dropped to avoid confusion with the son, now entering public office (cf. **3755** and the entry below for Flavius Julianus). It may be that Fl. Julianus' full name included alias Dioscurides, but there is no evidence of this as yet.

3 Mar. 323   XLI **2969** (for date cf. XLI **2993**). Dioscurides only.

29 Mar. 323   XXXVI **2767**. Dioscurides only.

324   P. Harr. II 214. Dioscurides only.

3–18 Mar. 325   **3758**. Dioscurides only (see ll. 3–4).

s.d.   XII **1509**. Dioscurides only; the logistes?

Latest attestation as logistes II:

Mar./Apr. 325   XLIII **3125**. Valerius Dioscurides only.

Out of office by:

July/Aug. 325   I **52**

Flavius Leucadius

Earlier career:

For the possibility of a connection with the prytanis of Feb./Mar. 325, see **3758** 18 n.

Commenced office after:

Mar./Apr. 325   XLIII **3125**

Earliest attestation as logistes:

July/Aug. 325   I **52**

Interim and undated attestations:

2 Oct. 325   **3759**

June/July 326   XLV **3265**

326?   **3760**?

Latest attestation as logistes:

Sept./Dec. 326   XLV **3249**

Out of office by:

16 Jan. 327   I **83** and **83a**

Flavius Thannyras

For the spelling of the name see **3765** 49 n.

Commenced office after:

Sept./Dec. 326   XLV **3249**

Earliest attestation as logistes:

16 Jan. 327   I **83** and **83a**. The date is not 16 February (= 22 Mecheir) as given in R. S. Bagnall and K. A. Worp, *Chron. Systems of Byzantine Egypt* 109.

Interim and undated attestations:

s.d.   **3765**

Latest attestation as logistes:

16 Jan. 327   I **83** and **83a** (see above)

Out of office by:

27 Oct. 329   **3766** (= XXXI **2570** re-ed.)

Flavius Julianus

Earlier career:

27 Sept. 320   Deputy-logistes? **3755**

Commenced office after:

16 Jan. 327   I **83** and **83a**

Earliest attestation as logistes:
    27 Oct. 329   **3766** (= XXXI **2570** re-ed.)
Interim and undated attestations:
    12 Jan. 330   XLVII **3350**
    s.d.   P. Harr. 73 (see *ZPE* 37 (1980) 229 ff.)
    iii–iv   P. Mich. inv. 411 (ed. H. C. Youtie, *ZPE* 37 (1980) 217–18 = *Script. Post.* ii
          581–2). Julianus, son of Dioscurides (no titles) appears in a possibly Oxyrhynchite
          name-list. Fl. Julianus the logistes seems a likely candidate for the identification
          (the script is a good official cursive, see *ZPE* 37 pl. VIIb) or at least a member of his
          family, conceivably his grandfather (see above under Val. Dioscurides alias
          Julianus), but I should be inclined to date the text iv rather than iii. This proposed
          identification strengthens the case for its Oxyrhynchite provenance. Further proof
          of that comes from recognizing the name of Eutonius alias Uranius (l. 4 in the
          Michigan text) in XLIV **3189** 5–6 (*Εὐτρυγίου* ed.), a tax-receipt assigned to the
          late third or early fourth century.
Latest attestation as logistes:
    13–14(?)
    June 331   XLIV **3195**
Out of office by:
    7 Nov. 331   PSI VII 767. 2 (see below under Fl. Hermias)
Out-of-office references:
    In PSI VII 767.28 (7 Nov. 331)]ιανου (so ed.) will surely be preceded by κληρο (νόμοι), cf. 23, and
    cannot therefore refer to Julianus as suggested in XLIV **3195** 3 n. Presumably Ammonianus
    was named, cf. p. 224. The Julianus son of Ammonianus in P. Ross.-Georg. V 28 (cited in
    XLIV **3195** 3 n.) is not to be identified with our Julianus, son of Dioscurides (cf. **3755** and the
    discussions above).
Later career:
    Feb./Mar. 334   Syndic. **3769** (Fl. Julianus)
    26 Mar. 334   Syndic. **3770** (Aur. Julianus)
    1 May 336   Acting syndic. **3771** and VI **901** (Fl. Julianus)
    Sept./Oct. 360   PSI V 467: a Fl. Julianus(?) held a post in the office of the *praeses* of Augustamnica.
          I am indebted to Dr Rosario Pintaudi for a photograph and an examination of the
          text; a reading (l. 1) *Φλαουΐ*[ω] *Ἰο*[υ]*λι*[*αν*ῷ seems possible. For the post held,
          perhaps cf. XLIX **3480** 1, *βενεφικιαρίῳ τάξεως*, which if abbreviated (*βφ*/) might
          conceivably fit the space in PSI 467. Nevertheless, it is not clear that this would be
          a likely step in the career of our Julianus, who would have been in his sixties (or
          more) at this date.

Flavius Hermias
  Earlier career:
    17 Aug. 323   Strategus. I **60**. See J. E. G. Whitehorne, *ZPE* 29 (1978) 184. Named Hermias
          only. See also **3746** 48 n.
    31? July 324   Strategus. XII **1430**. Hermias only.
    Mar./Apr. 325   Strategus. XLIII **3125**. Aur. Hermias. This then is a different Hermias from
          Claudius Hermias the later *ἔκδικος* (XLIV **3195**), and the other two strategus-
          references are likely to be to this same Aur. Hermias. There is possibly a reference
          to him as out of office in PSI III 201 (7 March 327: see P. J. Sijpesteijn and K. A.
          Worp, *ZPE* 26 (1977) 278), but in any case he was out of office by 11 February 327
          (Aur. Veronicianus in office: J. E. G. Whitehorne, *ZPE* 29 (1978) 184). It is
          possible, but much less likely, that it is Claudius Hermias who becomes Flavius
          Hermias the logistes: for other *gentilicia* at this period, see J. G. Keenan, *ZPE* 11
          (1973) 47, 51.
  Commenced office after:
    13–14(?)
    June 331   XLIV **3195**

Earliest attestation as logistes:

7 Nov. 331 — PSI VII 767. 2. In the introduction to that text the possibility was put forward of reading Mecheir for Hathyr in l. 2 and converting l. 1 to a post-consulate (thus 332); this possibility is hardly still open, because the consuls for 332 were already known in Mecheir 332, see R. S. Bagnall and K. A. Worp, *Chron. Systems of Byzantine Egypt* 110. (Conversely, a date to Mecheir 331 is excluded because Julianus was still logistes, see above. The 331 consuls were known this early, see Bagnall and Worp in *BASP* 17 (1980) 13.) The edition wrongly converts Hathyr 10 in 331 to 6 November instead of 7 November. μοι in 4 provides reasonable assurance for the restoration of Hermias' name in 3. The puzzle remains of the apparent later date in 7 (Hathyr 11, ed.) which ought to antedate Hathyr 10 in line 2. I have tried reading a different month (thanks to a photograph kindly supplied by Dr Rosario Pintaudi) but without success. It may be wrong to seek a date here, and we should rather look for an introductory formula on a par with those in 30 and 35. If so, 7 November 331 remains the earliest precise and reasonably secure date we have for Hermias as logistes.

Latest attestations as logistes:

332 (month and
day lost) — XII **1426**, XLIII **3127**

Out of office by:
s.d. — Tenure of Fl. Asclepiades (**3768**); or
26 Mar. 336 — X **1265**

Later career:
25 Oct. 336 — Syndic. P. Freib. 11 = SB III 6294

Flavius Asclepiades

The placing of Asclepiades, so far attested solely by the undated **3768**, at this point in the list is conjectural. See the discussion in **3768** introd.

Commenced office after:

332 (month and
day lost) — XII **1426**, XLIII **3127**

Only attestation as logistes:
s.d. — **3768**

Out of office by:
26 Mar. 336 — X **1265**

Flavius Paeanius alias Macrobius

For the correction of Paranius to Paeanius see P. Oxy. XXXVIII p. xiv.

Earlier career:

s.d. — Strategus. XXII **2344**. This text poses a problem, since Paeanius is styled Flavius and the evidence indicates that strategi in this period were not ex officio Flavii (J. G. Keenan, *ZPE* 13 (1974) 291 n. 171). On the other hand, the strategus was junior to the logistes (the logistae at this time were Flavii and may have retained the name on leaving office: cf. **3771** 3 n.), and tenure of the junior post subsequent to the senior post is hardly conceivable. Dr J. D. Thomas would now withdraw (personal communication of 30 July 1984) his suggestion in *CE* 34 (1959) 130 that Paeanius is in fact logistes in **2344**. We must, I think, conclude that Paeanius was entitled to the name Flavius on other grounds, possibly military service.

Commenced office after:

s.d. — Tenure of Fl. Asclepiades (**3768**); or
332 (month and
day lost) — XII **1426**, XLIII **3127**

Earliest attestation as logistes:
26 Mar. 336 — X **1265**

Interim and undated attestations:
    s.d.   X **1303**
Latest attestation as logistes:
    26 Mar. 336   X **1265** (see above)
Out of office by:
    13 Jan. 338   VI **892**

Flavius Eusebius
Commenced office after:
    26 Mar. 336   X **1265**
Earliest attestation as logistes:
    13 Jan. 338   VI **892**
Interim and undated attestations:
    28 Mar. 338   I **86**
    c. 338   **3772**
    There is no evidence that Eusebius was the addressee of the undated PSI III 202, although economic
    and scribal considerations (cf. Appendix III and Appendix IV below) mean that a dating *c.* 338 must
    be approximately right.
Latest attestation as logistes:
    26 Nov. 338   I **85**
Out of office by:
    341 (no month
    or day)   **3774**

Flavius Eulogius
Earlier career:
    There is a scant possibility of identity with the deputy strategus in early January 316 (XVII **2113**:
    J. E. G. Whitehorne, *ZPE* 29 (1978) 184), if this were a junior appointment held by Eulogius as a
    young man. The identity will hardly be compatible with identifying the ex-logistes with the
    πολιτευόμενος of 365 (XLVIII **3393**, see below). Given Eulogius' attested activity as *riparius* in 350
    (see below), it is more plausible to link him with his namesake of 365 than with the deputy strategus
    back in 316. Similar but less cogent arguments apply to identifying him with the πάρεδρος of **3757** 4
    (325) and elsewhere. There is no reason to associate the later logistes with the private person in
    P. Princ. II 79 (326).
Commenced office after:
    26 Nov. 338   I **85**
Earliest attestation as logistes:
    341 (no month
    or day)   **3774**
Interim and undated attestations:
    s.d.   XVII **2115**. The date previously attributed to this text, '*c.* 345' (*BASP* 13 (1976)
                          39), cannot stand.
Latest attestation as logistes:
    341 (no month
    or day)   **3774** (see above)
Out of office by:
    1 Mar. 342   I **87**: the unpublished second column is dated Phamenoth 5.
Out-of-office references:
    s.d.   XIX **2235**: ἀπὸ λογιϲτῶν, ῥιπαρίῳ. Cf. below.
    iv   P. Princ. II 98? See XIX **2233** 2 n., **2235** 1 n.
Later career:
    346   *Riparius.* VI **897**
    s.d.   *Riparius.* XIX **2229**
    s.d.   *Riparius.* XIX **2235**
    350   *Riparius.* P. Harr. II 218

7 June 350   *Riparius.* XIX **2233**
8 June 365   πολιτευόμενος. XLVIII **3393**. The possibility of identifying this Eulogius with the
                ex-logistes is discussed above under the heading of Eulogius' earlier career.

Flavius Dionysarius
    Commenced office after:
        341 (no month
        or day)   **3774**
    Earliest attestation as logistes:
        1 Mar. 342   I **87**: the unpublished second column is dated Phamenoth 5.
    Latest attestation as logistes:
        5 May 342   P. Harr. 65
    Out of office by:
        1 July 342   **3775**
    Later career:
        346   *Riparius.* VI **897**

Flavius Eutrygius
    Commenced office after:
        5 May 342   P. Harr. 65
    Earliest attestation as logistes:
        1 July 342   **3775**
    Interim and undated attestations:
        17(?) June 343 P. Harr. II 216
    Latest attestation as logistes:
        24 July 343   **3776**
    Out of office by:
        346 or 347 (no
        month or day)   P. Harr. II 217
    Out-of-office references:
        357   I **66**. Fl. Eutrygius, ἀπὸ λογιστῶν
        360   VIII **1103**. Eutrygius, ἀπὸ λογιστῶν
    I. F. Fikhman, *Le Monde grec.: hommages à Claire Préaux* 789, supposes that the plain Eutrygius who
    appears in I **93** (362), PIFAO II 13, and PSI III 217 may be the ex-logistes, but this is not
    compelling.

Flavius Heraclius
    Commenced office after:
        24 July 343   **3776**
    Only attestation as logistes:
        346 or 347 (no
        month or day)   P. Harr. II 217
    Out-of-office references:
        27 July 371   Dead by this date. XLVIII **3395**

APPENDIX II

THE GUILDS OF OXYRHYNCHUS

Despite the present volume's additions to our documentation, we are a long way from having declarations from all the guilds that must have made them, as a glance at a document such as PUG I 24 quickly makes clear. For a list of guilds and occupations see I. F. Fikhman, *Egipet na rubezhe dvukh epokh* (Moscow 1965) 25–34, 122–7. It is equally clear that the guilds did not always follow the same order: contrast e.g. LI **3624–6** with I **85** (re-ed. *ZPE* 39 (1980) 115–23). Nevertheless we now have several part-sequences and some overlaps and repeated sequences, and with the help of **3765** most of the declaring guilds can be put into a tentative order (which does not reflect that of the *Edictum de Pretiis*), although there are breaks in it (where we cannot yet calculate the number of intervening guilds) and other uncertainties such as those due to fragmentary declarations at the beginning or end of a sequence. It must also be admitted that the part-sequences we have may not come from the same overall sequence; indeed some of the part-sequences (e.g. the first two sections below) are incompatible. Some guilds appear in different positions in the tentative composite sequence I have constructed below; both occurrences are listed, with the second one bracketed.

χρυcοχόοι	3765 vii	3768			
ἀργυροκόποι		,,	3624		
ἀρτοκόποι			3625		
ταρcικάριοι			3626		
———					
?		85[1]			
χαλκοκολληταί		,,			
(ἀρτοκόποι)		,,			
ζυθοπῶλαι		,,			
———					
κεμιοπῶλαι		3737		3755	3744
ἐλαιουργοί		3738	3760		
ἀρτυματοπῶλαι	3765 i 1–2	3739	3761		
κάπηλοι	,, 3–4	3740	3762		
?	,, 5–7		3763		
———					
ἐκδοχεῖc	3772[2]				
ἐλαιοπῶλαι			85[3]		
μελιccουργοί		3747	,,		

σταγματοπῶλαι		**3748**	
γαροπῶλαι		**3749**	
ἁλοπῶλαι		**3750**	
ἐριοπῶλαι		**3751**	
λευκανταί	**3765** ii 8?	**3752**	**3743**
στιπποχειρισταί	,, 9–11	**3753**	
ὀθονιοπῶλαι	,, 12–15		**3776**
textile guild			,,

?	**3765** iii 16–17?	P. Harr. 73 i[4]
βαφεῖς	,, 18–23	,, ii
?[5]		,, iii

---

butchers of some kind?	**3765** iv 24–30

χοιρομάγειροι		PSI III 202
ἰχθυοπῶλαι	**3766**	,, ?[6]
κναφεῖς	,,	
κεραμεῖς	,,	
μυροπῶλαι	**3765** v 32–40[7] ,,	**3731**

?	**3765** vi 41–7

The following additional sequence is necessarily incompatible with the above:

?	**3732**
(μυροπῶλαι)	**3733**
(ἁλοπῶλαι)	**3734**
?	**3735** (a declaration in two columns)

We have effectively 'singleton' declarations from the following guilds (in alphabetical order) for which we also lack parallel guiding information, so that we have no clue to their place in any sequence of this sort:

ὀρβιοπῶλαι	**3745**
ὑελουργοί	**3742**

In the next Appendix on commodity-prices the guilds are listed in the sequence proposed here; the ὑελουργοί (no prices survive for the ὀρβιοπῶλαι) are tacked on at the end. For the φακοπῶλαι, not attested as such by a declaration and also tacked on at the end of the list, see note 35 to Appendix III.

Notes to Appendix II

¹ The placing of this group here is somewhat arbitrary. The other sections are held together by the framework of **3765**. I place the **85** guilds near the beginning on the uncertain grounds that metals and basic commodities come early in the sequence.

² It is not certain that the ἐκδοχεῖς immediately precede the ἐλαιοπῶλαι and ff.; see **3772** introd.

³ For the splitting of the sections of I **85**, see the re-edition of that papyrus in *ZPE* 39 (1980) 115 ff.

⁴ See the re-edition of P. Harr. 73 in *ZPE* 37 (1980) 229–36.

⁵ Might the guild here be the caγματοράφοι (for whom see *Rech. Pap.* 4 (1967) 82 n.) who follow the βαφεῖς in PUG I 24? Probably this is to put far too much weight on PUG I 24's list, since the βαφεῖς there are preceded (in reverse order) by the κναφεῖς, ταρcικάριοι, and λευκανταί, all of whom are established in different positions in the sequence above.

⁶ See *ZPE* 37 (1980) 230 and n. 1.

⁷ Seventeen more items would have followed, drawn from the declaration of the μυροπῶλαι. There can have been very few intervening items (and therefore even fewer guilds) before those preserved in ll. 41 ff. at the top of the next column.

APPENDIX III
COMPARATIVE COMMODITY PRICES

Commentary on the prices of the items declared by the guilds, in so far as they survive, has been reserved for this section from the notes on the individual texts above. The guilds are arranged in their projected order (see the preceding Appendix) rather than alphabetically, and the items declared follow the same order as in the declarations. Guilds for which no prices survive have been omitted; guilds with two positions in the sequence are given in the earlier position. I tabulate prices to cover the period from the *Edictum de Pretiis* (Nov./Dec. 301) until our latest declarations in 359, LI **3624–6**. Only prices derived directly or less directly (**3765, 3773**) from guild declarations are included; I use the previously published declarations (XXXI **2570** = **3766**, P. Harr. 73, I **85**, PSI III 202, and LI **3624–6**) as well as those in the present volume. This concentration on a single category of document avoids the problems of evaluating diverse evidence, e.g. the prices for (Tyrian) cτιχάρια in **3758** (see 21 n.) and especially the confrontation between open market prices and government refund levels. Prices are given throughout in talents (T) and denarii (d.). For consistent comparative purposes the solidus is understood throughout as = $\frac{1}{72}$ of a lb. of gold; I have recalculated values for the pre-Constantinian *aureus* (= $\frac{1}{60}$ lb. of gold) in terms of the later coin.

With each commodity for which the evidence admits it, I have calculated an annual compound inflation percentage for the period between the earliest and latest recorded prices. In most instances we have but one price for a commodity in a year, but the price fluctuations attested by **3773** show how unreliable these inflation percentages may be. Furthermore the pace of inflation was more irregular than is implied by my annual percentage figures. R. S. Bagnall, *Currency and Inflation in Fourth-century Egypt* (*BASP* suppl. 5 (1985))[1] explains 'inflation' in this period as due to the fluctuating but generally diminishing silver content of the coins in circulation, and analyses the changes not as gradual but as coming in stages, in line with the monetary changes. Nevertheless, in terms of the tariffed values of the coins, the inflation was real enough (so Bagnall, op. cit. 54–5). The percentages are given in two columns at the right edge of the table below: (A) covering the span from the Edict till our latest evidence, and (B) covering such spans as are available with the Edict's evidence excluded. I provide these latter figures to meet the comment of R. P. Duncan-Jones, *The Economy of the Roman Empire* (2nd edn., 1982) 367, that the Edict's prices are likely to be at least in part theoretical prices and not true market-prices.[2] These figures, totalled and divided by the number of the samples, provide averages of 13.91% including the Edict's evidence (column A, thus over the period 301–59) or 18.97% without the Edict's evidence (column B, effectively for the period from *c*. 310–11 till 359). These figures may be expected to correspond to the reduction in the silver content of the coinage; and, satisfyingly, I calculate the reduction from the 25 den. coin of 301 (Bagnall, *Currency* 30–1) to the introduction of the coin with 30 mg of silver in the early 350s (ibid. 44–5; also J.-M. Carrié, *Aeg.* 64 (1984) 224) as an annual decrease of approximately 13.75%. The discrepancy between my column A and column B figures needs some explanation. First, I have generally chosen the Edict's highest prices (cf. n. 4 below), while the goods listed in the Edict are often of a higher quality anyway than what was available locally in Oxyrhynchus; secondly, the increasing inflation in the later years covered by the samples pushes up the figures in column B, none of which derive from data earlier than *c*. 310–11. Such validity as these figures may have is of course only in terms of the buying power of talents and denarii; calculated in terms of the gold solidus or any other commodity, the results would be vastly different.[3]

I should like to thank Mr G. Mazzarino, of the Oxford University Institute of Economics and Statistics, and my father Romney Coles for help with the mathematics in this Appendix.

TABLE 2. *Commodity prices c.301–59*

Guild and substance	unit	Edictum de Pretiis[4] (Nov./Dec. 301)	3731 (c.310–11)	3732–5 3737–40 (312)	3742 (317)	3743–4 (318)	3747–53 (319)	3760–3 (326?)	3765 (c.327)	3766 (329)	P. Harr. 73 (329–31)	PSI 202 (c.338) 85 (338)	3773[5] (c.340)	3776 (343)	3624–6 (359)	(A) Including Edict	(B) Excluding Edict
Annual inflation (%)																	
χρυσοχόοι gold solidus (see above)	1	1,000 d.											190 T.(?) to 243⅓ T.[6]		45.333⅓ T.	16.33%[7]	28.07%[7]
ἀργυροκόποι ἀcίμου	1 lb.	4 T.											950 T.(?) to 1,213⅓ T.			17.46%	22.56%
ἀρτοκόποι cίτου	1 art.	327 d.[8]										24 T.	40 T. to 50 T.		1,366⅔ T.	16.27%[9]	21.22%[9]
χαλκοκολληταί χαλκοῦ ἐλατοῦ[10]	1 lb.	60 d.										6⅔ T.				14.82%	
χαλκοῦ χυτοῦ	1 lb.											4 T.					
ζυθοπῶλαι κριθῆς	1 art.	196 d.										13⅓ T.	15 T. to 25 T.			14.42%[9]	36.93%[9]
κεμιοπῶλαι ?	1 art.			1 T.													
φαcήλου	,,	327 d.		1 T.												14.85%	
ἐρεβίνθου	,,	327 d.		1 T.												14.85%	
τήλεως	,,	750 d.		750 d.												10.69%	
ὀρόβου	,,	327 d.		1,000 d.													
ἐλαιουργοί λαχανοcπέρμου	1 art.			2 T. 250 d.				15 T.					45 T. to 80 T.			9.96%[9]	
ἀρτυματοπῶλαι cηcάμου μελανθίου κορίου ξηροῦ ὀριγάνου																	

σινάπεως	1 art.?	490 d.				8 T.		13.08%		
μ-	1 art.					4 T.				
κνήκου	1 art.?					? T.				
φάβατος	1 art.	327 d.			500 d.	6? T.	6 T.	13.59%	13.48%	0%?
κυμίνου	1 art.	655 d.			375 d.	8 T.	8 T.	11.83%	11.32%	0%
κάπηλοι										
οἴνου Ὀασιτικ.	1 sext.	30 d.[11]	75 d.		400 d.			11.42%		
κυιδίου Θηβαικ.	,,		75 d.		375 d.					
?										
οἴνου Ὀξυρυγχ.	,,	30 d.[11]			375 d.	1 T. to 1⅔ T.[12]		12%[9]	15.71%[9]	
ὄξους Ὀξυρυγχ.	,,	6 d.			300 d.			16.23%		
μελισσουργοί										
?	?			1,150 d.?						
?										
σταγματοπῶλαι										
στάγματος	1 cnid.			500 d.						
γαροπῶλαι										
γάρου	1 sext.	16 d.		28 d.				3.1%		
ἁλοπῶλαι										
ἁλός	1 art.	327 d.[13]	250 d.	250 d.				-1.5%		0%
ἐριοπῶλαι										
ἐρίου λευκ. ἐντοπ.	1 lb.	25 d.?[14]		150 d.				10.46%		
ἰδιοχρώμων καὶ										
ἄλλων χρωμάτ.	,,			175 d.						
λευκανταί										
λίνου παντ. λευκ.										
τρυφεροῦ	1 lb.[15]			1 T. 100(+) d.	1 T. 125 d.					
κοινοῦ	,,			875 d.						
ὑποδεεστ. χωρ.	,,			500 d.	500 d.[16]					0%
στιπποχειρισταί										
στιππίου κεχειρ.										
τρυφ. ἐξόχου	1 lb.	24 d.[17]		450 d.				13.97%		6.05%
κοινοῦ	,,	20 d.		162 d.	720 d.[18]			13.79%		17.18%
ὑποδεεστ. χωρ.	,,	16 d.		100 d.	576 d.[18]			10.71%		

TABLE 2 (cont.)

Guild and substance	unit	Edictum de Pretiis[4] (Nov./Dec. 301)	3731 (c.310-11)	3732-5 3737-40 (312)	3742 (317)	3743-4 (318)	3747-53 (319)	3760-3 (326?)	3765 (c.327)	3766 (329)	P. Harr. 73 (329-31)	PSI 202 85 (c.338) (338)	3773[5] (c.340)	3776 (343)	3624-6 (359)	Annual inflation (%) (A) Including Edict	(B) Excluding Edict
ὀθονοπῶλαι																	
δαλμ. γυναικ.																	
ταρϲ. μεγ. μέτρ.	1 pr.																
1st quality		1 ἱϲτόϲ[19] 4⅔ T.							40 T.					400 T.			15.47%
2nd quality	,,	3 T.							?30 T. +					266⅔ T.			14.63%
3rd quality	,,	2 T.												200 T.			
ἀναβολαδίων	1 pr.																
1st quality		1 ἱϲτόϲ 3 T.												200 + T.			
2nd quality	,,	2 T.												200(+?) T.			
3rd quality	,,	1⅚ T.												100 + T.			
ϲτιχαρίων																	
3rd quality	,,	1 ἱϲτόϲ 1⅓ T.												133⅓ T.			
φακιαλίων																	
1st quality	,,	1 ἱϲτόϲ 1750 d.												160 T.			
2nd quality	,,	1 T.												120 T.			
3rd quality	,,	1250 d.												100 T.			
?																	
Νικαιῆϲ	1 lb.	1 T.[20]							80 T.		[ ]⅔ T.[21]					29.31%	
ῥιζίνηϲ	,,								3 T.								
?																	
Βαφεῖϲ																	
πορφ. ἐντοπίου 1st qu.	1 lb.	(33⅓ T.)[22]							2 T.		8 T.						41.42%
κοκκίνου 2nd quality	,,								8 T.		10 T.						5.7%
ϲανδυκ., χλωρ.,	,,								2 T.		5 T.						25.74%
καλλ., ϲυγχρ.,	,,								1 T.+		5 T.						49.53%
ῥοδίνου	,,	80 d.[23]							1 T.(+?)		7 T.					17.65%[23]	62.65%
?																	
ditto, 2nd qu.											100 T.						
πενταπηχ. ψιαθ.											80 T.						
ϲτιβ.	1										60 T.						
?																	

Commodity	Unit	Price 1	Price 2	Price 3	Price 4	Price 5	%	%
ditto, 2nd qu.	1 pr.							
ἐφιππίων	1 pr.					60 T.		
μοναυθρώπων	,,					40 T.		
ἐπιψελαρίων	?					60 T.		
?	1 pr.					80 T.		
?						300 T.		
θηλίων ὁμοίως		5,000 d.[24]		200 T.			17.05%	
α βόλου				150 T.				
β βόλου				100 T.				
τελείας				230 T.			17.68%	
ταύρου τελείου		5,000 d.		200 T.				
ὑποδεεστέρου				? d.?				
κρέως μοσχείου	1 lb.	8 d.[25]		100 T.			18.06%	
βοὸς τελείας		2000 d.						
χοιρομάγειροι								
κρέως χοιρίου	1 lb.	12 d.				1 T. 900 d.[26]	15.39%	
ἰχθυοπῶλαι								
ἰχθύων παντ.	1 lb.	24 d.			500 d.	1⅔ T.[27]	13.37%	19.58%
κναφεῖς								
νίτρου Ἀραβικ.	100 lb.				500 d.			
κεραμεῖς κερ. κερ.								
πίσσης ξηρᾶς	100 lb.	800 d.[28]	1 T.		3 T.		6.36%	
Cιρτικῆς	,,		200 d.					
Τρωαδησίας	,,		1 T.		2 T.			
μυροπῶλαι								
πιπέρεως	1 lb.	800 d.	1 T.		12 T.		11.76%	13.97%
λιβάνου	,,	100 d.	200 d.		2 T.		12.91%	15.31%
μαλαβάθρου	,,		1 T.		50 T.			22.86%
στύραχος		500 d.			20 T.			
ὑψηλοῦ	,,		1250 d.	4 T.	10 T.		24.47%	20.55%
ἐλαφροῦ	,,		750 d.(?)[29]	6 T.	6 T.		13.65%	19.26%
κόστου	,,	250 d.[30]	1 T.?	4 T.			17.22%	11.11%
μαστίχης	,,	175 d.	500(?) d.	8 T.			16.5%	19.6%
ἀμώμου	,,	125 d.[31]	? d.?	5 T.			18.08%	11.06%
Bδέλλης	,,	100 d.	250 d.	6 T.			19.16%	19.16%
κασίας	,,	120 d.[30]	500 d.		7 T.		18.06%	18.2%

TABLE 2 (cont.)

Guild and substance	unit	Edictum de Pretiis[4] (Nov./Dec. 301)	3731 (c.310–11)	3732–5 3737–40 (312)	3742 (317)	3743–4 (318)	3747–53 (319)	3760–3 (326?)	3765 (c.327)	3766 (329)	P. Harr. 73 (329–31)	PSI 202 85 (c.338) (338)	3773[5] (c.340)	3776 (343)	3624–6 (359)	Annual inflation (%) (A) Including Edict	(B) Excluding Edict
μυροπῶλαι (cont.)																	
κασάμου	1 lb.	375 d.		450 d.					1⅓ T.	2 T.?							11.56%
ψιμιτίου	,,	40 d.[32]								1⅔ T.						19.59%	
σανδυκίου	,,	400 d.								4 T.							
ζμίρνης	,,																
μόχλω.. [	,,	400 d.															
ζυνκιπέρεως	,,																
πατήματος	,,	25 d.		250 d.												10.5%	
ἀσφαλανθίου	,,	17[5?] d.[33]		75 d.												-1.41%	
ἀρραβωρατίου	,,			150 d.						1,000 d.							14.17%
σασέλεως	,,			105 d.[34]						1,000 d.							16.45%
σφαγνίου	,,			75 d.													11.8%
εἴρωνον	,,			150 d.						1,000 d.							10.79%
ἐλευδίου	,,	25 d.		175 d.						1,000 d.							16.45%?
ἀλκεωτίδων	,,			75 d.(?)												14.08%	
ὀνυχίου	,,			200 d.						1,000 d.							
ξυλομαστίχης	,,	50 d.		75 d.												3.75%	
ἁλμάστου?	,,			75 d.													
?																	
ὑποδεεςτ.									?20 T.								
βοίνης τελείας ὑποδεεςτ.		750 d.							20 T.							15.24%	
αἰγείου τελείου ὑποδεεςτ.		400 d.							15 T.							16.76%	
ὑποδεεςτ.		50 d.							4 T.							20.21%	
προβατείου τελ. ὑποδεεςτ.		30 d.							2 T.							19.37%	
									2 T.								
									1 T.								
ὑελουργοί																	
ὑέλου	100 lb.	2400 d.			4 T.											5.89%	
φακοπῶλαι?[235]																	
φακοῦ	1 art.												20 T. to 35 T.				75%[9]

Notes to Appendix III

¹ Bagnall's work was only available to me just as this volume was going to press.

² i.e., real prices in terms of denarii in 301 were already higher and the degree of inflation calculated for 301–59 should in reality stretch back over a longer period, thus pulling down the putative annual rate. Duncan-Jones also comments that the Edict does not distinguish between wholesale and retail prices. Given the extent to which the guilds declare the price paid for the raw materials of their trade (cf. **LI 3624–6** introd.), their prices are wholesale rather than retail in character so that the retail price and with it the inflation-rate can only have been higher.

³ For example, **3773** indicates that by *c.* 340 many items had fallen in price in terms of gold; a solidus would have bought roughly 3 art. of wheat or 5 art. of barley in 301, 5 art. of wheat or 10 art. of barley in *c.* 340.

⁴ Edict prices: where there are several grades potentially relevant to a commodity in this list, the highest price is given.

⁵ **3773** prices: those given are the lowest and highest prices recorded for each commodity during the period covered by the text. Lowest and highest are not necessarily equivalent to earliest and latest. See the table in **3773** introd.

⁶ Fractions of one-third and two-thirds are common in the pricing-structure, so that sums such as 266⅔ tal. (**3776** 18) are not as idiosyncratic as they may at first seem. 243 tal. 500 den. here is one-third of the way from 240 to 250 tal.

⁷ Calculated on the figure in the table of 243⅓ talents, which is not actually the latest figure in **3773** where the price per solidus in fact drops to 240 talents. A similar caution applies to all the other commodities in **3773** (cf. the table in the introd. ad loc.) except silver.

⁸ The Edict's price is 100 den. for 1 *castrensis modius*. For the conversion here and below to artabas (1 artaba = 3.2727 *castrenses modii*) see R. P. Duncan-Jones, *ZPE* 21 (1976) 56.

⁹ Cf. n. 7 above.

¹⁰ For χαλκοῦ ἐλατοῦ see E. J. Doyle, *Hesp.* 45 (1976) 97. The commentary there on I **85** is erroneous: see the revised text of that papyrus by R. A. Coles in *ZPE* 39 (1980) 117.

¹¹ The Edict's price-list does not include Oxyrhynchite or Oasitic wine; its grades range in price from 30 den. down to 8 den. the *sextarius*, M. Giacchero, *Edictum Diocletiani* 140–1. There is a brief list of Egyptian wine-prices and references in CPR VI p. 65; for the fourth century, Bagnall, *Currency* 66.

¹² Note that the type of wine is not specified in **3773**; this may therefore not be the strictly correct guild under which to place the **3773** prices.

¹³ The Edict's price is 100 den. for a *castrensis modius* (for the conversion see n. 8). The maintained drop in price evidenced by the papyri is surprising.

¹⁴ The Edict (§25 in both Giacchero and Lauffer) lists several prices for wool, reaching 400 den./lb. (this is for *lana marina*, see Lauffer's commentary (p. 264) on §19. 14 of the Edict). The specific varieties of wool listed seem inappropriate so that the cheapest grade (§25. 9) seems the best parallel.

¹⁵ The Edict's section περὶ λίνου is §26 in both Lauffer and Giacchero. The prices there (revised *ZPE* 34 (1979) 168) range from 1,200 down to 72 den./lb., in part exceeding papyrologically attested prices of nearly twenty years later. Because of the uncertainty over the way in which the declaration of λίνων παντοίων λευκῶν by λευκανταί (prima facie a service industry, not a retail trade) is to be understood, I do not tabulate the Edict's prices above or use them in calculations regarding inflation.

¹⁶ The price of 500 den./lb. in *c.* 327 is based on the assumption that **3765** 9–11 record the same items as **3753** 17–19 and therefore that **3765** 8 may record the same item as **3752** 19; nevertheless the unchanged price after eight years or so must cast doubt on the identification.

¹⁷ The prices for the three grades are those given in §26. 1a–3 of the Edict (ed. Giacchero), assuming equivalence of στιππίου κεχειρισμένου here and λίνου τοῦ καλουμένου στουπίου in the Edict.

¹⁸ These are not the prices as given in **3765**, which lists a 5-mina bundle at 2½ tal. for the best grade and 2 tal. for the ordinary grade. For the conversion (5 minas = 5.20833 lb.) see **3765** 9–11 n.

¹⁹ For the ἱστός/*tela* (translated '1 piece' by M. H. Crawford and J. M. Reynolds, *ZPE* 34 (1979) 195) see S. Lauffer, *Diokletians Preisedikt* 273; LI **3626** 16–17 n. No conversion to the ζεῦγος-based prices of the papyri has been attempted, and the Edict's prices have not been used to obtain an inflation figure.

²⁰ The Nicaean variety of purple, at 1 tal./lb., is one of the cheaper varieties in the Price Edict (§24. 8 ed. Giacchero), although the price relates not to the dyestuff but to the cost of a pound of wool dyed with it; so that

it may be unfair to compare this price with the 80 tal. for 1 lb. of the dyestuff itself (presumably) evidenced by **3765** 16. Nevertheless, 'cheaper' variety though the Nicaean might be, its price of 80 tal. is instructive for the quality of the local product (πορφύρας ἐντοπίου, **3765** 18) which is only 2 tal./lb. at the same date.

[21] For this figure see **3765** introd.

[22] This is the highest figure for πορφύρα in the Edict and it relates not to the substance but to the price of a pound of wool dyed with it. The much lower prices thirty years later in the papyri will surely relate to a cheap local substitute, as ἐντοπίου implies. I have therefore not taken account of the Edict's price(s) in assessing the inflation-factor.

[23] ῥοδίνου: listed by the Edict (ed. Giacchero, §34. 43–4) under the heading *De plantis/περὶ φύλλων*; this is likely to be a different substance from the dyestuff listed in our two papyri, despite the identical nomenclature, see S. Lauffer, *Diokletians Preisedikt* 287. The Edict's price ought perhaps therefore to be discounted in calculating inflation-rates.

[24] For the proposed identification of the animal here with the female donkey of the Price Edict (§30. 13 ed. Giacchero) cf. **3765** 24–6n. There is some uncertainty over the Edict's price, cf. *ZPE* 34 (1979) 178.

[25] This is the Edict's price for κρέως βοείου, §4.2 ed. Lauffer or Giacchero, and therefore perhaps not an exact parallel; in any case damage to the price in **3765** 29 prevents comparison.

[26] For the price see *ZPE* 39 (1980) 125.

[27] For the price c. 338 see *ZPE* 39 (1980) 125.

[28] The Edict (ed. Giacchero, §33. 7) gives 8 den./lb. as the price of πίσσης σκληρᾶς = *picis durae*. For the equivalence of σκληρᾶς:ξηρᾶς cf. S. Lauffer, *Diokletians Preisedikt* 283.

[29] On the price see **3733** 12n.

[30] For the price see M. H. Crawford and J. M. Reynolds, *ZPE* 34 (1979) 181.

[31] For the price see *ZPE* 34 (1979) 182.

[32] The price is given on the basis that σανδυκίου = the Edict's *sandugos* (§34. 79 Giacchero): see *ZPE* 34 (1979) 209 (*sandugos* in l. 78 in the text as edited here).

[33] For the substance and price see *ZPE* 34 (1979) 183.

[34] On this price note **3733** 23n.

[35] Not attested in our declarations, and therefore not included among the guilds arranged in the preceding Appendix. Conversely, none of our surviving declarations declare the price of lentils so as otherwise to identify the guild indirectly attested by the data in **3773**.

APPENDIX IV

SCRIBES AND SUBSCRIBERS

In *ZPE* 37 (1980) 230 I briefly discussed the phenomenon of the scribe in the logistes' bureau (in that case Aurelius Leontius, from P. Harr. 73) who was commissioned by the guilds' representatives to subscribe for them. Another such is Theon (I **85**, PSI III 202), see *ZPE* 39 (1980) 121, 124. ὑπογραφεῖς of this type are discussed by H. C. Youtie, *ZPE* 17 (1975) 216–18. The new texts in this volume enable us to recognize more such scribes.

Aurelius Theon in **3761** (?326) may be the same as the Theon just mentioned (338).

Only one subscription survives for Aurelius Nilus, as is the case for others (Aurelius Dionysius, **3760**; Aurelius Pathermouthis, **3742**), but in Nilus' case there is other proof that he was a scribe in the logistes' bureau, cf. **3733** introd.

Aurelius Sarmates in **3737**, put forward as a possible scribe in the bureau in the introduction to that text, will perhaps not be identical with his namesake in **3752** of nearly seven years later.

Finally there is Aurelius Horion, whose distinctive hand is widely found in subscriptions and elsewhere in several texts over a long period, from 312 to 329; he wrote the subscriptions in **3740** and possibly also **3739** (312), **3743** probably (the name is lost) of 318, **3748**, **3749**, and **3750** (all 319), possibly **3762** (?326), and **3766** iii–iv (329). The writing of **3762** is rather more cursive and flamboyant than the earlier examples, but there are nevertheless some particular resemblances and his continued activity in 329 can also argue for the identity. The tiny scrap P. Harr. inv. 190c (*ZPE* 37 (1980) 239) may also bear his hand.

INDEXES

Figures in small raised type refer to fragments, small roman numerals to columns. An asterisk shows that the word to which it is attached is not recorded in LSJ or Supplement. Square brackets indicate that a word is substantially restored, round brackets that it is expanded from an abbreviation or symbol. The article and (in the documentary texts) καί are not indexed.

I. NEW LITERARY TEXTS

(a) Commentary on ANACREON (**3722**)

ἀ[γ]γελλ[[6] 8?
ἄγε [15] ii [2?], 3, 5, [[25] ii 10?]
ἄδηλος [[3] 6?], [17] ii 8?
]αεκα[[7] 3
ἀθετεῖν [9] 2, [33] 7
ἆθλον [73] 8?
αιμ.[[27] 10
αἱματόεις [17] i 15
αἰνο- [25] i 6?
αἰόλος [73] 11?
Αἴολος [73] 11?
αἱρεῖν [16] i 7?
*ἀκρόμεστος [1] 8?
Ἀλκαῖος [1] 21?
ἀλκαῖος [1] 21?
αλλ[[51] ii 2
ἀλλά [14] 7?, [17] ii 10?, [21] i 8?
ἀλληγορεῖν [20] 8?
ἀλληγορία [52] 4
ἄλλος [15] ii [2?], 15?, [17] ii 10?, [18] 7
ἅμα [15] i 2?
Ἀμμώνιος [33] 7?
αμφ.[[54] ii 1
ἀμφίβολος [25] i 4?, [30] 5?
ἀμφοτερω- [25] i 5?
ἀνάγειν [1] 25
ἀναγιγνώσκειν [15] ii 13–14?
Ἀνακρέων [1] 19?, [15] i 18?, [27] 7?, [39] 4?, [73] 10
ἀνδάνειν [83] 1?
ἀνήρ [50] 6?
ἄνθος [[1] 26?]
ἄνθρωπος [15] ii 15?
ἄνομος [3] 7?
ἀντί [[15] ii 4?]
αντι[[5] 2?, [6] 4?, [51] ii 8?
ἀντιφέρειν [1] 17?
ἄξιος [25] ii 6

ἄοινος [25] i 7?
απ[[1] 28?
ἀπαρτίζειν [3] 4?
απειλ- [23] 7
ἀπείρων [17] i 19
ἀπέλαστος [3] 6?
Ἀπελλῆς [6] 2?, [28] 8?, [82] 2?
ἀπελλόν [6] 2?
ἀπιέναι [2] 3
ἀπό [1] 6, [2] 2, [16] ii 19?, [23] 5?
ἀπόδειξις [20] 7?
ἀποδιδράσκειν [21] i 6?
αποκε[[7] 10
ἀποκοπή [15] i 16?
Ἀπόλλων [16] ii [15?], 17
*ἀποποιμαίνειν [1] 5, [28] 3
ἀποσεύειν [[17] i 15]
απατ[[50] 9?
]απτα[[4] 11
αρετη[[4] 4
ἄρθμιος [3] 3
Ἀρι- [21] i 9?
Ἀριστάρχειος [33] 7?
Ἀρίσταρχος [20] 4
Ἀριστοτέλης [16] ii 15–16?
Ἀριστοφάνης [1] 16?
ἅρμα [5] 3, 9
αρχ[[50] 13
αρχο[[52] 3?
ἄσημος [15] i 3
ἀσθενής [16] i 3?
Ἀστερίς [30] 6?
ἄτοπος [[3] 4?]
ατωλ[[77] 6
αὐτός [1] 22?, [2] 2?, [7] 5?, [15] i 13?, ii 16?, [16] i 5?, [19] 2, [33] 7a, 7b, [50] 12?, [55] 5?, [83] 3
αὔτως [15] ii 16?

ἐπί ¹ 18?, 20?, 22?, 23?, ² [3?], 5?, ⁵ 5?, ¹⁷ i 10?, [19],
   ²¹ i 6?, ²⁹ 4, ⁵⁰ 13, ⁵⁴ ii 12?, ¹⁰⁷ 3?
ἐπιγιγνώσκειν ²¹ i 10?
επιθεμ[¹⁶ ii 3
ἐπιρρηματικός [¹⁵ ii 3?]
ἐπισχετικός ²⁵ ii 8
ἐπιτίθεσθαι? επιθεμ[¹⁶ ii 3
ἐπιφέρειν ¹⁵ ii 4, 17, ²⁶ 4?
ἐπιχειλής ¹ 20?, 22?
ἐρεῖν ¹⁵ ii 5, ¹⁶ ii 9–10?
Ἐρινύς [¹⁷ i 17]
ἕρμα [¹⁵ i 4?]
Ἔρως (or ἔρως) ¹ 26, ⁷ 7?, ¹⁴ 5?, ²⁵ ii 11, ⁸² 17?, ¹⁰² 3?
ἐρωτικός ² 6, ¹⁰² 3?
ἐς ²⁵ ii 7?
ἑταῖρος ⁸³ 3?
εὔπεπλος ⁸² 3?
εὔπυργος ¹⁶ ii 12?
εὑρίσκειν [¹⁵ i 6?]
Εὐρυπύλη ²⁷ 6a

Ζεύς [⁵ 8?]
ζῷον ¹⁹ 6?

ἤ ¹⁵ i 16?, [ii 4?]
ἥβη ²⁵ i 6?
ἡδύς ¹⁶ i 10
ἡμέτερος ⁴⁸ 2?
ἡμίονος [¹⁵ i 7?]
]ηρακλ.[⁴⁴ 4
Ἡσίοδος ¹⁵ ii 8?, [¹⁷ i 13]
ἤτοι ²⁵ i 4?
ητοι.[⁴ 5

θεός ¹⁶ ii 6?, ¹⁸ 6
θεράπων ² 1
θεσμός ⁹⁹ 4?
θρην[⁶ 5?
θρηνητικός ¹⁹ 5?

ἰέναι ¹ 28?, ⁵ 4?, ¹⁶ i 7?, ²⁵ ii 7
ἰέναι [¹⁵ ii 9?], [⁸⁸ 4?]
ἱερεύς ¹⁶ ii 15?
ινα[⁵⁰ 11
ιναι ¹⁶ ii 7
ἱπποθόρος ¹⁵ i 5?, 8–9?
ἵππος ¹⁵ i 6?, 9?
ἰχθῦς [⁷⁰ 5?]
ἴψ ⁵¹ i 8?

καθά ⁵ 7?
καθεύδειν ²⁶ 8–9?
καί ¹ 24, ² 7, ³ 2, [7?], ⁵ 6?, 7, ⁶ 6?, ⁷ 8?, ¹⁵ ii 2?, [3?],
   8, 18, ¹⁶ i 3, 10?, 19?, ii 9, ¹⁷ i 12?, ¹⁹ 2, ²¹ i 9?, ²⁵ i
   14?, ²⁶ 4?, ³³ 11, ⁴⁰ 5?, ⁷¹ 2a?, ⁸² 20?

καίειν ⁵⁵ 3?
καίπερ ¹⁶ ii 2?
κακός ¹ 26
καλεῖν ¹⁷ i [14], [19], ³³ 7b?
κατά ⁶ 7?, [¹⁵ i 16?], ²⁵ i 17?, ²⁸ 9?
κατακοιμᾶν ¹⁵ ii 11?, ²⁶ 8?
καταλαμβάνειν ⁵⁰ 18?
καταρράπτειν ²⁵ ii 17–18?
κεῖσθαι ³² 4?
]κερ...[¹⁷ ii 6
κινεῖν ²⁷ 8?
Κλεαρίστη ⁵⁷ 4?
Κλεάριστος ⁵⁷ 4?
Κλέαρχος ¹ 17?, ⁵⁷ 4?
κλεεννός ¹⁶ ii 12?
κοκκύζειν ¹⁷ ii 3?
κόκκυξ ¹⁷ ii 3?
κόριον ¹ 24
κόρος ¹⁷ ii 4?
κόσμος ⁹⁹ 4?
κρατερός ¹⁷ i 17–18
κτ.[⁷³ 12?
κυανῶπις ¹⁶ i 9?
Κυθέρεια ²⁵ i 25–6?
Κυπρογενής ¹⁴ 10?
κυρτός ⁷⁰ 5?
κώμη ²⁵ i 7?

λαμβάνειν ⁵² 2?
λεγε.[¹ 9
λέγειν ¹ 18?, ² 1?, ¹⁵ [i 9?], ii 9, ²⁰ 4?, [⁵³ 5?]
λέξις ⁵⁰ 14?
λεπτήκης ¹⁵ i 2?
]ληρος ²⁹ 3
λίαν ² 7, [⁶ 6?]
λόγος ³ 6?, ⁵⁷ 1?
λοιπάζειν ³⁰ 7?
λοιπός ³⁰ 7?
λόφος ⁵² 7?

μαινάς ³³ 7b
μαίνειν ² 1
μάντευμα ¹⁶ ii 17?
μας.η.[²³ 6
μέγας ¹⁰ 3, [¹⁷ i 18]
μεθυ[¹⁵ ii 10
μεθύειν ¹⁶ ii 11
μεθύσκειν ² 8
μει- ³³ 12?
μειδιᾶν ²⁹ 2
Μελίαι ¹⁷ i 13, [19]
μέμφεσθαι ³ 5 (bis?)
μέν ² 4, 7?, [⁶ 6?], ¹⁵ i 14?, ii 7?, 13?, ¹⁶ ii 12, ¹⁷ ii 6,
   ²⁵ ii 5?, 10, ²⁶ 10?, ²⁸ 3

πύργος ¹⁶ ii 12?
πῶς ¹⁶ ii 14?, ³⁰ 5?

ῥαθάμιγξ ¹⁷ i 14-15
ῥυθμός ¹⁷ i 2

Cάμιος ¹⁸ 8?
Cάμος ¹⁵ i 18?
Cάρδις ²⁵ i 15
cείειν ²⁵ ii 12?
cημεῖον ¹ 25?
cίδηρος ³¹ 5?
Cικελία ⁴ 6?
Cιληνός ²⁵ ii 17?
Cιμ[⁵⁷ 3?
cτεφανηφόρος ¹⁶ ii 6-7?
cύ ¹⁶ ii 12, ¹⁷ i 12?, ii 6, ²⁵ ii 10, 12?
cυβώτης ¹⁵ i 17
cυγγράφειν ¹⁹ 7?
cυλλαβή [²⁰ 3?]
cυμβαίνειν ⁴ 1
cυμπόcιον ² 2
cύν ¹⁶ i 8?
cυναινεῖν [¹⁵ ii 8?]
cυναλιφή ¹⁵ i 16?
cφάλλειν ⁵¹ ii 9?
cχεδόν ⁸² 16?
cωφρονίζειν ¹⁵ ii 12, 14-15?

ταμίας ¹⁸ 8?
τανύπεπλος ⁸² 3?
ταπει[³⁰ 4
ταῦρος ⁸³ 2
ταυτολογία ⁵⁴ i 19a-b?
τε ⁷ 6?, ¹⁷ i 17, [18], 18, ⁷⁰ 5?
τέκνον ¹⁹ 4?
τέμνειν ¹⁶ i 21?
Τέως ⁷³ 8?, 9
τερπ[²² ii 6
τέρπειν ³⁴ 1
τέρψις ⁴ 3?
τέτρατος [¹⁵ ii 9?], ⁸⁸ 4?
]τεως[⁷² 1
τήκειν ¹⁵ i 2?
της[⁵ 10
τι[⁵ 2?
τίκτειν ¹⁵ i 7?
τις ¹⁵ i 15?, ⁵⁷ 5?
τίς ¹⁷ ii 7, ⁵³ 5?, ⁵⁷ 5?
]τραπ[⁸⁵ 3
τρεῖς ¹⁵ ii 9, ⁸⁸ 3?
τριετής ⁸² 16?
τριτο[¹⁴ 8?
τρόπος ¹⁷ ii 7, ⁸⁴ 2

τρυγᾶν ¹ 26?
τύραννος ³ 6

ὕδρη ¹⁶ i 24?
ὕδωρ ¹⁵ ii 1, [6?], [7?], 9?, ⁸⁸ 3?
ὑπέρ [¹⁵ i 4?]
υπερες.[³³ 4
ὕπνος ¹⁴ 4?
ὑπό ¹ 16?, [¹⁵ i 7?], ¹⁶ ii 8, ³¹ 5?
υπομε- ¹⁶ i 12?
υψ[¹² 4?
ὑψιμέδων ⁵ 8?
ὑψιχαίτης ⁵ 10?

φαίνεcθαι ¹⁶ i 5-6?, ³³ 6, ⁸⁷ 10
φάναι ² 5, ¹⁵ ii 16, ¹⁶ ii 14, 16?, [¹⁷ i 13], ²⁵ ii 18?
φέρειν ¹⁵ ii 1 (bis), [1?], [2?], 4
φιλίη ⁴⁸ 2?
φίλος ¹⁶ i 13?, ¹⁷ ii 2, [²⁹ 2], ⁵³ 5
φιλότης ⁴⁸ 2?, ⁵⁰ 15
φοβερός ²⁵ ii 5?
φόβος ²⁵ ii 5?, 6
φοινός ⁸⁸ 6?
φορεῖν [¹⁵ i 4?]
φρήν ²⁵ ii 5?
φῶς [²⁹ 2]

χαίρειν [²⁹ 2]
χαμ.[⁷³ 4?
χαρίεις ¹⁶ ii 10, [²⁹ 2]
χεῖλος ¹ 9?, 18?, 20?, 22?, ¹⁹ 3?, ⁵¹ ii 10
χειμάζειν ¹⁵ i 4?
χεῖν ¹ 23?
χείρ ¹ 7
χελιδών ¹⁹ 3?, 5?
χιάζειν ⁵³ 4?
χιτών ³² 5
χορός [⁷⁰ 5?]
χρόα ²⁸ 2
χρόνος [⁸² 16?]
χρυσοχαίτης ⁵ 10?

ψαρός ⁵² 7?
ψυ- ³³ 11

ὦ [¹⁵ ii 1?], ¹⁶ ii 10?, ²⁵ i 6?, ⁵¹ ii 4?
ᾠδή [¹⁵ ii 2?]
Ὠκεανός [⁵¹ ii 9?]
*ῷοι ¹⁷ ii 7
ὥρα ²⁵ i 6?
ὡραῖος ²⁵ i 6?
ὡς ¹⁵ ii 11?, ¹⁷ ii 8?, ²¹ i 9?
ὡcαύτως ⁷ 5?
ὥστε ¹⁷ ii 3?

(*b*) Elegy and Epigram (**3723–3726**)

The first two digits of the item number (always **37**) have been omitted.

εἶναι **23** 5?, 10?   **24** ¹ iii 16?, 21?, iv 23?, (26), v 10,
   vii 16?, 20?, (21), viii 10?   **25** ¹ ii [8], [11]   **26** ¹ 26
εἰπεῖν **24** ¹ iv 9, viii 8?
εἰς **24** ¹ iv 4, 11   **25** ¹ ii 4
εἰς ⟦**24** ¹ iii 5⟧   [**26** ¹ 26]
εἰσαίρειν **24** ¹ iv 23?
ἐκεῖνος **24** ¹ i 2?, 19
ἐκλέγειν **24** ¹ viii 5
ἐκτιθέναι **24** ¹ iii 22?
*ἐκτονεῖν **24** ¹ iv 30?
ἐλέφας **24** ¹ i 7
ἕλκειν **24** ¹ v 28
ἐλπ[**24** ² 11?
ἐμβάλλειν **24** ¹ v 25   **25** ³ 4?
ἐμός **24** ¹ iv 12?, vi 5
ἐν **24** ¹ vii 11, viii 3   **25** ¹ ii 7, ² 5?
ἐναίρειν **23** 18
ἐνδημεῖν **25** ² 5?
ἐνθάδε **24** ¹ iv 18
ἐνοίκιον [**25** ¹ ii 5]
ἔξ **24** ¹ vii 22?
ἐξειδέναι **24** ¹ vii 22?
ἐξήκοντα **24** ¹ vii 25?
ἑός **23** 1, 22?
ἐπέκεινα **24** ¹ i 2?
ἐπηλυσία **23** 22?
ἐπί **24** ¹ i 2?   **25** ¹ ii 9, ² 8?   **26** ¹ 23?
ἐπίσχειν **23** 16?
ἑπτά **24** ¹ ii 14
ἐρᾶν **24** ¹ i 17, iii 10?
ἔρασθαι **24** ¹ v 11, vii 7
ἐρύεσθαι **23** 22
ἔρως **23** 15, 20   **24** ¹ iii 10?
Ἔρως **24** ¹ ii 26, iv 30
ἐς [**25** ¹ ii 8]
ἔτι **24** ¹ ii 1?
εὕδειν **24** ¹ iii 20
εὔιος [**23** 13?]
εὔμοιρος **24** ¹ i 7?
*εὐπάταγος **23** 14
εὑρίσκειν **24** ² 6?   **25** ¹ ii 8
εὐτακτεῖν **25** ¹ ii 5
εὐφρόσυνος [**25** ¹ ii 4]
εὔχαρις **24** ¹ vii 20
ἔχειν **23** 23   **24** ¹ iv 27, v 6, vi 12, ² 10
ἐχθές **24** ¹ iii 22?, vi 11
ἐχίδνη [**23** 17?]

ζάθεος **23** 4?
Ζεύς **24** ² 12
ζῆν **23** 10?
ζωροπότης **24** ¹ iv 20

ἤ **25** ¹ ii 12

ἠδέ **23** 12, 18
ἤδειν **24** ¹ vii 22?
ἤδη **24** ¹ ii 6, iv 9, v 30, vii 2?, 21
Ἡδύλιον **24** ¹ viii 6
ἡδύς **24** ¹ ii 26, v 28
ἥκειν **24** ¹ iv 28
ἠλακάτη **24** ¹ vi 16?
ἡλικίη [**25** ¹ ii 8]
ἡμάτιος [**25** ¹ ii 6]
ἡμέτερος **24** ¹ iv 5
ἤν **23** 5?   **24** ¹ viii 1   [**25** ¹ ii 5]
ἡνίκα **24** ¹ vi 14
ἠΰκομος **23** 19
ἠχή **23** 14

Θεόδωρος [**25** ¹ ii 10]
Θεόκριτος **26** ¹ 25
θέρος **24** ¹ v 28
θηλυ( ) **24** ¹ v 10
θνητός **24** ¹ vii 11?
θορυβεῖν [**25** ¹ ii 7]
θρῆϊξ **23** 19
θυ(γατ-?) **24** ¹ iii 12
θύειν **24** ¹ iv 33?
θυμε(λη?) **24** ¹ iv 16
θυμός **23** 22
θύρη **24** ¹ i 18
θύρσος **23** 16
θυσία **25** ³ 6?

ἰάχειν **23** 13?
ἰέναι [**23** 14?]   [**25** ¹ ii 8]
Ἴκαρος **24** ¹ vi 9
*ἱκετηριάς **23** 10?
Ἰνδός **23** 15
Ἰνώ **24** ¹ iv 19
ἰξένειν **24** ¹ ii 12
ἰξός **24** ¹ vi 12

κα[**26** ¹ 21?
κάδος **24** ¹ iii 22?
καί **24** ¹ i 1?, 21?, 23?, ii 19, 23?, iii ⟦7⟧, 12, 15,
   iv 25?, v 14, 16, 17, 22, 23, 24, 31, vi 2, 5 (*bis?*),
   10, vii 6, 15?, 21, viii 9, 12?   **25** ¹ ii [3], 6, 10   **26**
   ² 5
καίειν **24** ¹ vi 3?, 5?
καινός [**23** 13?]
Καῖσαρ **24** ¹ iv 25?
κακο[**24** ² 3?
κακός **23** 8?
καλεῖν **24** ¹ ii 22?
Καλλικρα( ) **24** ¹ iii 20
κάλλος [**23** 19?]
καλός [**23** 8?]   **24** ¹ ii 22?, iii 17, viii 5, 8?   [**25** ¹ ii 11]

ὅδε **24** ¹ i 15, viii 7? **26** ¹ 25
ὄζειν [**25** ¹ ii 10]
οἶνος **24** ¹ vi 10
ὀκταπλοῦς **24** ¹ iii 23?
ὀκτώ **24** ¹ iii 16?
ὀκτωκαιδεκέτις **24** ¹ iii 14
ολη[**25** ³ 4
ὄλλυσθαι **24** ¹ vii 3
ὄμβρος **24** ¹ i 11
ὄμμα **24** ¹ i 17
ὁμοίως **25** ² 3?, ³ 5
ὁμολογεῖν **24** ¹ iv 28
ὀνομάζειν **26** ² 4?
ὁρᾶν **24** ¹ i 18, ² 9?
ὄρνυσθαι [**23** 14?]
ὀρχεῖσθαι **24** ¹ vi 7, vii 14
ὅς **23** 5?, 10?, 13? **24** ¹ ii 7, ² 10?
ὅτι **24** ¹ iv 25?, vii 6
οὐ **24** ¹ ii 3, 26, iii 18, iv 1, 8, v 10, vi 15, vii 10 [**25** ³ 4?] **26** ¹ 24
οὐδέπω **24** ¹ v 25
οὔπω **24** ¹ ii ⟦4⟧, 24
οὖς **24** ¹ v 23?
οὔτε [**23** 8? (*bis?*)] **24** ¹ iv 6
οὔτις **23** 7?
οὗτος [**23** 20?] **24** ¹ i 4?, ii 9, 29?, iv 29?, vi 13, viii 3, 11, ² 13
οὕτω(ς) **24** ¹ iii 16?
οὐχί **24** ¹ v 11
ὀφιῆτις [**23** 17?]
ὀχληρός **24** ¹ ii 20
ὀψωνεῖν **24** ¹ vii 8

πα( ) **24** ¹ v 23
πάθος **23** 8, [22?]
παιδάριον **24** ¹ i 8?
παῖς **23** 16 **24** ¹ v 9
πάϊς [**23** 17?]
παλλίολον **24** ¹ v 29
*παντομέδων **24** ¹ iii 23?
παρά **25** ² 7?
παραί **23** 9
παρθένιος **24** ¹ v 19
Παρθενόπη **24** ¹ iv 14, 15
πᾶς **23** 21 **24** ¹ i 12?, vii 5 **25** ¹ ii 3
παύειν **24** ¹ vi 16
Παφίη **24** ¹ ii 10, iv 13, 24
πέζα **23** 11
πείθειν **24** ¹ v 7?, 21
πειρᾶν [**25** ¹ ii 5]
πέμπειν **24** ¹ iv 31
πέμπτος **24** ¹ vii 2, 16
πέντε **24** ¹ ii 18, ⟦iii 7⟧
περί **24** ¹ i 23

περισσός [**25** ¹ ii 5]
πιθα(νός) **24** ¹ v 8, viii 1
πίνειν **24** ¹ v 7?
πλη( ) **24** ¹ iv 15?
πλο( ) **24** ¹ iii 18
πλόκαμος **24** ¹ iii 13
πλου( ) **24** ¹ ii 17?
πο( ) **24** ¹ v 2
πόθεν **25** ¹ ii 8
πόημα **24** ¹ iv 8
πόθος [**23** 22?]
ποῖος **25** ¹ ii 4, [12 (*bis*)]
πολλάκις **24** ¹ v 30
πολύς **26** ¹ 26
πολυτρη( ) **24** ¹ v 9
ποτε **23** [17?], 18 **24** ¹ vii 11
πούς **23** 9, 14 **24** ¹ v 20
πρίν **24** ¹ ⟦iii 7⟧, v 31
πρό **24** ¹ ii 2
προιέναι **24** ¹ i 1
Πρόκνη **24** ¹ vii 1?
προλέγειν **24** ¹ iv 17
πρός **23** 14, 20, 23 [**25** ¹ ii 3]
πρόςω(πον?) **24** ¹ ii 27
πρός(ωπον?) **24** ¹ vii 6
πρότερον **24** ¹ ii 15, 16, 21, iv 16, vii 4
προφα( ) **24** ¹ ii 3?
πρῴην **24** ¹ ii 7
πρωκτός **25** ¹ ii 10, [12]
Πρωτεύς **24** ¹ v 18
πρῶτος **24** ¹ iv 13
πτερυ[**25** ³ 1
πτωχός **24** ¹ iv 27
πυκάζειν **23** 3?
πῦρ **23** 1
πω **24** ¹ viii 8?
πῶς **26** ² 6?

ῥόδινος **24** ¹ vi 10
ῥόδον **24** ¹ vii 21
Ῥωμαία **24** ¹ viii 4?

σαπρόστομος **25** ¹ ii 9?
Σάρδεις **24** ¹ iv 25?
σαυτοῦ [**25** ¹ ii 3]
σβεννύναι **23** 1
σηκός **23** 5
σιγᾶν **24** ¹ iv 10
σιμός **24** ¹ ii 27
σκευή ⟦**24** ¹ iii 1⟧
σκοπιά [**23** 12?]
σκῦλον **23** 15
σμύρνα **24** ¹ v 16
σός **23** 10? **24** ¹ iii 16?

The first two digits of the item number (always **37**) have been omitted from Indexes II to XII.

II. EMPERORS AND REGNAL YEARS

Diocletian and Maximian
 οἱ κύριοι ἡμῶν Αὐτοκράτορες Διοκλητιανὸς καὶ Μαξιμιανὸς Cεβαστοὶ καὶ Κωνστάντιος καὶ Μαξιμιανὸς οἱ
 ἐπιφανέστατοι Καίcαρες Cεβαστοί (oath formula) **27** 7–10
Constantius and Galerius
 . . . κύριοι ἡμῶν Αὐτοκράτορες . . . **28** 10
Constantine I and Licinius
 οἱ δεσπόται ἡμῶν Αὐτοκράτορες καὶ Καίcαρες (oath formula) **46** 27–8, 52–3
19/9 (= AD 324/5)
 57 1 **58** 3, 39, 78, [98], 134, 156, 181
20/10/2 (= AD 325/6)
 59 1, 42
24/14/6 (= AD 329/30)
 67 [1]?
25/15/7 (= AD 330/1)
 67 [1]?

III. CONSULS

AD 303 ἐπὶ ὑπάτων τῶν κυρίων ἡμῶν Αὐτοκρατόρων Διοκλητιανοῦ τὸ η // καὶ Μαξιμιανοῦ τὸ ζ // Cεβαστῶν **27** 1–3

AD 306 ἐπὶ ὑπάτων τῶν κυρίων ἡμῶν Αὐτοκρατόρων Κωνσταντίου καὶ Μαξιμιανοῦ Cεβαστῶν τὸ ϛ´ **28** 1–2

AD 307 ἐπὶ ὑπάτων τῶν κυρίων ἡμῶν Αὐτοκράτορος Cεουήρου Cεβαστοῦ καὶ Μαξιμίνου τοῦ ἐπιφανεστάτου
 Καίcαρος **29** 2–5

AD 312 ὑπατείας τῶν δεσποτῶν ἡμῶν Φλαυίου Οὐαλερίου Κωνσταντίνου καὶ Λικινιανοῦ Λικινίου Cεβαστῶν τὸ β´
 [**32** 1–3] **33** 1–2 **34** 1–3 [**35** 1–2] **36** 1–4 **37** 1–4 **38** 1–4 **39** 1–4 **40** 1–4

AD 313 ὑπατίας τοῦ δεσπότου ἡμῶν Φλαυίου Οὐαλερίου Κωνσταντίνου Cεβαστοῦ τὸ γ´ **41** (front) 1

AD 317 ὑπατείας Ὀουίνίου Γαλλικανοῦ καὶ Καιcωνίου Βάccου τῶν λαμπροτάτων **42** 14–16

AD 318 ὑπατείας τῶν δεσποτῶν ἡμῶν Λικινίου Cεβαστοῦ τὸ εϛ´ καὶ Κρίcπου τοῦ ἐπιφανεστάτου Καίcαρος τὸ αϛ´
 43 1–4 **44** 1–4 **45** 1–4

AD 319 ὑπατείας τῶν δεσποτῶν ἡμῶν Κωνσταντίνου Cεβαστοῦ τὸ εϛ´ καὶ Λικινίου τοῦ ἐπιφανεστάτου Καίcαρος
 τὸ αϛ´ **46** 18–20, 44–6

— ὑπατείας τῶν δεσποτῶν ἡμῶν Κωνσταντίνου Cεβαστοῦ τὸ εϛ´ καὶ Λικινίου Καίcαρος τὸ αϛ´ **48** 1–3 **49** 1–3
 50 1–3 **51** 1–3 **52** 1–3 **53** 1–3

AD 320 ὑπατείας τῶν δεσποτῶν ἡμῶν Κωνσταντίνου Cεβαστοῦ τὸ ϛ´ καὶ Κωνσταντίνου τοῦ ἐπιφανεστάτου Καίcαρος
 τὸ α´ **54** 1–2 **55** 19–23 (beginning lost)

AD 324 [κεχρονιc]μένου εἰς ὑπατείαν τῶν δεσποτῶν ἡμῶν Κρίcπου καὶ Κωνσταντίνου τῶν ἐπιφανεστάτων [Καιcάρων
 τὸ γ´ **58** 203–5

AD 325 ὑπατίας Πρόκλου καὶ Παυλίνου **56** 26 **58** 39

— ὑπατείας Πρόκλου καὶ Παυλίνου τῶν λαμπροτάτων **58** 132

— ὑπατείας Παυλίνου καὶ Ἰουλιανοῦ τῶν λαμπροτάτων **57** 1–2

AD 326 . . . Καίcαρος τὸ α´ **60** 1?

AD 329 ὑπατείας τῶν δεσποτῶν ἡμῶν Κωνσταντίνου Αὐγούστου τὸ η´ καὶ Κωνσταντίνου τοῦ ἐπιφανεστάτου
 Καίcαρος τὸ δ´ **66** 23–8, 49–55, 77–8

AD 334 ὑπατείας Φλαουΐου Ὀπτάτου πατρικίου καὶ Ἀνικίου Παυλίνου τῶν λαμπροτάτων **69** 1–2 **70** 18–19

AD 336 ὑπατείας Οὐιρίου Νεπωτιανοῦ καὶ Τεττίου Cεκούνδου (l. Φακούνδου) τῶν λαμπροτάτων **71** 1–2

AD 341 ὑπατείας Ἀντωνίου Μαρκελλίνου καὶ Πετρωνίου Προβίνου [τῶν λαμ(προτάτων)] **74** 1–2

AD 342 ὑπατείας τῶν δεσποτῶν ἡμῶν Κωνσταντίου τὸ γ´´ καὶ Κώνσταντος τὸ β´´ Αὐγούστων **75** 1–3, 15
 (fragmentary)

AD 343 ὑπατείας Φουρίου Πλακίδου καὶ Φλαουΐου Ῥωμώλου τῶν λαμπροτάτων **76** 32–3

IV. MONTHS AND DAYS

(a) Months

(b) Days

V. PERSONAL NAMES

VI. GEOGRAPHICAL

(a) Countries, Nomes, Cities, Etc.

Αἴγυπτος **56** $_9$ **57** $_5$, 18 **58** 10, 15, [37], 80, 92 **59** 6,
  13 **64** 6, 8 **67** [5], 7, 17
Ἀλεξάνδρεια **56** 7 **58** 120-1
Ἀλεξανδρέων, πόλις τῶν **56** 2
Ἀραβικός **66** 44
Αὐγουσταμνική **74** 12-13 **75** 9
Ἑπτανομία (**41** 3-4?)
Θηβαϊκός **40** 17 **62** 16 **65** 4
Λαδικηνός **76** 41
Λίβυς **58** 100, 101, 121
Λίβυσσα **41** 5
Μαρεώτης **56** 3
Μαστίτης **56** 3, 4, 5 **57** 6 **58** 81
Μέμφις **27** 7
Νικαϊνός **65** 16
Ὄασις **58** 161, 168
Ὀασιτικός **40** 16 **62** 15 **65** 3
Ὀξυρυγχίτης (nome) [**27** 4] [**28** 3] **30** 2 [**32** 5]

33 3 **34** 5 [**35** 3] **37** 6 **39** 6 **40** 6 **41** (front)
  2, 3 **42** 2 **43** 6 **44** 6 **45** 6 **48** 5 [**53** 5] **54** 4
  65 50 **66** 57, [79] **67** 8 **68** 2, 11, [22] [**69** 3]
  71 3 **72** 2 [**74** 3] **76** 2
(Ὀξυρυγχίτης) (nome) **29** 7 **46** 22, 48 **49** 5 **50** 5
  51 5 **52** 5 [**60** 2] **66** 29 **75** 4
Ὀξυρυγχιτικός **65** 5, 6, 7?
Ὀξυρυγχιτῶν πόλις **27** 6 **29** 10-11 **30** 4 **31** 4-5
  41 (front) 4 **46** 50-1 **53** 7 [**54** 6] **60** 4-5 **70** 1
Ὀξ(υρυγχιτῶν) πόλις **42** 4 **43** 8-9 [**44** 8-9] **45** 8
  48 7 [**49** 7] **51** 7 **52** 7 **55** 31-2, [43-4] **65** 53
  66 6, 31, 60-1, 80
Ὀξ(υρύγχων) πόλις **46** 24
πάγος **46** 25 (8th) **71** 5 (5th) [**74** 4 (7th)?]
Cιριτικός **66** 71-2
Ταρcικός **65** 12-13 **76** 16
Τρωαδήcιος **66** 73
Τύρος **58** 19

(b) Villages

Δωcιθέου **46** 25
Ἰcίον Παγγᾶ **58** 100, 222

Cεφώ **74** 4
Τααμπεμοῦ **71** 4-5

(c) Miscellaneous

ἄμφοδον Παμμένους Παραδείcου **54** 11
εἶ γράμμα (district of Alexandria) **56** 2

Cίγμα (district of Alexandria?) **56** 2

VII. RELIGION

Ἁδριανεῖον **58** 134 **64** 14 **67** 1
Ζεύς see Index IV (b) s.v. Διός
ἱερόν **42** introd. **59** 1
ἱερός **59** 38
Ἰcίον see Index VI (b)

Καπιτώλιον **57** 3 **58** 78, 156
Κορεῖον **42** introd. **59** 1
κυριακή **59** 38, 39
τύχη (genius) [**27** 10]

VIII. OFFICIAL AND MILITARY TERMS AND TITLES

ἄρχειν [**57** 9] **58** 85, 182
ἀρχοντικός **58** 5?
βιβλιοφύλαξ **58** 139
βουλευτής **58** 8, 16, 158, 188 (**64** 15)
γυμνάσιον **58** 181
δημόσιος **59** 8 **74** 5

διαδέχεσθαι (**46** 22, 48)
διάδοχος **29** 8 **55** [8], 28
διαιτητής **64** 15, [17], 22-3, 23
διασημότατος **31** 6 (**46** [10], 34, 59) **56** 9 **57** 4, 18
  58 10, 15, 18, 35, 37, 80, 92 **59** (5), [12?] **64** (6),
  7 **67** (4), (7), [(17)], 24 **74** 11-12 **75** 8

IX. PROFESSIONS, TRADES, AND OCCUPATIONS

X. MEASURES

(*a*) Weights and Measures

(ἀρτάβη) [**34** 14] **37** 15–19 **38** 14 **39** 15–17, 19–23 **50** 14 **60** 13 **61** [10], 11?, 12?, 13, 14 **65** 1, 2 **73** 16–19, 27–31, 35–8, 43–6, 54–7, 61–4, 68–71, 82, 98

δεςμίδιον (**39** 18) **65** 9

(κεντηνάριον) **42** 13 **66** 44, 72, 73

λίτρα **56** 22?

(λίτρα) **31** 9–12, 14–19 **33** 8–20, 22–30 **43** 20–2 **51** 15, 17 **52** 17–19 **53** 18–20 **65** 8, 16–20, 22, 23, 29, 32–9 **66** 18, 84–97, 103–10 **73** 15, 26, 34, 42, 53, 60, 67, 81

(μνᾶ) **65** 9

(ξέςτης) **40** 16, 17 **49** 15 **62** 15, 16 **65** 3–6 **73** 13, 20, 39, 47, 51, 58, 65, 72

(*b*) Money

ἀccάριον **56** 12, 23 **58** 11, 30, 38

(δηνάριον) **31** 10, 15–19 **32** 13–15 **33** 9, 11, 12, 15?, 16–20, 22–30 **34** 14 **37** 18, 19 **38** 14 **39** 16–21, 23 **40** 16, 17 **43** 20 **47** 15 **48** 15 **49** 15 **50** 14 **51** 15, 17 **52** 17–19 **53** 18–20 **58** 21, 33, 34 **62** 15, 16 **65** 3–6, 8, 10, 14?, 22, 38 **66** [18], 44, 95, 105–9 **73** 14, 15, 23, 25, 26, 33–5, 41, 42, 47, 49, 51–3, 58–60, 65–7, 72–4, 80, 81, 89, 97 **76** 18, 27

νομιςμάτιον **73** [7], 14, [22], [25], 33, 41, 49, 52, 59, (66), (73), 80, 88, 96

τάλαντον **56** 14 (*bis*), 15, 16 (*ter*), 17, 19, 20 **58** 90, 96

(τάλαντον) **31** 9, 11 **33** 8, 10, 13? **37** 15–17 **38** 14 **39** 16, 22, 23 **41** 21? **42** 13 [**43** 20] **52** 17 **57** 16, 22 **58** 32 **60** 13 **61** [10–12], 13, [14] **65** 1, 2, 10, 11, 13, [14], 16–20, 22–8, 30–8, 41–7 **66** 72, 84–97, [103] **73** *passim* **76** 17–19, 21–3, 26, 27, 29–31

XI. TAX

ἰχθυηρά **41** 14

XII. GENERAL INDEX OF WORDS

ἀγανακτεῖν **58** 62

ἄγειν **57** 19 **58** 32, 93, 120, 167 **65** 9

ἄγροικος *see* Index IX

ἀγχίνοια **58** 63

ἀγωγή **41** 56

ἀδελφός **46** (back) 38–9 **56** 3 **57** 8 **58** 84, 114, 117 **65** 56

ἀδικεῖν **71** 12?

αἴγειος **65** 44

αἰδεςιμώτατος **58** 187–8

αἱρεῖςθαι **64** 17

αἰτεῖν [**28** 5] **30** 7?

αἰτιᾶςθαι **41** 46

αἴτιον **64** 22

*ἀκμινάλιος **41** 45

ἀκοή **58** 47

ἀκολούθως [**28** 6] **31** 5 [**32** 8?] (**33** 5) (**34** 8) [**35** 5?] **37** 10 **38** 9 **39** 9 **40** 10–11 **42** 6 [**43** 12] [**44** 11] [**45** 11] [**47** 8] **48** 9 **49** 9 **50** 8 **51** 8–9 **52** 10 **53** 11 **55** 35 **56** 8, 11, 13, 23 **74** 10

ἀκούειν **58** 47 (*bis*)

ἀλήθεια **67** 24

ἁλιεύς *see* Index IX

*αλιμαςτου **33** 30? **66** 112?

*ἀλκεωτίδων **33** 27 **66** 109

ἀλλά **58** 25, 57, 161 **64** 6, 18 **70** 7

ἀλλοδαπός **70** 8?

ἄλλος **41** 5, 9, 59 **46** 42 **51** 16 **56** 23? **58** 7

ἀλλότριος **58** 28, 129

ἀλλοτριοῦν **70** 17?

ἁλοπώλης *see* Index IX

ἅλς **34** 14 **50** 14

ἄμφοδον *see* Index VI (*c*)

ἀμφότερος [**30** 6?] **57** 20 **58** 94 **59** 39? **64** 11 **67** 26?

ἄμωμον **31** 16 **33** 15 **65** 35 **66** 91

ἄν **46** [9], 33, 58 **58** 50

ἀναβολάδιον **76** 20?

ἀναγινώςκειν **57** [13–14], 14 **58** 54, 55 (*bis*), 88, 89, 150, 151, [201], 202, 205–6, 210 **59** 14, 15, 26 (*bis*) **67** 6?, [8]

ἀνάγκη **58** 58

XIII. CORRECTIONS TO PUBLISHED PAPYRI

PLATE I

3722 frr. 1–13

PLATE II

PLATE III

PLATE IV

3722 frr. 32, 34–67

PLATE V

3722 frr. 68–96

PLATE VI

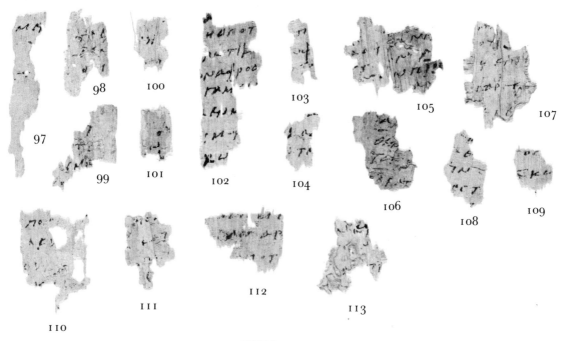

3722 frr. 97–113

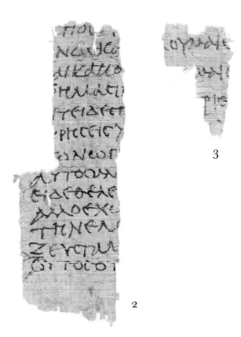

3724 frr. 2–3

PLATE VII

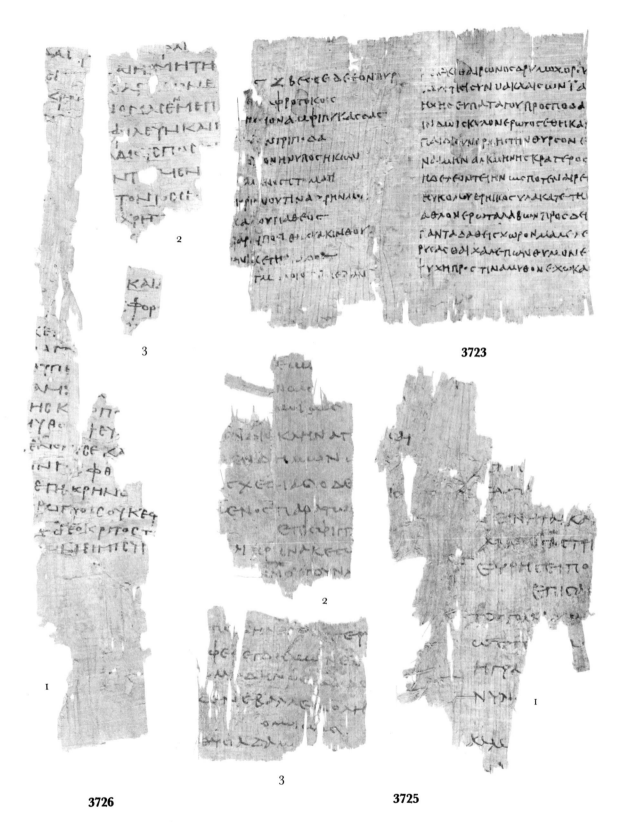

2

3

3723

2

1

3

1

3726

3725

PLATE VIII

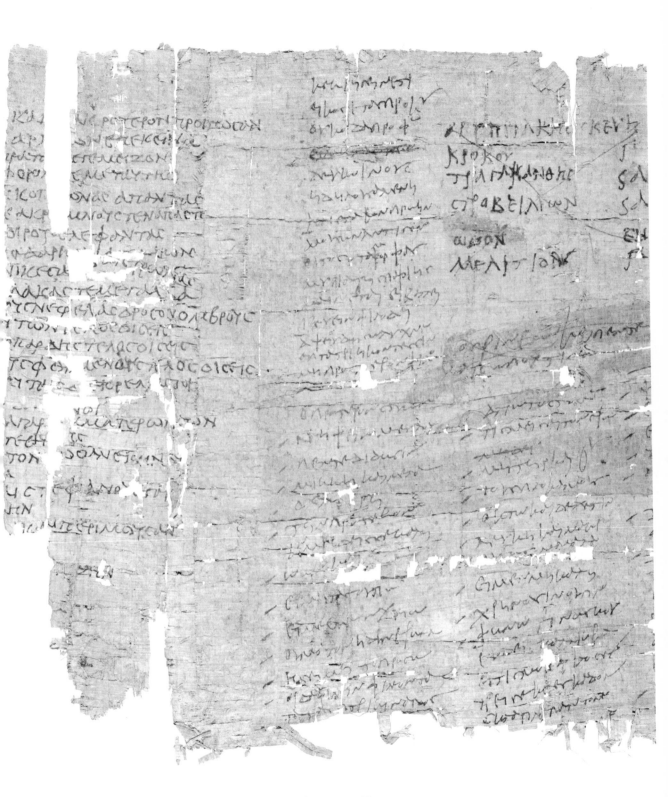

3724 fr. 1 i–iii

PLATE IX

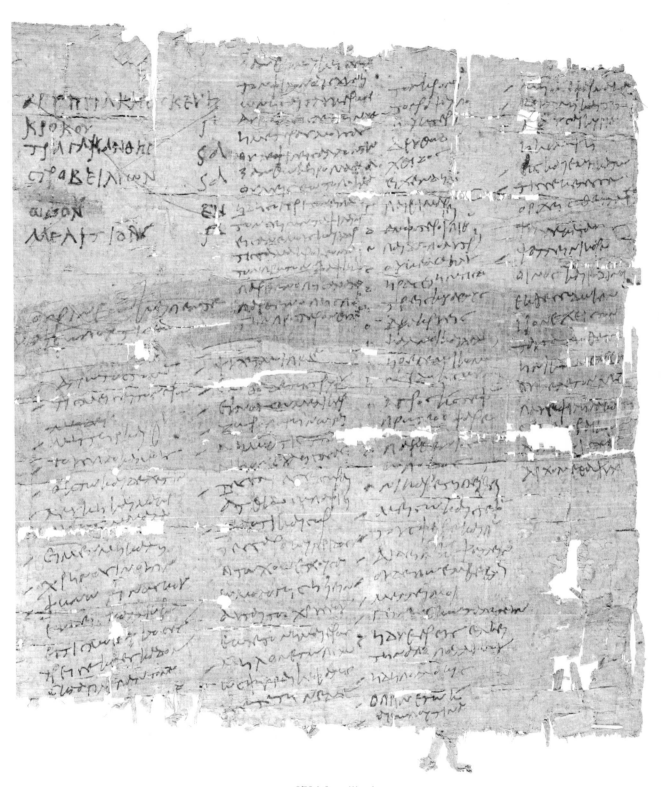

3724 fr. I iii–vi

PLATE X

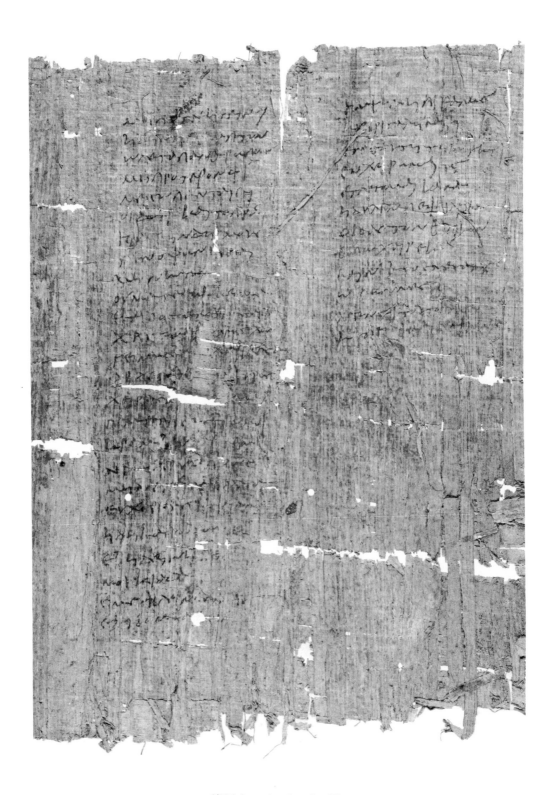

3724 fr. 1 back vii–viii

PLATE XI

3741 part

PLATE XII

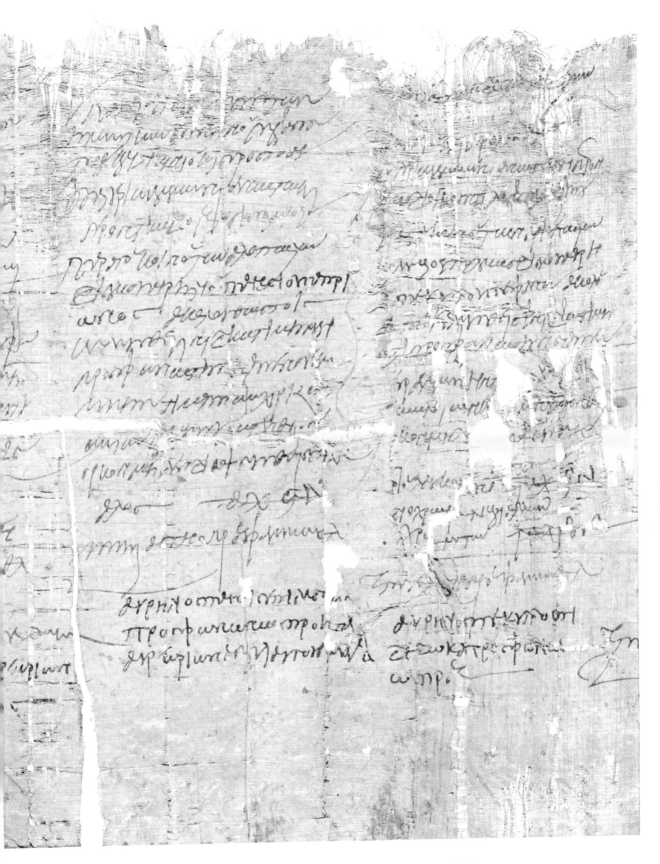

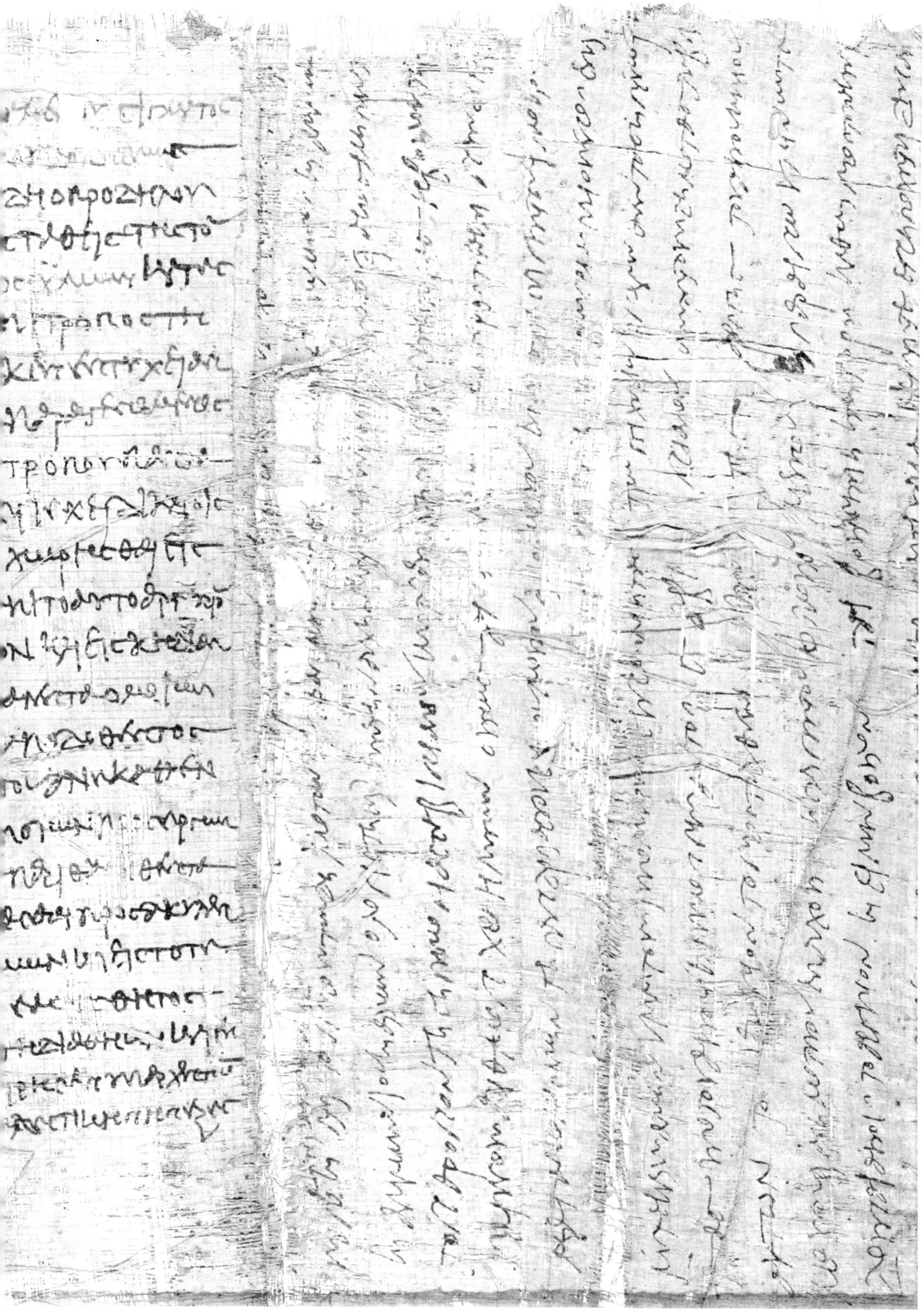

3756 part

3758 part

PLATE XIV

PLATE XV

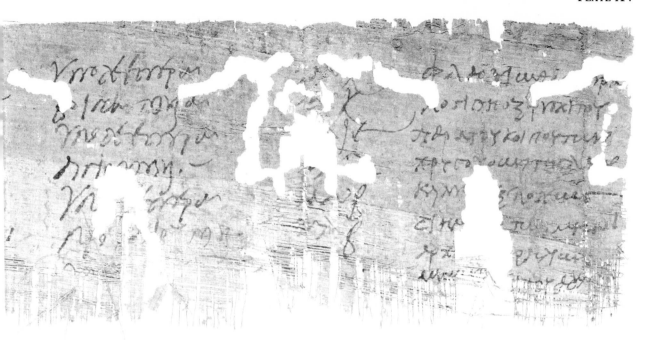

3765 part

3771

PLATE XVI

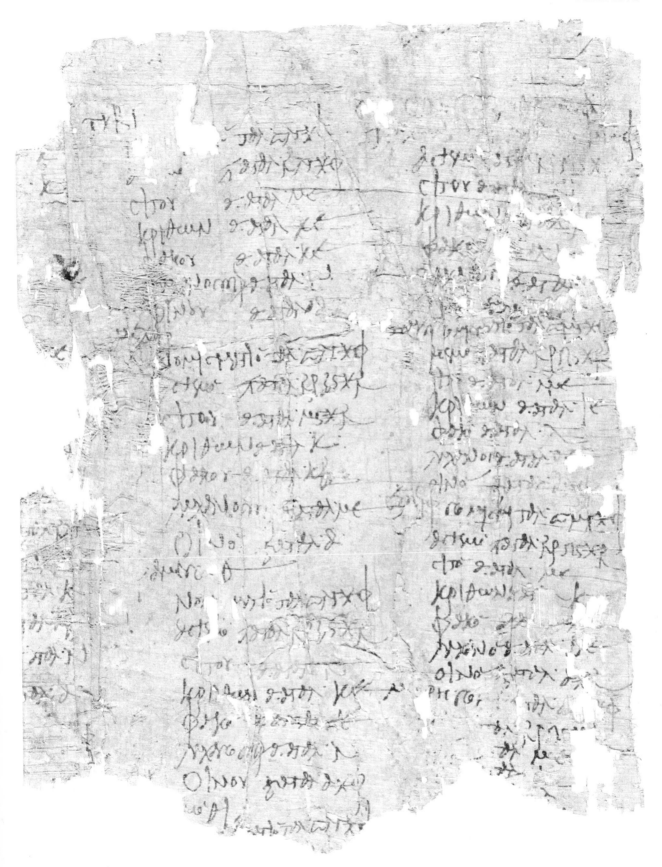

3773 front